THE Z80®
MICROPROCESSOR

Hardware, Software, Programming, and Interfacing

Barry B. Brey

DeVry Institute of Technology
Columbus, Ohio

Prentice-Hall International, Inc.

ISBN 0-13-983982-8

© 1988 by Prentice-Hall, Inc.
A Division of Simon & Schuster
Englewood Cliffs, NJ 07632

Printed in the United States of America

10 9 8 7 6 5 4 3 2

ISBN 0-13-983982-8 NBZI

Prentice-Hall International (UK) Limited, *London*
Prentice-Hall of Australia Pty. Limited, *Sydney*
Prentice-Hall Canada Inc., *Toronto*
Prentice-Hall Hispanoamericana, S.A., *Mexico*
Prentice-Hall of India Private Limited, *New Delhi*
Prentice-Hall of Japan, Inc., *Tokyo*
Simon & Schuster Asia Pte. Ltd., *Singapore*
Editora Prentice-Hall do Brasil, Ltda., *Rio de Janeiro*
Prentice-Hall, Inc., *Englewood Cliffs, New Jersey*

To Sheila:

*May this book bring you pride and joy
as we treasure each day together.*

Contents

Preface

It is important for students of computer science, engineering, technology, and technician programs to understand how to program and interface a microprocessor. Programming requires an understanding not only of high-level languages, but also of how to manipulate data at the assembly or machine language level. Today the microprocessor is used to control many different processes in almost all industries. It has replaced the mainframe computer, and in many instances the minicomputer, for process control. It is therefore essential for future and present success that low-level control software be fully understood by students in any of the aforementioned disciplines.

This text not only presents the instruction set for a very common microprocessor, the Zilog Z80, but also provides a sound foundation in structured programming at the assembly or machine language level, and also in microprocessor interfacing. You will learn all the basic machine language building blocks that are used to construct modern process control systems along with many of the interfaces used in these systems. Interfacing is also presented, and it is also very important if one is to succeed in the field of microprocessor technology.

In Chapters 1 and 2 the basic fundamentals are detailed so that the microprocessor can be programmed and so that some of the applications can be understood. In addition, the architecture of the Z80 is introduced.

After these first two chapters introduce the basics, Chapters 3 through 5 describe the operation of each of the Z80 instructions.

Once the instruction set is understood, Chapters 6 and 7 introduce the assembler and the concepts of structured programming. These are important topics that are often neglected.

Chapters 8 and 9 detail some of the many programming concepts that are used to design modern programs. These concepts include data manipulation, multiplication, division, code conversion, and time delays.

Chapters 10 through 15 detail interfacing for the Z80 microprocessor. First Chapter 10 completely covers the system architecture of the Z80, and then Chapter 11 covers memory interfacing. Once memory interfacing, which includes dynamic RAM, is covered, I/O interfacing is described in Chapters 12 through 15. In these chapters, the 8255A (programmable peripheral interface adapter), the 8251A (programmable communications interface), the 8254 (timer), analog-to-digital converters, and digital-to-analog converters are completely presented with applications.

Chapter 16 introduces 16- and 32-bit microprocessors which include the Intel 8086 and 80386 and the Motorola 68000 and 68020. Although these more powerful versions of 8-bit microprocessors are finding widespread application, they will not replace the 8-bit microprocessor for many years to come.

After completing this text the student is prepared to use the microprocessor in further studies on control systems and digital data communications. The student is also prepared to pursue the study of the microprocessor further with the 16- or 32-bit versions that are currently filling the market.

chapter 1

Introduction
to Microprocessors

This chapter introduces you to the microprocessor—the ninth wonder of the modern world. It is absolutely critical that the programming of the microprocessor be understood to compete successfully in today's complex job market. It is to this end that this first chapter introduces you to this intricate modern electronic marvel. Imagine, an entire book devoted to a single integrated circuit that occupies less than 2 square inches of space! Just a few decades ago a device of this complexity would have occupied at least a 2-square-yard area.

1-1 OBJECTIVES

Upon completion of this chapter, you will be able to:

1. Trace the history of the microprocessor from its meager beginnings to the present day.
2. Identify some of the major microprocessor manufacturers and the microprocessors they produce.
3. Define what a microprocessor is and describe the function of the main components of a microprocessor based system.
4. Describe the basic operations performed by the microprocessor.
5. List some commonly found microprocessor input/output (I/O) equipment.

1-2 HISTORY OF THE MICROPROCESSOR

The first microprocessor was conceived by Intel Corporation in California in 1971 as a 4-bit microcontroller designed for use in an electronic calculator. It did not take long before other applications for this device were dreamed up by inventive minds at such companies as Balley Corporation. One of the early applications was a video game produced by Balley.

The Intel 4004

This early computer on a chip was the Intel 4004 microprocessor, which could add two 4-bit binary numbers and perform many other operations. (A bit is a binary digit capable of storing a 1 or a 0.) You might think that a 4-bit microprocessor has very limited application today, but believe it or not, it still has wide application. If you were to buy a microwave oven or similar device, you would probably find that it contained a 4-bit microprocessor. Two of the most common microprocessors used in applications such as microwave ovens are the TMS-1000, which is manufactured by Texas Instruments, and the Intel 4040, which is an updated version of the original 4004.

   The 4004 was a fairly primitive device by today's standards, capable of addressing 4096 different memory locations. For many applications this is not enough memory. In addition to memory size, the word size (4 bits) of the 4004 proved to be too restrictive in many cases. A 4-bit number can store only 16 possible codes. For many applications that handle alphabetic information, 4 bits proves to be too limiting because there are 26 letters in the alphabet plus a variety of special characters and numbers. It normally takes at least a 6-bit and often 7-bit binary number to encode all of these different characters. To solve this problem the 8-bit microprocessor (8008) was introduced by Intel Corporation.

The Intel 8008

The Intel 8008 could handle 8-bit numbers (called bytes), which was a great enhancement over the 4004. (A byte is usually equal to 8 bits.) In addition to the increased word size, the memory size was increased from 4096 four-bit words in the 4004 to 16K eight-bit words in the 8008. (A computer K is equal to 1024.) The 4004 and the 8008 could both add numbers at the rate of 20,000 per second, which at the time was fast enough for many of the early applications. With engineers dreaming up new tasks for the microprocessor every day, this speed eventually began to limit the application of these early microprocessors. The main reason these early devices were so slow is that they were constructed of the then state-of-the-art PMOS logic circuitry. (PMOS is an acronym for P-channel metal-oxide semiconductor.) PMOS logic is inherently slow, and in addition to being slow, it is fairly difficult to interface to standard TTL logic circuitry because it uses a negative power supply. (TTL is an acronym for Transistor-Transistor Logic.)

   Then, at about the same time, there was a breakthrough in the fabrication of NMOS logic circuitry. (NMOS is an acronym for N-channel metal-oxide semiconductor.) NMOS logic is much faster than PMOS, and it also uses a positive power supply, which makes it more readily adaptable to be connected to TTL logic circuitry. This is important because many of the ancillary integrated circuits connected to a microprocessor are TTL. NMOS allows the speed of the microprocessor to be increased by a factor of about 25 times, which is significant. This new technology was used in the construction of the now famous Intel 8080 microprocessor.

The Intel 8080

The Intel 8080 was introduced in 1973, and its introduction is responsible for catapulting the world into the age of microprocessors. The 8080 was a greatly enhanced version of the 8008 that could perform 500,000 operations per second and address 64K bytes of memory. This device was also responsible for ushering in the age of the home computer, which was first introduced by MITS in 1974. This first hobby or home computer was the Altair 8800, which generated keen interest in microprocessing.

Although the Altair 8800 computer is no longer manufactured, it did represent a change in the way that people viewed the computer. A computer was no longer a mystical device suited only for large corporations or the military. It was a device that would, in a few short years, begin to populate American homes in the form of Apples, Ataris, Commodores, IBMs, and various other microprocessor-based computer systems.

The Zilog Z80

Soon after Intel introduced the 8080, Zilog introduced an enhanced version called the Z80. The Z80 could also address 64K bytes of memory and execute 500,000 instructions per second. The main advantage of the Z80 over the 8080 is that it can perform many additional instructions. In addition to performing more instructions it can also use the same instructions that are written for the 8080. Software that is developed on the 8080 is able to execute without complications on the Z80. Many of the 8-bit home computers in existence today use the Z80 microprocessor. If the computer is CP/M compatible, then it contains a Z80 in most cases. (CP/M is an acronym for Control Program/Microprocessor introduced by Digital Research Corporation.)

A few important hardware features of the Z80 include an enhanced register array when compared to the 8080 microprocessor. The Z80 also incorporates a mechanism that is used to automatically refresh dynamic RAM memory in a system. These two additional features make the Z80 superior to the Intel 8080.

Other Early Microprocessors

Up until 1973, Intel was the major producer of microprocessors; then other manufacturers began to see that this new device had a future and started manufacturing their own modified versions of the Intel 8080 microprocessor. Many of the early microprocessors are no longer actively produced because of the popularity exhibited by the Intel 8080 micro- processor. Some of these early microprocessors, together with their manufacturers, are listed in Table 1-1. You may notice from the list of microprocessors in Table 1-1 that

TABLE 1-1. EARLY 8-BIT
MICROPROCESSORS

Manufacturer	Part number
Fairchild	F-8
Intel	8080
MOS Technology	6502
Motorola	MC6800
National Semiconductor	IMP-8
Rockwell International	PPS-8

not all these microprocessors are in production today, and in fact some of these companies no longer produce microprocessors.

Microprocessors of Today

The thrust in recent microprocessor development seems to come from three different manufacturers: Intel, Motorola, and Zilog. Each company continues to market improved versions every year or two. Microprocessors today vary in size from 4 bits all the way up to 32-bit versions. Table 1-2 lists many of the microprocessors being manufactured by these three companies, together with their basic word size.

TABLE 1-2. MICROPROCESSORS MANUFACTURED
BY INTEL, MOTOROLA, AND ZILOG

Manufacturer	Part number	Word size
Intel	8048	8
	8051	8
	8085A	8
	8086	16
	8088	16
	8096	16
	80186	16
	80188	16
	80286	16
	80386	32
Motorola	6800	8
	6805	8
	6809	8/16
	68000	16/32
	68008	16/32
	68010	16/32
	68020	32
Zilog	Z8	8
	Z80	8
	Z8000	16
	Z80000	32

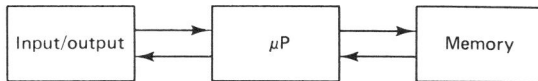

Figure 1–1   The block diagram of a microprocessor based computer system.

1-3 THE MICROPROCESSOR

What is a microprocessor? The microprocessor is a device that can be commanded to perform a wide variety of various functions—it is a programmable controller. All microprocessors perform the same three basic functions: data transfer, arithmetic and logic, and decision making. These are the same three tasks that can be performed by any microprocessor, minicomputer, or mainframe computer system.

Figure 1-1 illustrates a typical block diagram of a computer system with the microprocessor at the center. The microprocessor is pictured at the center because it controls the operation of the memory and the input/output (I/O) blocks. The interconnections between the microprocessor and these ancillary devices are the data bus, the address bus, and the control bus.

Buses

The address bus connections are used to supply the memory address or an I/O address to the memory and I/O blocks. The address, which is a binary number, is used to point to a unique memory location or I/O device. Memory can be envisioned as a series of numbered (addressed) boxes that each hold an 8-bit number in an 8-bit microcomputer.

The data bus connections, which would be 8 bits wide in an 8-bit microprocessor, are used to carry the information between the microprocessor and the memory or I/O. Data bus connections are, in most cases, bidirectional lines capable of transmitting information in either direction.

The control bus connections are used to control both the memory and I/O systems. The control bus consists of four signals: $\overline{RD}$ (read), $\overline{WR}$ (write), $\overline{MREQ}$ (memory request), and $\overline{IORQ}$ (I/O request). The $\overline{RD}$ and $\overline{WR}$ signals are used to cause data to be read or written to memory or I/O. The $\overline{MREQ}$ signal qualifies $\overline{RD}$ or $\overline{WR}$ as memory read or memory write and the $\overline{IORQ}$ signal qualifies them as I/O read or I/O write.

Data Transfer

The microprocessor spends a great deal of its time transferring data between itself and the I/O and memory. About 50% of its time is spent fetching instructions from the memory and executing them. Computers today store the commands or instructions in their memory so that they can be executed at a very high rate of speed. This is called the stored program concept.

TABLE 1-3. ARITHMETIC AND LOGIC
OPERATIONS FOUND IN MANY
MICROPROCESSORS

Operation	Notes
Addition	—
Subtraction	Two's complement addition
AND	Logical multiplication
OR	Logical addition
XOR	Exclusive-OR
NOT	Inversion
Shift	Either arithmetic or logical
Rotate	—

Arithmetic and Logic

A small portion of the microprocessor's time is spent performing arithmetic or logic operations. These operations can be executed in 1 to 2 microseconds (μs) in most microprocessors. Table 1-3 illustrates the typical arithmetic and logic operations performed by most microprocessors. Notice that multiplication and division have been omitted from this listing. This is done because not all of the currently available microprocessors are capable of these two operations.

Decisions

The ability of the microprocessor to make decisions allows it to process information more efficiently. It also allows the programmer to develop software that can choose different paths through a program. This ability has made the computer system the powerful device that it is today.

Microprocessors make decisions based upon numerical facts. Table 1-4 lists some testable conditions that microprocessors use to make decisions.

TABLE 1-4. COMMON TESTABLE
CONDITIONS USED BY
MICROPROCESSORS TO MAKE DECISIONS

Numeric condition	Testable condition
Zero	Equal to zero
	Not equal to zero
Sign	Positive
	Negative
Parity	Odd parity
	Even parity
Carry	Carry of one
	Carry of zero

1-4 THE MEMORY SYSTEM

The memory system in a computer performs two very important tasks: (1) memory is used to store the instructions of a program, and (2) memory is used to store the data used by the program. In many systems the program is stored in a read-only memory (ROM), and the data are stored in a random access memory (RAM), the term used for a read and write memory.

The Program

The program in a computer system is made up of various instructions that direct the operation of the microprocessor. Instructions are binary numbers that are interpreted by the microprocessor as various operations that are to be executed by the microprocessor. A grouping of these instructions is called the program. Programs vary in length from a few hundred instructions in simple systems to thousands of instructions in very complex systems.

A simple example of a program is adding the numbers 2 and 3 together. To direct the computer to perform this addition, a series of instructions are stored in the memory as a program. The first instruction of this program fetches a 3 from the memory. This is comparable to writing the 3 down on a piece of paper. The second instruction gets the 2 out of memory and adds it to the 3. This is comparable to writing the 2 beneath the 3 and adding the two numbers together in your mind. Finally, the third instruction is required to store, or save, the answer in the memory—the same thing that you do whenever you write the answer down on a piece of paper. Notice how this simple task of adding two numbers together seems more difficult than normal. This is because each step must be thought of and written down as separate instructions in the program.

Types of Memory

As mentioned earlier, the ROM, or some form of ROM such as an EPROM (erasable/programmable read-only memory), is often used to store the program, and the RAM is used to store the data. This is not always true, of course, but it is in many cases.

The ROM memory that is commonly found associated with the microprocessor is typically a factory– or mask–programmed ROM. The ROM is programmed with the information at the factory where it is manufactured. The EPROM is programmed in the field by a device called an EPROM programmer (sometimes EPROM burner). In addition to being programmable, the EPROM is also erasable in case a mistake is discovered. To erase an EPROM it is exposed to a high intensity ultraviolet light which erases it in a few minutes.

The RAM memory is most often some form of NMOS or CMOS memory device. In small memory systems, memory is often constructed with static RAM devices (SRAM), and in large memory systems, memory is often constructed with dynamic RAM devices (DRAM). The SRAM requires more power to operate, but its interface to a microprocessor is easier than the DRAM. The DRAM memory requires less power and is more compact,

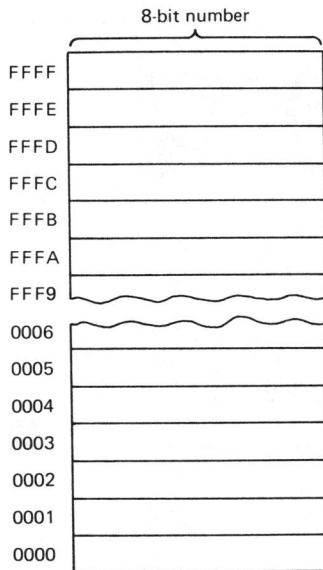

8-bit number

Address
FFFF
FFFE
FFFD
FFFC
FFFB
FFFA
FFF9
0006
0005
0004
0003
0002
0001
0000

Figure 1–2 A symbolic representation of a computer system memory. Each box (memory location) contains a binary number and each location is addressable by a number (memory address).

but it also requires additional circuitry to function with the microprocessor. For this reason small memory systems use SRAM, and large systems use DRAM.

Figure 1-2 illustrates a symbolic memory which shows the address of each memory location and also some binary data stored in each memory address or memory location. It makes the task of programming much easier if you think of the memory as a row of mailboxes that each hold a number. Each mailbox also has an address that is used to locate the data stored in it.

1-5 INPUT/OUTPUT DEVICES

The input/output (I/O) block in a computer system is the microprocessor's connection to the outside world. The microprocessor communicates to humans and/or machines through the I/O block. Without this communications path, the computer would truly be a worthless device.

I/O devices are defined as devices that can either accept an electrical signal for processing or generate an electrical signal to accomplish work. Just about any device in use by today's modern society could be, and often is, interfaced to a microprocessor as an I/O device. This has largely been made possible since analog-to-digital (ADC) and digital-to-analog (DAC) converters are available. Some of the more common I/O devices are listed in Table 1-5.

TABLE 1-5.   COMMON INPUT/OUTPUT DEVICES

Device	Type	Common usage
Switch	Input	Used to sense events such as key strokes on a keyboard, limits in mechanical systems, etc.
ADC	Input	Converts any analog voltage into a digital signal that can be processed by the microprocessor
Indicator	Output	An LED or similar device that indicates a single condition, or a display that indicates a number or alphabetical character
Motor	Output	Used to position mechanical devices; may be a stepper, AC, or DC motor
Solenoid	Output	Used to control electrical contacts or physically move an external device
DAC	Output	Used to convert a digital output from the microprocessor into an analog voltage

1-6 MICROPROCESSOR TRAINING AIDS

Microprocessor training aids (trainers) are devices that contain a keyboard, a set of numeric displays, and usually a method of connecting the trainer to an outside circuit. A typical training aid is pictured in Figure 1-3. This device is designed to train people on the operation and programming of the microprocessor. Microprocessor trainers are probably the least expensive method of learning the operation and programming of a

Figure 1–3 The Micromodule 85, a microprocessor trainer. (Courtesy of DeVry Inc.)

microprocessor. Most training aids cost less than $500 and are fairly easy to operate. The trainer is used to introduce the student to the microprocessor in the laboratory.

Trainer Functions

The trainer normally contains a hexadecimal keypad for data entry plus some additional keys for control. The control keys that are often found control:

1. The reading of data from the memory
2. The writing of data to the memory
3. The displaying and modifying of the contents of the microprocessor's registers
4. The execution of a program that is stored in the memory
5. The debugging of a faulty program by the use of a single-instruction execution mode of operation
6. The resetting of the microprocessor if the program becomes entangled in an infinite loop

The trainer also contains a set of hexadecimal displays that are capable of displaying hexadecimal data as a two-digit and a four-digit number. The displays normally indicate:

1. A sign-on message such as 80, which is displayed when the trainer is first turned on or reset
2. An address and data from any memory location
3. The contents of an internal register and its letter designation
4. Some indication that a user's program is being executed
5. Breakpoint addresses during debugging

In addition to the keyboard and displays, the trainer also should have an area that can be used for expanding the circuit of the trainer. For example, suppose that you wished to add an analog-to-digital converter to the trainer for an experiment. This is accomplished by wiring up the circuit on the breadboard area of the trainer or on an external breadboard that is connected to the trainer.

1-7 SUMMARY

1. Intel Corporation developed the first microprocessor, the 4004, a 4-bit machine that could directly address 4K nibbles of memory.
2. Four-bit microprocessors still find wide application in such systems as microwave ovens, dishwashers, and even automobiles.
3. Eight-bit microprocessors are much more useful in many applications because al-

phabetic data require at least a 6-bit code for representation and more often a 7-bit code.

4. PMOS logic, which was used in early microprocessors, proved to be too slow. This led to the development of NMOS logic and the modern gender of the microprocessor.

5. As early as 1974, the home computer began to appear on the scene in the form of the Altair 8800 computer system.

6. Today microprocessors are available in 4-, 8-, 16-, and 32-bit versions.

7. The Z80 microprocessor is an enhanced version of the popular Intel 8080 microprocessor.

8. The microprocessor is a device that performs arithmetic and logic, data transfer, and some rudimentary decisions based upon numerical facts.

9. Buses interconnect the blocks in a computer system block diagram. All microprocessors contain an address bus, a data bus, and a control bus.

10. The memory in a microprocessor-based system is used to store the instructions of a program and the data used by the program.

11. A program is a collection of instructions that are used to perform a useful task in a computer.

12. RAM (random access memory) is used to store temporary data and user programs, and ROM (read-only memory) is used to store programs and more permanent data.

13. An input/output (I/O) device is a device that will either accept an electrical signal or generate one.

14. A microprocessor trainer is a device that is used to learn how to program the microprocessor. Most trainers allow the user to enter data or commands, view the data from the memory or internal registers, and execute or single-step through a program.

1-8 GLOSSARY

Address bus   A set of connections that are used to select a memory and I/O location.

Bit   One binary digit (0 or 1) or position in a binary number. A contraction formed from binary (BI) and digit (T).

Buses   Common paths that interconnect the many components in a computer system.

Byte   Generally, an 8-bit binary number. A contraction formed from binary (B) and eight (YTE).

CMOS   Complementary metal-oxide semiconductor technology.

Control bus   A set of connections that provide the control signals for the memory and I/O. The control bus selects memory or I/O and also causes a read or a write operation.

Data bus   A set of connections that contain all of the data transferred between the microprocessor and the memory or I/O in a computer.

DRAM   Dynamic random access memory.

EPROM   An erasable programmable read-only memory is a device that can be erased with an ultraviolet lamp and reprogrammed electrically.

Input device   A device, such as a keyboard or switch, that sends data to the computer.

I/O   The input/output equipment provides the computer with its interface to the outside world.

K   In computer terminology a K is generally equal to 1024 decimal.

Mainframe computer   A mainframe computer system is a large computer designed to handle extremely large jobs. The term mainframe comes from the fact that the machine is often mounted in one or more rack panels or frames.

Memory   A device that stores binary information for the microprocessor.

Microcomputer   A computer system constructed around a microprocessor.

Microprocessor   A device that is programmed to control just about any situation. It is a programmable controller.

Microprocessor trainer   A system that is used to learn the operation and programming of a particular microprocessor.

Minicomputer   A scaled-down version of a mainframe computer that is losing its definition today because of the microprocessor-based microcomputer.

NMOS   N-channel metal-oxide semiconductor technology.

Output device   A device, such as a printer or numeric display, that accepts data from the computer.

PMOS   P-channel metal-oxide semiconductor technology.

Program   A collection of instructions that are organized to direct the computer to perform a useful task.

RAM   Random access memory is a device that allows data to be written or read.

ROM   Read-only memory is a device that has been permanently programmed with data at the factory during its construction.

SRAM   Static random access memory.

TTL   Transistor-transistor bipolar semiconductor technology.

Word size   Generally, the word size of a computer is determined by the width of the microprocessor's internal arithmetic circuitry.

QUESTIONS AND PROBLEMS _____

1-1. What corporation developed the first microprocessor?

1-2. What were some of the early applications for the microprocessor?

1-3. What led to the development of the 8-bit microprocessor?

1-4. One byte is normally equal to _____ bits.

1-5. A 4K memory device contains how many decimal memory locations?

1-6. What breakthrough ushered in a faster and more versatile microprocessor?

1-7. List three different 8-bit microprocessors.

1-8. List three different 16-bit microprocessors.

1-9. What software enhancements made the Z80 microprocessors more powerful than the 8080?

1-10. Give a brief definition of the microprocessor.

1-11. What three main blocks comprise the block diagram of a computer system?

1-12. What three main operations are performed by the microprocessor?

1-13. What buses interconnect the blocks in the block diagram of a computer system, and what are their function?

1-14. List four common arithmetic and logic operations performed by microprocessors.

1-15. List three common factors that the microprocessor uses to make decisions.

1-16. What type of memory is often used to store the program in a microprocessor-based system?

1-17. Data of a transitory nature are stored in which type of memory?

1-18. Define the term "program."

1-19. What types of RAM are found in various computer systems?

1-20. Define the term input/output.

1-21. List four common I/O devices.

1-22. What hardware features are usually found in a microprocessor trainer?

1-23. What functions are most often found in a typical microprocessor?

chapter 2

Z80 Architecture

Before a detailed study of the Z80 can be undertaken, its architecture must be understood. This chapter explains the Z80's internal operation, programming model, memory and I/O structure, and data and command words, and presents an overview of the instruction set.

2-1 OBJECTIVES

Upon completion of this chapter, you will be able to:

1. Draw the Z80 programming model and explain the purpose of each register.
2. Describe the purpose of each flag bit and explain what its contents indicate.
3. Draw the memory and I/O maps of the Z80 and explain the purpose of any special memory locations.
4. Convert decimal numbers into binary integers, binary fractions, binary-coded decimal (BCD), and binary floating-point numbers.
5. Convert the following into decimal numbers: binary integers, binary fractions, binary-coded decimal (BCD), and binary floating-point numbers.
6. Encode and decode ASCII-coded alphanumeric characters.
7. List the basic types of Z80 instructions.

2-2 THE Z80 ARCHITECTURE _____

The Z80 is an 8-bit general-purpose microprocessor that is ideally suited to many applications. In this section we introduce the internal architecture of the Z80 microprocessor.

The Z80 Block Diagram

Figure 2-1 illustrates the internal block diagram of the Z80 microprocessor. Although a detailed understanding of the internal block diagram and operation of the Z80 is not required for programming, it does help to explain why some of the instructions operate in a particular fashion.

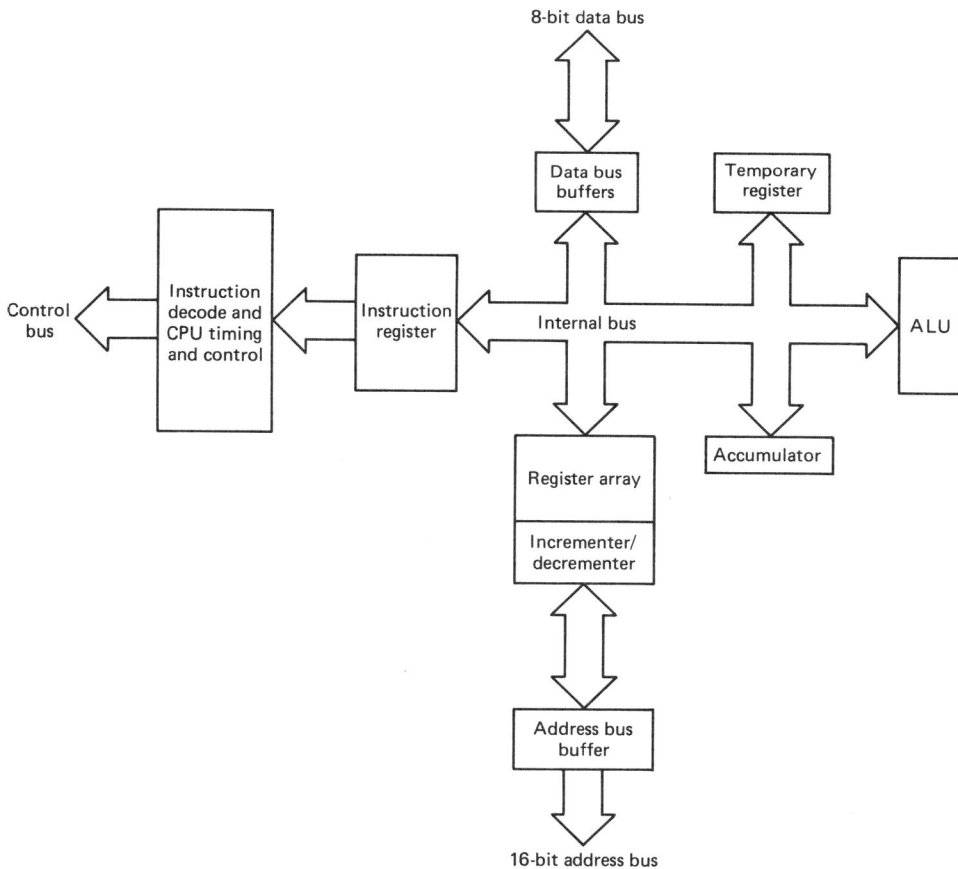

Figure 2–1   The internal structure of the Z80 microprocessor.

The Z80 contains a register array, a timing and control section, an arithmetic and logic unit (ALU), an instruction register and decoder, and bus connections to the outside world. Notice that there are 16 address bus connections A_0—A_{15} and 8 data bus connections D_0—D_7. The 16-bit address bus allows the Z80 to address 2^{16} (64K) different memory locations and the 8-bit data bus allows the Z80 to access a byte of data at a time. The address bus is used to address either memory data or I/O data and contains either a memory address or an I/O address. The data bus is used to transfer data between the Z80 and the memory or I/O.

The Registers

The Z80 contains a variety of internal registers that are used to hold temporary data, memory addresses, instructions, and information about the status of the Z80. The function of some of these registers will be explained here, and the remainder will be explained in Section 2-3 together with the programming model of the Z80.

Instruction register.   This register is used to hold the instruction that the Z80 is currently executing. Its outputs are connected to the instruction decoder, which decodes the instruction and controls the rest of the microprocessor, memory, and I/O through the timing and control block and external pin connections.

Temporary register.   The temporary register is used to hold information from the memory or the register array for the ALU. The other input to the ALU comes from the accumulator. The result, available at the output of the ALU, is fed to the internal 8-bit data bus for distribution to the accumulator, register array, or the memory.

Incrementer/decrementer address latch.   This block is used to hold the address of data to be accessed in the memory or I/O. It is also used to add one or subtract one from any of the 16-bit registers in the register array.

Miscellaneous Sections

The interrupt control section is used to determine the priority of the interrupt control inputs and also to supply, in some cases (NMI pin), an interrupt instruction to the instruction register. An interrupt is an operation where the external circuitry interrupts a program. When the program is interrupted, the microprocessor executes another program that responds to the external interrupt.

The timing and control section provides the basic control bus signals $\overline{\text{MREQ}}$, $\overline{\text{IORQ}}$, $\overline{\text{RD}}$, and $\overline{\text{WR}}$. In addition to these basic system control signals, other signals are also supplied to control the external hardware and also accepted to control some internal functions. More detail on these control signals and the system architecture is provided in later chapters of this text. At that time the signals are again explained with detail given to their application in a system.

Main registers		Alternate registers	
B	C	B′	C′
D	E	D′	E′
H	L	H′	L′
A	F	A′	F′
IX			
IY			
SP			
PC			
I	R		

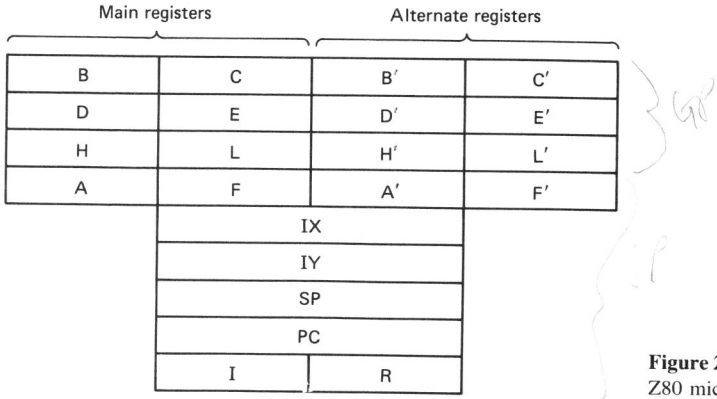

Figure 2–2   The programming model of the Z80 microprocessor.

2-3 THE PROGRAMMING MODEL

Before an instruction can be understood or a program can be written, the structure of the internal register set must be fully known. This section details the programming model of the Z80—the set of available registers that can be affected by a program.

Figure 2-2 illustrates the programming model (register set) of the Z80 microprocessor. The register set can be broken into two general areas: general-purpose registers and special-purpose registers.

General-Purpose Registers

The Z80 contains a double set of general-purpose registers: main registers and alternate registers. These registers are selected as a group, and either the main set or alternate set is available. The instruction set contains instructions (EXX and EX AF,AF′) that allow the sets of registers to be exchanged.

The six Z80 general-purpose registers are B, C, D, E, H, and L. These registers are called general-purpose because they can be used in any manner by the person programming the microprocessor. The general-purpose registers can be used to hold numeric, BCD, or ASCII data, and in fact, any type of information that may be required. They are flexible enough so that they can be used as six 8-bit registers or as three 16-bit register pairs.

The valid register pairs are BC, DE, and HL. Register pairs can be used to hold 16-bit numeric data or any other 16-bit coded information. In addition to being used to hold 16 bits of data, register pairs can also be used to address data in the memory. If a memory address is placed into a register pair, certain instructions allow the contents of the location addressed by the register pair to be manipulated.

Special-Purpose Registers

The special-purpose registers—A, F, SP, PC, IX, IY, I, and R—are used for accumulating results from arithmetic and logic operations, for addressing memory, and also for house-keeping. The term housekeeping is used to refer to tasks that are required by the micro-processor for proper operation, but normally occur without the intervention of the programmer.

The accumulator register (A).   The accumulator is a very important register in the Z80 microprocessor because it is used to accumulate the answer after almost every arithmetic and all logic operations. You might call the A register the answer register because the answer is normally found in it.

The flag register (F).   The flag register contains 6 bits that are used as flags or indicators for the ALU. Any time the Z80 executes most arithmetic or logic instructions, the flags will be modified. (Refer to Figure 2-1 for the placement of the flag register.) The results reflected by the flag bits indicate the condition of the result from the ALU. Figure 2-3 illustrates the contents of the flag byte. Notice that only 6 of the 8 flag bits actually contain information. The 6 flag bits and their uses are as follows:

1. The sign flag bit (S) is used to indicate whether the result of an arithmetic or logic operation is positive or negative. A logic 1 in this bit indicates a negative outcome and a logic 0 a positive outcome.
2. The zero flag bit (Z) indicates whether the outcome of an ALU operation is zero or not zero. A logic 1 in this bit indicates a zero result and a logic 0 indicates a non-zero result.
3. The half-carry flag bit (H) holds the carry that occurs between the least significant and most significant half bytes of the result from the ALU. (This flag is normally only used by the DAA command.)
4. The parity/overflow flag bit (P/V) is a dual function bit that indicates parity or arithmetic overflow. The P/V bit indicates an overflow condition for arithmetic operations and parity of logic operations. Parity is the count of the ones in a number expressed as even or odd, and overflow is an arithmetic condition that occurs if

FLAG REGISTER

S	Z		H		P/V	N	C

S = Sign
Z = Zero
H = Half-carry
P/V = Parity/overflow
N = Add/subtract
C = Carry

Figure 2–3 The Z80 flag register.

the result of a signed arithmetic operation exceeds the limits $+127$ and -128. Parity is even if P/V is a logic 1 and odd if it is a logic 0.

5. The negative flag bit (N) indicates whether the arithmetic operation is a subtraction or an addition. It is used with the H flag bit for BCD correction.

6. The carry flag bit (C) holds the carry that occurs from the most significant bit of the ALU after an addition, borrow after a subtraction, or a logic zero after all logic operations.

The interrupt vector register (I).   The interrupt vector register is used when an external signal interrupts the microprocessor. The interrupt vector register provides the high-order part of the interrupt address and the external interrupt provides the low-order portion.

The memory refresh register (R).   This register is used to refresh dynamic memory devices that are connected to the Z80. Each time that the Z80 runs a refresh cycle the count in the register is incremented so that eventually, after enough refresh cycles occur, the entire dynamic memory is refreshed.

The index registers (IX and IY).   These memory pointers are used by instructions that support indexed addressing. More on these in later sections of the text.

The program counter (PC).   The program counter does not count programs. The program counter is used by the Z80 to locate the next instruction to be executed. Why is it called a counter? It is called a counter because it is a counter. It counts up through the memory, allowing the microprocessor to sequentially execute the next instruction in the program. The importance of this register and a greater discussion appear in Chapter 5.

The stack pointer (SP).   The stack pointer allows the Z80 to track its last-in, first-out (LIFO) stack. The stack in the Z80 processes data so that the first data into the stack are the last data out of the stack. For example, if a 2, a 3, and a 4 are placed on the stack, they come off the stack in reverse order, as a 4, a 3, and a 2. You might think that this is a strange way to store information. It is, unless subroutine nesting is important. Subroutines, and the importance of this type of stack, are discussed in Chapter 5.

2-4 MEMORY AND I/O

As mentioned earlier, the memory is used to store programs and data, and the I/O system is used to allow humans and machines to communicate with the microprocessor. Both areas are very important, and it is critical that they are understood before a program is written.

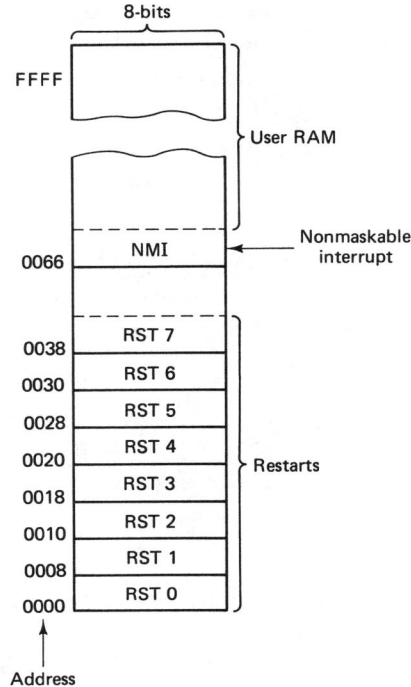

Figure 2–4 The memory map of the Z80 microprocessor showing RST and user RAM areas.

The Z80 Memory Map

The memory map of the Z80 is depicted in Figure 2-4. Notice that the memory locations are numbered in hexadecimal from 0000 through location FFFF. This means that the capacity of the memory system is 64K locations. Each memory location holds one byte of information, which can be an instruction or any form of data.

In addition to the numbered memory locations, there are also some restart (RST) locations listed at certain memory locations. The restart (RST) instruction is explained in Chapter 5.

The memory in the Z80 is most often segmented into two areas. One area of the memory is devoted to the system program and is most often populated with ROMs. The other area is used to store data and also programs and microprocessor-based training systems, and usually populated with semiconductor RAMs.

The reset location is a very important location in the Z80 memory map. The reset location (0000) is where the Z80 will begin to execute a program after the reset button, or input, of the Z80 is activated. If you are developing software for a Z80 system, you must begin the system software at memory location 0000. If you are using a microprocessor trainer, its system software begins at location 0000. This means that your program must

FF

8-Bit
user
I/O ports

00

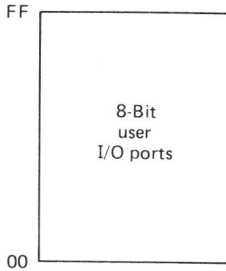

Figure 2–5 The I/O port map of the Z80 microprocessor showing the I/O port numbers.

begin elsewhere in the RAM memory of the trainer. The exact memory location of the RAM varies from trainer to trainer.

The Z80 I/O Map

The Z80 can directly address 256 different input devices and 256 different output devices. External I/O devices are called I/O ports in a Z80-based system. An input port is an external device that passes information to the microprocessor, and an output port is an external device that accepts information from the microprocessor. The port number is like a memory address because it is used to address an external I/O device and is often called the port address.

Figure 2-5 depicts the I/O map of the Z80 microprocessor. Notice that the I/O map is isolated from the memory system, and therefore this type of I/O system is called isolated I/O. The I/O ports are numbered from 00 to FF, and all ports are available to the user unless a microprocessor-based trainer is in use. A complete discussion of the I/O instructions, IN and OUT, is presented in Chapter 3.

2-5 DATA WORD FORMATS

There are many different data word formats that must be understood before a program can be written. This section covers unsigned integers, signed integers, ASCII-coded alphanumeric characters, binary coded decimal (BCD) data, binary fractions, and floating-point numbers. If one looks into the memory at an 8-bit number it is impossible to determine if it is an integer or any of these other forms of data. The type of data stored in a memory location must be known before it is used.

The Unsigned Integer

Unsigned integers, in the Z80 microprocessor, are most often either 8 or 16 bits in width, but they could be any multiple of 8 bits in width. The 8-bit unsigned integers are found

2^7	2^6	2^5	2^4	2^3	2^2	2^1	2^0
(128)	(64)	(32)	(16)	(8)	(4)	(2)	(1)

Note: Weights are in parentheses.

Figure 2–6 The format of an 8-bit unsigned integer in a register or a memory location.

stored in the memory system and also in any single register. The 16-bit unsigned integers are found stored in two contiguous bytes of memory and also in register pairs.

8-bit unsigned integer. Figure 2-6 shows the binary format of an 8-bit unsigned integer that is stored in either the memory or a register. All 8-bits are used to hold the value of a number with the binary weights of each bit position as indicated in this illustration.

Some examples of 8-bit unsigned integers are $0000\ 0001_2$ (01H) = 1, $1000\ 0000_2$ (80H) = 128_{10}, $1100\ 0000_2$ (C0H) = 192_{10}, and $1111\ 1111_2$ (FFH) = 255_{10}. The allowable range of 8-bit unsigned integers is 0—255_{10} (0—FFH). (Note: Hexadecimal quantities are always denoted with the letter H following the hexadecimal number. For example, 67H is equal to a 67 hexadecimal.)

16-bit unsigned integer. Figure 2-7 shows the format of the 16-bit unsigned integer in a register pair and also in two contiguous bytes of the memory. Notice that when a 16-bit unsigned integer is stored in the memory it is always stored with the least significant 8 bits in the lowest-numbered memory location and with the most-significant 8 bits stored in the highest-numbered location. The least significant portion is called the low-order part, and the most significant portion is called the high-order part.

Some examples of 16-bit unsigned integers are $0000\ 0000\ 0010\ 0000_2$ (0020H) = 32_{10}, $0010\ 0000\ 1000\ 1110_2$ (208EH) = 8334_{10}, and $1111\ 1010\ 0000\ 1011_2$ (FA0BH) = $64,011_{10}$. The allowable range of the unsigned 16-bit integer is 0—$65,535$. Note: When this text uses binary numbers they are always presented in BCH (binary-coded hexadecimal). A BCH number is a binary number that is grouped in 4-bit segments: for example, $0000\ 1100_2$ = 0CH.

Signed Integers

Single-byte signed integers are 7-bit numbers plus a sign bit. Positive numbers are stored with a 0 in the sign bit followed by a 7-bit magnitude, and negative numbers are stored with a 1 in the sign bit followed by a 7-bit two's complement of the magnitude. Both the positive and negative 8-bit integers are illustrated in Figure 2-8.

Positive numbers range in value from 0 to $+127$ and negative numbers range in value from -1 to -128. Some examples of positive signed 8-bit numbers are $0000\ 1000_2 = +8_{10}$, $0111\ 1111_2 = +127_{10}$, and $0101\ 0000_2 = +80_{10}$. Negative numbers are not quite as easy to calculate, so it may pay to become familiar with Figure 2-9, which can be used to determine the value of a positive or a negative number. The weight

(a)

2^{15}	2^{14}	2^{13}	2^{12}	2^{11}	2^{10}	2^9	2^8	2^7	2^6	2^5	2^4	2^3	2^2	2^1	2^0
(32768)	(16384)	(8192)	(4096)	(2048)	(1024)	(512)	(256)	(128)	(64)	(32)	(16)	(8)	(4)	(2)	(1)

(b)

1001H (High-order)

2^{15}	2^{14}	2^{13}	2^{12}	2^{11}	2^{10}	2^9	2^8
(32768)	(16384)	(8192)	(4096)	(2048)	(1024)	(512)	(256)

1000H (Low-order)

2^7	2^6	2^5	2^4	2^3	2^2	2^1	2^0
(128)	(64)	(32)	(16)	(8)	(4)	(2)	(1)

Figure 2-7 Sixteen bit unsigned integer word formats: (a) in a register; (b) in the memory.

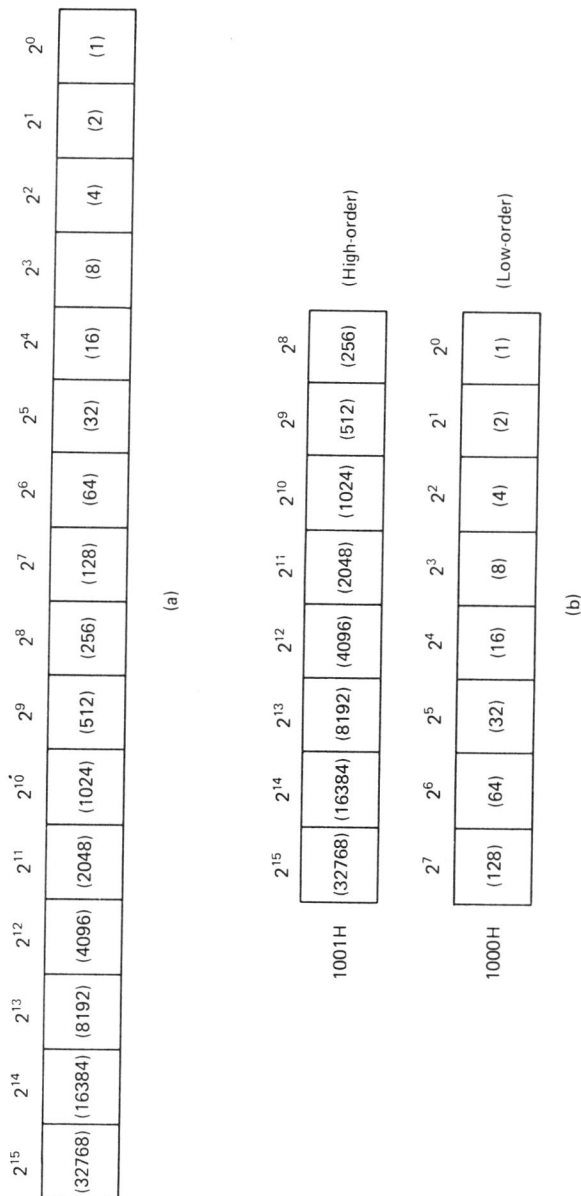

Note: Weights are in parentheses.

23

Sign

| 0 | 7-bit magnitude |

(a)

Sign

| 1 | 7-bit two's complement |

(b)

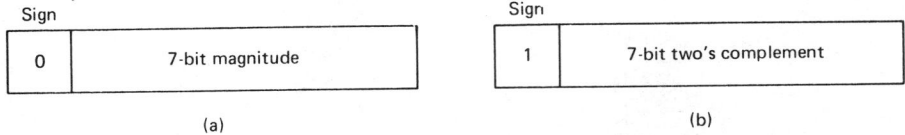

Figure 2–8   Signed 8-bit integers formats: (a) a positive integer; (b) a negative integer.

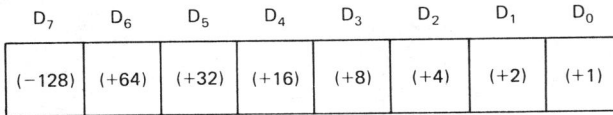

D_7	D_6	D_5	D_4	D_3	D_2	D_1	D_0
(−128)	(+64)	(+32)	(+16)	(+8)	(+4)	(+2)	(+1)

Note: Weights are in parentheses.

Figure 2–9   The binary weights of each bit position in a signed 8-bit integer.

(value) of the sign bit is −128. If a 1 appears in the sign bit, it is equal to −128, and if a 0 appears it is equal to a 0. The remaining bit positions are numbered +64, +32, +16, +8, +4, +2, and +1. If a number such as $1000\ 0011_2$ is converted to decimal using Figure 2-9, a −128, +2, and a +1 are added together to arrive at a value of −125$_{10}$ for this number. If a number such as $0001\ 0101_2$ is converted to decimal, a +16, +4, and a +1 are added together to arrive at +21.

Sixteen-bit signed numbers are treated in the same manner as 8-bit signed numbers. The extreme left-hand bit is the sign bit, and the remaining bits contain the magnitude for positive numbers and the two's complement of the magnitude for negative numbers. Figure 2-10 depicts the weights of a 16-bit signed number for conversions between binary and decimal.

ASCII Data Format

Refer to Appendix C for a complete listing of the ASCII-coded characters. ASCII is an acronym for American Standard Code for Information Interchange. This code is used by virtually all American and Japanese manufacturers of computer peripheral equipment, and it is therefore an excellent idea to become familiar with this code.

The first 32 codes are used for control purposes and are numbered from 00H to 1FH. To obtain any of these codes, on most computer keyboards, hold the control key down and type a letter A for 01H, a letter B for 02H, and so forth. The 00H code is most often obtained by holding the control and shift keys down while typing the letter P.

It is important to notice that ASCII code is a 7-bit code. The eighth and most significant bit is used to hold the parity in a data communications system. In computer systems this bit is often a logic 0. In some printers a 0 in the eighth bit causes the printer to print ASCII characters, and a 1 causes it to print graphics characters.

D_{15}	D_{14}	D_{13}	D_{12}	D_{11}	D_{10}	D_9	D_8	D_7	D_6	D_5	D_4	D_3	D_2	D_1	D_0
(−32768)	(+16384)	(+8192)	(+4096)	(+2048)	(+1024)	(+512)	(+256)	(+128)	(+64)	(+32)	(+16)	(+8)	(+4)	(+2)	(+1)

Figure 2–10 The binary weights of each bit position in a signed 16-bit integer.

Note: Weights are in parentheses.

TABLE 2-1. BCD CODES FOR
THE NUMBERS 0 THROUGH 9

Decimal	Unpacked BCD
0	0000 0000
1	0000 0001
2	0000 0010
3	0000 0011
4	0000 0100
5	0000 0101
6	0000 0110
7	0000 0111
8	0000 1000
9	0000 1001

BCD Data Format

In many systems that do not contain an ASCII keyboard, data are entered on a numeric keyboard and encoded by the keyboard circuitry as a binary-coded-decimal (BCD) number. This number is usually processed as an unpacked BCD number. An unpacked BCD number is a number that is stored as one digit per byte. In other words, to store a 76 in unpacked BCD code would take two bytes of memory. The first byte contains a 0000 0111 (7) and the second byte a 0000 0110 (6). (Refer to Table 2-1 for a list of valid BCD codes.)

In certain cases it is desirable to conserve memory space. When this is the case, BCD numbers are stored as a packed number which contains a two-digit BCD number per byte. To store a 76 in packed BCD code would take one byte of memory (0111 0110).

Signed BCD numbers are not nearly as common as unsigned BCD numbers. If they are used, the negative numbers are stored in the ten's complement form. For example, a -14 is stored as a 1000 0110 (86), which is the ten's complement of a 14. To form a ten's complement number, first subtract each digit of the number from a 9 and then add a 1 to the result. Subtracting a 14 from a 99 would yield an 85 plus the 1 equals an 86.

Binary fractions. Binary fractions can also be stored in either byte or two-byte form for use by the Z80, although they are not very commonly found. Usually, they are unsigned numbers that use the leftmost bit position as a bit which has a weight of 2^{-1}. For example, if the binary number 1100 0000 is found in a memory location and it is known that it is an unsigned fraction, its value is 0.75_{10}. The left hand bit is equal to 0.5 (2^{-1}) and the next bit is equal to 0.25 (2^{-2}) or a total of 0.75_{10}.

Floating-point data

How are numbers that are not integers or fractions stored in a computer system's memory? The floating-point format is used to store noninteger as well as integer data in many computer systems. Floating-point numbers are similar to scientific notation in decimal. They have a mantissa and an exponent. The mantissa is a normalized number between

1 and less than 2. The exponent is a power of 2 that represents the position of the binary point in the original number. Examples 2-1 through 2-3 illustrate a few binary numbers converted to normalized floating-point numbers.

Example 2-1

$$1110010 = 1.11001 \times 2^6$$

Example 2-2

$$11.10001 = 1.110001 \times 2^1$$

Example 2-3

$$0.001101 = 1.101 \times 2^{-3}$$

Floating-point numbers are often stored in four bytes of memory. Figure 2-11 illustrates the format of a four-byte (single-precision) floating-point number. The left-hand bit position is used to indicate the sign of the mantissa; the next eight bit positions are used to store the exponent; and the last 23 bits are used to store the magnitude of the mantissa.

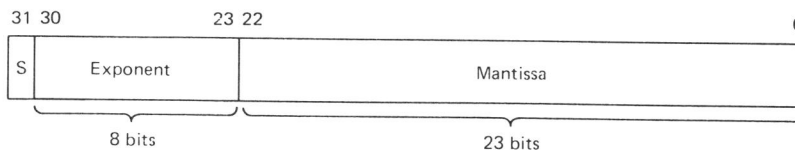

Figure 2–11   The format of the four byte single precision floating point number.

The excess 127 notation is an unsigned integer that is equal to the exponent plus 127 (7FH). For example, if the value of the exponent is a 6, the exponent is coded as a 133 in the excess 127 notation. $(127 + 3)$ If the exponent is determined to be a -2 then it is encoded as a 125.

The mantissa is a 23-bit number with a hidden or implied twenty-fourth bit position. Notice that when a number is normalized, the left-hand bit is always a logic 1. Because this 1 is always present, we do not need to store it in the memory. (A zero is the only case where the implied 1 is missing. In this case all four bytes of the number are zero, to indicate a value of zero.) Examples 2-4 through 2-7 illustrate some decimal numbers that have been converted to floating-point numbers.

Example 2-4

$$100_{10} = 1100100_2$$
$$1100100_2 = 1.1001 \times 2^6$$

```
S Exponent  Mantissa

0 10000101  10010000000000000000000
```

Example 2-5

$$-12.75_{10} \quad = \quad -1100.11_2$$

$$-1100.11_2 \quad = \quad -1.10011 \times 2^3$$

```
S Exponent   Mantissa

1 10000010   10011000000000000000000
```

Example 2-6

$$2.1_{10} \quad = \quad 10.000110011001100110011 0$$

$$1.0001100110011001100110 \times 2^1$$

```
S Exponent   Mantissa

0 10000000   00001100110011001100110
```

Example 2-7

$$0 \quad = \quad 0$$

$$0 \quad = \quad 0 \times 2^0$$

```
S Exponent   Mantissa

0 00000000   00000000000000000000000
```

2-6 COMMAND WORD FORMATS

There are basically four different command word formats used by the Z80: one-, two-, three-, and four-byte-long instructions. The one-byte commands represent a majority of the instructions for the Z80 microprocessor. In all four formats the first byte is always the opcode. The opcode tells the microprocessor which operation to perform and also whether a second, third, and fourth byte are required.

One-Byte Commands

The one-byte commands, which are the most numerous, are used for most of the instructions in a program. They are used for moving numbers between registers or between registers and memory, and also to accomplish most of the arithmetic and logic operations.

Two-Byte Commands

In the two-byte command the first byte is the opcode and the second contains data, a displacement, an extension to the opcode, or an I/O port number.

Figure 2-12 illustrates the basic formats of the two-byte command. Notice that the second byte contains 8-bits of immediate data (Figure 2-12 (a)), an 8-bit displacement

| Op-code | | Immediate data |

(a)

| Op-code | | 8-bit displacement |

(b)

| Op-code | | Op-code extension |

(c)

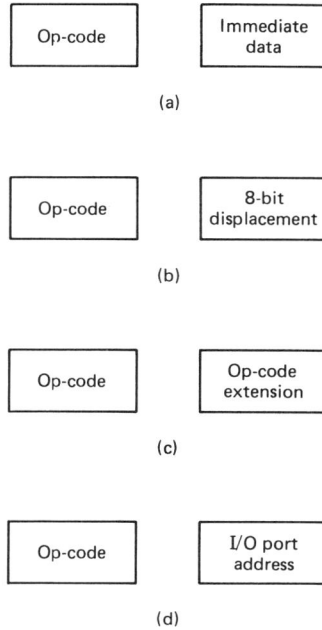

Figure 2–12   The two-byte command format. (a) A two-byte instruction using immediate data; (b) a two-byte instruction using a signed 8-bit displacement; (c) a two-byte instruction using a 16-bit opcode; and (d) a two-byte instruction using an I/O port address.

| Op-code | | I/O port address |

(d)

(Figure 2-12 (b)), an extension to the opcode (Figure 2-12 (c)), or an I/O port address (Figure 2-12 (d)).

Three-Byte Commands

The three-byte commands contain an opcode for the first byte and then data or a memory address. Figure 2-13 illustrates both forms of the three-byte-long commands.

Refer to Figure 2-13 (a) for a three-byte-long instruction that uses data for an operand. (The operand is the data used by an opcode.) Notice that the data are encoded so that the least significant 8 bits (low-order data) follow the opcode and the most

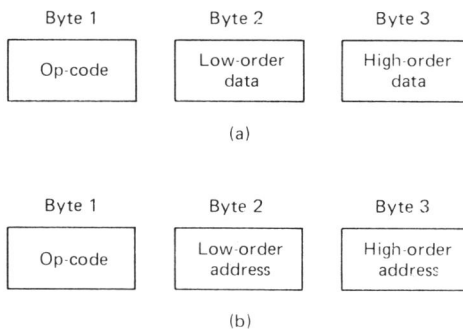

| Byte 1 | Byte 2 | Byte 3 |
| Op-code | Low-order data | High-order data |

(a)

| Byte 1 | Byte 2 | Byte 3 |
| Op-code | Low-order address | High-order address |

(b)

Figure 2–13   The three-byte command format: (a) a three-byte instruction using 16 bits of immediate data; (b) a three-byte instruction using a 16-bit memory address.

TABLE 2-2. HEXADECIMAL DATA OR ADDRESSES
CONVERTED TO LOW- AND HIGH-ORDER FORM
FOR A THREE-BYTE-LONG INSTRUCTION

Hexadecimal data	Low-order	High-order
0023	23	00
1000	00	10
1234	34	12
ABCD	CD	AB
10EC	EC	10

significant 8 bits (high-order data) follow the low-order byte. It may take some time to get used to this, because this is different from the way that a number is normally written. Some examples of 16-bit hexadecimal data broken down into low- and high-order parts are written in Table 2-2.

Figure 2-13 (b) shows a three-byte command that requires a memory address (operand address) in place of data. Just as with the data, a memory address must also be coded with the low-order portion first, followed by the high-order portion.

Four-Byte Commands

The last form of instruction for the Z80 is the four-byte command. The first byte of a four-byte-long command contains the opcode, and the second byte contains the opcode extension. The remaining bytes are used for displacements and various other data. Figure 2-14 illustrates the form of a four-byte-long command.

Figure 2-14   The four-byte instruction format.

2-7 THE INSTRUCTION SET

The instruction set of the Z80 microprocessor can be broken into three main categories: data transfer instructions, arithmetic instructions, and program control instructions. This section introduces these three forms of instructions, and they are covered in complete detail in Chapters 3, 4, and 5.

Data Transfer Instructions

Data transfer instructions represent a lot of processing time in most software systems. For this reason it is important that these instructions are understood. There are actually six types of data transfer instructions available in the Z80 instruction set. These types are register-to-register moves, move immediates, indexed moves, direct moves, input/

output, and block data transfers. (None of the data transfer instructions affect the flag register.)

Arithmetic and Logic Instructions

Another common operation in a microprocessor-based system is some simple arithmetic or logic operations. The Z80 is capable of a wide assortment of arithmetic and logic operations. Instructions that the Z80 is capable of executing are addition, subtraction, AND, OR, NOT, Exclusive-OR, shifting, and various forms of rotation. Most of these operations can be used to function with most internal registers or the contents of any memory location. They even can be performed using immediate data, and there is also a block compare instruction that allows data in a block of memory to be compared. (Most of the arithmetic and logic instructions affect the flag register.)

Program Control Instructions

The Z80 microprocessor can execute four different types of program control instructions: unconditional and conditional jumps, indirect jumps, unconditional and conditional calls, and unconditional and conditional subroutine returns. The conditional instructions are used to test the flag bits. If the condition under test is true, a jump occurs to some other instruction in the program, and if the condition is false, the program continues with the next sequential step in the program.

2-8 SUMMARY

1. The Z80 microprocessor is a general-purpose 8-bit microprocessor that is ideally suited for many control applications.
2. The Z80 microprocessor contains a register array, a timing and control section, an arithmetic and logic unit (ALU), and bus connections to the outside world.
3. The Z80 microprocessor is capable of addressing 64K bytes of memory through an 8-bit data bus via a 16-bit address bus.
4. The timing and control section generates the major system control signals: $\overline{RD}$ (read), $\overline{WR}$ (write), and IO/$\overline{M}$ (I/O or memory).
5. The programming model of the Z80 contains two banks of registers and also two sections: a general-purpose section and a special-purpose section. The general-purpose section contains six registers (B, C, D, E, H, and L), which are used as 8-bit registers or in pairs as 16-bit registers (BC, DE, and HL). The special-purpose registers include the accumulator (A), the stack pointer (SP), the flag register (F), the program counter (PC), the index registers (IX and IY), the interrupt vector register (I), and the refresh register (R).
6. The accumulator is used to hold an operand before and the result after most arithmetic and logic instructions.

7. The stack pointer (SP) register is used by the Z80 to address data that are pushed onto the LIFO stack.

8. The flag register is used to hold information about the result after most arithmetic and logic instructions. The flag bits are zero (Z), sign (S), parity/overflow (P/V), carry (C), half carry (H), and negate (N).

9. The program counter (PC) addresses the next instruction to be executed by the Z80. It always points to the next instruction in the program.

10. The IX and IY index registers are used by many instructions to indirectly address memory data.

11. The interrupt vector register (I) and the refresh register (R) are used for system control and operation and are mainly hardware dependent registers.

12. The Z80 is capable of directly addressing 256 different input and 256 different output devices. External I/O devices are often called I/O ports in a Z80-based system.

13. Data used by the Z80 takes many forms: unsigned and signed binary integers, binary fractions, packed and unpacked BCD, ASCII, and floating-point.

14. Instructions for the Z80 are one, two, three, or four bytes in length.

15. Instruction types are data transfer, arithmetic and logic, and program control.

2-9 GLOSSARY

Accumulator register   The accumulator is used to hold the operand before an arithmetic or logic operation and the result after the operation.

Address bus   A common set of connections that are used to convey the address to the memory or I/O port number to I/O.

ALU   Arithmetic and logic unit.

ASCII code   ASCII data consist of an alphanumeric code used in many computer systems.

Bank   A set of registers that are switched with another set. The Z80 contains two banks of registers: the main bank and the alternate bank.

BCD   Binary-coded-decimal (BCD) is stored in groups of 4 bits that represent the decimal numbers 0 through 9.

Exponent   The binary power of 2 in a floating-point number that is used to reference the position of the binary point in the mantissa.

Flag register   A register that holds the condition of the ALU after most arithmetic and logic operations.

Floating-point number   A number that is used to store very large or very small integers, fractions, or mixed numbers.

General-purpose registers   A set of registers that are used by the programmer in any way that is deemed proper.

Housekeeping   Tasks that are normally processed by the microprocessor without intervention from the programmer.

Instruction register   A register used to hold the instruction so that the microprocessor can decode and execute it.

$\overline{IORQ}$ The $\overline{IORQ}$ signal is used to request an I/O read or write operation. This signal becomes a logic zero for the IN and OUT instructions.

LIFO   A LIFO (last-in, first-out) stack memory is used to store data and return addresses in the memory as tracked by the stack pointer register.

Mantissa   The part of the floating-point number that holds a value of 1 through less than 2.

$\overline{MREQ}$ The $\overline{MREQ}$ (memory request) signal is used to request a memory read or write operation.

Opcode   The opcode is the part of an instruction that specifies the operation to be performed by the microprocessor.

Opcode extension   In the Z80 microprocessor some opcodes are two bytes in length. The second byte of the opcode is called the opcode extension.

Operand   The data used by the opcode.

Operand address   The address of the data used by the opcode.

Parity   A count of the number of ones in a number expressed as even or odd.

Port, I/O   An external I/O device.

Program counter   A register that holds the address of the next instruction to be executed.

Programming model   A model of the internal user-affected registers in a microprocessor.

$\overline{RD}$ The $\overline{RD}$ (read) signal is used to cause the memory or I/O to read or send data to the microprocessor.

Signed integer   A whole number that can be either positive or negative.

Special-purpose registers   A group of registers that are used for processor housekeeping and also program use.

Stack   See LIFO

Stack pointer register   A register that is used to address the LIFO stack.

Unsigned integer   A whole number that has no arithmetic sign.

$\overline{WR}$ The $\overline{WR}$ (write) signal is used to enable the memory or I/O.

QUESTIONS AND PROBLEMS _____

2-1. The Z80 address bus contains how many bits?

2-2. The Z80 can directly address how many bytes of memory?

2-3. What is the purpose of the instruction register in Figure 2-1?

2-4. List the four main Z80 control signals.

2-5. Draw the programming model of the Z80 microprocessor.

2-6. List at least three types of data normally held in the general-purpose registers.

2-7. When two general-purpose registers are connected together to form a 16-bit register, what is this new register called?

2-8. What is the answer register?

2-9. List each of the flag bits and briefly describe their function.

2-10. Why is the program counter (PC) called a counter?

2-11. The stack pointer (SP) register is used to reference what type of stack memory?

2-12. What is the purpose of the IX and IY registers?

2-13. Describe the memory of the Z80 microprocessor.

2-14. Where is the ROM in a Z80 system normally found?

2-15. How many different external input devices can be accessed by the Z80?

2-16. What is an I/O port?

2-17. Convert the following decimal numbers to 8-bit unsigned binary integers: 12, 33, 55, 100, 155, 196, and 212.

2-18. Convert the following decimal numbers to 16-bit unsigned binary integers: 156, 522, 1000, 2009, and 10,000.

2-19. Convert the following 8-bit signed binary integers to decimal: 1111 1111, 1000 0111, 0110 1000, and 0111 0000.

2-20. Convert the following decimal numbers to 8-bit signed binary integers: 12, -12, 32, -63, and -100.

2-21. Using the ASCII coding chart in Appendix C, convert your name to ASCII code.

2-22. How is an ASCII BS (backspace) obtained on many keyboards? (Not by using the backspace key!)

2-23. Write the following decimal numbers as both packed and unpacked BCD numbers: 12, 3, 10, 99, 12, and 712.

2-24. Convert the following decimal numbers to four-byte binary floating-point form: 12, -22, 10.5, 0.002, and -4.25.

2-25. Convert the following three four-byte binary floating-point numbers into decimal numbers:

0100 0001   0100 0000   0000 0000   0000 0000
1011 1111   1000 0000   0000 0000   0000 0000
0100 1000   1110 1000   0000 0000   0000 0000

2-26. What is an opcode?

2-27. What is an operand?

2-28. What is an operand address?

2-29. Explain the order of the data in a three-byte command.

2-30. Convert the following hexadecimal numbers into the correct form for data storage in the second and third bytes of a three-byte-long command: 1234H, ACDCH, 87FFH, 3443H, and 9080H.

2-31. What three main categories of instructions comprise the Z80 instruction set?

2-32. Which types of instructions do not affect the flags?

2-33. What type of instruction will affect the flags?

chapter **3**

Data Transfer Instructions

One of the most common types of instructions in the Z80 microprocessor's instruction set is the data transfer instruction. Data transfer instructions come in many forms: register to register, register to memory, memory to register, block transfers, and stack operations.

In this chapter we present the various addressing modes available for all instructions and also all the data transfer instructions, including the machine language and assembly language versions.

3-1 OBJECTIVES

Upon completion of this chapter, you will be able to:

1. Explain how the Z80 responds to each of the following addressing modes: direct, register, indexed, register indirect, and block transfers.
2. Use the LD (load) instruction to load any internal register or memory location.
3. Explain the operation of the BC, DE, and HL register pairs for the register indirect mode of addressing.
4. Explain the use of IX and IY in indexed addressing.
5. Describe the operation of the block transfer instruction.
6. Explain the operation of the stack by the PUSH, POP, and EX (SP), HL, EX (SP), IX, and EX (SP), IY instructions.
7. Briefly describe the operation of the IN, OUT, and remaining EX instructions.

3-2 ADDRESSING MODES

The Z80 microprocessor uses five different addressing modes for most instructions: direct, register, register indirect, indexed, and immediate. Before a particular instruction is examined, it is essential that each of these addressing modes is completely understood. In this section of the text we detail the addressing modes so that the subsequently explained instructions can be understood.

Direct Addressing

Instructions that directly address the memory always include the operand address which is stored following the opcode in a program. The form of each instruction that uses direct addressing is illustrated in Figure 3-1.

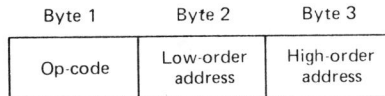

Byte 1	Byte 2	Byte 3
Op-code	Low-order address	High-order address

Figure 3-1 A direct addressed instruction showing the opcode, low and high order addresses.

Notice that with this type of addressing the instruction contains an opcode followed by a 16-bit memory address in the two additional bytes of memory following the opcode. (All instructions that use direct addressing are three bytes in length.) It is also important to note that the operand address is stored so that the least significant byte follows the opcode and the most significant byte follows the least significant byte. This was discussed in Chapter 2 in the section that illustrated a three byte instruction that stored 16-bit data in the memory. Table 3-1 shows how various addresses are stored following an opcode in machine language. If this form of addressing is used by a particular instruction, an a16 is found in the assembly language listing provided in Appendix A and also throughout this and the next two chapters.

TABLE 3-1. VARIOUS ADDRESSES CONVERTED TO MACHINE CODE FOR THE DIRECT ADDRESSING MODE OF OPERATION

Hexadecimal address	Machine-coded form
	B1 B2 B3
1234H	XX 34 12
1000H	XX 00 10
4BCDH	XX CD 4B

Notes: XX is any opcode that allows direct addressing; B1, B2, and B3 are used to indicate byte 1, byte 2 and byte 3.

Register Addressing

Register addressing is one of the more common forms of addressing data in the Z80 microprocessor. The opcode specifies the register (B, C, D, E, H, L, or A), register pair, (BC, DE, HL, or SP), or index register (IX or IY). All register addressed instructions are one byte in length except those dealing with either IX or IY. This mode of addressing is heavily illustrated later in this chapter with the LD (load) instructions.

Register Indirect Addressing

With register indirect addressing, a register pair holds the address of the memory location accessed by the instruction—the memory location is indirectly addressed by the register pair. If the HL register pair is used to address memory indirectly, the HL is surrounded by parentheses as (HL). For example, suppose that the HL register pair contains a 1000H and the (HL) is used as a register. An instruction using (HL) will access memory location 1000H because the HL register pair points to that memory location.

There are also a few instructions that allow memory to be addressed indirectly through the BC and DE register pairs. The addressing mode uses (BC) or (DE) like (HL) is used to address memory data indirectly. These instructions are discussed later in this chapter. The SP is also used to indirectly address memory through a few commands—the stack operations—which are also discussed late in this chapter.

Indexed Addressing

Indexed addressing is very similar to indirect addressing except that the address is held in index register IX or IY rather than BC, DE, or HL. In addition, the value held in either of these two index registers is modified by the addition of a displacement. The form of the operand is either (IX + dd) or IY + dd) where dd is a signed 8-bit displacement. A displacement is a distance. Here it is the distance from the address placed in the index register and may range in value from − 128 to + 127 (a signed 8-bit number).

For example, if the IX register contains a 1000H and the operand is a (IX + 0AH) then the actual memory address referenced by the operand is 100AH. Likewise if the operand is a (IY + 0F8H) and IY contains a 2200H then the actual address is 2200H plus a − 8. (F8H is a − 8.) Here the address is 21F8H. If the displacement is 0, this text indicates it by using either (IX) or (IY).

Immediate Addressing

The immediate addressing mode is used if constant data are used in a program. The data are encoded immediately following the opcode in program memory. (See Figure 3-2.) The Z80 microprocessor has two forms of immediate addressing: 8- and 16-bit immediate addressing. The 8-bit form uses the notation d8 in Appendix A and the instruction listing in this and the next two chapters, and the 16-bit form uses a d16.

Byte 1   Byte 2

Op-code	Immediate data

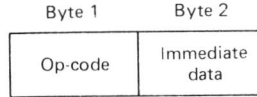

Figure 3–2 An LD instruction showing the placement of the 8 bits of immediate data.

Table 3-2 illustrates some 8- and 16-bit immediate data instructions. The 8-bit immediate instructions are always two bytes in length, and the 16-bit immediate instructions are always three bytes in length. Notice from Table 3-2 that if 16-bit data are used, the data are stored in the same form as an address, as discussed earlier in this section on direct addressing.

TABLE 3-2. EXAMPLE IMMEDIATE INSTRUCTIONS

Assembly	Machine	Comment
LD B, 12H	06 12	12H is loaded to B.
LD A, 60	3E 3C	3CH is loaded to A.
LD BC, 100	11 64 00	64H is loaded to BC.
LD IY, 1234H	DD 21 34 12	1234H is loaded to IY.

3-3 IMMEDIATE DATA TRANSFER INSTRUCTIONS

The Z80 microprocessor has two basic forms of the immediate data transfer instruction. One form is used to transfer an 8-bit number into a register, the memory location indirectly addressed by the HL register pair (HL), or the memory location addressed by the IX and IY index register with a displacement (IX + dd) or (IY + dd). The other form is used to load any 16-bit register pair, the stack pointer, or any index register with 16 bits of immediate data. Table 3-3 illustrates all of the immediate data transfer instructions with their assembly language and machine language forms. The term immediate is used to indicate that the data immediately follow the opcode in the program.

The 8-bit Load Immediate Instruction

The LD (load) instruction is used to place any 8-bit number into any register, any memory location indirectly addressed by HL, or any memory location indexed by IX or IY. Example 3-1 shows how a 12H is placed into the B register in both hexadecimal machine language (06 12) and in symbolic assembly language (LD B,12H).

Example 3-1

```
06 12          LD B,12H        ;moves 12H into B
```

TABLE 3-3. IMMEDIATE DATA TRANSFER INSTRUCTIONS

Assembly	Machine	Comment
LD B,d8	06 d8	d8 is moved into B
LD C,d8	0E d8	d8 is moved into C
LD D,d8	16 d8	d8 is moved into D
LD E,d8	1E d8	d8 is moved into E
LD H,d8	26 d8	d8 is moved into H
LD L,d8	2E d8	d8 is moved into L
LD (HL),d8	36 d8	d8 is moved into (HL)
LD A,d8	3E d8	d8 is moved into A
LD (IX + dd),d8	DD 36 dd d8	d8 is moved into (IX + dd)
LD (IY + dd),d8	FD 36 dd d8	d8 is moved into (IY + dd)
LD BC,d16	01 ll hh	d16 is moved into BC
LD DE,d16	11 ll hh	d16 is moved into DE
LD HL,d16	21 ll hh	d16 is moved into HL
LD SP,d16	31 ll hh	d16 is moved into SP
LD IX,d16	DD 21 ll hh	d16 is moved into IX
LD IY,d16	FD 21 ll hh	d16 is moved into IY

Notes: d8, 8-bits of data; d16, 16-bits of data; hh, high-order data byte; ll, low-order data byte; dd, signed 8-bit displacement.

Just as a number can be loaded into the B register (see Example 3-1), a number can be moved into any internal Z80 register. Example 3-2 shows some additional load immediate instructions with comments that explain the operation of each instruction.

Example 3-2

```
1E 64        LD E,64H      ;moves a 64H into E
0E 64        LD C,100      ;moves a 100 into C
3E FF        LD A,-1       ;moves a -1 into A
2E 33        LD L,33H      ;moves a 33H into L
```

The LD (HL),d8 instruction is used to store a byte of data in the memory. This instruction uses the HL register pair to refer to (point to) a location in the memory. (Refer to section 3-1 on indirect addressing.)

Suppose that the HL register pair contains 1000H and the LD (HL),11 instruction is executed. This instruction loads the immediate byte of data (11H) into the memory location addressed by the HL register pair (1000H). In other words, an 11H is stored in memory location 1000H. Example 3-3 illustrates how this instruction is stored in the memory together with the instructions that place a 1000H into the HL register pair.

Example 3-3

```
26 10        LD H,10H      ;moves a 10H into H
2E 00        LD L,00H      ;moves a 00H into L
36 11        LD (HL),11H   ;moves an 11H into 1000H
```

The 16-bit Load Immediate Instruction

The 16-bit LD (load) immediate instruction is used to load a 16-bit number into any register pair (BC, DE, or HL), the stack pointer (SP), or any index register (IX or IY). Each 16-bit load immediate instruction is three or four bytes in length with the last two bytes containing the 16 bit data that are loaded into a register pair, stack pointer, or index register. The data are always stored with the low-order part (11) first, followed by the high-order part (hh) last. Example 3-4 shows how a 10CDH is placed into the HL register pair using a 16-bit LD instruction. Notice how the least significant byte (CD) immediately follows the opcode (21), and the most significant byte (10) follows the least significant byte. Of course, in symbolic assembly language, the number appears as a 10CDH.

Example 3-4

```
21 CD 10        LD HL,10CDH     ;moves a 10CDH into HL
```

If Example 3-3 is redone using the 16-bit LD in place of the two 8-bit loads used to load HL with a 1000H, the resulting program (see Example 3-5) is a much simplified version.

Example 3-5

```
21 00 10        LD HL,1000H     ;moves 1000H into HL
36 11           LD (HL),11H     ;store 11H into 1000H
```

Example 3-6 uses the indexed instructions to move a 01H into memory locations 1000H, 1001H, and 1002H. Notice how the displacement is used to accomplish this operation. IX is first loaded with a 1000H, and then indexed load immediate instructions are used to store a 01H in each of these three memory locations.

Example 3-6

```
DD 21 00 10     LD IX,1000H     ;load IX with 1000H
DD 36 00 01     LD (IX),01H     ;load 1000H with 01H
DD 36 01 01     LD (IX+1),01H   ;load 1001H with 01H
DD 36 02 01     LD (IX+2),01H   ;load 1002H with 01H
```

3-4 DIRECT DATA TRANSFER INSTRUCTIONS

The direct data transfer instructions are most useful if only one byte or word of data are transferred between a register or register pair and the memory. Otherwise it is best to use either indirect addressing or indexed addressing which makes it easier to transfer many bytes between the memory and a register. The Z80 has two forms of direct addressed instructions: one loads the accumulator to memory or from memory, and the other loads the register pairs or index registers to or from the memory. These instructions

TABLE 3-4. DIRECTLY ADDRESSED INSTRUCTIONS

Assembly	Machine	Comment
LD A,(a16)	3A ll hh	A is loaded from a16
LD (a16),A	32 ll hh	a16 is loaded from A
LD (a16),BC	ED 43 ll hh	a16 is loaded from BC
LD (a16),DE	ED 53 ll hh	a16 is loaded from DE
LD (a16),HL	22 ll hh	a16 is loaded from HL
LD (a16),IX	DD 22 ll hh	a16 is loaded from IX
LD (a16),IY	FD 22 ll hh	a16 is loaded from IY
LD (a16),SP	ED 73 ll hh	a16 is loaded from SP
LD BC,(a16)	ED 4B ll hh	BC is loaded from a16
LD DE,(a16)	ED 5B ll hh	DE is loaded from a16
LD HL,(a16)	2A ll hh	HL is loaded from a16
LD IX,(a16)	DD 2A ll hh	IX is loaded from a16
LD IY,(a16)	FD 2A ll hh	IY is loaded from a16
LD SP,(a16)	ED 7B ll hh	SP is loaded from a16

Notes: a16, 16-bit memory address; ll, low-order address; hh, high-order address.

are listed in both the machine and assembly language versions in Table 3-4. All directly addressed instructions are three or four bytes in length with the last two bytes containing the 16-bit memory address (a16) of the operand.

The 8-Bit Direct Addressed Instructions

Two instructions, the first two in Table 3-4, directly address the memory and transfer an 8-bit number between the accumulator (A) and the memory. In both cases, the opcode is followed by a 16-bit memory address. In the LD A,(a16) instruction a byte of data is removed from the memory and loaded into the accumulator. The LD (a16),A instruction transfers a copy of the contents of the accumulator into the memory.

Example 3-7 shows how a number is copied from memory location 1000H and stored into 1200H using the LD A,(A16) and LD (a16),A instructions.

Example 3-7

```
3A 00 10        LD  A,(1000H)    ;load A from 1000H
32 00 12        LD  (1200H),A    ;load 1200H from A
```

The 16-Bit Direct Addressed Instructions

There are many more 16-bit direct addressed instructions than 8-bit direct addressed instructions. Data may be transferred between the memory and BC, DE, HL, IX, IY, or SP. These instructions store or read data from two consecutive bytes of memory beginning with the byte addressed by a16 in the instruction. In all cases the two bytes from the 16-bit register are stored or read from memory so that the lowest numbered

memory address contains the low-order byte and the highest numbered memory location
contains the high-order byte. For example, if a LD (1000H),DE instruction is executed,
the E register (low-order part) is loaded into memory location 1000H, and the D register
(high-order part) is loaded into location 1001H.

Example 3-8 illustrates how the contents of BC, DE, and HL are stored in 6
consecutive bytes of memory beginning at address 1000H. Here three load instructions
are used to store these three register pairs in the memory.

Example 3-8

```
ED 43 00 10     LD (1000H),BC   ;load 1000H with BC
ED 53 02 10     LD (1002H),DE   ;load 1002H with DE
22 04 10        LD (1004H),HL   ;load 1004H with HL
```

3-5 INDIRECT DATA TRANSFER INSTRUCTIONS

Although HL is used to indirectly address the memory, there are other ways to indirectly
address memory data. In this section we will not cover HL as it is used to address
memory data because it is presented in Section 3-3 and also in later sections of this
chapter. Instead this section explains the use of the BC and DE register pairs which
are also used to indirectly address memory data.

Table 3-5 lists the different forms of the LD instruction that use BC and DE to
indirectly address memory data. Notice that each of these instructions is only one byte
in length because the address of the data is stored in either the BC or DE register pairs.

To illustrate the operation of these indirect instructions, Example 3-7 will be
repeated using the BC and DE register pairs to indirectly address memory locations
1000H and 1200H. Example 3-9 illustrates how the BC and DE register pairs are loaded
with these memory addresses and also how LD instructions are used to transfer data
from location 1000H into 1200H.

Example 3-9

```
01 00 10     LD BC,1000H   ;loads BC with 1000H
11 00 12     LD DE,1200H   ;loads DE with 1200H
02           LD A,(BC)     ;loads A with (1000H)
1A           LD (DE),A     ;loads (1200H) with A
```

TABLE 3-5.   INDIRECTLY ADDRESSED INSTRUCTIONS

Assembly	Machine	Comment
LD A,(BC)	02	loads A from (BC)
LD A,(DE)	12	loads A from (DE)
LD (BC),A	0A	loads (BC) from A
LD (DE),A	1A	loads (DE) from A

LD   rd, rs   (LD B, C)

rd = Destination register
rs = Source register

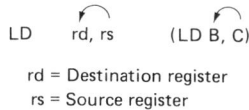

Figure 3–3   The LD instruction illustrating both the source and destination registers and the direction of the data transfer.

3-6 REGISTER DATA TRANSFER INSTRUCTIONS

The largest group of data transfer instructions is the register data transfer group, which includes indexed addressing and also indirect addressing via the HL register pair. These forms of addressing, indexed and indirect, have been included here for ease of understanding. The basic form of this instruction is listed in Figure 3-3. The rightmost register is called the source register and the leftmost the destination register. These instructions copy the contents of the source register into the destination register. Note that the contents of the source register never change and the contents of the destination register always change. The direction of the flow is indicated by the arrow in Figure 3-3.

A complete list of all the register instructions is provided in Table 3-6 together with a comment about the operation of each of these instructions. Notice that some of these instructions use register addressing, indirect addressing via HL, or indexed addressing via IX and IY. Also notice that not all of these instructions have a useful purpose such as LD B,B. The LD B,B instruction will copy the contents of register B into register B, but this does not serve any useful function.

Example 3-10 shows how a number in the accumulator is moved into both the D and E registers. The first instruction copies the contents of the accumulator into the D register, and the second copies the accumulator into the E register.

Example 3-10

```
57              LD D,A          ; loads D from A
5F              LD E,A          ; loads E from A
```

Another example (Example 3-11) uses the load instructions to clear the contents of all the internal 8-bit registers. Here the accumulator is first cleared to zero by loading it with a 00H. Next, load instructions are used to load all the 8-bit registers from the accumulator.

Example 3-11

```
3E 00           LD A,00H        ; loads A with 00H
47              LD B,A          ; clear B
4F              LD C,A          ; clear C
57              LD D,A          ; clear D
5F              LD E,A          ; clear E
67              LD H,A          ; clear H
6F              LD L,A          ; clear L
```

TABLE 3-6. REGISTER DATA TRANSFER INSTRUCTIONS

Assembly	Machine	Comment
LD B,B	40	loads B from B
LD B,C	41	loads B from C
LD B,D	42	loads B from D
LD B,E	43	loads B from E
LD B,H	44	loads B from H
LD B,L	45	loads B from L
LD B,(HL)	46	loads B from (HL)
LD B,A	47	loads B from A
LD B,(IX + dd)	DD 46 dd	loads B from (IX + dd)
LD B,(IY + dd)	FD 46 dd	loads B from (IY + dd)
LD C,B	48	loads C from B
LD C,C	49	loads C from C
LD C,D	4A	loads C from D
LD C,E	4B	loads C from E
LD C,H	4C	loads C from H
LD C,L	4D	loads C from L
LD C,(HL)	4E	loads C from (HL)
LD C,A	4F	loads C from A
LD C,(IX + dd)	DD 4E dd	loads C from (IX + dd)
LD C,(IY + dd)	FD 4E dd	loads C from (IY + dd)
LD D,B	50	loads D from B
LD D,C	51	loads D from C
LD D,D	52	loads D from D
LD D,E	53	loads D from E
LD D,H	54	loads D from H
LD D,L	55	loads D from L
LD D,(HL)	56	loads D from (HL)
LD D,A	57	loads D from A
LD D,(IX + dd)	DD 56 dd	loads D from (IX + dd)
LD D,(IY + dd)	FD 56 dd	loads D from (IY + dd)
LD E,B	58	loads E from B
LD E,C	59	loads E from C
LD E,D	5A	loads E from D
LD E,E	5B	loads E from E
LD E,H	5C	loads E from H
LD E,L	5D	loads E from L
LD E,(HL)	5E	loads E from (HL)
LD E,A	5F	loads E from A
LD E,(IX + dd)	DD 5E dd	loads E from (IX + dd)
LD E,(IY + dd)	FD 5E dd	loads E from (IY + dd)
LD H,B	60	loads H from B
LD H,C	61	loads H from C
LD H,D	62	loads H from D
LD H,E	63	loads H from E
LD H,H	64	loads H from H
LD H,L	65	loads H from L
LD H,(HL)	66	loads H from (HL)

TABLE 3-6.   (continued)

Assembly	Machine	Comment
LD H,A	67	loads H from A
LD H,(IX + dd)	DD 66 dd	loads H from (IX + dd)
LD H,(IY + dd)	FD 66 dd	loads H from (IY + dd)
LD L,B	68	loads L from B
LD L,C	69	loads L from C
LD L,D	6A	loads L from D
LD L,E	6B	loads L from E
LD L,H	6C	loads L from H
LD L,L	6D	loads L from L
LD L,(HL)	6E	loads L from (HL)
LD L,A	6F	loads L from A
LD L,(IX + dd)	DD 6E dd	loads L from (IX + dd)
LD L,(IY + dd)	FD 6E dd	loads L from (IY + dd)
LD (HL),B	70	loads (HL) from B
LD (HL),C	71	loads (HL) from C
LD (HL),D	72	loads (HL) from D
LD (HL),E	73	loads (HL) from E
LD (HL),H	74	loads (HL) from H
LD (HL),L	75	loads (HL) from L
LD (HL),(HL)	—	invalid instruction
LD (HL),A	77	loads (HL) from A
LD A,B	78	loads A from B
LD A,C	79	loads A from C
LD A,D	7A	loads A from D
LD A,E	7B	loads A from E
LD A,H	8C	loads A from H
LD A,L	7D	loads A from L
LD A,(HL)	7E	loads A from (HL)
LD A,A	7F	loads A from A
LD A,(IX + dd)	DD 7E dd	loads A from (IX + dd)
LD A,(IY + dd)	FD 7E dd	loads A from (IY + dd)
LD (IX + dd),B	DD 70 dd	loads (IX + dd) from B
LD (IX + dd),C	DD 71 dd	loads (IX + dd) from C
LD (IX + dd),D	DD 72 dd	loads (IX + dd) from D
LD (IX + dd),E	DD 73 dd	loads (IX + dd) from E
LD (IX + dd),H	DD 74 dd	loads (IX + dd) from H
LD (IX + dd),L	DD 75 dd	loads (IX + dd) from L
LD (IX + dd),A	DD 77 dd	loads (IX + dd) from A
LD (IY + dd),B	FD 70 dd	loads (IY + dd) from B
LD (IY + dd),C	FD 71 dd	loads (IY + dd) from C
LD (IY + dd),D	FD 72 dd	loads (IY + dd) from D
LD (IY + dd),E	FD 73 dd	loads (IY + dd) from E
LD (IY + dd),H	FD 74 dd	loads (IY + dd) from H
LD (IY + dd),L	FD 75 dd	loads (IY + dd) from L
LD (IY + dd),A	FD 77 dd	loads (IY + dd) from A

Note: dd, 8-bit signed displacement; ( ), address of memory data.

Indirectly Addressing Memory Using HL

Suppose that Example 3-9 is again repeated, but this time a LD using (HL) will be used. Refer to Example 3-12 for the program that moves a number out of memory location 1000H into memory location 1200H via the HL register pair.

Example 3-12

```
21 00 10        LD HL,1000H     ;address 1000H
7E              LD A,(HL)       ;get data from 1000H
26 12           LD H,12H        ;change address to 1200H
77              LD (HL),A       ;save at 1200H
```

Using the Index Registers to Address Memory

The index register can also be used to accomplish the task of Example 3-12. Example 3-13 shows how IX and IY are used to address memory location 1000H and 1200H. The data are then moved from 1000H to A and back to 1200H from A.

Example 3-13

```
DD 21 00 10     LD IX,1000H     ;address 1000H
FD 21 00 12     LD IY,1200H     ;address 1200H
DD 7E 00        LD A,(IX)       ;load A from 1000H
FD 77 00        LD (IY),A       ;load 1200H from A
```

3-7 STACK DATA TRANSFER INSTRUCTIONS

As mentioned in Chapter 2, the Z80 microprocessor has a LIFO (last-in, first-out) stack memory that is used to store return addresses for subroutines and also data temporarily. This section of the text covers data storage on the stack, and Chapter 5 covers subroutines. Table 3-7 lists the stack data transfer instructions available in the Z80 microprocessor's instructions set. This set of instructions consists of PUSHs, POPs, and EXs (Exchanges).

Stack Memory Operation

Before the stack data transfer instructions are covered, it is important that the operation of the stack memory is understood. The microprocessor doesn't know where the stack memory is located when the power is first applied to the system; it must be told. This is normally accomplished by first loading the stack pointer (SP) register with an address in the memory. (Loading the stack pointer at the beginning of the program is essential if any of the stack operations are used within the program.) The address loaded to the stack pointer is selected so that the stack resides in the read/write RAM memory. The stack pointer is always loaded with the memory address that is one byte above the top of the stack. The stack pointer always points to the current entry/exit point on the stack. (Refer to Figure 3-4 for a pictorial view of the stack memory and the stack pointer.)

TABLE 3-7. STACK DATA TRANSFER INSTRUCTIONS

Assembly	Machine	Comment
PUSH AF	F5	AF is stored on the stack
PUSH BC	C5	BC is stored on the stack
PUSH DE	D5	DE is stored on the stack
PUSH HL	E5	HL is stored on the stack
PUSH IX	DD E5	IX is stored on the stack
PUSH IY	FD E5	IY is stored on the stack
POP AF	F1	AF is loaded from the stack
POP BC	C1	BC is loaded from the stack
POP DE	D1	DE is loaded from the stack
POP HL	E1	HL is loaded from the stack
POP IX	DD E1	IX is loaded from the stack
POP IY	FD E1	IY is loaded from the stack
EX (SP),HL	E3	HL is exchanged with stack data
EX (SP),IX	DD E3	IX is exchanged with stack data
EX (SP),IY	FD E3	IY is exchanged with stack data

Operation of the PUSH and POP Instructions

The stack memory in the Z80 is a LIFO stack or, more descriptively, a push-down, pop-up stack. The name push-down, pop-up describes how the stack memory functions. If data are pushed (placed) onto the stack, they move into the memory at locations SP − 1 and SP − 2. (Note that data are always stored as pairs of bytes on the stack.) The high-order byte is always stored first at the highest numbered memory location (SP − 1), and then the low-order byte is stored at the lowest numbered memory locations (SP − 2). Once data are pushed onto the stack, the contents of the stack pointer register are decremented by 2 (SP = SP − 2). The next push will occur below the last one, in other words.

The POP instruction functions in the reverse order of the PUSH. POP causes data to be removed from the stack starting with the low-order byte at memory location SP.

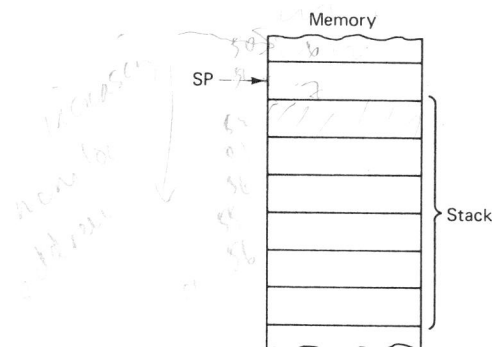

Figure 3–4 The stack memory which begins at one memory location below the SP address.

| | |
| Memory
(before PUSH BC) | Memory
(after PUSH BC) |

SP →

| 1000 |
| 0FFF |
| 0FFE |
| 0FFD |
| 0FFC |
| 0FFB |
| 0FFA |
| 0FF9 |

? 0FFF
? 0FFE

(B)
(C) ← SP

(a)   (b)

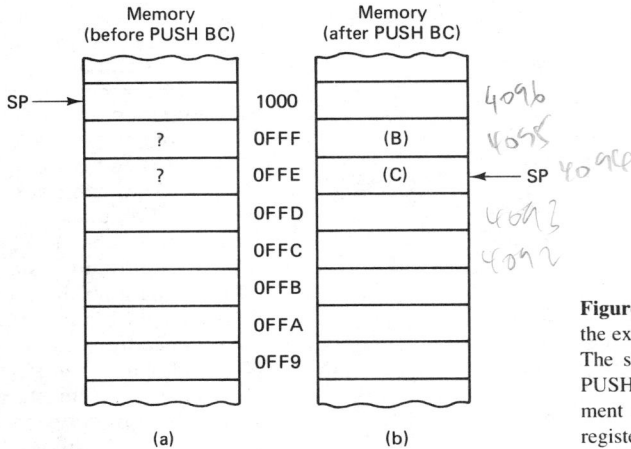

Figure 3–5 (a) The stack and SP before the execution of a PUSH BC instruction. (b) The stack and SP after the execution of a PUSH BC instruction illustrating the placement of the contents of both the B and C registers on the stack.

The high-order byte is next removed from memory location SP + 1, and finally the contents of the SP are incremented by two (SP = SP + 2).

Suppose that the SP is loaded with 1000H, and BC contains a 1234H. A PUSH BC instruction places the contents of BC (1234H) onto the stack. Here B (12H) is stored at memory location 0FFFH (SP − 1), and the contents of C (34H) are stored at memory location 0FFEH (SP − 2). The SP is then decremented by a two to 0FFEH. If this is followed by a POP AF, data from location 0FFEH (SP) are moved into the flags and data from 0FFFH (SP + 1) are moved into the accumulator. Figure 3-5 illustrates the foregoing series of events.

Example 3-14 illustrates how the stack can be used to exchange the contents of the DE and BC register pairs. Here the BC pair is first pushed on the stack followed by the DE pair. Because DE was the last information placed on the stack it is the first to come off the stack. The POP BC instruction removes the prior contents of the DE register from the stack and places it into the BC register pair. This is followed by the POP DE instruction which removes the prior contents of the BC register pair from the stack and places it into the DE register pair. The contents of the two register pairs have now been swapped. Another interesting thing is that the SP is now back where it started. The stack operations use the same section of the memory (the stack) over and over again in a program.

Example 3-14

```
C5        PUSH  BC      ;BC to stack
D5        PUSH  DE      ;DE to stack
C1        POP   BC      ;get BC
D1        POP   DE      ;get DE
```

The PUSH and POP instructions should always occur in pairs in a program or a subroutine. If there is one PUSH there must normally be one POP; two PUSHs should have two POPs, etc. If this rule is broken, the stack will eventually occupy the entire memory.

The Stack Exchange (EX) Instructions

These instructions exchange the most recent data placed on the stack with the contents of HL, IX, or IY. For example, if a 1000H is PUSHed onto the stack and IX contains a 2000H, an EX (SP),IX instruction will exchange these two values. After execution, IX equals a 1000H and the stack contains a 2000H. These instructions and their application are illustrated in later chapters of this text.

3-8 MISCELLANEOUS DATA TRANSFER INSTRUCTIONS

In previous sections of this chapter we have observed the operation of most of the data transfer instructions except for I/O instructions, block transfers, and some of the special purpose instructions. Table 3-8 lists the remaining data transfer instructions together with a brief description of their operation.

Load SP Instructions

The Z80 has instructions that transfer the contents of HL, IX, or IY into the stack pointer register. Although these instructions do not have wide application they are found in certain circumstances. The most common approach to loading the stack pointer is with the LD SP,d16 immediate instruction.

Exchange Instructions

There are quite a few exchange instructions in the Z80 instructions set. A few of these have already been explained in the last section under stack operations because they exchanged stack data with HL, IX, or IY. The remaining exchange instructions, EX AF,AF′ and EXX, are used to exchange the main and alternate registers. The EX AF,AF′ instruction exchanges the contents of the main and alternate accumulator and flags. The EXX instruction is used to exchange the main and alternate BC, DE, and HL register pairs.

The last exchange instruction is the EX DE,HL i instruction. This instruction exchanges the contents of the DE register pair with the HL register pair. Suppose that this instruction is used to copy a number from memory location 1000H and store it in 1200H. (It is not actually used for that, but instead is used to position these addresses in the HL pair so that indirect addressing can be used.) Refer to Example 3-15 for this program.

Example 3-15

```
21 00 10    LD    HL,1000H    ;address location 1000H
11 00 12    LD    DE,1200H    ;address location 1200H
7E          LD    A,(HL)      ;get data at 1000H
EB          EX    DE,HL       ;exchange memory pointers
77          LD    (HL),A      ;save data at 1200H
```

TABLE 3-8.   MISCELLANEOUS DATA TRANSFER INSTRUCTIONS

Assembly	Machine	Comment
LD SP,HL	F9	SP is loaded from HL
LD SP,IX	DD F9	SP is loaded from IX
LD SP,IY	FD F9	SP is loaded from IY
EX AF,AF'	O8	Exchange AF with AF'
EX DE,HL	EB	Exchange DE with HL
EXX	D9	Exchange main and alternate BC, DE, and HL
LDD	ED A8	(DE) is loaded to (HL) after which decrement BC, DE, and HL
LDDR	ED B8	same as LDD, but repeated until BC = O
LDI	ED AO	(DE) is loaded with (HL) after which DE and HL are incremented and BC is decremented
LDIR	ED BO	same as LDI, but repeated until BC = O
IN A,d8	DB d8	input to A from port d8
IN B,(C)	ED 40	input to B from port (C)
IN C,(C)	ED 48	input to C from port (C)
IN D,(C)	ED 50	input to D from port (C)
IN E,(C)	ED 58	input to E from port (C)
IN H,(C)	ED 60	input to H from port (C)
IN L,(C)	ED 68	input to L from port (C)
IN A,(C)	ED 78	input to A from port (C)
IND	ED AA	input to (HL) from port (C) after which decrement B and HL
INDR	ED BA	same as IND, but repeated until B = O
INI	ED A2	input to (HL) from port (C) after which HL is incremented and B is decremented
INIR	ED B2	same as INI, but repeated until B = O
OUT d8,A	D3 d8	output A to port d8
OUT (C),B	ED 41	output B to port (C)
OUT (C),C	ED 49	output C to port (C)
OUT (C),D	ED 51	output D to port (C)
OUT (C),E	ED 59	output E to port (C)
OUT (C),H	ED 61	output H to port (C)
OUT (C),L	ED 69	output H to port (C)
OUT (C),A	ED 79	output A to port (C)
OUTD	ED AB	output (HL) to port (C) after which HL and B are decremented
OTDR	ED BB	same as OUTD, but repeated until B = O
OUTI	ED A3	output (HL) to port (C) after which HL is incremented and B is decremented
OTIR	ED B3	same as OUTI, but repeated until B = O

Block Data Transfers

The block data transfer instructions are very powerful in the Z80 microprocessor. Each of them takes the contents of the memory location addressed by the DE register pair and transfers it to the location addressed by the HL register pair. These instructions move data from one part of the memory to another. In addition to transferring the data, the DE and HL register pairs are also incremented or decremented depending upon which block transfer instruction is chosen. LDD will decrement the pointers, and LDI will increment them. The BC register pair is also always decremented by these instructions. Therefore, the LDD instruction transfers a byte of data from (HL) to (DE), then decrements HL, DE, and BC. LDI transfers a byte of data from (HL) to (DE), then increments HL and DE and decrements BC.

Both the LDD and LDI instructions can be repeated. If the LDDR instruction is executed, it is repeated until the contents of the BC register are decremented to a 0000H. If the LDIR instruction is executed it also repeats until BC becomes a 0000H.

Example 3-16 illustrates the use of the LDIR instruction to transfer the contents of a block of data from one section of the memory to another. Here HL (source address) is loaded with a 1000H, DE (destination address) is loaded with a 2000H, and BC (count) is loaded with a 0100H before the LDIR instruction. This means that this short program will transfer 100H (256) bytes of data from a block of memory beginning at 1000H into a block of memory beginning at 2000H. In all the bytes between 1000H and 10FFH are copied into bytes 2000H—20FFH.

Example 3-16

```
21 00 10      LD    HL,1000H    ;address source at 1000H
11 00 20      LD    DE,2000H    ;address destination at 2000H
01 00 01      LD    BC,0100H    ;load count of 100H
ED B0         LDIR              ;transfer data
```

Input/Output Data Transfer Instructions

The I/O instructions allow data to be transferred between the Z80 and external I/O devices. These external devices are addressed with an 8-bit I/O port number or address. Two basic types of I/O instructions exist in the Z80. One is a fixed I/O instruction where the I/O port number is stored in the memory following the opcode, and the other is a variable I/O port number that is stored in the C register. These I/O instructions are called fixed because often instructions are stored in a ROM or called variable because the contents of the C register can be changed by the program.

The IN instruction inputs data to any register (A, B, C, D, E, H, or L) from an external I/O port and the OUT sends data from any register to an external I/O port. For example, the IN A,(C) instruction inputs data from the I/O port whose address is stored in C to the accumulator. The OUT (C),L instruction copies the contents of the L register to the I/O port whose address is stored in C.

In addition to these I/O instructions there are also block I/O instructions. The block I/O instructions allow data to be output from a block of memory or read into (input) to a block of memory. In both cases, the block of memory is addressed by the HL register pair, and the I/O port number is held in the C register. As with the block data transfer instructions the block I/O instructions may also be automatically repeated. The only difference is that the counter is an 8-bit count in the B register instead of a 16-bit count in the BC register pair.

3-9 SUMMARY

1. Data transfer instructions are used to transfer information from register to register, from register to memory, from memory to register, between the microprocessor and the stack, between the microprocessor and the I/O, and between blocks of memory.

2. Five addressing modes are used in the Z80 microprocessor: direct, register, register indirect, indexed, and immediate.

3. Direct addressing is used whenever a memory location is accessed by storing the address in the memory immediately following the opcode.

4. Register addressing is used to address either a single 8-bit register (B, C, D, E, H, L, and A), a 16-bit register pair (BC, DE, HL, and SP), or an index register (IX or IY).

5. Register indirect addressing allows the memory data to be addressed via the contents of the BC, DE, or HL register pair.

6. Indexed addressing allows the microprocessor to address memory data through the address stored in either IX or IY. In addition the index register may also have an 8-bit signed displacement attached to it so that the index address may be referenced via the displacement.

7. Immediate instructions allow an 8-bit immediate byte or a 16-bit immediate word to be loaded into a register, register pair, or an index register.

8. If a memory address is specified in an instruction it is surrounded by parentheses. For example, the LD A,(HL) instruction loads A with the contents of the memory locations addressed by HL.

9. In addition to using HL to address memory data the contents of BC, DE, IX, and IY may also be used to address memory data.

10. The register data transfer instructions are by far the most numerous type of data transfer instruction. Most are one byte in length.

11. The stack memory in the Z80 is a LIFO (last-in, first-out) memory that is used to store return addresses for subroutines and also to store data temporarily.

12. The stack pointer (SP) register is used to indirectly address the stack memory. It is used to address the stack for PUSHes, POPs, and some EX (exchange) instructions.

13. The block data transfer instructions use the HL register pair to address the source block, the DE register pair to address the destination block, and in a repeated transfer the BC register pair to hold the count.

14. The IN and OUT instructions either use the C register to hold the I/O port number or the byte following the IN or OUT opcode. If the C register holds the port number it is a variable I/O instruction, and if the port number is in C, then it is a fixed I/O instruction.

3-10 GLOSSARY

Destination register   The register that receives a copy of the data in the execution of an instruction.

Direct addressing   If memory data are directly addressed, the memory address is stored with the instruction in a program. The address is stored so that the last byte of the instruction is the high-order portion of the address and the second to last byte is the low-order portion of the address.

Displacement   A number that is added to an index register to locate the data. It may be positive or negative to reference forward or backwards in the memory.

Immediate addressing   An immediate instruction contains the data used with the instruction in the form of the second byte (8-bit immediate data) or second and third bytes (16-bit immediate data) following the opcode or opcode and its extension of the instruction.

Immediate data   8- or 16-bit data that are stored with the instruction.

Indexed addressing   An addressing mode where the index register (either IX or IY) contains the memory address of the data used by the instruction. In addition, an 8-bit signed displacement may be added to form the address.

Indirect addressing   Data are indirectly addressed through the address held in HL, DE, or BC.

Port   An I/O device in the Z80 is called an I/O port.

Port address   An 8-bit number that is used to address a unique I/O device.

Register addressing   A register-addressed instruction specifies the register or register pair where the data are located.

Source register   The register that supplies the data in an instruction. The source is never changed by the instruction.

QUESTIONS AND PROBLEMS

3-1. What five addressing modes are available for use with the Z80 microprocessor?

3-2. Direct addressed instructions use _____ bytes to store the address.

3-3. Describe how the memory address is stored with a direct addressed instruction.

3-4. Convert the following 16-bit memory addresses into the form required when stored with a direct addressed instruction: 1000H, 234AH, ABCDH, 5000H, and 456FH.

3-5. What 8-bit registers are available for use with register addressed instructions? What 16-bit registers are available?

3-6. How does one use the HL pair in an instruction to indirectly address the memory?

3-7. Explain how 16-bit immediate data are stored with an instruction.

3-8. Convert the following symbolic instructions into hexadecimal machine language instructions: LD DE,1200H, LD C,90H, LD SP,1234H, LD (HL),10, and LD (HL),10H.

3-9. Write a sequence of immediate instructions that will place a 0000H into the BC register pair and a 12H into the accumulator.

3-10. Write a sequence of immediate instructions that will place a 16H into memory location 1200H and a 17H into memory location 1201H.

3-11. Explain how the LD A,(1000H) instruction functions.

3-12. Explain what answer is found in memory location 1200H and 1201H in the following sequence of instructions:

$$
\begin{array}{ll}
\text{26 22} & \text{LD H,22H} \\
\text{2E 44} & \text{LD L,44H} \\
\text{22 00 12} & \text{LD (1200H),HL}
\end{array}
$$

3-13. Which register indirect instruction is used to store the contents of the accumulator in the memory location indirectly addressed by the BC register pair?

3-14. Explain what answer is found in memory location 1200H after the following sequence of instructions:

$$
\begin{array}{ll}
\text{06 12} & \text{LD B,12H} \\
\text{0E 00} & \text{LD C,00H} \\
\text{3E 77} & \text{LD A,77H} \\
\text{12} & \text{LD (BC),A}
\end{array}
$$

3-15. Write a sequence of instructions that will use register indirect addressing to transfer the number stored in memory location 1300H to memory location 1301H.

3-16. If IX = 1200H and the following instruction is executed: LD A,(IX + 12H), what memory location is loaded into the accumulator?

3-17. Why is it rare to find an LD B,B instruction in a program?

3-18. Explain what the LD (HL),C instruction accomplishes if HL = 1233H and C = 34H.

3-19. Write a sequence of instructions that swap the contents of the BC register pair with the DE register pair.

3-20. Write a sequence of instructions that store a 00H into memory locations 1000H through 1003H.

3-21. If a 1000H is pushed onto the stack followed by a 2000H, which number comes off the stack first?

3-22. The push instruction is used to place the contents of a _____-bit register onto the stack.

3-23. What is placed on the stack by a PUSH AF instruction?

3-24. What number appears in the BC register pair after the following sequence of instructions?

$$
\begin{array}{ll}
\text{21 00 30} & \text{LD HL,3000H} \\
\text{11 00 20} & \text{LD DE,2000H} \\
\text{E5} & \text{PUSH HL} \\
\text{D5} & \text{PUSH DE} \\
\text{E1} & \text{POP HL} \\
\text{C1} & \text{POP BC}
\end{array}
$$

3-25. If a PUSH AF is immediately followed by a POP BC instruction where does the contents of the flag register appear?

3-26. Write a short program that uses the block transfer instruction to transfer 50H bytes of data from a block beginning at memory location 0000H to a block beginning at memory location 2000H.

3-27. Explain the operation of an EXX instruction.

3-28. Explain the operation of the OUT 12H,A instruction.

3-29. Explain the operation of the IN B,(C) instruction.

3-30. Which instructions are used to place a number into the stack pointer register? List all of them.

chapter 4

Arithmetic and Logic Instructions

The Z80 arithmetic and logic instructions described in this chapter include the following operations: addition, addition with carry, subtraction, subtraction with borrow, inversion, negation, AND, OR, Exclusive-OR, set, reset, bit test, shift, and rotates. In addition to the operations performed by these instructions this chapter details the operation of the flag bits with each instruction. None of the instructions described in Chapter 3 affected the flags. The flags are only generally affected by an arithmetic or a logic operation.

4-1 OBJECTIVES

Upon completion of this chapter, you will be able to:

1. Explain the operation of the Z80 arithmetic and logic instructions and their effect on the flags.
2. Write short programs that use arithmetic and logic operations.
3. Use the instructions in the instruction set to set, clear, invert, and test any bit.
4. Test the contents of the accumulator using the AND A or OR A instructions.
5. Explain the operation of the shift and rotate instruction and their effect on the flag bits.

4-2 ADDITION

Addition takes several forms in the Z80 microprocessor: 8-bit binary, 16-bit binary, and two digit binary-coded-decimal (BCD). In binary addition either signed or unsigned numbers are added, and in BCD addition only unsigned numbers are added. The instruction set supports additions using register addressing, register indirect addressing, indexed addressing, and immediate addressing, but not direct addressing.

8-Bit Binary Addition

Because the Z80 is basically an 8-bit microprocessor, most of the addition instructions are 8-bit additions. Table 4-1 lists all of the possible 8-bit addition commands. Notice that all the addressing modes are represented except for direct addressing. It is also very important to recognize that the flag bits will always be affected by any of these addition instructions. All of these instructions add the operand data to the contents of the accumulator.

Example 4-1 illustrates a sequence of instructions that add a 12H to the contents of the accumulator, which initially contains a 55H. After the Z80 adds the 12H and the 55H together, the result (67H) is placed into the accumulator. The flags change as follows:

Z = 0   The result is not zero.

S = 0   The result is positive.

H = 0   No half-carry.

V = 0   No overflow.

N = 0   Indicates addition.

C = 0   No carry.

TABLE 4-1.   Eight-bit binary addition instructions

Assembly	Machine	Comment
ADD A,d8	C6 d8	A = A + d8
ADD A,B	80	A = A + B
ADD A,C	81	A = A + C
ADD A,D	82	A = A + D
ADD A,E	83	A = A + E
ADD A,H	84	A = A + H
ADD A,L	85	A = A + L
ADD A,(HL)	86	A = A + (HL)
ADD A,A	87	A = A + A
ADD A,(IX+dd)	DD 86 dd	A = A + (IX+dd)
ADD A,(IY+dd)	FD 86 dd	A = A + (IY+dd)

Notes: d8, 8-bit immediate data; dd, 8-bit signed displacement.

Example 4-1

```
3E 55          LD   A,55H        ;load A with 55H
C6 12          ADD  A,12H        ;add 12H to A
```

Suppose that it is desirable to add the number in the B register to the number in the A register. This is accomplished by using the ADD A,B instruction, which adds the contents of the B register to the contents of the A register and places the sum in the A register. This sequence, together with the loading of both the A and B registers, is illustrated in Example 4-2. In this example, a 40H and an EEH are added together to produce a sum of 2EH. The carry out of the accumulator is held in the carry flag after this addition. The flags are changed to the following conditions:

Z = 0   The result is not zero.

S = 0   The result is positive.

H = 0   No half-carry.

V = 0   No overflow.

N = 0   Indicates addition.

C = 0   A carry occurred.

Example 4-2

```
3E 40          LD   A,40H        ;load A with 40H
06 EE          LD   B,0EEH       ;load B with EEH
80             ADD  A,B          ;add B to A
```

Suppose that it is desirable to add the number in the B register to the number in the C register and place the sum in the D register. This addition is accomplished by using the ADD A,B instruction, which add the contents of the B register to the contents of the A register. Before the addition takes place, the number in C must be loaded into A. After the addition, the answer must be copied from A into the D register. Example 4-3 illustrates this sequence of instructions and also the instructions required to load both the B and C registers. A 2FH is added to an 8 to generate a result of 37H. Notice the extra instructions required to position C before the addition and also position the result in D after the addition. The flags change as indicated:

Z = 0   The result is not zero.

S = 0   The result is positive.

H = 1   A half-carry occurred.

V = 0   No overflow.

N = 0   Indicates addition.

C = 0   No carry.

Example 4-3

```
06 2F           LD   B,2FH      ;load B with 2FH
OE 08           LD   C,8        ;load C with 8
79              LD   A,C        ;position C
80              ADD  A,B        ;add B to C
57              LD   D,A        ;save sum in D
```

Suppose that it is required to add the contents of 1000H, 1001H, 1002H, and 1003H. This is accomplished by using the indexed mode of addressing as illustrated in Example 4-4. Here IX is used to initially hold the address of 1000H, and the displacement is then used to add each of these numbers to the A register. (A is initially cleared to zero so that the correct sum results.)

Example 4-4

```
3E 00           LD   A,OOH        ;clear A
DD 21 00 10     LD   IX,1000H     ;load IX with 1000H
DD 86 00        ADD  A,(IX)       ;add 1000H
DD 86 01        ADD  A,(IX+1)     ;add 1001H
DD 86 02        ADD  A,(IX+2)     ;add 1002H
DD 86 03        ADD  A,(IX+3)     ;add 1003H
```

Add with Carry

Whenever large numbers are added—numbers wider than eight bits—the carry must be propagated from one 8-bit portion to the next. Propagation from one byte to another is illustrated in Figure 4-1. To accomplish a carry in multiple-byte addition, the add with carry instruction is used to propagate the carry. It is important to note that this instruction is only used if numbers wider than 8-bits are added. Table 4-2 lists all of the add with carry instructions.

Suppose that the DE register pair contains a 16-bit number that is to be added to the number in the BC register pair. To accomplish this multiple-byte addition, it is necessary to add E and C together and then add D and B together with the carry that may have occurred from the addition of E and C. The sequence of instructions required to accomplish this addition is listed in Example 4-5. Notice that the ADD A,E instruction

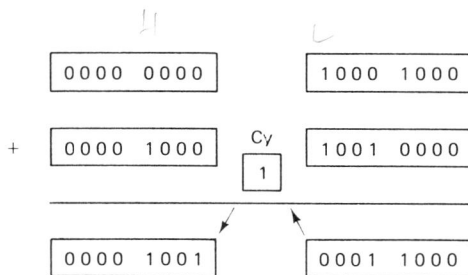

Figure 4–1 Multiple byte addition illustrating the carry propagation through the carry bit.

TABLE 4-2. ADD WITH CARRY INSTRUCTIONS

Assembly	Machine	Comment
ADC A,d8	CE d8	A = A + d8 + carry
ADC A,B	88	A = A + B + carry
ADC A,C	89	A = A + C + carry
ADC A,D	8A	A = A + D + carry
ADC A,E	8B	A = A + E + carry
ADC A,H	8C	A = A + H + carry
ADC A,L	8D	A = A + L + carry
ADC A,(HL)	8E	A = A + (HL) + carry
ADC A,A	8F	A = A + A + carry
ADC A,(IX+dd)	DD 8E dd	A = A + (IX+dd) + carry
ADC A,(IY+dd)	FD 8E dd	A = A + (IY+dd) + carry

Notes: d8, 8-bit immediate data; dd, 8-bit signed displacement.

generates a carry which is added to the most significant byte of the answer with the ADC A,D instruction. The answer, which is found in the BC register pair, is 030FH.

Example 4-5

```
01 10 01    LD  BC,0110H   ; load BC
11 FF 01    LD  DE,01FFH   ; load DE
79          LD  A,C        ; C = C + E
83          ADD A,E
4F          LD  C,A
78          LD  A,B        ; B = B + D + carry
8A          ADC A,D
47          LD  B,A
```

16-Bit Addition

Although Example 4-5 illustrates 16-bit addition, the Z80 instruction set contains special instructions that allow a 16-bit addition. Table 4-3 lists these 16-bit addition instructions. Notice that both add and add with carry instructions are available so that 32-bit and larger additions are possible.

Suppose that Example 4-5 is repeated and modified so that the number in the BC register pair is added to the number in the HL register pair. Example 4-6 illustrates this new sequence required to accomplish this 16-bit addition. Unlike other addition instructions which affect all the flags, the 16-bit addition instructions affect only the carry flag.

Example 4-6

```
01 10 01    LD  BC,0110H   ; load BC
21 FF 01    LD  HL,01FFH   ; load HL
09          ADD HL,BC      ; add BC to HL
```

The 16-bit addition with carry instructions proves useful for adding large numbers together. Suppose that the 32-bit number in BC and DE is added to the 32-bit number

TABLE 4-3. SIXTEEN-BIT ADDITIONS INSTRUCTIONS

Assembly	Machine	Comment
ADD HL,BC	09	HL = HL + BC
ADD HL,DE	19	HL = HL + DE
ADD HL,HL	29	HL = HL + HL
ADD HL,SP	39	HL = HL + SP
ADD IX,BC	DD 09	IX = IX + BC
ADD IX,DE	DD 19	IX = IX + DE
ADD IX,HL	DD 29	IX = IX + HL
ADD IX,SP	DD 39	IX = IX + SP
ADD IY,BC	FD 09	IY = IY + BC
ADD IY,DE	FD 19	IY = IY + DE
ADD IY,HL	FD 29	IY = IY + HL
ADD IY,SP	FD 39	IY = IY + SP
ADC HL,BC	ED 4A	HL = HL + BC + carry
ADC HL,DE	ED 5A	HL = HL + DE + carry
ADC HL,HL	ED 6A	HL = HL + HL + carry
ADC HL,SP	ED 7A	HL = HL + SP + carry

in HL and IY. This is accomplished as illustrated in Example 4-7. Notice that the second 16-bit addition is an add with carry instruction. Here an 0101FFFFH is added to a 02003303H.

Example 4-7

```
01 01 01      LD   BC,0101H   ;load BC
11 FF FF      LD   DE,0FFFFH  ;laod DE
21 00 02      LD   HL,0200H   ;load HL
FD 21 03 33   LD   IY,3303H   ;load IY
FD 19         ADD  IY,DE      ;add DE to IY
ED 4A         ADC  HL,BC      ;add BC to HL with carry
```

BCD Addition

BCD addition is like binary addition except the numbers that are added together can only range in value from 0 through 9. In the Z80 a special instruction is provided that allows BCD addition to be accomplished using the regular binary addition instructions. The DAA (decimal accumulator adjust) instruction is used after a BCD addition (and subtraction as depicted in the next section) in order to adjust the binary result to BCD. Example 4-8 illustrates the summation of the packed BCD numbers 11 and 19. After the addition, the accumulator contains a 2AH, which is not a valid BCD number—the answer should be a 30_{BCD}. DAA corrects the answer and yields a 30_{BCD} after the instruction is executed. (Note that a 30H is the same as a 30_{BCD} when stored in the memory.) The DAA instruction changes the result through a series of two tests by adding a 00H, 06H, 60H, or a 66H to the accumulator.

Example 4-8

```
3E 11              LD   A,11H        ;load A with 11 BCD
C6 19              ADD  A,19H        ;add 19 BCD
27                 DAA               ;adjust the answer
```

1. If the least significant half-byte is greater than 9 or the H flag bit (half-carry) is set a 06H is added to the accumulator.
2. If the most significant half-byte is greater than 9 or the C flag bit (carry) is set, a 60H is added to the accumulator.

Increment

The last form of addition available in the Z80 instruction set is increment or add 1. The increment command (INC) is either an 8- or 16-bit add 1 instruction. (Table 4-4 lists all of the versions of the increment instruction.) The 8-bit increments affect all the flags except the carry flag, and the 16-bit increment affects none of the flags. Although there is no example of these instructions at this point in the text, the increment instruction is extremely useful, as we shall discover in later chapters on programming and interfacing.

4-3 SUBTRACTION

The Z80 microprocessor supports 8-bit binary subtraction, 8- and 16-bit binary subtraction with borrow, BCD subtraction, and decrement. Each type of subtract command is detailed in this section of the text.

8-bit Binary Subtraction

Table 4-5 lists all of the various forms of 8-bit binary subtraction instructions, which include register, register indirect, indexed, and immediate addressing, but not direct addressing. Each of these instructions affects the flag bits so that they reflect the various conditions about the difference after a subtraction.

Example 4-9 illustrates a simple sequence of instructions that find the difference between 2EH and 3FH. The accumulator equals an EFH after the subtraction which is a valid answer ($46 - 63 = -17$). The flags change as indicated:

$Z = 0$	The result is not zero.
$S = 1$	The answer is negative.
$H = 1$	A half-borrow occurred.
$V = 0$	No overflow occurred.
$N = 1$	Set for subtraction.
$C = 1$	A borrow occurred.

TABLE 4-4. INCREMENT INSTRUCTIONS

Assembly	Machine	Comment
INC B	04	B = B + 1
INC C	0C	C = C + 1
INC D	14	D = D + 1
INC E	1C	E = E + 1
INC H	24	H = H + 1
INC L	2C	L = L + 1
INC (HL)	34	(HL) = (HL) + 1
INC A	3C	A = A + 1
INC BC	03	BC = BC + 1
INC DE	13	DE = DE + 1
INC HL	23	HL = HL + 1
INC SP	33	SP = SP + 1
INC IX	DD 23	IX = IX + 1
INC IY	FD 23	IY = IY + 1
INC (IX + dd)	DD 34 dd	(IX + dd) = (IX + dd) + 1
INC (IY + dd)	FD 34 dd	(IY + dd) = (IY + dd) + 1

Note: dd, an 8-bit signed displacement; 8-bit instructions affect all the flags except carry, otherwise no flags affected.

TABLE 4-5. EIGHT-BIT BINARY SUBTRACTION

Assembly	Machine	Comment
SUB d8	D6 d8	A = A − d8
SUB B	90	A = A − B
SUB C	91	A = A − C
SUB D	92	A = A − D
SUB E	93	A = A − E
SUB H	94	A = A − H
SUB L	95	A = A − L
SUB (HL)	96	A = A − (HL)
SUB	97	A = A − A
SUB (IX + dd)	DD 96 dd	A = A − (IX + dd)
SUB (IY + dd)	FD 96 dd	A = A − (IY + dd)

Notes: d8; 8-bits of data; dd, 8-bit signed displacement.

Example 4-9

```
3E 2E       LD  A,2EH      ;load A with 2EH
D6 3F       SUB 3FH        ;subtract 3FH
```

Notice that the borrow is held in the carry flag, and the half-borrow is held in the H flag (half-carry) after the subtraction. Borrows that occur for 8-bit subtraction are most

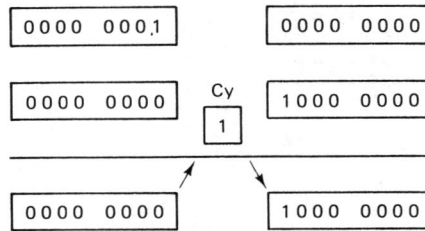

Figure 4–2 Multiple byte subtraction illustrating the borrow propagation through the carry flag.

often ignored, but borrows that occur for multiple-byte subtractions are cascaded through the more significant bytes of the difference.

Subtract with Borrow

Whenever multiple-byte numbers are subtracted, the borrow (held in carry) must be subtracted from one 8-bit portion into another. Borrow propagation is illustrated in Figure 4-2 for a multiple byte subtraction. To develop a program that propagates the borrow, a new instruction is required. The subtract-with-borrow instructions are listed in Table 4-6. Notice that in addition to 8-bit subtract-with-borrow instructions there are also 16-bit subtract-with-borrow instructions.

Suppose that the number in the DE register pair is subtracted from the number in the BC register pair. Just as with addition, the least significant byte is operated upon first. Once the difference of C and E is determined, the D register is subtracted from the B register with the borrow. This effectively propagates the borrow through the most

TABLE 4-6. SUBTRACT-WITH-BORROW INSTRUCTIONS

Assembly	Machine	Comment
SBC A,d8	DE d8	A = A − d8 − carry
SBC A,B	98	A = A − B − carry
SBC A,C	99	A = A − C − carry
SBC A,D	9A	A = A − D − carry
SBC A,E	9B	A = A − E − carry
SBC A,H	9C	A = A − H − carry
SBC A,L	9D	A = A − L − carry
SBC A,(HL)	9E	A = A − (HL) − carry
SBC A,A	9F	A = A − A − carry
SBC A,(IX + dd)	DD 9E dd	A = A − (IX + dd) − carry
SBC A,(IY + dd)	FD 9E dd	A = A − (IY + dd) − carry
SBC HL,BC	ED 42	HL = HL − BC − carry
SBC HL,DE	ED 52	HL = HL − DE − carry
SBC HL,HL	ED 62	HL = HL − HL − carry
SBC HL,SP	ED 72	HL = HL − SP − carry

Notes: d8, 8-bits of data; dd, 8-bit signed displacement.

significant byte of the result. Example 4-10 illustrates the sequence of instructions required for this subtraction.

Example 4-10

```
01  00  01        LD    BC,0100H       ;load BC
11  01  00        LD    DE,1           ;load DE
79                LD    A,C            ;C = C - E
93                SUB   E
4F                LD    C,A
78                LD    A,B
9A                SBC   A,D            ;B = C - D - carry
47                LD    B,A
```

In this example the 01H in E is subtracted from the 00H in C. This generates a result in C of FFH with a borrow, which is held in the carry flag. When the 00H in D is subtracted from the 01H in B with borrow, the result is 00H. The difference after this sequence is a 00FFH, and it is found in the BC register pair.

BCD Subtraction

As with BCD addition, there is no special instruction. Instead the normal subtract instruction is used followed by the DAA instruction. The DAA instruction, as with BCD addition, corrects the result. The result is corrected as follows:

1. If the value of the least significant half-byte is larger than 9 or the H flag is set a 06H is subtracted from the accumulator.
2. If the value of the most significant half-byte is larger than 9 or the H flag is set a 60H is subtracted from the accumulator.

Decrement

The final form of subtraction available in the Z80 is decrement or subtract 1. The decrement command (DEC) is either 8- or 16-bits as listed in Table 4-7.

The 8-bit DEC instruction affects all the flag bits except carry, and the 16-bit DEC instruction affects no flags. Although there is no example of the decrement instructions at this point in the text, they are extremely useful as will be demonstrated later in this textbook.

Compare Instructions

The compare instruction is a modified subtraction instruction. It performs 8-bit subtraction with one very unique modification—the difference is not routed into the accumulator. This instruction only changes the flags to reflect the outcome of the subtraction. You might wonder why this is done. Suppose that you are required to determine if the number

TABLE 4-7.   DECREMENT INSTRUCTIONS

Assembly	Machine	Comment
DEC B	05	B = B − 1
DEC C	0D	C = C − 1
DEC D	15	D = D − 1
DEC E	1D	E = E − 1
DEC H	25	H = H − 1
DEC L	2D	L = L − 1
DEC (HL)	35	(HL) = (HL) − 1
DEC A	3D	A = A − 1
DEC (IX + dd)	DD 35 dd	(IX + dd) = (IX + dd) − 1
DEC (IY + dd)	FD 35 dd	(IY + dd) = (IY + dd) − 1
DEC BC	0B	BC = BC − 1
DEC DE	1B	DE = DE − 1
DEC HL	2B	HL = HL − 1
DEC SP	3B	SP = SP − 1
DEC IX	DD 2B	IX = IX − 1
DEC IY	FD 2B	IY = IY − 1

in the accumulator is a 12H. You could subtract a 12H from the accumulator and look at the zero flag bit. The problem with this is that the contents of the accumulator are destroyed (lost). The compare allows this comparison and preserves the contents of the accumulator.

In addition to 8-bit comparisons there are also block comparisons. Table 4-8 lists all the forms of the compare instruction.

Block comparisons.   The block compares are similar to the block data transfer instructions presented in the previous chapter. In all forms the contents of the memory location indirectly addressed by HL are compared with the contents of the accumulator. There are two basic compare instructions (CPD and CPI) that can be repeated (CPDR and CPIR). All of these instructions compare A with (HL), then they decrement the BC pair and CPD or CPDR decrement HL while CPI or CPIR increment HL. If they are repeated (end with an R) then they repeat until an equal condition exists (A − (HL)) or until the BC register becomes a 0000H.

Example 4-11 illustrates a short program that used the CPIR instruction to search through a list of numbers for a value in the accumulator. Here the list of numbers begins at memory location 1200H and is 50 bytes in length. The number (23H) being searched for is loaded to the accumulator.

Example 4-11

```
21 00 12        LD HL,1200H     ;address 1200H
3E 23           LD A,23H        ;load search value
01 32 00        LD BC,50        ;load count
ED B1           CPIR            ;search for 23H
```

TABLE 4-8. COMPARE INSTRUCTIONS

Assembly	Machine	Comment
CP d8	FE d8	A − d8
CP B	B8	A − B
CP C	B9	A − C
CP D	BA	A − D
CP E	BB	A − E
CP H	BC	A − H
CP L	BD	A − L
CP (HL)	BE	A − (HL)
CP A	BF	A − A
CP (IX + dd)	DD BE dd	A − (IX + dd)
CP (IY + dd)	FD BE dd	A − (IY + dd)
CPD	ED A9	A − (HL), then decrement HL and BC.
CPDR	ED B9	same as CPD, but repeated until A = (HL) or BC = 0.
CPI	ED A1	A − (HL), then increment HL and decrement BC.
CPIR	ED B1	same as CPI, but repeated until A = (HL) or BC = 0.

Notes: d8, 8-bits of data; dd, 8-bit signed displacement.

4-4 LOGIC INSTRUCTIONS

The Z80 microprocessor is capable of executing four basic logic instructions: invert, AND, OR, and Exclusive-OR. Why does the microprocessor instruction set contain logic instructions? One reason is that logic instructions are sometimes used to replace discrete logic gates. Today, program storage costs about 1/20 of a cent per byte. If an instruction can be used to replace an external logic gate, imagine the amount of money saved by programmed logic! Another reason is that system control software usually requires bit manipulation—a logic operation.

Inversion

The CPL instruction, 2FH in machine language, is used to one's complement or invert the contents of the accumulator. This operation, which affects no flag bits, causes each bit of the accumulator to be inverted (changed from a 1 to a 0 or from a 0 to a 1). CPL causes the accumulator to appear as eight inverters. This means that this one-byte instruction can be used to replace eight discrete inverters provided that the speed is not too great. The amount of circuitry replaced by the CPL instruction is 1⅓ of a 7404 TTL hex inverter. Cost advantage: software = $0.0005 versus hardware = $0.40, a savings of 80,000 percent.

In addition to the invert (often called NOT) instruction which performs the one's complement there is an instruction that performs the two's complement called NEG (ED 44 in machine language). The NEG instruction is used to negate (change the sign) of the accumulator for signed numbers.

The AND Operation

The AND operation, whose symbolic notation is a $\wedge$, actually has two separate functions in a microprocessor-based system: selectively clearing bits of the accumulator and replacing discrete logic gates.

The logical multiplication, or AND instruction, functions as eight independent two-input AND gates, as illustrated in Figure 4-3. This instruction is used to replace two 7408 quad two-input AND gates. The cost advantage: software = $0.0005 versus hardware = $0.80, a savings of 160,000 percent. The effect on the flag bits is as follows: Z, S, and P are set or reset depending on the outcome of the AND operation. The C and H flag bits are always cleared, and the N flag bit is set.

In addition to replacing external logic circuitry, the AND function can also be used to selectively clear (mask) any number of bit positions in the accumulator. This command will, in other words, turn off individual bits in the accumulator. The 8 bits of the accumulator are available to use as eight switches for controlling external hardware.

Figure 4-4 illustrates this effect by using X's (don't cares) to represent each bit position of the accumulator and 0000 1111 as a test pattern ANDed with the accumulator. The outcome clearly indicates that the 0's in the test pattern force the corresponding bit positions to 0 and the 1's in the test pattern allow the corresponding bit positions to pass through to the result unchanged. All the possible AND instructions are listed in Table 4-9.

The AND A instruction has a special function. With AND A, the accumulator is ANDed with the accumulator, and as a result the value in the accumulator does not change. This instruction does change the flags, so that a number in the accumulator can be tested for a zero–not zero, positive–negative, or an odd–even parity condition. For this reason the AND A instruction should be thought of as a TEST A instruction.

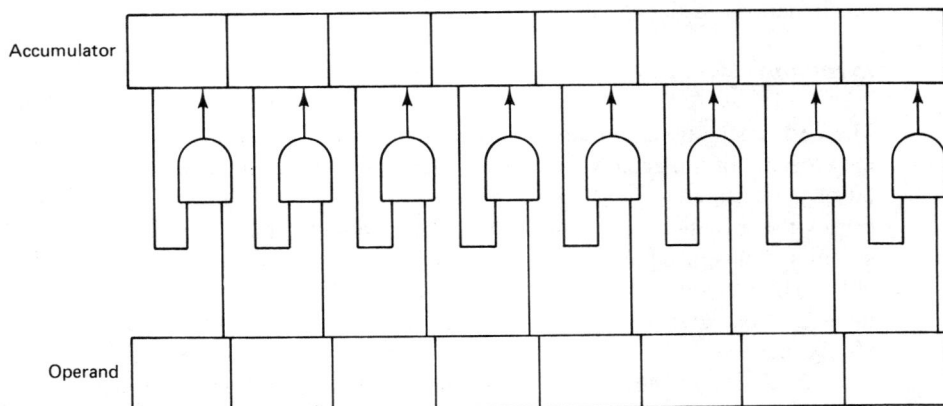

Figure 4–3   Notice how the 8-bit number in the operand is ANDed with the accumulator bit position by bit position.

```
      X X X X  X X X X      Accumulator
  ∧   0 0 0 0  1 1 1 1      Operand
      ────────────────
      0 0 0 0  X X X X      Result
```

Figure 4–4 The AND operation illustrating the effect on the result. A 0 ANDed with anything results in a 0. A 1 ANDed with anything results in no change.

TABLE 4-9. AND INSTRUCTIONS

Assembly	Machine	Comment
AND d8	E6 d8	A = A ∧ d8
AND B	A0	A = A ∧ B
AND C	A1	A = A ∧ C
AND D	A2	A = A ∧ D
AND E	A3	A = A ∧ E
AND H	A4	A = A ∧ H
AND L	A5	A = A ∧ L
AND (HL)	A6	A = A ∧ (HL)
AND A	A7	A = A ∧ A
AND (IX + dd)	DD A6 dd	A = A ∧ (IX + dd)
AND (IY + dd)	FD A6 dd	A = A ∧ (IY + dd)

Notes: d8, 8-bits of data; dd, 8-bit signed displacement.

The OR Operation

The inclusive-OR instruction, whose symbolic notation is represented by a V, actually has two separate functions in a microprocessor-based system: selectively setting bits of the accumulator and replacing discrete OR gates.

The binary logical addition or inclusive-OR instruction functions as eight indepen-

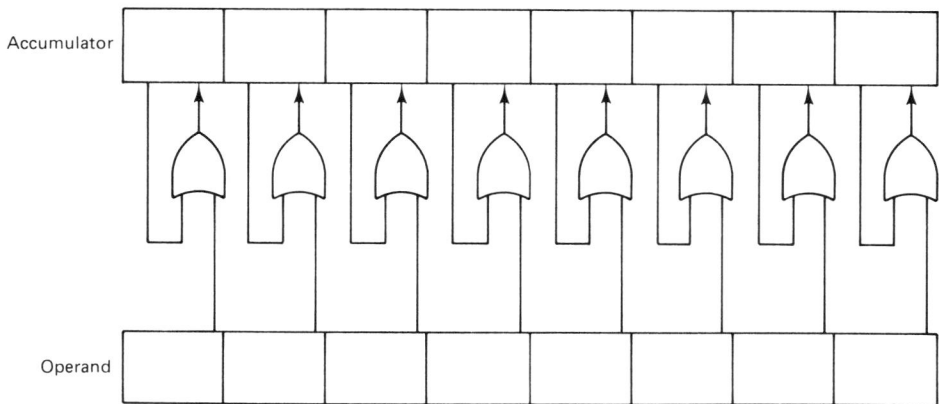

Figure 4–5 The OR operation showing how the 8-bit number in the operand is ORed with the accumulator bit position by bit position.

```
        X X X X   X X X X   Accumulator
    V   0 0 0 0   1 1 1 1   Operand
        X X X X   1 1 1 1   Result
```

Figure 4–6 The OR operation illustrating the effect on the result. A 1 ORed with anything results in a 1. A 0 ORed with anything results in no change.

dent two input OR gates, as illustrated in Figure 4-5. This instruction is used to replace two 7432 quad two-input OR gates. The cost advantage: software = $0.0005 versus hardware = $0.80, a savings of 160,000 percent. The effect on the flag bits is as follows: Z, S, and P are set or reset depending on the outcome of the OR operation; C and H are always cleared; and N is always set.

In addition to replacing external logic circuitry, the OR function can also be used to selectively set any number of bit positions in the accumulator. This command will, in other words, turn on individual bits in the accumulator. The 8 bits of the accumulator are available to use as eight switches for controlling external hardware. The AND operation is used to turn bits off, and the OR operation is used to turn bits on.

Figure 4-6 illustrates this effect by using X's (don't cares) to represent each bit of the accumulator and 0000 1111 as a test bit pattern ORed with the accumulator. The outcome clearly indicates that the 1's in the test bit pattern force the corresponding bit positions to 1, and the 0's in the test pattern allow the corresponding bit positions to pass through to the result unchanged. All the possible OR instructions are listed in Table 4-10.

The OR A instruction, as the AND A instruction, has a special function. With the OR A instruction, the accumulator is ORed with the accumulator and the value of the result does not change. This instruction does change the flags so that a number in the accumulator and the value of the result does not change. This instruction does change the flags so that a number in the accumulator can be tested for a zero–non zero, positive–negative, or even–odd parity condition. For this reason, the OR A and AND A instructions should both be thought of as TEST A instructions.

TABLE 4-10. OR INSTRUCTIONS

Assembly	Machine	Comment
OR d8	F6 d8	A = A V d8
OR B	B0	A = A V B
OR C	B1	A = A V C
OR D	B2	A = A V D
OR E	B3	A = A V E
OR H	B4	A = A V H
OR L	B5	A = A V L
OR (HL)	B6	A = A V (HL)
OR A	B7	A = A V A
OR (IX + dd)	DD B6 dd	A = A V (IX + dd)
OR (IY + dd)	FD B6 dd	A = A V (IY + dd)

Notes: d8, 8-bits of data; dd, 8-bit signed displacement.

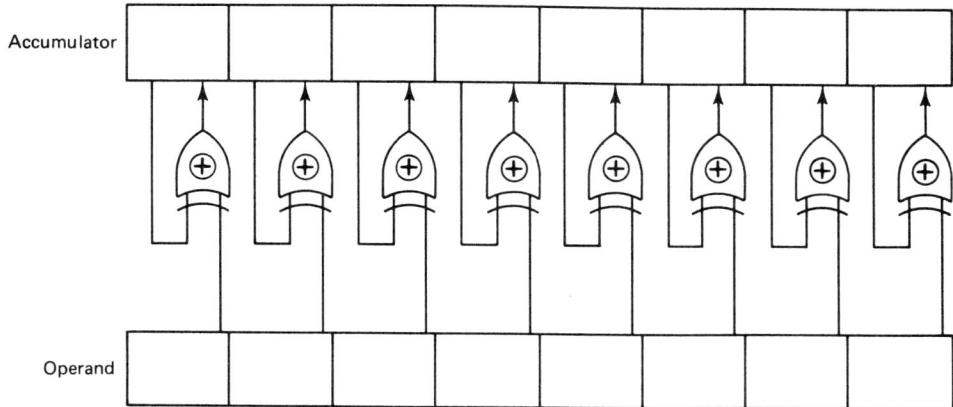

Figure 4–7   The exclusive-OR operation showing how the 8-bit number in the operand is exclusive-ORed with the accumulator bit position by bit position.

The Exclusive-OR Operation

The exclusive-OR instruction, whose symbolic notation is represented by a ⊻, actually has two separate functions in a microprocessor-based system: selectively inverting bits of the accumulator and replacing discrete exclusive-OR gates.

The exclusive-OR instruction as eight independent two-input exclusive-OR gates, as illustrated in Figure 4-7. This instruction is used to replace two 7486 quad two-input exclusive-OR gates. The cost advantage: software = $0.0005 versus hardware = $0.80, a saving of 160,000 percent. The effect on the flag bits is as follows: Z, S, and P are set or reset depending on the outcome of the exclusive-OR operation; C and H are cleared; and N is set.

In addition to replacing external logic circuitry, the exclusive-OR function can also be used to selectively invert any number of the bit positions in the accumulator. This command will, in other words, complement individual bits in the accumulator. The 8 bits of the accumulator are available to use as eight switches for controlling external hardware. The AND operation is used to turn bits off, the OR operation is used to turn bits on, and the exclusive-OR operation is used to invert bits.

Figure 4-8 illustrates this effect by using X's (don't cares) to represent each bit of the accumulator and 0000 1111 as a test pattern exclusive-ORed with the accumulator. The outcome clearly indicates that the 1's in the test pattern force the corresponding bit positions to invert, and the 0's in the test pattern allow the corresponding bit positions

```
      X X X X   X X X X    Accumulator
  ⊻   0 0 0 0   1 1 1 1    Operand
      ───────────────
      X X X X   X̄ X̄ X̄ X̄    Result
```

Figure 4–8   The exclusive-OR operation illustrating the effect on the result. A 1 exclusive-ORed with anything results in inversion. A 0 exclusive-ORed with anything results in no change.

TABLE 4-11. EXCLUSIVE-OR INSTRUCTIONS

Assembly	Machine	Comment
XOR d8	EE d8	A = A ∀ d8
XOR B	A8	A = A ∀ B
XOR C	A9	A = A ∀ C
XOR D	AA	A = A ∀ D
XOR E	AB	A = A ∀ E
XOR H	AC	A = A ∀ H
XOR L	AD	A = A ∀ L
XOR (HL)	AE	A = A ∀ (HL)
XOR A	AF	A = A ∀ A
XOR (IX + dd)	DD AE dd	A = A ∀ (IX + dd)
XOR (IY + dd)	FD AE dd	A = A ∀ (IY + dd)

Notes: d8, 8-bits of data; dd, 8-bit signed displacement.

to pass through to the result unchanged. All the possible exclusive-OR instructions are listed in Table 4-11. An added bonus is the XOR A instruction, which clears the contents of the accumulator to zero. This command should be thought of as a CLEAR A instruction.

Bit Reset, Set, and Test Instructions

The Z80 microprocessor contains a complete set of bit reset, set, and test instructions that allow any bit of the memory or register (A, B, C, D, E, H, or L) to be reset to a logic 0, set to a logic 1, or tested for a 1 or 0. It is true that reset and set are also performed by the AND and OR instructions, but those instructions allow multiple bits to be affected. These instructions allow only one bit to be addressed and then modified or tested.

TABLE 4-12. RES (RESET) INSTRUCTIONS

Register	Bit positions							
	0	1	2	3	4	5	6	7
A	87	8F	97	9F	A7	AF	B7	BF
B	80	88	90	98	A0	A8	B0	B8
C	81	89	91	99	A1	A9	B1	B9
D	82	8A	92	9A	A2	AA	B2	BA
E	83	8B	93	9B	A3	AB	B3	BB
H	84	8C	94	9C	A4	AC	B4	BC
L	85	8D	95	9D	A4	AD	B4	BD
(HL)	86	8E	96	9E	A6	AE	B6	BE
(IX + dd)	86	8E	96	9E	A6	AE	B6	BE
(IX + dd)	86	8E	96	9E	A6	AE	B6	BE

Notes: Instructions are two-bytes long (CB XX) except for index addressing which are 4-bytes long (DD CB dd XX for (IX + dd) and FD CB dd XX for (IY + dd)); XX, byte from the table; dd, 8-bit signed displacement.

TABLE 4-13.   SET INSTRUCTIONS

Register	Bit positions 0	1	2	3	4	5	6	7
A	C7	CF	D7	DF	E7	EF	F7	FF
B	C0	C8	D0	D8	E0	E8	F0	F8
C	C1	C9	D1	D9	E1	E9	F1	F9
D	C2	CA	D2	DA	E2	EA	F2	FA
E	C3	CB	D3	DB	E3	EB	F3	FB
H	C4	CC	D4	DC	E4	EC	F4	FC
L	C5	CD	D5	DD	E4	ED	F4	FD
(HL)	C6	CE	D6	DE	E6	EE	F6	FE
(IX + dd)	C6	CE	D6	DE	E6	EE	F6	FE
(IX + dd)	C6	CE	D6	DE	E6	EE	F6	FE

Notes: Instructions are two-bytes long (CB XX) except for index addressing which are 4-bytes long (DD CB dd XX for (IX + dd) and FD CB dd XX for (IY + dd)); XX, byte from the table; dd, 8-bit signed displacement.

Table 4-12 illustrates all of the RES (reset), Table 4-13 all of the SET, and Table 4-14 all of the BIT (test) instructions. RES and SET do not affect any of the flag bits, but the BIT instruction allows a bit in the memory or register to be tested. The Z flag bit indicates if the tested bit is a 1 or a 0.

These instructions are in the form of BIT b,r, where b is the bit position of the register (r) to be tested, set, or reset. The register/memory data are ordered so that the right-most bit position is numbered 0 and the left-most is 7.

A RES 2,B instruction will reset (0) bit position 2 of the B register. The opcode for this instruction is located in Table 4-12 as CB with the second byte as 90.

TABLE 4-14.   BIT (TEST) INSTRUCTIONS

Register	Bit positions 0	1	2	3	4	5	6	7
A	47	4F	57	5F	67	6F	77	7F
B	40	48	50	58	60	68	70	78
C	41	49	51	59	61	69	71	79
D	42	4A	52	5A	62	6A	72	7A
E	43	4B	53	5B	63	6B	73	7B
H	44	4C	54	5C	64	6C	74	7C
L	45	4D	55	5D	64	6D	74	7D
(HL)	46	4E	56	5E	66	6E	76	7E
(IX + dd)	46	4E	56	5E	66	6E	76	7E
(IX + dd)	46	4E	56	5E	66	6E	76	7E

Notes: Instructions are two-bytes long (CB XX) except for index addressing which are 4-bytes long (DD CB dd XX for (IX + dd) and FD CB dd XX for (IY + dd)); XX, byte from the table; dd, 8-bit signed displacement.

4-5 SHIFT AND ROTATE INSTRUCTIONS

In certain applications it is desirable that information be shifted or rotated. The Z80 microprocessor is capable of all types of logical rotations and also logical and arithmetic shifts.

Rotate Instructions

There are six rotate instructions that allow the contents of the register or memory location to be rotated right or left and that allow the contents of the right half-byte of the accumulator to be rotated 4 places through the address pointed at by the HL register pair.

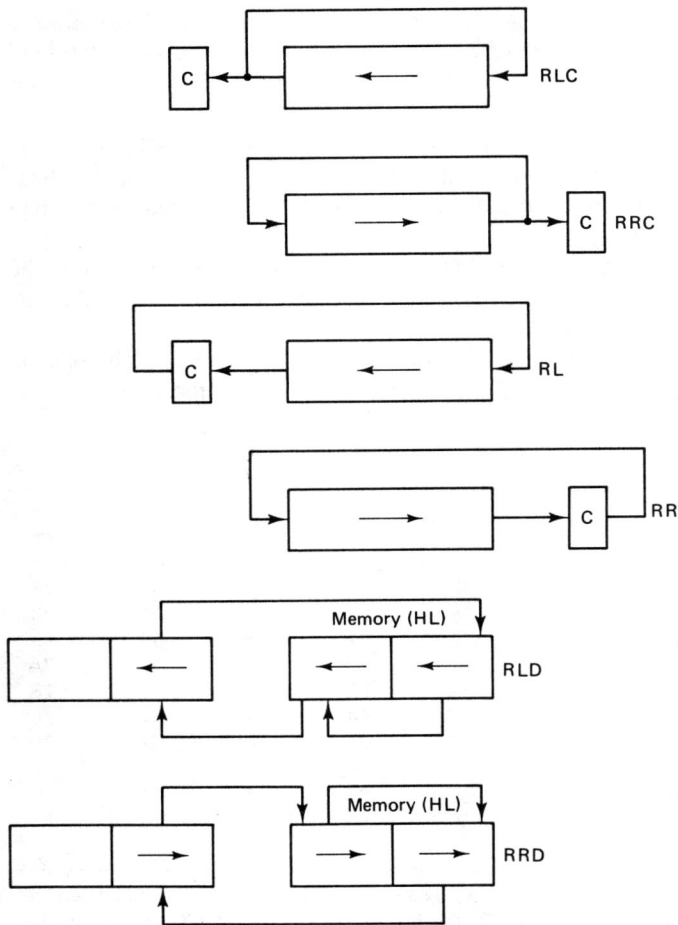

Figure 4–9   The six rotate instructions: RLC, RRC, RL, RR, RLD, and RRD.

Figure 4-9 illustrates the operation of the six rotate instructions: RLC, RRC, RL, RR, RLD, and RRD. The RLC and RRC instructions rotate the contents of the 8-bit register or memory location right or left one place. Whatever is rotated in the loop is also copied into the carry flag. The RL and RR instructions treat the register or memory location and carry flag as a 9-bit register. The RLD and RRD instruction rotate data four places between the accumulator's right hand half-byte and the contents of the memory location addressed by the HL register pair. Table 4-15 lists each rotate instruction and its machine language and assembly language forms.

TABLE 4-15. ROTATE INSTRUCTIONS

Assembly	Machine	Comment
RRC B	CB 08	rotate B right
RRC C	CB 09	rotate C right
RRC D	CB 0A	rotate D right
RRC E	CB 0B	rotate E right
RRC H	CB 0C	rotate H right
RRC L	CB 0D	rotate L right
RRC (HL)	CB 0E	rotate (HL) right
RRC A	CB 0F	rotate A right
RRCA	0F	same as RRC A
RRC (IX + dd)	DD CB dd 0E	rotate (IX + dd) right
RRC (IY + dd)	FD CB dd 0E	rotate (IY + dd) right
RLC B	CB 00	rotate B left
RLC C	CB 01	rotate C left
RLC D	CB 02	rotate D left
RLC E	CB 03	rotate E left
RLC H	CB 04	rotate H left
RLC L	CB 05	rotate L left
RLC (HL)	CB 06	rotate (HL) left
RLC A	CB 07	rotate A left
RLCA	07	same as RLC A
RLC (IX + dd)	DD CB dd 06	rotate (IX + dd) left
RLC (IY + dd)	FD CB dd 06	rotate (IY + dd) left
RR B	CB 18	rotate B right with carry
RR C	CB 19	rotate C right with carry
RR D	CB 1A	rotate D right with carry
RR E	CB 1B	rotate E right with carry
RR H	CB 1C	rotate H right with carry
RR L	CB 1D	rotate L right with carry
RR (HL)	CB 1E	rotate (HL) right with carry
RR A	CB 1F	rotate A right with carry
RRA	1F	same as RR A
RR (IX + dd)	DD CB dd 1E	rotate (IX + dd) right with carry
RR (IY + dd)	FD CB dd 1E	rotate (IY + dd) right with carry
RL B	CB 10	rotate B left carry
RL C	CB 11	rotate C left carry
RL D	CB 12	rotate D left carry

TABLE 4-15. (Cont.)

Assembly	Machine	Comment
RL E	CB 13	rotate E left carry
RL H	CB 14	rotate H left carry
RL L	CB 15	rotate L left carry
RL (HL)	CB 16	rotate (HL) left carry
RL A	CB 17	rotate A left carry
RLA	17	same RL A
RL (IX + dd)	DD CB dd 16	rotate (IX + dd) left carry
RL (IY + dd)	FD CB dd 16	rotate (IY + dd) left carry
RRD	ED 67	rotate digit right
RLD	ED 6F	rotate digit left

Suppose the accumulator contains two four-bit BDC numbers and software is required to reposition them so that the most significant digit is exchanged with the least significant digit. This is easily accomplished by using any 8-bit rotate instruction. Example 4-12 illustrates the RRC A instruction used four times to rotate the accumulator four places. The RLC A instruction is also able to accomplish the same result by rotating the number to the left instead of the right.

Example 4-12

```
OF          RRCA            ;rotate 4 places
OF          RRCA
OF          RRCA
OF          RRCA
```

Shift Instructions

The Z80 has three shift instructions: SLA, SRA, and SRL. The SLA and SRL instructions are used to logically shift the contents of a register or memory location to the right or the left. If the SLA instruction is used, a 0 is moved into the right bit and if the SRL instruction is used, a 0 is moved into the left bit. The SRA instruction is a logical shift right instruction that copies the sign bit through the number toward the right. Figure 4-10 illustrates the operation of these three instructions, and Table 4-16 lists all the shift instructions.

The shift left instruction is used to multiply a number by two. If a number is shifted left two places it is multiplied by four, by three places by eight, etc. The shift logical right instruction is used to divide an unsigned number by two, and the arithmetic shift right instruction divides a signed number by two. As with left shifts, each shift right shift divides by another power of two.

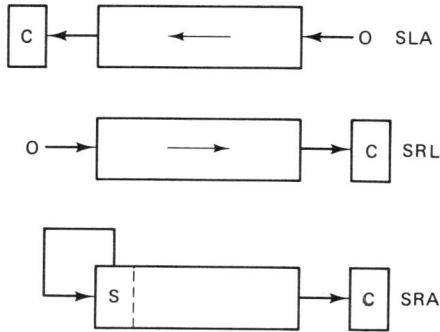

Figure 4–10 The three shift instructions: SLA, SRL, and SRA.

TABLE 4-16. SHIFT INSTRUCTIONS

Assembly	Machine	Comment
SLA B	CB 20	shift B left
SLA C	CB 21	shift C left
SLA D	CB 22	shift D left
SLA E	CB 23	shift E left
SLA H	CB 24	shift H left
SLA L	CB 25	shift L left
SLA (HL)	CB 26	shift (HL) left
SLA A	CB 27	shift A left
SLA (IX + dd)	DD CB dd 26	shift (IX + dd) left
SLA (IY + dd)	FD CB dd 26	shift (IY + dd) left
SRL B	CB 38	shift B right
SRL C	CB 39	shfit C right
SRL D	CB 3A	shift D right
SRL E	CB 3B	shift E right
SRL H	CB 3C	shift H right
SRL L	CB 3D	shift L right
SRL (HL)	CB 3E	shift (HL) right
SRL A	CB 3F	shift A right
SRL (IX + dd)	DD CB dd 3E	shift (IX + dd) right
SRL (IY + dd)	FD CB dd 3E	shift (IY + dd) right
SRA B	CB 28	shift arithmetic B right
SRA C	CB 29	shift arithmetic C right
SRA D	CB 2A	shift arithmetic D right
SRA E	CB 2B	shift arithmetic E right
SRA H	CB 2C	shift arithmetic H right
SRA L	CB 2D	shift arithmetic L right
SRA (HL)	CB 2E	shift arithmetic (HL) right
SRA A	CB 2F	shift arithmetic A right
SRA (IX + dd)	DD CB dd 2E	shift arithmetic (IX + dd) right
SRA (IY + dd)	FD CB dd 2E	shift arithmetic (IY + dd) right

4-6 SUMMARY

1. The arithmetic and logic instructions affect the flag bits, whereas the data transfer instructions of Chapter 3 did not affect the flags.

2. Most of the arithmetic and logic instructions gate the result into the accumulator.

3. Most arithmetic and logic instructions use register, immediate, register indirect, and indexed addressing.

4. Addition is available as add 1 (increment) to any register, memory location, or register pair; 8- and 16-bit binary; 8- or 16-bit binary with carry; and binary-coded-decimal (BCD).

5. Subtraction is available as subtract 1 (decrement) from any register, memory location, or register pair; 8 binary, 8- and 16-bit with borrow; as a compare (a form of subtraction); and binary-coded-decimal (BCD).

6. The logic operations are AND, OR, exclusive-OR, and invert. The NEG (negate) instruction performs inversion plus one which is a two's complement.

7. The logic instructions are used to control external events that require more than one bit change. The AND instruction is used to clear bits, the OR instruction is used to set bits, and the exclusive-OR instruction is used to invert bits.

8. Programmed logic uses the AND, OR, exclusive-OR, and invert functions to replace discrete logic circuitry at a tremendous cost advantage.

9. Individual bits are set, reset, or tested with the bit control instructions SET, RES (reset) and BIT (test).

10. Some of the Z80 instructions have hidden functions. For example the AND A instruction does not modify the contents of the accumulator, but it does change the flags to reflect its contents.

11. The rotate commands are used to position data in any register or memory location.

12. The shift instructions are used to multiply a number by two or divide by two.

4-7 GLOSSARY

Accumulator adjust   The act of correcting the result after a BCD addition or subtraction. The result of each BCD digit is correct by adding (for BCD addition) or subtraction (for BCD subtraction) a 6 if a carry occurred or the result is greater than 9.

AND   The logical multiplication operation (AND) is: $0 \wedge 0 = 1$, $0 \wedge 1 = 0$, $1 \wedge 0 = 0$, and $1 \wedge 1 = 1$.

Arithmetic right shift   Whenever a number is shifted right, the sign bit is copied through the number for an arithmetic right shift.

Borrow   A borrow into the most significant bit off the result after a subtraction is held in the carry flag. Carry is a 1 for a borrow, and a 0 for no borrow.

Compare   A special form of subtraction where the value of the difference is lost, but the flag bits reflect the difference.

Decrement   To decrement is to subtract a one from a register, memory location, or a register pair.

Don't care   A don't care is a binary bit that may be either a one or a zero. Don't cares are represented as an X.

Exclusive-OR   The exclusive-OR operation is: $0 \veebar 0 = 0$, $0 \veebar 1 = 1$, $1 \veebar 0 = 1$, and $1 \veebar 1 = 0$.

Increment   To increment is to add a 1 to a register, memory location, or a register pair.

Inversion   Whenever a bit is inverted, it is changed from a 1 to a 0 or from a 0 to a 1.

Logical shift   When a number is shifted, a zero is moved into the left- or right-most bit for a logical shift.

Mask   The act of removing part of a number, usually through the AND operation. The portion that is removed is cleared to 0.

Multiple-byte number   A number that is more than one byte in width.

OR   The logical addition (OR) operation is: $0 \vee 0 = 0$, $0 \vee 1 = 1$, $1 \vee 0 = 1$, and $1 \vee 1 = 1$.

Programmed logic   Software that is used to replace hardware.

Rotate   Whenever a number is shifted to the right or the left, a bit drops off the end of the register or memory location. If this bit is recirculated through the register or memory location, the number is said to be rotated.

QUESTIONS AND PROBLEMS _____

4-1. What forms of addressing are used with most of the arithmetic and logic instructions?

4-2. List all the flag bits and indicate their contents after the following addition: 12H + 33H, F0H + 33H, 0FH + 40H, and 3FH + ABH.

4-3. Develop a sequence of instructions, in both machine and assembly language, that will add a 55H to the number in the B register.

4-4. Develop a sequence of instructions, in both machine and assembly language, that will add the number in the H register to the number in the L register.

4-5. Develop a sequence of instructions, in both assembly language and machine language, that will add the number in the memory location addressed by the HL register pair to the number in the C register. Store the result in the D register.

4-6. Where would the add-with-carry instruction find most of its application?

4-7. Develop a sequence of instructions, in both machine and assembly language, that will add the number in the DE register pair to the HL register pair. (You must use only 8-bit addition instructions.)

4-8. Explain what the ADD HL,DE instruction accomplishes.

4-9. The 16-bit ADD instructions affect which flag bits?

4-10. The Z80 has a special command for BCD addition and subtraction. Does this command precede or follow the addition or subtraction instruction?

4-11. Develop a program, in both machine and assembly language, that will add the BCD number in the B register to the BCD number in the L register.

4-12. What instruction is used to add a 1 to HL register pair? Which flag bits are affected by this instruction?

4-13. Convert the following assembly language instructions into hexadecimal machine language:
   (a) ADD HL,BC
   (b) ADD A,(IX + 22H)
   (c) DAA
   (d) INC B
   (e) ADC A,B

4-14. List all the flag bits and indicate their contents after the following subtractions: 12H − 33H, F0H − 33H, 0FH − 40H, and 3FH − ABH.

4-15. Where is the borrow found after a subtraction, and what does it indicate?

4-16. What instruction is used to subtract the contents of the memory location pointed to by the HL register pair from the accumulator?

4-17. Develop a sequence of instructions, in both assembly and machine language, that will subtract the number in the D register from the number in the E register.

4-18. Develop a sequence of instructions, in both assembly and machine language, that will subtract the number in the DE register pair from the number in the BC register pair.

4-19. True or false: If the DEC B instruction is executed, all the flags will change.

4-20. What is the main difference between a compare and a subtract instruction?

4-21. Why is the compare instruction useful?

4-22. Explain the operation of the CPIR instruction.

4-23. What Z80 instruction is used to invert the contents of the accumulator?

4-24. What instruction is used to two's complement the contents of the accumulator?

4-25. Write a sequence of instructions, in both assembly and machine language, that will one's complement the contents of the DE register pair.

4-26. The AND operation is used to _____ bits in the accumulator.

4-27. The OR operation is used to _____ bits in the accumulator.

4-28. The exclusive-OR operation is used to _____ bits in the accumulator.

4-29. Since the NAND operation is a NOT AND, is it possible to replace a NAND gate with programmed logic? If so, how?

4-30. What special function is performed by the AND A instruction?

4-31. Write a sequence of instructions, in both assembly and machine language, that will set bits 7,6 and 5 and clear bit 0 without changing any other bit in the accumulator. (You must use the logic instructions to accomplish this.)

4-32. Repeat question number 4-31 using the SET and RES instructions.

4-33. Why can the RLC instruction be used in place of the RRC in the program listed in Example 4-12?

4-34. What is the difference between an arithmetic and a logic shift right?

4-35. Develop a sequence of instructions, in both assembly and machine language, that will shift the number in the BC register pair to the left one bit position.

chapter 5

Program Control Instructions

The Z80 has a variety of program control instructions which allow the flow of the execution of a program to be altered. This ability is one of the main reasons that computer systems are so powerful. Program control instructions allow the computer to make decisions and modify the flow of the program based upon the outcome of the decision.

There are two basic forms of program control instructions available: jump and call. The jump instructions allow the program to jump to any location in the memory to continue a program. The call instructions allow a group of instructions (subroutine) to be reused by the program from many different points.

5-1 OBJECTIVES

Upon completion of this chapter, you will be able to:

1. Explain the operation of the unconditional and conditional jump instructions.
2. Describe which flag bits are tested by each of the conditional jump instructions.
3. Explain the operation of the unconditional and conditional call instructions.
4. Indicate how the stack functions when used by the call and return instructions.
5. Define the term subroutine and describe its importance in software development.
6. Describe the operation of such instructions as NOP, RST, CCF, SCF, and HALT.

5-2 UNCONDITIONAL JUMP INSTRUCTIONS

The unconditional jump instructions are available in three forms: a three-byte command (JP) that allows the program to transfer control to an instruction at any memory location, a two-byte command (JR) that allows the program to continue up to +127 to -128 bytes from the address of the next instruction, and an indirect jump (JP) that allows the program to continue at the address pointed to by HL, IX, or IY. Before these instructions are used in a program, some additional detail must be given to both machine and assembly language versions of a program. Example 5-1 illustrates how the jump instruction is coded in the memory in both machine and assembly language forms. Notice that a new component, the address, exists for both versions. The address of the instruction appears to the left in machine language (1000 and 2000, both in hexadecimal), and a label takes the place of the address in assembly language (WILD and NEXT).

Example 5-1

```
1000 C3 00 20     WILD: JP NEXT        ; go to NEXT
                        •
                        •
                        •
2000 C3 00 10     NEXT: JP WILD        ; go to WILD
```

Both instructions, in this example, are of the three-byte form. The first instruction jumps to memory location NEXT for the next instruction, and then the instruction at memory location NEXT jumps to location WILD. This sequence is repeated without interruption and is called an infinite loop because it never ends. A label is used as a symbolic memory address (NEXT and WILD), and a hexadecimal number (1000 and 2000) is used as the actual address. The importance of the jump is that a task can be repeated over and over without reprogramming the computer.

Table 5-1 illustrates the unconditional jump instructions that are available in the Z80 instruction set.

Relative Jumps (Two-Byte Jumps)

The prior example illustrated the three-byte jump (JP). Example 5-2 illustrates the same sequence of instructions (closer together) that use the relative or two-byte unconditional jumps (JR). The relative jump does not contain the memory address of the next instruction. Instead, the second byte of this instruction contains the displacement (distance) to the next instruction. The displacement is an 8-bit signed number that is added to the program counter to generate the address of the next instruction.

Example 5-2

```
1000 18 0E        WILD: JR NEXT        ; go to NEXT
1002                    •
                        •
                        •
1010 18 EE        NEXT: JR WILD        ; go to WILD
1012
```

TABLE 5-1.   UNCONDITIONAL JUMP INSTRUCTIONS

Assembly	Machine	Comment
JP a16	C3 ll hh	Program continues at a16
JP (HL)	E9	Program continues at (HL)
JP (IX)	DD E9	Program continues at (IX)
JP (IY)	FD E9	Program continues at (IY)
JR dd	18 dd	Program continues at PC + dd

Notes: a16, 16-bit memory address; dd, 8-bit signed displacement; ll, low-order portion of the address; and hh, high-order portion of the address.

In this example the first jump (JR NEXT) jumps to memory location 1010H because the program counter (which always points to the address of the next instruction) contains a 1002H and the displacement is a 0EH. The sum of 1002H and 000EH is 1010H. The second jump jumps to memory location 1000H because the PC contains a 1012H and the displacement is an EEH. The sum of 1012H plus FFEEH is 1000H. When the displacement is negative (80H—FFH) it is sign-extended to a 16-bit number and added to the PC. The carry that may occur from this addition is dropped.

The Indirect Jump

The final form of the jump instruction is the indirect jump. The indirect jump allows the program to continue at the memory address pointed to by HL, IX, or IY. A JP (IX) instruction, for example, transfers the contents of IX into the PC so that the next instruction to be executed is the location that is contained in IX.

Example 5-3 illustrates how the JP (HL) instruction is used in a program. Here the JP (HL) instruction causes the program to continue execution at memory location 1000H. It does this because HL is loaded with a 1000H before the JP (HL) instruction is executed. Notice that this program never ends because it continually jumps to 1000H.

Example 5-3

```
1000 21 00 10    LOOP: LD HL,1000H    ;address 1000H
1003 E9                JP (HL)         ;jump to LOOP
```

5-3 CONDITIONAL JUMP INSTRUCTIONS _____

The conditional jump instructions are in many aspects the same as the unconditional jumps except that they allow the programmer to make a choice. Conditional jump instructions are available in the long form, three-bytes, and also in the relative form, two-bytes. A condition can be tested by the microprocessor to determine whether or not a jump occurs. The conditions that are tested by the conditional jumps are the same con-

TABLE 5-2.   CONDITIONAL JUMP INSTRUCTIONS

Assembly	Machine	Comment
JP Z,a16	CA ll hh	Jump if zero
JP NZ,a16	C2 ll hh	Jump if not zero
JP C,a16	DA ll hh	Jump if carry set
JP NC,a16	D2 ll hh	Jump if carry cleared
JP M,a16	FA ll hh	Jump if minus
JP P,a16	F2 ll hh	Jump if positive
JP PE,a16	EA ll hh	Jump if parity even (overflow)
JP PO,a16	E2 ll hh	Jump if parity odd (no overflow)
JR Z,dd	28 dd	Jump if zero
JR NZ,dd	20 dd	Jump if not zero
JR C,dd	38 dd	Jump if carry set
JR NC,dd	30 dd	Jump if carry cleared
DJNZ dd	10 dd	Decrement B and jump if B is not zero

Notes: a16, 16-bit address; dd, 8-bit signed displacement; ll, low-order address; and hh, high-order address.

ditions that are held in the flag bits. The long form of the conditional jump allows the carry, zero, parity/overflow, and sign flags to be tested. The relative form allows the carry and zero flag to be tested. The conditional jump instructions, and the conditions they test, are listed in Table 5-2.

Testing the Zero Flag Bit

The zero flag bit is tested by the JP Z,a16, JP NZ,a16, JR Z,dd, and the JR NZ,dd instructions. The JP NZ,a16 or JR NZ,dd instructions execute a jump if the zero flag indicates a nonzero ($Z = 0$) condition. The program continues with the next sequential instruction if the zero flag indicates a zero result ($Z = 1$). If the condition is true, the jump occurs, and if the condition is false, the next sequential step in the program is executed. The JP Z,a16 or the JR Z,dd instruction jumps if zero and continues with the next instruction if not zero.

Example 5-4 shows how the JR NZ,dd instruction can be used to repeat the shift-left instruction (ADD HL,HL) ten times. Notice that the B register is used to hold a count of 10 in this program. This program continues to shift the HL register pair left until the contents of the B register become a zero. As long as B is not a zero, the program continues to jump to memory location loop because the JR NZ,LOOP instruction tests the zero flag bit. The zero flag bit is modified by the DEC B instruction, causing the JR NZ,LOOP instruction to jump to LOOP as long as B is not a zero. In addition to illustrating the first program in the text, this sequence also serves to show a programmed loop and a wait loop. The wait loop uses the unconditional jump instruction (JP ENDP) so that the microprocessor stops executing new instructions at the end of the program.

Example 5-4

```
2000  06  0A        START:  LD   B,10        ;load count
2002  29            LOOP:   ADD  HL,HL       ;shift HL left
2003  05                    DEC  B           ;decrement count
2004  20  F4                JR   NZ,LOOP     ;LOOP if B not 0
2006  C3  06  20    ENDP:   JP   ENDP        ;end program
```

Testing the Carry Flag Bit

The carry flag bit is tested by the JP C,a16, JR C,dd, JP NC,a16, and the JR NC,dd instructions. JP C,a16 and JR C,dd jump to the address or displacement location if the carry is set and JP NC,a16 or JR NC,dd jump if the carry is cleared to zero. In both cases, if the condition being tested is false, then no jump occurs.

The carry is most often tested after a comparison. If the magnitude of the accumulator is greater than or equal to the number being compared with it, no carry is generated. This conditional test is illustrated in the programming Example 5-5. In this example, a partial program tests the accumulator to see if the contents are greater than or equal to a 50H, and if they are, a jump occurs to memory location 3000H. Otherwise, the instruction stored at memory location 2005H is executed. The JP C,a16 and JR C,dd are used to test if the accumulator is less than the number being compared with it.

Example 5-5

```
2000  FE  50             CP 50H         ;test for 50H
2002  D2  00  30         JP NC,3000H    ;jump if A >= 50H
```

Testing the Sign Flag Bit

The sign flag bit is tested with the JP M,a16 and JP P,a16, instructions. JP M,a16 is used to test a number for a negative condition and JP P,a16 is used to test for a positive condition. Suppose that the number stored at memory location 0100H is to be tested for its arithmetic sign. Example 5-6 illustrates the sequence of instructions that are used to accomplish this test. Notice on this program that the number is loaded into the accumulator and then tested. Merely moving a number to the accumulator does not affect the flag bits. The flags will change only when an arithmetic or logic instruction is executed. Here, the OR A instruction, is used to modify the flag bits to reflect the contents of the accumulator without changing the contents of the accumulator. If, after testing A, the contents are negative, the next sequential instruction is executed. If positive, then a jump occurs to memory location 3000H.

Example 5-6

```
2000  3A  00  01         LD A,(0100H)   ;get data
2003  B7                 OR A           ;test A
2004  F2  00  30         JP P,3000H     ;jump if A = +
```

Testing the Parity/Overflow Flag Bit

This flag bit serves two functions. It indicates parity after logic instructions and overflow after addition or underflow after subtraction. An overflow or underflow condition occurs when the signed result exceeds the $+127$ or -128. Parity is a count of the number of ones expressed as even or odd.

The parity/overflow flag bit is tested with the JP PO,a16 (parity odd) or the JP PE,a16 (parity even) instruction. (There are no relative jumps to test this flag bit in the Z80 instruction set.)

Suppose that the data stored at memory location 0110H must be tested for even parity. The program that accomplishes this is similar to the one listed in Example 5-6 except the conditional jump is different. (see Example 5-7). Here the number is loaded to the accumulator and tested with an OR A instruction, just as in Example 5-6. This time the test is followed by the JP PO instruction. If the data at location 0110H have odd parity, a jump to an error-handling program (known as ERROR here) occurs, and if parity is even then the next sequential instruction is executed.

Example 5-7

```
2000 3A 10 01          LD  A,(0110H)  ;get data
2003 B7                OR  A          ;test it
2004 E2 XX XX          JP  PO, ERROR  ;if parity odd
```

Testing for an overflow.   These instructions are also used to test for an overflow (JP PE,a16) or no overflow (JP PO,a16). Example 5-8 illustrates how an overflow is tested after adding the contents of memory location 1000H to the contents of memory location 1001H. Notice that the HL register pair is loaded with these data directly from the memory and then they are added together. The JP PE,a16 instruction follows the addition of these signed numbers to test for an overflow.

Example 5-8

```
2000 2A 00 10          LD   HL,(1000H)  ;get data
2003 7C                LD   A,H         ;sum data
2004 85                ADD  A,L
2005 EA XX XX          JP   PE,OVER     ;if overflow
```

The DJNZ Instruction

The DJNZ dd instruction is a very powerful instruction that is a combination of two instructions: DEC B and JR NZ,dd. The reason that this instruction appears in the instruction set is because a counter is often decremented and tested for a zero condition. This was noticed by Zilog, and they incorporated the instruction in the instruction set. This instruction does not affect any of the flag bits; instead the Z80 decrements the contents of B without a change to the flags as normally would occur.

To illustrate the usefulness of this instruction, Example 5-4 is repeated in Example 5-9 using the DJNZ instruction in place of the DEC B and JR NZ,LOOP instructions. Notice that this saves some memory space in a program.

Example 5-9

```
2000 06 0A        START: LD   B,6      ;load count
2002 29           LOOP:  ADD  HL,HL    ;shift-left
2003 10 FD               DJNZ LOOP     ;repeat B times
2005 C3 05 20     ENDP:  JP   ENDP     ;wait
```

5-4 SUBROUTINES

One of the most important programming features of any microprocessor is the subroutine. A subroutine is a short sequence of instructions that performs a single task. Subroutines are special because they are used as many times as necessary in a program without being stored more than once. The advantages afforded by subroutines are a significant savings in memory space, and the task of writing a program is simplified because subroutines are written once and used many times.

Linking to a Subroutine

A group of instructions are provided that allow the programmer to use a subroutine from any point in a program. These instructions are named CALL instructions. Table 5-3 lists all the possible conditional and unconditional CALL instructions.

When the Z80 executes a CALL instruction, two things occur: (1) the contents of the program counter are pushed onto the stack, and (2) the program jumps to the memory address stored with the CALL instruction. The CALL instruction is a combination of the PUSH and JP instructions.

Why is the CALL instruction different from the jump? The main difference is the

TABLE 5-3. CALL INSTRUCTIONS

Assembly	Machine	Comment
CALL a16	CD 11 hh	Calls the subroutine at a16
CALL C,a16	DC 11 ah	Call the subroutine on a carry = 1
CALL NC,a16	D4 11 hh	Call the subroutine on a carry = 0
CALL Z,a16	CC 11 hh	Call the subroutine on a zero
CALL NZ,a16	C4 11 hh	Call the subroutine on not zero
CALL M,a16	FC 11 hh	Call the subroutine on minus
CALL p,a16	F4 11 hh	Call the subroutine on positive
CALL PE,a16	EC 11 hh	Call the subroutine on parity even (overflow)
CALL PO,a16	E4 11 hh	Call the subroutine on parity odd (no overflow)

Notes: a16, 16-bit memory address; 11, low-order address; and hh, high-order address.

PUSH that occurs before the jump portion of the CALL. The PUSH stores the contents of the program counter on the stack. Because the program counter always points to the next instruction in the program, the stack contains the address of the instruction that follows the CALL. This is called the subroutine return address. The return address is used by the subroutine to return to the point of interruption in the main program. It is for this reason that subroutines must be called rather than jumped to in a program. A jump to a subroutine would afford no method of returning to the main program at the proper point. The CALL allows this because the return address is placed on the stack and it can be accessed within the subroutine so that a return can be made to the program.

Notice that Table 5-3 contains both conditional and unconditional CALL instructions. The conditional CALL instructions test the flag bit indicated by the instruction. If the condition tested is true, a call occurs, and if the condition tested is false, no call occurs and the next sequential instruction in the program is executed. Suppose that the Z flag contains a 1. This indicates that the outcome of an arithmetic or logic operation was a zero. If the CALL NZ,a16 instruction is executed, the program continues with the next instruction in the program. If the CALL Z,a16 instruction is executed, the program continues at the subroutine addressed by the CALL Z,a16 instruction.

Returning from a Subroutine

As mentioned, the CALL instruction places a copy of the contents of the program counter on the stack (the return address). The RET (return) instruction is used to return to the main program at the instruction that follows the CALL. This can be accomplished because the address of this instruction is stored on the stack—the CALL placed it there. The return occurs by removing the return address from the stack and placing it back into the program counter. The RET instruction POPs a number from the stack and places it into the program counter. A list of the available return instructions appears in Table 5-4. As with the CALL instructions, there are both conditional and unconditional returns. If the condition is true, the conditional return instruction removes a number from the stack and places it into the program counter. If the condition is false, the return instruction has no effect and the program continues with the next sequential instruction.

TABLE 5-4.   RETURN INSTRUCTIONS

Assembly	Machine	Comment
RET	C9	Return from subroutine
RET C	D8	Return if carry set
RET NC	DO	Return if carry cleared
RET Z	C8	Return if zero
RET NZ	CO	Return if not zero
RET M	F8	Return if minus
RET P	FO	Return if positive
RET PE	E8	Return if parity even (overflow)
RET PO	EO	Return if parity odd (no overflow)

Using the CALL and RET Instructions

To truly understand the operation of the CALL and RET instructions, an example is required. Suppose that a subroutine is written to two's complement the contents of the accumulator. (Although this is a trivial task, it can be coded as a subroutine.) Example 5-10 illustrates this subroutine, which is stored at memory address 2040H. The one's complement is formed by inverting all the bits of the accumulator with the CPL instruction, and then the result is incremented to obtain the two's complement. The RET instruction changes this task from a sequence of instructions, in a program, to a subroutine. All subroutines must always terminate execution with the RET instruction.

Example 5-10

```
2040 2F          COMP:   CPL           ;invert A
2041 3C                  INC A         ;form 2's complement
2042 C9                  RET           ;return from subroutine
```

Example 5-11 shows how the subroutine of Example 5-10 is used in a program. The first instruction loads the stack pointer register. It is very important that the stack pointer is initialized if a program uses a subroutine or a PUSH or POP instructions. In the program the accumulator is next loaded with a +1. This is followed by two CALL COMP instructions, which call the subroutine twice and change the sign (two's complements) of the contents of the accumulator twice. Although this program has no real application it does illustrate how a subroutine is used from a program.

Example 5-11

```
2000 31 00 21    START:  LD    SP,2100H  ;load SP
2003 3E 01               LD    A,1       ;load a 1 to A
2005 CD 40 20            CALL  COMP      ;change sign
2008 CD 40 20            CALL  COMP      ;change sign
200B 18 FE       ENDP:   JR    ENDP      ;wait
```

The first CALL COMP instruction places the contents of the program counter (2008H) onto the stack. Recall that the CALL instruction places a copy of the program counter on the stack and the program counter always contains the address of the next step in a program. Next, the first CALL COMP jumps to memory location 2040H (COMP). The Z80 executes the CPL and INC A, and when it executes the RET, it removes the 2008H from the stack and places it back into the program counter so that the instruction following the RET is located at 2008H. This instruction is the second CALL COMP.

When the second CALL COMP is executed, the program counter contains a 200BH—the address of the instruciton following the CALL. This becomes the address returned to after the subroutine is called for the second time. Notice that the same group of instructions (subroutine) is used from two different locations in the program. Transfer to and from the subroutine is illustrated in Figure 5-1.

Subroutines are critically important in developing software that is efficient and easy to write. Suppose that a sequence of instructions, 50 bytes long, is required to print data

```
START:  LD    A, 1

        CALL  COMP ─────────────►  COMP:  CPL

        CALL  COMP ◄─ ─ ─ ─                INC A

END:    JP    END  ◄─ ─ ─ ─ ─ ─          RET
```

Notes: ────► = First subroutine pass
        ─ ─► = Second subroutine pass

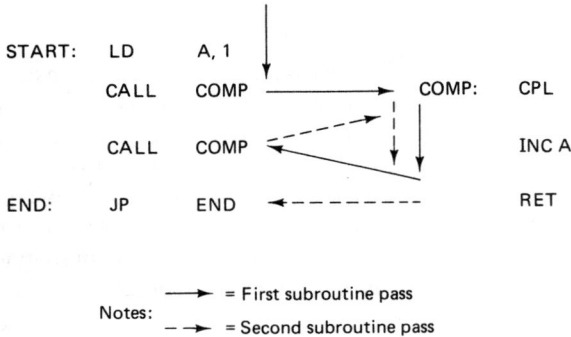

Figure 5–1 Program flow diagram illustrating the path of this program as a subroutine called twice by the main program.

on a printer, and a program is required to print the data 15 times. If the program does not use a subroutine for printing, it takes 15 times 50 bytes or 750 bytes of memory to store a program to print 15 times. If, on the other hand, a subroutine is used for printing, it takes 51 bytes of memory for the subroutine (RET must be added) and 45 bytes for the 15 CALL instructions, or a total of 96 bytes for the program using a subroutine. Programs utilizing subroutines are considerably shorter and take much less time to code.

The Restart Instructions

The restart instructions, as listed in Table 5-5, are actually special unconditional CALL instructions. The reason is that they call a subroutine that begins at a fixed memory location in the Z80 instead of a variable location as addressed by the CALL instruction. Notice that a RST 10H instruction calls the subroutine which begins at memory location 0010H. This is the same as a CALL 0010H except the RST 10H takes one byte of memory to store and the CALL 0010H instruction takes three bytes.

RST instructions are used for system subroutines because of the reduced amount of memory required for their storage in a program. Remember that every time an RST is used in place of a CALL, two bytes of memory are saved. It is also important to note that since system software is often stored in a ROM these RST instructions may not be available to the user. This is true on many of the microprocessor trainers that are available.

TABLE 5-5. RESTART INSTRUCTIONS

Assembly	Machine	Comment
RST 0	C7	Calls subroutine at 0000H
RST 8	CF	Calls subroutine at 0008H
RST 10H	D7	Calls subroutine at 0010H
RST 18H	DF	Calls subroutine at 0018H
RST 20H	E7	Calls subroutine at 0020H
RST 28H	EF	Calls subroutine at 0028H
RST 30H	F7	Calls subroutine at 0030H
RST 38H	FF	Calls subroutine at 0038H

One other important fact about the RSTs is that they are spaced eight bytes apart in the memory. This means that a RST subroutine must normally contain a JP instruction if the subroutine is more than eight bytes in length so that it can be continued elsewhere in the memory.

5-5 MISCELLANEOUS INSTRUCTIONS

The last instructions to be discussed either control the Z80 or the hardware interrupt structure of the Z80. A list of these instructions and a brief comment about each appear in Table 5-6.

Microprocessor Control Instructions

The first instructions covered are the instructions that control the operation of the Z80 microprocessor.

The NOP instruction.   NOP is the symbolic opcode for no operation. What is a no operation instruction? This instruction is used to waste time (4 system clocking periods) in programs that require time delays. (It takes this amount of time to execute a NOP.) NOPs are also used when writing machine language programs in order that room can be left within a program for future additions. Today the NOP is of little use because software is most often written in assembly language.

The SCF and CCF instructions.   SCF and CCF are used to control the state of the carry flag bit. SCF sets carry, and CCF complements carry. If the carry flag needs to be cleared, an SCF followed by a CCF is used, or in most cases the AND A or OR A instruction is found. (Remember all the logic instructions clear the carry flag bit.) Why is it important to be able to modify the carry flag? Carry is used whenever many numbers

TABLE 5.6.   MISCELLANEOUS CONTROL INSTRUCTIONS

Assembly	Machine	Comment
NOP	00	Performs no operation
SCF	37	Set carry flag
CCF	3F	Complement carry flag
HALT	76	Halt until reset or interrupt
IM 0	ED 46	Select interrupt mode 0
IM 1	ED 56	Select interrupt mode 1
IM 2	ED 5E	Select interrupt mode 2
EI	FB	Enable interrupts
DI	F3	Disable interrupts
RETI	ED 4D	Return from interrupt
RETN	ED 45	Return from non-maskable interrupt

are added or subtracted, and both operations require that it is cleared before they begin. In addition to this, the carry flag is at times used to indicate an error condition at a return from a subroutine.

The HALT instruction.   The HALT instruction is used to stop program execution. The only way that execution can continue after a HALT is to reset the Z80 or have an interrupt occur. Both the reset and the interrupt must come from the external hardware. It is for this reason that this command must be reserved for special purposes such as catastrophic system failure.

The Interrupt Control Instructions

There are 5 interrupt control instructions: IM 0, IM 1, IM 2, EI, and DI. The first three are used to select the mode of operation for the interrupt structure of the Z80 microprocessor, and the last two turn the interrupt pin ($\overline{\text{INT}}$) on (EI) or off (DI). Another interrupt input, non-maskable interrupt ($\overline{\text{NMI}}$), automatically calls the interrupt service subroutine that begins at memory location 0066H.

Mode 0 operation is selected by executing the IM 0 instruction. Once the Z80 is operating in mode 0 it expects the external hardware to apply a RST instruction to the data bus in response to an $\overline{\text{INTA}}$ (interrupt acknowledge) signal (the combination of $\overline{\text{IORQ}}$, $\overline{\text{RD}}$, and $\overline{\text{M1}}$) from the microprocessor.

Mode 1 operation is selected by executing the IM 1 instruction. Once operating in mode 1, the Z80 responds to an interrupt input by automatically executing an RST 38 instruction. If only one interrupt is present in the system this is the best mode of operation to select.

Mode 2 operation is selected by executing the IM 2 instruction. Once operating in mode 2, the Z80 automatically vectors to the location held in the I (interrupt) register. The I register holds the high-order 8 bits of interrupt address, and the low-order 8 bits of the interrupt address come from the interrupting device. When the $\overline{\text{INT}}$ signal is activated, the Z80 calls the subroutine that begins at this address. Another load instruction (LD I,A), not mentioned in the chapter on data transfer instructions, is used to load the I register from the accumulator.

The RETI and RETN Instructions

These instructions are used with the $\overline{\text{INT}}$ pin and the $\overline{\text{NMI}}$ pin. Both the RETI and the RETN instructions perform a return just as the RET instruction.

The RETI instruction is used to end the interrupt service subroutine for the $\overline{\text{INT}}$ input pin. The execution of the RETI instruction, which is decoded by the Z80 peripheral, causes the Z80 external peripheral to internally cause the interrupt request to be reset. RETI only causes a normal return as far as the Z80 is concerned. The RETN instruction has the same function. It returns from an interrupt just as a RET would, but it is not decoded by an external device as an RETI. Instead it is decoded as an RETN for a $\overline{\text{NMI}}$ input.

5-6 SUMMARY

1. Program control instructions allow a program to jump around unused sections of the memory and also allow the program to test the flag bits in order to make decisions.

2. The unconditional jumps (JP and JR) are either two- or three-bytes in length. The JP instruction uses its second and third byte to hold the address of the next instruction to be executed in the program. The JR instruction is a relative instruction that jumps forward or backward in the memory. This relative jump can jump up to $+127$ or -128 bytes from the address of the next instruction.

3. The conditional jump instructions allow the flags (Z, C, P, and S) to be tested. If the outcome of the test is true, a jump occurs, and if the outcome is false, the next sequential instruction is executed. The JP instructions can test all the flags, and the JR instructions test only the C and Z flags.

4. Subroutines are short programs that perform one task, are ended with a return instruction, and can be used many times at many different points within a program.

5. The CALL instruction is used to link to a subroutine. It does this by pushing the contents of the program counter onto the stack and jumping to the memory location stored in bytes 2 and 3 of the instruction.

6. The return address is the contents of the program counter that are placed on the stack by the CALL instruction. The return address is removed from the stack by the return (RET) instruction, which places it back into the program counter from the stack.

7. Conditional CALL and RET instructions work just like conditional jump instructions. If the condition being tested is true, the call or return occurs, and if the condition being tested is false the next sequential instruction is executed.

8. Restarts (RST) are special one-byte CALL instructions. The RST instructions call subroutines that begin at memory locations 0, 8, 10H, 18H, 20H, 28H, 30H, and 38H.

9. The NOP instruction performs no operation and is sometimes used in time delay software because it takes 4 clocking periods to do nothing.

10. SCF and CCF are used to set and complement the carry flag, respectively.

11. The HALT instruction is used to stop execution until either a system reset or interrupt occurs.

12. The Z80 contains two interrupt inputs: $\overline{\text{NMI}}$ and $\overline{\text{INT}}$.

13. EI (enable interrupts) and DI (disable interrupts) are used to turn the $\overline{INT}$ pin on and off.

14. IM 0, IM 1, and IM 2 are used to select three different modes of operation for the $\overline{INT}$ pin. Mode 0 causes the $\overline{INT}$ pin to fetch an RST instruction from the data bus; mode 1 causes an RST 38H; and mode 2 uses the I (interrupt) register to supply the high-order address and the data bus to supply the low-order address of the interrupt service subroutine.

15. The RETI instruction is used to end an $\overline{INT}$ interrupt service subroutine and the RETN instruction is used to end an $\overline{NMI}$ interrupt service subroutine.

5-7 GLOSSARY

CALL instructions   CALL instructions are special instructions that perform two tasks: (1) The contents of the program counter are pushed onto the stack, and (2) a jump to the subroutine occurs.

Conditional jump   An instruction that tests a flag bit to determine whether or not to jump to another part of a program. If the condition under test is true, the jump occurs, and if the condition under test is false, the next sequential instruction in the program is executed.

Displacement   The distance from the next instruction is the displacement. A displacement is used with the JR instruction to address a location for the jump.

Halt   A condition arising from the execution of the HALT instruction. The only way to exit a halt is via a hardware reset or interrupt.

Infinite loop   A programmed loop that has no ending which is often used to terminate the execution of a program.

Interrupt   A hardware-initiated subroutine call that interrupts the currently executing program and calls an interrupt service subroutine.

Interrupt service subroutine   A subroutine that is called by a hardware interrupt. The interrupt service subroutine services the interrupt.

Relative addressing   A relative addressed instruction adds a displacement to the program counter to form the address. In the Z80 relative addressing is used with the jump (JR) instructions.

Restart instruction   A restart (RST) instruction is a one-byte CALL.

Return address   The return address is the contents of the program counter which is saved on the stack by a CALL instruction and removed from the stack by the return (RET) instruction.

Return instruction   A special instruction that is used to terminate a subroutine. The return instruction removes a number from the stack and places it into the program counter. Three forms of return exist in the Z80: RET, RETI, and RETN.

Subroutine   A group of instructions that perform a single task which can be called from any location in a program. Subroutines are always terminated with the RET instruction.

Unconditional jump   An unconditional jump is an instruction that will always jump to another point in the program. The JP instruction is three bytes in length and has the address stored with it, and the JR instruction is two bytes long and contains a displacement.

QUESTIONS AND PROBLEMS _____

5-1. Explain the operation of the unconditional (JP) instruction.

5-2. Explain the operation of the unconditional (JR) instruction.

5-3. What is the difference between a JP a16 instruction and the JP (HL) instruction?

5-4. Why is the short program illustrated in Example 5-2 called an infinite loop?

5-5. The conditional (JP) instruction is used to test which 4 flag bits?

5-6. Which flag bits are tested by the conditional (JR) jump instructions?

5-7. If two numbers are compared and it is desired to determine whether they are equal, which conditional jump instruction is used?

5-8. Why is the carry flag tested with conditional jump instructions?

5-9. Why is the OR A instruction called a test accumulator instruction in Example 5-5?

5-10. The JP PO,a16 instruction tests for an overflow after what operations?

5-11. What is a subroutine?

5-12. Which instruction is used to link to a subroutine?

5-13. List the two operations performed by the CALL instruction.

5-14. What is a return address and where is it found?

5-15. The CALL Z,a16 instruction will call the subroutine if the outcome of an arithmetic or logic operation is _____.

5-16. The return (RET) instruction removes data from the stack and places it into which register?

5-17. Write a short subroutine that will triple the contents of the accumulator.

5-18. Use the subroutine of question 5-17 in a program that will multiply the contents of the accumulator by 9.

5-19. Explain what the RST 20H instruction accomplishes.

5-20. Just exactly what does the NOP instruction accomplish?

5-21. Show how the carry flag is cleared using two techniques.

5-22. What two ways are used to exit a HALT instruction?

5-23. What is an interrupt?

5-24. What is an interrupt service subroutine?

5-25. Explain each of the interrupt modes of operations.

5-26. What is an RETI instruction?

5-27. What is an RETN instruction?

5-28. The EI and DI instructions control which Z80 pin?

chapter 6

Assembly Language

Assembly language is used for most programming today because it is extremely difficult to program a microprocessor in its native hexadecimal machine language. The assembly language program or assembler is a program that takes the input (the source program) coded in mnemonic or symbolic machine language language and converts it into a hexadecimal machine language program (object program).

The main reason that software is not written in hexadecimal machine language directly is that whenever a program is modified in machine language, the addresses must be relocated. For example, if a JP 1000H appears in the program and a two-byte instruction is added prior to the JP 1000H, address 1000H must be incremented by 2. Imagine a program that contains 10 or 15 JP instructions and the amount of work required to relocate them. The assembler does this work automatically for the user.

6-1 OBJECTIVES

Upon completion of this chapter, you will be able to:

1. Define the terms: assembler, assembly language, source program, and object program.
2. Briefly describe the operation of a two-pass assembler.
3. Define the purpose of each field in an assembly language statement and indicate the type of information typically found in each field.
4. Explain the purpose of the following assembly language pseudo operations: DB, DW, DS, ORG, and EQU.

5. Identify common assembly language errors so that you do not repeat these errors.

6. Describe the purpose of a macro assembler and explain the directives that are found in a Z80 macro assembler.

6-2 THE ASSEMBLER

As mentioned in the introduction to this chapter, an assembler is a program that converts software written in symbolic machine language into hexadecimal machine language. The symbolic version of the software is called a source program and the hexadecimal version is the object program. The source program provides the assembler with the source of conversion, and the hexadecimal machine language output of the assembler is its object. See Figure 6-1 for an illustration of this process.

The Two-Pass Assembler

Most assemblers convert the source code into object code by passing or scanning through the source code twice. This type of assembler is called a two-pass assembler. Early in the development of computers, and the assembler program, some computer systems were supplied with a one-pass assembler, but it had many limitations. The most notable limitation of the one-pass assembler is that it does not allow forward addressing. This means that the software cannot jump ahead to an instruction in a program, which makes programming difficult at times and sometimes virtually impossible. The reason a forward reference is difficult for a one-pass assembler to accomplish is that the assembler does not know the forward reference memory location. The two-pass assembler corrects this problem by adding an extra pass to the process that corrects the problem of forward references.

Pass one.   During the first pass of the assembler, the source program is scanned and a label table is constructed by the assembler. Figure 6-2 illustrates a short source

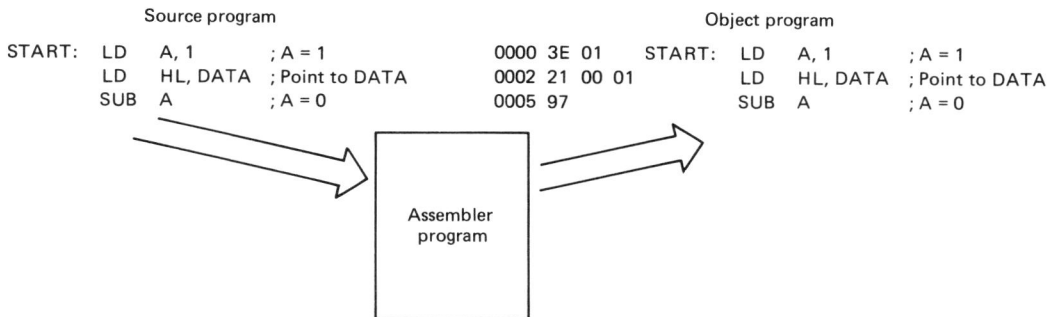

```
        Source program                          Object program

START:  LD   A, 1      ; A = 1      0000 3E 01   START:  LD   A, 1      ; A = 1
        LD   HL, DATA  ; Point to DATA  0002 21 00 01       LD   HL, DATA  ; Point to DATA
        SUB  A         ; A = 0      0005 97              SUB  A         ; A = 0

                              ┌──────────────┐
                              │  Assembler   │
                              │   program    │
                              └──────────────┘
```

Figure 6–1   The assembler program shown converting a source program into an object program.

Label table

Label	Address
START	0000
LOOP	0006
ENDP	000C
DATA	000F

Source program

START:	LD	HL, DATA	; Point to DATA
	XOR	A	; Clear A
	LD	B, 5	; Load count
LOOP:	ADD	A, (HL)	; Add data
	INC	HL	; Point next
	DEC	B	; decrement count
	JP	NZ,LOOP	; if count not zero
ENDP:	JP	ENDP	; Wait
DATA:	DB	1, 2, 3, 4, 5	; Define data

Figure 6–2   The source program and the Label Table that is generated by the assembler.

program and the label table that is generated by the assembler from the program. Each entry in the label table contains the label and the address at which the label appears in the program. The assembler always assumes that the first address of the program is stored at memory location 0000H unless it is otherwise directed with the ORG command. (ORG is discussed in Section 6-4.)

During the first pass, the assembler determines the length of each instruction by updating an internal program counter. The internal program counter allows the assembler to complete the label table by equating each label to this internal program counter. Once the label table is complete, the assembler begins its second pass of the source program.

Pass two.   During the second pass of the source program through the assembler, an object program is formed by referring to the label table for any labels that appear in the program. The assembler also references another table (an instruction table) that contains all the valid opcodes. The instruction table contains all the valid opcodes allowed by the assembler in both symbolic and hexadecimal machine language forms. These tables are used to convert the source program into the object program. Example 6-1 illustrates the final version of the object program that is presented in Figure 6-2.

Example 6-1

```
(OBJECT)                (SOURCE)

ADDR B1 B2 B3 B4

0000 21 0D 00           START: LD   HL,DATA   ;point to data
0003 AF                        XOR  A         ;clear A
0004 06 05                     LD   B,5       ;load counter
0006 86                 LOOP:  ADD  A,(HL)    ;add data
0007 23                        INC  HL        ;point to next datum
0008 10 FC                     DJNZ LOOP      ;repeat LOOP
000A C3 0A 00           ENDP:  JMP  ENDP      ;end program
000D 01 02 03 04        DATA:  DB   1,2,3,4   ;define data
0011 05                        DB   5
```

In addition to building the object program, the second pass also lists the program in both source and object forms on the printer or CRT terminal. If any errors are detected—such as invalid opcodes—the assembler also lists them so that they can be corrected by the programmer. A list of error codes and a discussion of each type appears in Section 6-5. The assembler does not write the program for you, but it does make it a lot easier to write and debug.

6-3 THE ASSEMBLY LANGUAGE STATEMENT

Before it is possible to write assembly language source programs, the basic assembly language statement must be thoroughly understood. This statement contains four distinct fields or parts—label, opcode, operand, and comment—that are meant to contain certain types of information (see Example 6-2). Each of these fields must contain either a space or some alphanumeric characters, and each field must be separated by at least one space. Otherwise the data as entered are in free form.

Example 6-2

```
LABEL       OPCODE      OPERAND     COMMENT

START:      CALL        SUBR        ;call subroutine
```

The Label Field

The label field contains a symbolic memory address that is used to refer to the statement on a program. Labels are optional and must end with a colon (:) in some Z80 assemblers. Labels are constructed from alphanumeric characters and must begin with a letter. The remaining digits can be numbers or letters, and with some assemblers a limited number of special characters may also be used. Table 6-1 lists a number of valid and invalid labels.

A comment can also be specified in the label field in most Z80 assemblers. If the

TABLE 6-1.   VALID AND INVALID LABELS

Label	Valid/invalid	Comment
DOGGY:	Valid	All alphabetic characters
DOG12:	Valid	All alphanumeric characters
SUB:	Invalid	An opcode
D:	Invalid	A register
DOG6.5	Invalid	A special character (.)
4DOG:	Invalid	Begins with a number
DOG_HOUSE:	Valid	The underscore (_) is often valid in a label
*WATER:	Valid	This is a valid comment
; WELL	Valid	This is a valid comment

first character of the label field is an asterisk (*) or a semicolon (;), the entire statement is considered by the assembler as a comment. Comments are not assembled by the assembler; instead they are listed during pass-two for the sake of documentation. Example 6-3 illustrates how asterisks can be used to identify a segment of a program for documentation.

Example 6-3

```
*************************************************************
*********** The system software begins here ***********
*************************************************************
*
START:  LD   HL,DATA
        JP   START           ;loop to start
```

It is also very important to remember that many assemblers do not allow the use of opcodes are register names as labels. For example, if an ADD is used as a label, most assemblers will indicate a label error. Similarly, if the letter A, B, or any other valid Z80 register is specified as a label, an error will occur.

The Opcode Field

The opcode field must always contain a valid Z80 opcode or pseudo opcode. If it does not, the assembler will indicate an error. The valid opcodes for the Z80 have been covered in previous chapters and are also listed in Appendix A, and the valid pseudo opcodes are listed in Section 6-4. Any other entry into this field will result in an error.

The Operand Field

The operand field may contain register names, data, or labels. If more than one operand is present (LD A,B for example), they must be separated with a comma. Data must be encoded as decimal, binary, octal, hexadecimal, or ASCII. Table 6-2 lists the different forms of data allowed in the operand field. When using hexadecimal data it is important to include a leading zero if any hexadecimal data begin with a letter (0A9H, for example). If you do not include this leading zero, the assembler will assume that it is a label and issue an error in most cases. ASCII data may also be used as an operand, and if they are, they must be surrounded by apostrophes.

In addition to specifying the number system of the operand data, the assembler is also capable of performing some arithmetic on the operand data. Table 6-3 illustrates the types of arithmetic operations available and some examples of their usage.

The Comment Field

The comment field must begin with the semicolon or the asterisk in most Z80 assemblers and continues to the end of the line. If it is continued to the next line, the next line must begin with a semicolon or an asterisk. Example 6-4 illustrates some example comments.

TABLE 6-2.   VALID FORMS OF OPERAND DATA

Operand	Type	Comment
100	Decimal	8- or 16-bit quantity
1000	Decimal	16-bit quantity
50D	Decimal	8- or 16-bit quantity
10H	Hexadecimal	8- or 16-bit quantity
23AFH	Hexadecimal	16-bit quantity
0FFH	Hexadecimal	8- or 16-bit quantity
120	Octal	8- or 16-bit quantity
11001111B	Binary	8- or 16-bit quantity
"A"	ASCII	8-bit quantity
"AB"	ASCII	16-bit quantity
"HELLO"	ASCII	Multiple-byte quantity

TABLE 6-3.   OPERAND ARITHMETIC OPERATORS

Operation	Example	Comment
+	LABEL+2	Points to address LABEL plus two bytes
−	LABEL-1	Points to address LABEL minus one byte
*	DOG*3	Equates to the value of DOG times 3
/	SEVEN/2	Equates to the value of SEVEN divided by 2; if SEVEN equals 7, it equates to a 3, the unrounded integer portion of the result
NOT	NOT TRUE	NOT generates the ones complement of TRUE
AND	DI AND FI	AND generates the logical product of DI and FI
OR	DD OR FF	OR generates the logical sum of DD and FF
XOR	TG XOR HU	XOR exclusive-ORs TG with HU
MOD	COW MOD 8	COW is divided by 8 and the remainder of the division is generated; for example, if COW equals 9, the result is 1

Example 6-4

```
;
;this is a comment
;
START:  LD  DE,DATA    ;comment
*
*this is a comment
*
;all of the above are comments except for START: ....
```

6-4 ASSEMBLER PSEUDO OPERATIONS

The assembler pseudo operations are directives to the assembler program that may or may not generate hexadecimal machine code. For example, the END pseudo opcode indicates to the assembler that the end of the program has been reached. This pseudo opcode generates no machine code. Other pseudo opcodes used by many Z80 assemblers include DB, DW, DS, ORG, EQU, IF, ENDIF, SET, GLB, EXT, TITLE, and SPC. All pseudo opcodes are placed in the opcode field of the assembly language statement.

Define Byte (DB)

The DB (define byte) pseudo opcode is used to define 8-bit memory data for a program. The DB opcode stores a byte of bytes of data in the memory for use by the program. Example 6-5 illustrates many examples of the use of the DB opcode.

Example 6-5

```
DATA:     DB  1,2,3,4    ;define DATA as four bytes
DATA1:    DB  100        ;define DATA1 as 100 decimal
DATA2:    DB  0A0H       ;define DATA2 as A0 hexadecimal
DATA3:    DB  1111B      ;define DATA3 as 1111 binary
DATA4:    DB  'D'        ;define DATA4 as an ASCII D
DATA5:    DB  'HELLO'    ;define DATA5 as 10 ASCII bytes
          DB  'THERE'
DATA6:    DB  ''''       ;define DATA6 as an ASCII '
```

Define Word (DW)

The DW (define word) pseudo opcode is used to store a 16-bit number in the memory for use by a program. Example 6-6 illustrates many examples of the usage of the DW directive.

Example 6-6

```
DATA:     DW  1000H      ;define DATA as 1000H
DATA1:    DW  10H        ;define DATA1 as 0010H
DATA2:    DW  10101B     ;define DATA2 as 10101 binary
DATA3:    DW  'AB'       ;define DATA3 as an ASCII BA
DATA4:    DW  START      ;define DATA4 as label START
```

Define Storage (DS)

The DS (define storage) directive is used to reserve space in a program for variable data. The DS opcode always defines the number of bytes to be reserved. Some examples of this opcode are listed in Example 6-7.

Example 6-7

```
DATA:     DB  10         ;define DATA as 10 decimal
          DS  10         ;reserve 10 bytes of memory
DATA1:    DB  0DH        ;define DATA1 as 13
```

Origin (ORG)

The ORG (origin) pseudo opcode is used to change the starting point of the program from location 0000H to any other address. The ORG statement can be used at any point in a program to change the location of the assembled machine language instructions. Some examples of ORG and its application are listed in Example 6-8.

Example 6-8

```
                        ORG  1000H     ;set origin to 1000H
1000 3E 01      START:  LD   A,1       ;set A to 01
1002 C3 00 10           JP   1000H     ;jump to START
                ;
                ;set new origin
                ;
                        ORG  2000H     ;set origin to 2000H
2000 01 02 03   DATA:   DB   1,2,3     ;define DATA
2003 41 42 43   DATA1:  DB   'ABC'     ;define DATA1
```

Equate (EQU)

The EQU (equate) directive is used to equate a label to another label or a value. This pseudo opcode generates no machine code but instead loads the label table in pass-one of the assembly process with the value or the address of the label. An example of the equate statement appears in Example 6-9.

Example 6-9

```
                        ORG  100
0064 3E 01              LD   A,ONE     ;A = 1
0066 21 00 01           LD   HL,DATA   ;address DATA
0069 C3 64 00           JP   START
006C 01 00      ONE:    EQU  1
006C 00 01      DATA:   EQU  100H
006C 64 00      START:  EQU  100
```

IF and ENDIF

The IF and ENDIF directives allow the programmer to conditionally assemble portions of a program. The IF statement evaluates the argument included with the IF statement to determine if it is true or false. True and false conditions are determined by the value of the argument (True; least significant bit of 1 and false; least significant bit of 0). If the argument is true, the assembler generates the object code for the statements between the IF and the ENDIF statements. If the argument is false, the assembler does not generate object code for the statements between IF and ENDIF.

A useful application of these two pseudo operations is in certain types of setup programs. For example, suppose that a computer system will output data that is either 80 or 120 columns wide to a printer. The setup program allows the programmer to change the setup information by answering some simple true-and-false questions before the program is assembled. The source program listed in Example 6-10 illustrates some simple questions.

Example 6-10

```
***** Setup program *****
*****
FALSE:    EQU   0
TRUE:     EQU   1
*****
***** Printer page width *****
***** C80 = true for 80 columns
***** C80 = false for 132 columns
*****
C80:      EQU   TRUE
```

Example 6-11 illustrates the portion of the setup program that uses the IF and ENDIF directives to set the width of the printer to 80 or 120 columns. Notice how the IF C80 is used for TRUE (1) and the IF NOT C80 is used to cause the FALSE (0) condition. The information assembled for PWIDE causes the printer to setup to print either 80 or 120 columns.

Example 6-11

```
          IF   C80       ;(true) for 80 columns
PWIDE:    DB   1BH,11H   ;PWIDE = 1BH, 11H
          ENDIF
          IF   NOT C80   ;(false) for 132 columns
PWIDE:    DB   1BH,21H   ;PWIDE = 1BH, 21H
          ENDIF
```

SET

The SET directive is used in the same manner as the EQU directive except that the SET directive is temporary. A label may be equated to a value only once during assembly, whereas the SET directive may be used to reset the same label to a different value in the assembly process. In most cases SET is used only for special cases in an assembly language program.

Global (GLB) and External (EXT)

Global (GLB) and external (EXT) are used in a programming environment that contains a linker program to link software modules together. The linker is a program that is used to connect (link) different assembly language program segments (modules) together. One problem that arises when modules are linked together is that the variables in each modules are defined only in the module. This prevents other modules from using the same variables.

The GLB statement is used to allow a software module to make local variables available to other software modules. Example 6-12 shows how the variables DOG and CAT and the subroutine named DOGCAT are made available to other software modules.

Example 6-12

```
*
***** define global labels *****
*
          GLB   DOGCAT      ;make DOGCAT global
          GLB   DOG         ;make DOG global
          GLB   CAT         ;make CAT global
*
***** DOG times two plus CAT subroutine *****
*
DOGCAT:   LD    A,(DOG)     ;double DOG
          ADD   A,A
          LD    B,A
          LD    A,(CAT)
          ADD   A,B         ;double DOG plus CAT
          RET
DOG:      DB    0
CAT:      DB    0
```

If module DOGCAT is used in another module, the EXT statement is used so that the linker knows that DOGCAT is external to the module. This allows the linker to search other modules for labels that are defined as global. If a label is external, it must always be defined as a global. If a label is external, it must always be defined as a global label in another module. An example of a module that uses DOGCAT and its variables DOG and CAT, which are defined as global labels in Example 6-12, is listed in Example 6-13.

Example 6-13

```
*
***** Make MODULE1 global *****
*
          GLB   MODULE1     ;make MODULE1 global
*
***** Define DOGCAT, DOG, and CAT as external *****
*
          EXT   DOGCAT      ;make DOGCAT external
          EXT   DOG         ;make DOG external
          EXT   CAT         ;make CAT external
*
***** Subroutine MODULE1 *****
*
MODULE1:  LD    A,12H
          LD    (DOG),A     ;set DOG = 12H
          LD    A,2
          LD    (CAT),A     ;set CAT = 2
          CALL  DOGCAT      ;do subroutine
          RET
```

TITLE and SPC

In addition to all of the previous pseudo operations, some assemblers also contain the listing control directives TITLE and SPC.

The TITLE directive allows the programmer to (1) feed to the top of a new page, (2) place a title on the top of the new page, and (3) continue to print the title on the top of each subsequent page until another TITLE directive appears in the program.

The SPC directive allows the programmer to insert blank lines of paper between sections of a program. The number of blank lines is specified by the argument of the SPC directive. Example 6-14 illustrates the TITLE and SPC directives.

Example 6-14

```
TITLE 'THIS IS A TITLE'
SPC   7
```

6-5 ASSEMBLER ERROR DETECTION

Most Z80 assembler programs are capable of detecting errors in certain portions of the assembly language source program. Unfortunately, assemblers cannot detect errors in the order of the statements in a program. If this were possible, programmers would not be needed because the assembler could automatically correct any errors in the program.

Table 6-4 lists the error codes detected by the assembler and a brief description of each type of error. When an error is detected by the assembler, it is printed together with the source and object programs in the listing. Example 6-15 illustrates some statements that are in error along with the error codes.

TABLE 6-4. ERROR CODES FOR THE Z80 ASSEMBLER

	Code Name	Comment
D	Duplicate label error	This label at appears at some other point in the program in the label field
E	Expression error	The expression (argument) is too complex to compute
L	Label error	The label is incorrectly used or inconsistently used in the program
N	Not implemented	The expression applies to a different version of the assembler
O	Opcode error	Invalid opcode specified
P	Phase error	The value of a label changed between passes 1 and 2 of the assembler
R	Register error	You specified a nonexistent register
S	Syntax error	Occurs for a typographical error

Example 6-15

```
0000 00 00 00   U   START:  LD   HL,DATA
0003 00 00 00   0           LO   A,B
0006 80                     ADD  A,B
0007 3E 00      V           LD   A,1000
0009 00 00 00   E           ADD  B
000C C6 10      D   START:  ADD  A,10H
000E 00 00 00   N           IF   TRUE
0011 01             TRUE:   DB   1
```

6-6 MACRO ASSEMBLERS

A macro assembler is a special form of the standard assembler that allows the programmer to define new opcodes. For example, the Z80 cannot switch the contents of the HL register pair directly with the BC register pair. It may be common in a particular program to require this task. The task can be programmed as a subroutine or as a macro if a macro assembler is available. With the subroutine (see Example 6-16), a CALL SWITCH instruction is used inserted in the main program each time that the contents of HL are switched with BC. If the same task is developed as a macro, the program contains the opcode SWITCH each time that the HL and BC pairs are exchanged.

Example 6-16

```
SWITCH:    PUSH HL    ;save HL
           PUSH BC    ;save BC
           POP  HL    ;BC to HL
           POP  BC    ;HL to BC
           RET
```

Macros

To convert the subroutine listed in Example 6-16 into a macro*, the macro is first defined and then all the steps of the subroutine except for the RET follow the macro definition statement (see Example 6-17). The MEND statement is used to end the macro. From this point forward the assembler automatically inserts the macro coding into the program each time that this new opcode SWITCH is found in a program. Example 6-18 illustrates the SWITCH macro used in a short program. Notice from this example that the assembler inserts the steps between MACRO and MEND of the original macro into the program. The assembler precedes each step of the macro with a plus sign (+) so that it can be identified in the listing.

---

*The macros defined here are used in the Hewlett-Packard HP64000 logic development system. Other systems may use slightly different definitions.

Example 6-17

```
SWITCH:   MACRO        ;define new opcode SWITCH
          PUSH HL      ;save HL
          PUSH BC      ;save BC
          POP  HL      ;BC to HL
          POP  BC      ;HL to BC
          MEND         ;end new opcode SWITCH
```

Example 6-18

```
              ;
              ;source program
              ;
              START:    LD  BC,1000H   ;load BC
                        LD  HL,2000H   ;load HL
                        SWITCH         ;envoke macro
                        JP  START      ;repeat
              ;
              ;assembled version
              ;
0000 01 00 10 START:    LD  BC,1000H   ;load BC
0003 21 00 20           LD  HL,2000H   ;load HL
0006                    SWITCH         ;envoke macro
0006 E5         +        PUSH HL       ;save HL
0007 C5         +        PUSH BC       ;save BC
0008 E1         +        POP  HL       ;BC to HL
0009 C1         +        POP  BC       ;HL to BC
000A C3 00 00           JP  START      ;repeat
```

Macros with Parameters

One of the most useful features of the macro is its ability to pass parameters to the macro from a program. Suppose that a program is required to add two 16-bit numbers located in memory and store the sum in the memory. A macro can be written that will allow these data to be added and defined in the macro calling sequence. Variable macro data must be defined in the operand field, and each variable must be preceded by an ampersand (&). The macro is illustrated in Example 6-19.

Example 6-19

```
DADD:    MACRO &VAR1,&VAR2,&VAR3
         PUSH  AF            ;save registers
         PUSH  HL
         PUSH  DE
         LD    HL,(&VAR1)    ;get first variable
         EX    DE,HL
         LD    HL,(&VAR2)    ;get second variable
         ADD   HL,DE         ;generate sum
         LD    (&VAR3),HL    ;save sum
         POP   DE            ;restore registers
         POP   HL
         POP   AF
         MEND
```

In this example, the new opcode (macro) is DADD for double addition. Associated with it are three variables that are used within the macro to define the memory locations where the data are stored and where the sum is stored. The 16-bit number at memory location &VAR1 and &VAR2 are added, and the result is stored at location &VAR3. Example 6-20 shows how this macro is used in a short program. As you can see from this example, the macro assembler can provide the programmer with a new set of options. It is even possible to write a simple high-level language using macro instructions.

Example 6-20

```
                        ;
                        ;source program
                        ;
                        START: DADD   ONE,TWO,THREE
                               JP     START
                        ONE:   DW     9
                        TWO:   DW     4
                        THREE: DW     O
                        ;
                        ;assembled program
                        ;
    0000                START: DADD   ONE,TWO,THREE
    0000 F5           +        PUSH   AF          ;save registers
    0001 E5           +        PUSH   HL
    0002 D5           +        PUSH   DE
    0003 2A 14 00     +        LD     HL,(&VAR1)  ;get first variable
    0006 EB           +        EX     DE,HL
    0007 2A 16 00     +        LD     HL,(&VAR2)  ;get second variable
    000A 19           +        ADD    HL,DE       ;generate sum
    000B 22 1B 00     +        LD     (&VAR3),HL  ;save sum
    000E D1           +        POP    DE          ;restore registers
    000F E1           +        POP    HL
    0010 F1           +        POP    AF
    0011 C3 00 00              JP     START
    0014 09 00        ONE:     DW     9
    0016 04 00        TWO:     DW     4
    0018 00 00        THREE:   DW     O
```

6-7 SUMMARY

1. Assemblers are programs that convert symbolic machine language into hexadecimal machine language.

2. The source program, which is input to the assembler, is a program written in symbolic machine language, and the object program, which is the output of the assembler, is on hexadecimal machine language.

3. Most assemblers are two-pass, which means that they look at the source program twice. The first pass generates a label table, and the second pass develops the assembled hexadecimal version of the source program.

4. An assembly language statement is composed of four fields: label, opcode, operand, and comment. The label field is used to address a statement, the opcode field holds the symbolic opcode, the operand field holds the address or object of the opcode, and the comment field is for comments by the programmer.

5. Assembler labels must begin with an alphabetic character and may be followed by any combination of alphabetic or numeric characters. The last portion of a label must be a colon in most Z80 assemblers.

6. The operand may contain labels, registers, or numbers. If numbers are contained they may be binary, decimal, octal, hexadecimal, or ASCII.

7. The assembler has some additional directives called pseudo operations. The most common pseudo operations are DB, DW, DS, ORG, EQU, IF, ENDIF, SET, GLB, EXT, TITLE, and SPC.

8. The assembler is capable of detecting errors in form. The most common errors include duplicate labels, expression, opcode, register, syntax, and undefined label.

9. A macro assembler is a standard assembler that allows the user to specify new opcodes. This is done by defining the new opcode with the MACRO statement and ending it with the MEND statement.

10. Macros can be written to pass parameters through to the code contained between the MACRO and MEND statements. All the parameters must begin with an ampersand (&), which is used to distinguish a parameter from a label.

6-8 GLOSSARY

Assembler A program that converts symbolic machine language (sometimes called assembly language) into hexadecimal machine language.

Comment A portion of an assembler statement that starts with a semicolon (;) or an asterisk (*) that is used by the programmer to comment about a program.

Conditional assembly A factor in the assembler that allows code to be generated if a particular condition is true.

Directive See Pseudo operation.

External variable In modular programming, labels that do not exist in the current module are considered external to the module.

Global variable In modular programming, labels that exist in the current module that will be used in others are declared global.

Label A symbolic address that is used in an assembly language program to address statements. If it appears in the label field, it is most often followed by a colon (:).

Label table A table of labels that is generated during pass one in a two-pass assembler containing each label and its relative address in the program.

Linker A program that takes assembly language or high-level-language modules and connects or links them together. The linker is an important tool in modular programming.

Macro assembler A special form of the assembler that allows the user to define new opcodes.

MOD   Specifies the remainder after a division. MOD 10, for example, divides by 10 and yields the remainder after the division.

Object program   The output of the assembler which is listed and stored in the memory in hexadecimal machine language.

Operand   The data acted on by the opcode.

Origin   The starting point or address of a program that is defined to the assembler using the ORG directive.

Pseudo operation   A directive that commands the assembler to perform certain special functions. Pseudo operations may or may not generate machine code.

Source program   The input to the assembler written in symbolic machine language and often called the assembly language program.

Syntax error   An error in form, usually a typographical error.

Two-pass assembler   An assembler that looks at a program twice: the first time to generate a label table and the second time to generate the object program.

QUESTIONS AND PROBLEMS _____

6-1. Why is software written in assembly language instead of machine language?

6-2. A symbolic program is called the _____ program and the machine-coded version is called the _____ program.

6-3. What events occur during each pass of a two-pass assembler?

6-4. Why is it rare to find a one-pass assembler?

6-5. What four fields are found in an assembly language statement?

6-6. From the following list of labels, determine which are valid and which are invalid. For all invalid labels, give the reason why it is invalid.
  (a) DOGGY.3:
  (b) COW33:
  (c) 33WATER:
  (d) WINTER__SNOW:
  (e) MELLOW PILLOW:

6-7. If the first character of the label field is an asterisk, the entire statement becomes a _____ .

6-8. Code a 12 as decimal, octal, and hexadecimal operand.

6-9. Why is an FFH coded as an OFFH when used as an operand?

6-10. Write your name in ASCII code.

6-11. Why is a semicolon found in an assembly language statement?

6-12. The operand 19 MOD 8 evaluates to _____ .

6-13. What pseudo operation is used to store an ASCII-coded name such as WATERLOO in memory using the assembler?

6-14. What does the DS directive cause the assembler to accomplish?

6-15. Form an assembly language statement that will start to assemble a program at memory location 0800H.

6-16. Explain the difference between the EQU and SET statements.

6-17. True or false: The IF statement checks the variable in the operand field to determine if it is even or odd. If even, the statements between IF and ENDIF are assembled.

6-18. GLB and EXT are used in modular programming for what reason?

6-19. What is a linker?

6-20. Given the following statements, determine which error code is listed if each statement is assembled by the assembler.
  (a) LD A,666
  (b) POP X
  (c) LD A.B
  (d) JP START.X

6-21. Where are the error codes listed in the output of the assembler?

6-22. What is a macro assembler?

6-23. What is the difference between a subroutine and a macro?

6-24. The _____ statement defines the macro and the _____ statement ends the definition.

6.25. What appears in the output listing of the assembler to distinguish macro instructions?

6-26. How can parameters be passed through to a macro?

chapter 7

Structured Assembly Language Programming

What is structured assembly language programming? It is a programming methodology that aids in the development of complicated software with a minimum amount of effort. In this chapter, we present the basic structures, programming techniques, and basic approaches required to solve problems through software. We also develop an understanding of flowcharting, which aids in the development and documentation of complex programs.

7-1 OBJECTIVES

Upon completion of this chapter, you will be able to:

1. Describe the purpose of each common flowcharting symbol.
2. List the basic structured programming constructs and briefly describe each construct.
3. Explain how the programmed loop functions.
4. Convert a word problem into flowcharting using the basic constructs of structured programming.

7-2 FLOWCHARTING

Flowcharts are used to design the control flow of a software-based system and are always included in program documentation so that future software modifications can be made

Symbol	Name	Function
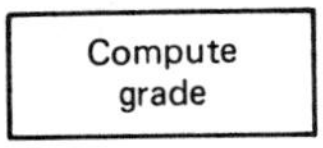 Compute grade	Process	Used to indicate any type of arithmetic or procedural operation
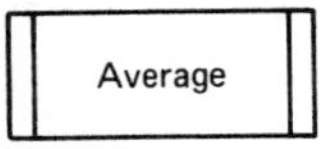 Average	Predefined process	Used to invoke a subroutine which is normally used as a predefined process in assembly language
 Read score	Input/output	Used for any input or output operation
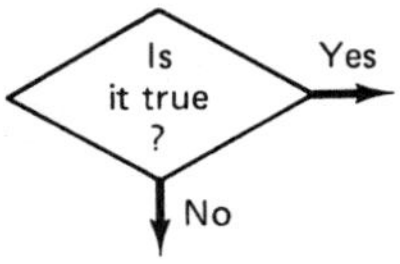 Is it true ? Yes No	Decision	Used to·ask a question in a program with either two or three outcomes
3	Connector	Allows the flowchart to be drawn without crisscrossed flow lines
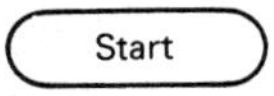 Start	Terminal	Indicates the starting or ending point of the program or predefined process

Figure 7–1   The commonly used flowcharting symbols.

with a minimal amount of effort. Before flowcharting symbols are used to implement software control structures, the flowcharting symbols must be understood.

Flowcharting Symbols

Figure 7-1 depicts the most common flowcharting symbols (process, predefined process, input/output, decision, connector, and terminal) that are used in flowcharts of assembly language programs. Although this is not a complete list of all the possible flowcharting symbols, it is generally understood to be a list of the most pragmatic subset for structured assembly language programming.

The process symbol.   The process flowcharting symbol is used to indicate any type of process in a program. The process depicted by this symbol can be either arithmetical or procedural in nature and is always written inside the symbol as an equation or a simple phrase in English describing the process. Do not write assembly language instructions in the process or any of the other flowcharting symbols. Each block in a flowchart should represent many assembly language instructions. If a flowchart is understandable by a nonprogrammer, it has all the requirements for being capable of documenting the program and making the program easier to code into assembly language.

The predefined process.   This block is very important when writing software because it allows the programmer to indicate the need for subroutines in the completed program. The predefined process block usually contains the name of the subroutine. Recall that a subroutine is a grouping of instructions that perform a task. Subroutines need be stored in the memory once, after which they may be used many times by the program. This reduces coding time and makes software (and flowcharts) easier to construct and maintain.

The input/output symbol.   Whenever data are input to a program or output from a program, the input/output symbol is used. This specially shaped symbol makes it easier to identify an input/output operation in the flowchart. Usually, the type of data and the direction of data flow are indicated within the symbol. Some examples include input character, output character, output line, send data, and receive data.

The decision symbol.   Because a computer system's power comes from its ability to make decisions, the decision flowcharting symbol is indeed very important. In most cases this symbol is used to ask and answer a question about the flow of a program. The question is always written inside the symbol. The symbol itself has one input and up to three output points (answers to the question). In most cases two outputs are used to answer yes–no, true–false, 1–0, or similar questions, and three outputs to answer the arithmetic, 0, +, or − .

The connector.   The connector symbol is used to eliminate crisscrossed connecting lines in a complicated flowchart. Its use is optional, but using it makes the flowchart more readable, which is very important. Connectors usually contain a number or letter and usually come in pairs. One of the connectors in the pair has a flow arrow into it and the other has a flow arrow out of it.

The terminal symbol.   Programs all start somewhere and require a symbol to indicate where they start. The terminal symbol is used to indicate the start of a program and also the starting and ending points of a predefined process (subroutine) flowchart. This symbol usually contains the word START, END, RETURN, or the name of a subroutine.

An Example Flowchart

Figure 7-2 illustrates the flowchart that might be used to compute the class average grade on a test. Notice that this simple program contains every type of flowcharting symbol listed in Figure 7-1.

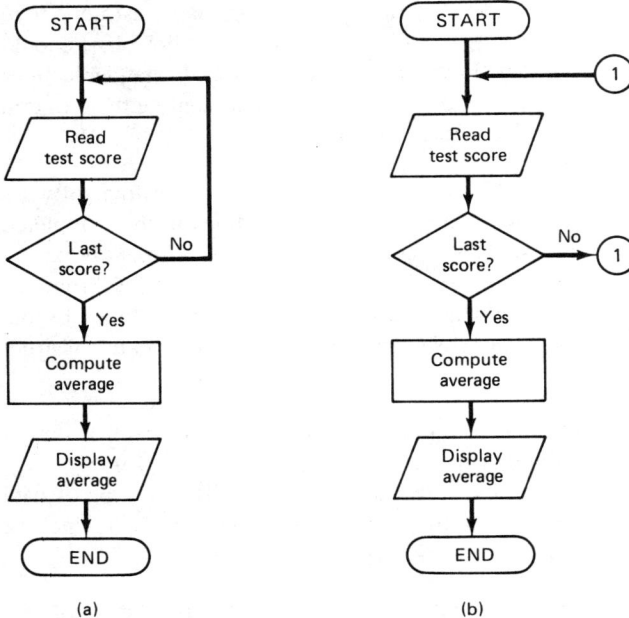

Figure 7–2 A sample flowchart of a program which illustrates how a test average is computed for a class group.

In addition, the operations performed by each symbol are written in clear and concise English so that anyone can understand the sequence of events in this flowchart. Notice that the flowchart flows from top to the bottom, a technique that is often called top-down programming. Also notice that the flow of the program is illustrated with arrows that move from symbol to symbol. This allows the programmer to more easily construct the assembly language version of the program. How easy is it to find the beginning and ending point of this flowchart? Easy, because the terminal symbols clearly show the starting and ending points of this simple program's flowchart.

Figure 7-2 (b) is provided so that the connector symbol can be illustrated. In this example, it is probably better not to use the connector symbol because the flow lines do not cross. Again as mentioned previously, the connector is normally used only to prevent flow lines from crossing.

7-3 BASIC CONSTRUCTS

A construct is a sequence of steps that has one input or entrance point and one output or exit point. There is a group of basic constructs that is used to solve virtually all programming problems. If these constructs are learned well, programming tends to become much easier—it is easier because of the handful of techniques (constructs) that allow a flowchart to be created with a great deal of efficiency. The constructs are all converted into assembly language in the same manner that makes coding a program into assembly

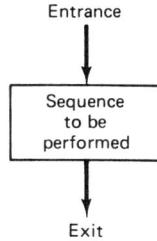

Figure 7–3   The flowchart sequence for the sequence construct.

language much easier. The basic constructs of structured programming include: sequence, if–then, if–then–else, repeat–until, do–while, and programmed loop (a special case of repeat–until.

The Sequence Construct

The sequence construct, illustrated in Figure 7-3, is one of the most basic of all structures. With this structure, control is transferred to it, a process is performed, and control exits it.

A simple sequence structure that will compute the average and standard deviation of a test and print the results is illustrated in Figure 7-4 (a). Here four steps are required to solve for the average and standard deviation and print the results: two are predefined processes and two are output functions. Figure 7-4 (b) illustrates the assembly language source equivalent of the flowcharted structured sequence of Figure 7-4 (a). In the assembly

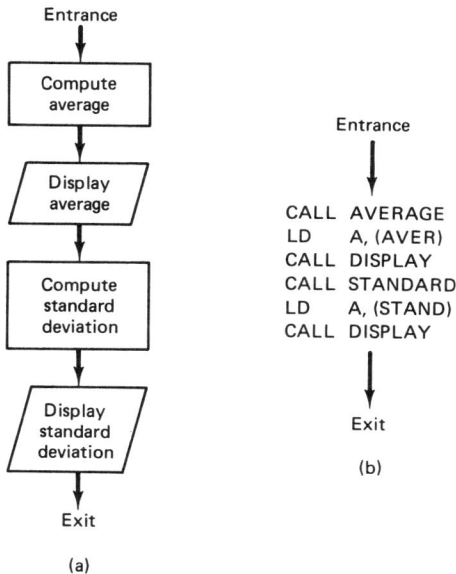

```
CALL  AVERAGE
LD    A, (AVER)
CALL  DISPLAY
CALL  STANDARD
LD    A, (STAND)
CALL  DISPLAY
```

Figure 7–4   (a) The flowchart used to compute and print the average and standard deviation using the sequence construct; (b) the assembly language version of the sequence construct.

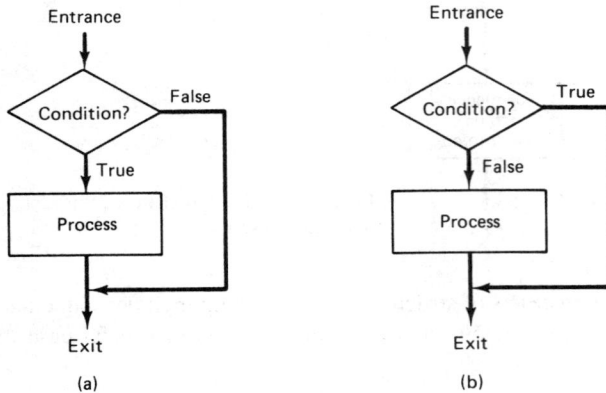

Figure 7–5   (a) The flowchart sequence for the if-true-then construct; (b) the flowchart sequence for the if-false-then construct.

language version of this program, subroutines are utilized because these basic operations are common and are probably used in other programs.

The If–Then Construct

The if–then construct is used to test a condition and then perform the sequence if the result of the test is true or false. The two basic forms of this construct are these: if the condition is true, then perform a sequence (if–then–true), and if the condition is false, then perform a sequence (if–then–false). The if–then–true construct is illustrated in Figure 7-5 (a), and the if–then–false construct is illustrated in Figure 7-5 (b). Notice that both structures of the if–then construct have one entrance point and one exit point, as do all constructs.

Figure 7-6 (a) shows how both constructs are used in an example flowchart for controlling a heating system, and Figure 7-6 (b) shows the listing of the assembly language source version of the program. Notice that the more complicated tasks are written as subroutines that are referenced by the assembly language source version of the program. Also notice that in the assembly language source version, the jump occurs if the condition is met, as when the temperature is tested and found that it is too cool to affect the heater. In many cases of the if–then construct, the compare instruction is used to test for a condition.

The If–Then–Else Construct

From the flowchart of Figure 7-6 it is easy to see that a new construct can be treated that handles the case where both true and false conditions cause a different event to occur. This new construct is the if–then–else construct, which takes the form of if–true do one sequence, else (false) do another sequence. The if–then–else construct is depicted in Figure 7-7. As you can see, this structure allows both sequences to occur with only one test, which makes the flowchart and often the assembly language program easier to construct.

Entrance

Temperature greater than thermostat?

No

Yes

Turn heater off

Temperature greater than thermostat?

Yes

No

Turn heater on

Exit

(a)

```
                Entrance

        LD    A, (TEMP)    ; Get temperature
        LD    B, A
        LD    A, (THERM)   ; Get thermostat
        CMP   B
        JR    NC, ONE      ; TEMP > THERMOSTAT
        LD    A, 1
        OUT   HEATER       ; HEATER OFF
ONE:    LD    A, (TEMP)    ; Get temperature
        LD    B, A
        LD    A, (THERM)   ; Get thermostat
        CMP   B
        JR    C, TWO       ; TEMP > THERMOSTAT
        LD    A, 0
        OUT   HEATER       ; HEATER ON
TWO:

                Exit

                 (b)
```

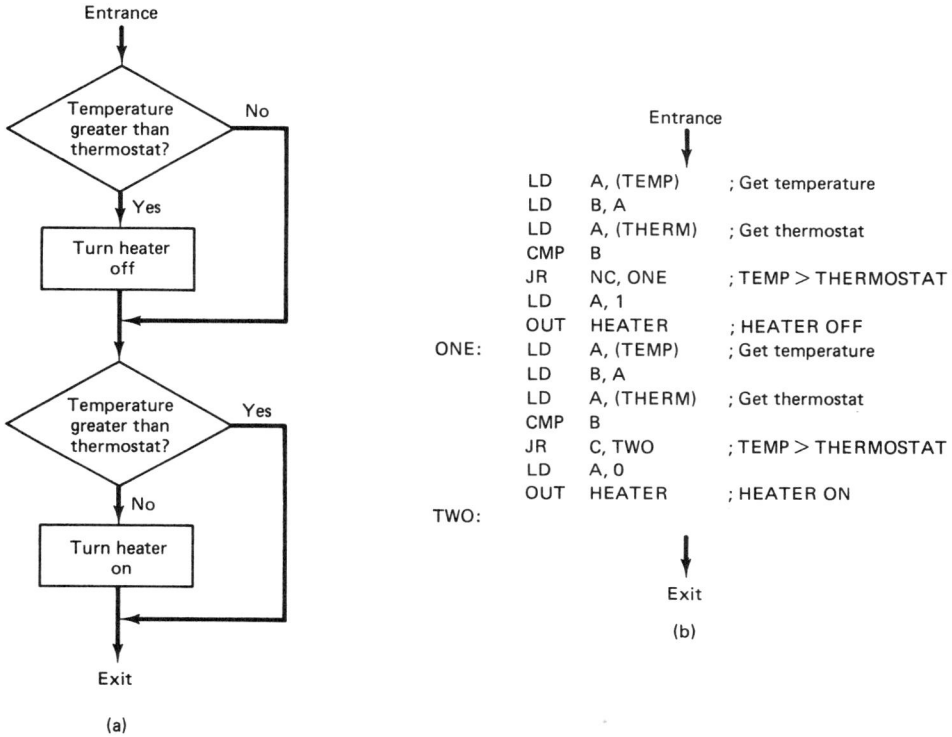

Figure 7–6   (a) The flowchart used to control a heater illustrating both the if-true-then and if-false-then constructs; (b) the assembly language version of the heater control sequence.

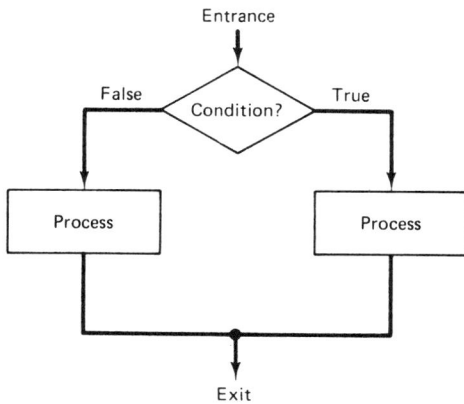

Entrance

False   Condition?   True

Process   Process

Exit

Figure 7–7   The flowchart sequence for the if-then-else construct.

```
          Entrance

       LD    A, (TEMP)      ; Get temperature
       LD    B; A
       LD    A, (THERM)     ; Get thermostat
       CMP   B
       JR    C, TWO         ; IF TEMP > THERM
       JR    NC, ONE        ; IF TEMP < THERM
TWO:   LD    A, 1
       OUT   HEATER         ; HEATER OFF
       JR    THREE
ONE:   LD    A, 0
       OUT   HEATER         ; HEATER ON
THREE:

          Exit
```

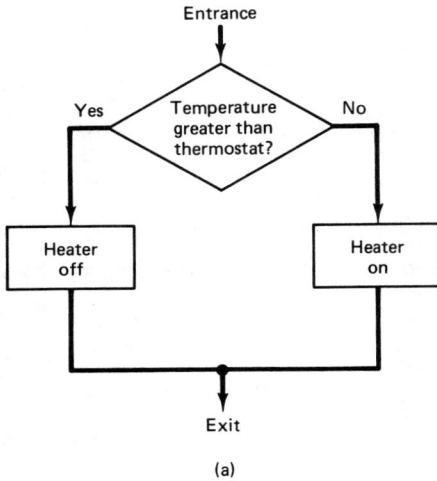

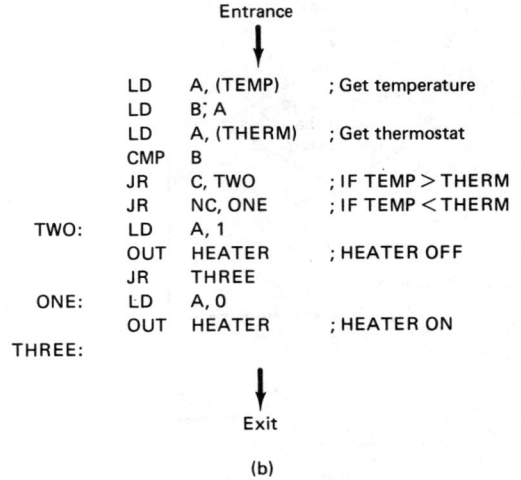

Figure 7–8 (a) The flowchart used to control a heater illustrating the if-then-else construct; (b) the assembly language version of the heater control sequence using the if-then-else construct.

Suppose that the example in Figure 7-6 is modified so that it uses the if–then–else construct. Notice from Figure 7-8 (a) that the length of the flowchart is shorter and easier to understand and the software of Figure 7-8 (b) is slightly shorter. The software is shorter because only one test is made instead of the two tests of Figure 7-6.

The Repeat–Until Construct

The repeat–until construct allows a process to be executed or repeated until an event occurs. Whenever this construct is used, the process is first executed and then a condition

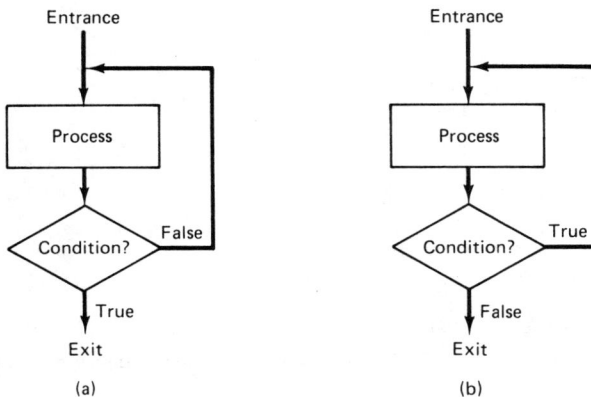

Figure 7–9 (a) The flowchart sequence for the repeat-until-true construct; (b) the flowchart sequence for the repeat-until-false construct.

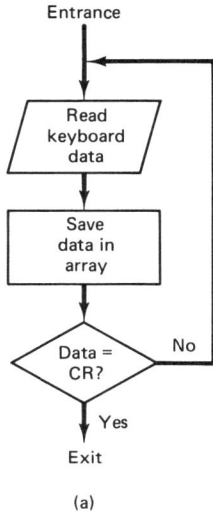

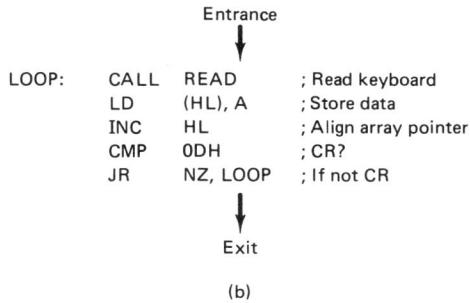

Figure 7-10 (a) The flowchart used to read a key from a keyboard, save the keycodes in a memory array and repeat-until a CR (carriage return) is detected; (b) the assembly language source version of the flowchart.

is tested for a true or a false. It is important to remember that with this construct the process is executed even if the loop is not repeated. Figure 7-9 (a) illustrates the repeat –until–true construct, and Figure 7-9 (b) illustrates the repeat–until–false construct.

An example of the repeat–until construct is depicted in the flowchart of Figure 7-10 (a) and the assembly language version of Figure 7-10 (b). Suppose that software is required to read a keyboard and store the keyboard data in a memory array until the CR (carriage return) character is detected by the program. Figure 7-10 (a) shows how the repeat—reading the keyboard until a CR is detected—flowchart is constructed. Notice that the software of Figure 7-10 (b) is as simple to develop as the flowchart.

The Do–While Construct

The do–while construct is comparable to the repeat–until construct except for one basic difference. The repeat–until construct performs the process before checking a condition, and the do–while construct checks the condition and then, if required, performs the process and repeats the check. There are two forms (see Figure 7-11) of the do–while construct: (1) do–while–false and (2) do–while–true.

Again let us use the keyboard as an example for this construct. Figure 7-12 illustrates both the flowchart and assembly language software for the keyboard. If Figure 7-12 is compared with Figure 7-10, the only difference is that in Figure 7-10 the CR is stored in memory together with the other characters entered into the keyboard, and in Figure 7-12 only the characters entered before the CR are stored in the memory. Notice that the

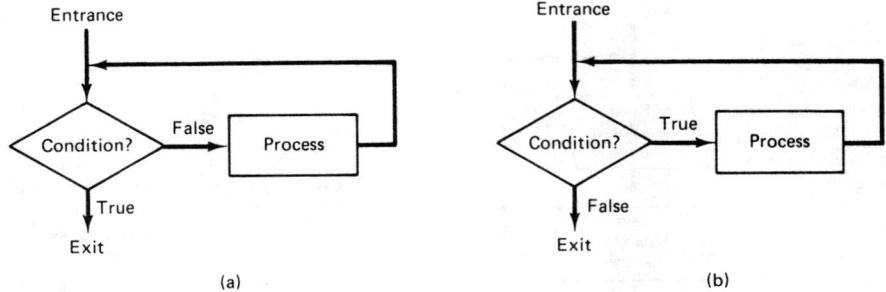

Figure 7–11 (a) The flowchart sequence of the do-while-false construct; (b) the flowchart sequence of the do-while-true construct.

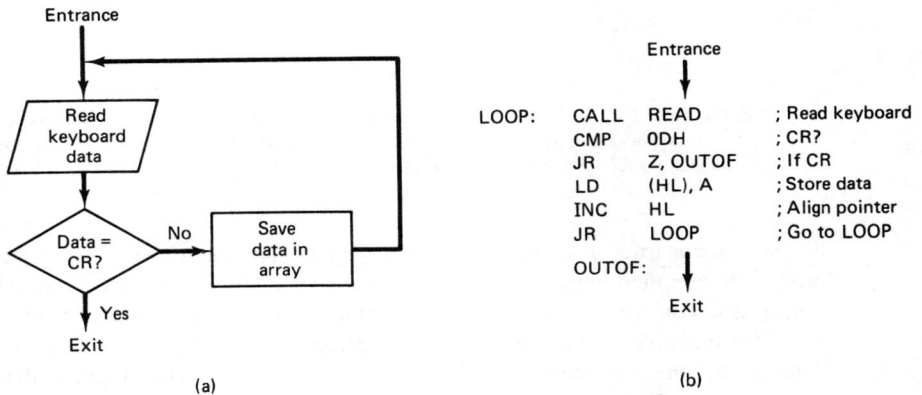

Figure 7–12 (a) The flowchart used to read a key from a keyboard, save the keycodes in a memory array using the do-while-false construct; (b) the assembly language source version of the flowchart.

read keyboard data process block seems to be misplaced in Figure 7-12. It is not misplaced—it is really a part of the testing of the condition to determine if the keyboard data contains a carriage return.

The Programmed–Loop Construct (A Special Case of Repeat–Until)

Although this structure is not normally considered a construct, it is included here because of its common use in assembly language programming. Some textbooks call this a for–next construct, but the name does not really fit its function in assembly language programming. It may be argued that this construct is a form of the repeat–until construct, and it is, but again it is presented separately because of its common application.

Entrance

Load
counter

Process

Decrement
counter

Count =
0?

No

Yes

Exit

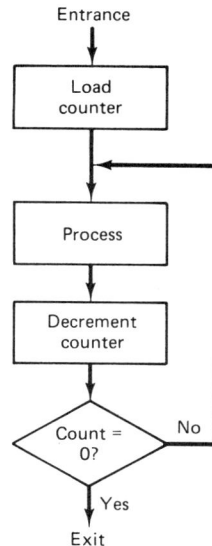

Figure 7–13   The flowchart sequence of the programmed-loop construct which loops through the process counter number of times.

Figure 7-13 shows how the flowchart of this construct appears. The first step loads a counter with the number of iterations required for the process block that follows. After the process is executed, the next flowchart block decrements the counter, and finally a test is made to determine if the counter has reached zero. If the counter has not reached zero the loop is repeated—repeat–until the counter equals zero. The significance of this construct is that a process is repeated the number of times originally loaded into a counter.

Suppose that exactly 12 characters are to be read from a keyboard and stored in a memory array. About the only way that this task can be easily accomplished is with the programmed–loop construct presented in Figure 7-13. Here the counter is loaded with a 12 so that the process—read keyboard and store the character read in a memory array—is repeated exactly 12 times. Figure 7-14 illustrates the flowchart and assembly language version of the programmed–loop construct.

In the Z80 microprocessor, the value of the number loaded into the counter determines whether the counter is a single 8-bit register or a 16-bit register pair. The software used with the single register counter and the register pair counter differs somewhat, as illustrated in Figure 7-15. In Figure 7-15 (a) a DJNZ instruction is used to decrement the count stored in a register, and in Figure 7-15 (b) the DEC BC instruction is used to decrement the count stored in a register pair. Notice that a few instructions follow the DEC BC instruction. These are required because the 16-bit DEC instruction does not change the flag bits. Recall that the flags are tested by the conditional jump instruction, so the software must modify the flags when the counter is decremented to determnine if the counter has reached a zero value. The LD A,B and OR C instructions that follow DEC BC allow the flags to reflect the condition of the BC register pair—the counter. The only time that the zero flag indicates a zero condition is when both B and C contain zeros. Remember that 0 OR 0 equals 0 and 1 OR anything equals 1.

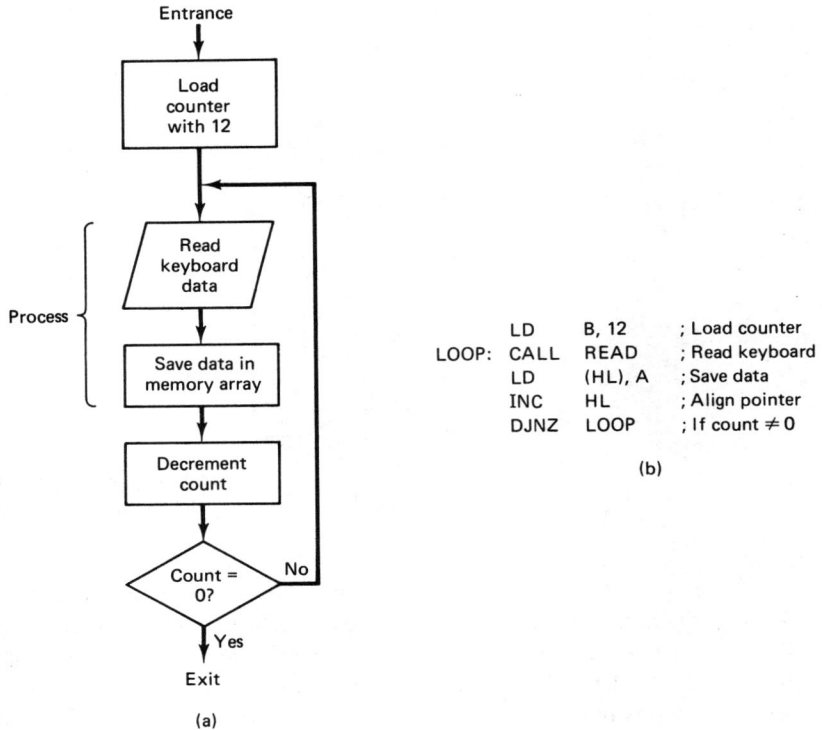

```
           LD    B, 12       ; Load counter
LOOP:  CALL  READ        ; Read keyboard
           LD    (HL), A     ; Save data
           INC   HL          ; Align pointer
           DJNZ  LOOP       ; If count ≠ 0

                    (b)
```

Figure 7-14   The flowchart used to read 12 keys from a keyboard and save the keycodes in a memory array; (b) the assembly language source version of the flowchart.

7-4 EXAMPLE PROGRAM STRUCTURES

To become proficient with structured flowcharting using the constructs presented in Section 7-2, some example flowcharts are needed. In this section we present three structure flowcharting examples using the basic constructs.

Program Example 1

This example illustrates how a flowchart is developed for reading a series of grades from a keyboard, finding the average of the series of grades, and listing the average on a CRT screen. Before this flowchart can be developed, more detail is required. The number of grades to be entered is probably variable in size. It is therefore necessary that some code be entered following valid grades so that the program can count the number of grades entered into the program. For this example the number 101 (larger than 100 percent, or perfect) is typed to indicate that all grades are entered. This is enough detail to begin developing the flowchart.

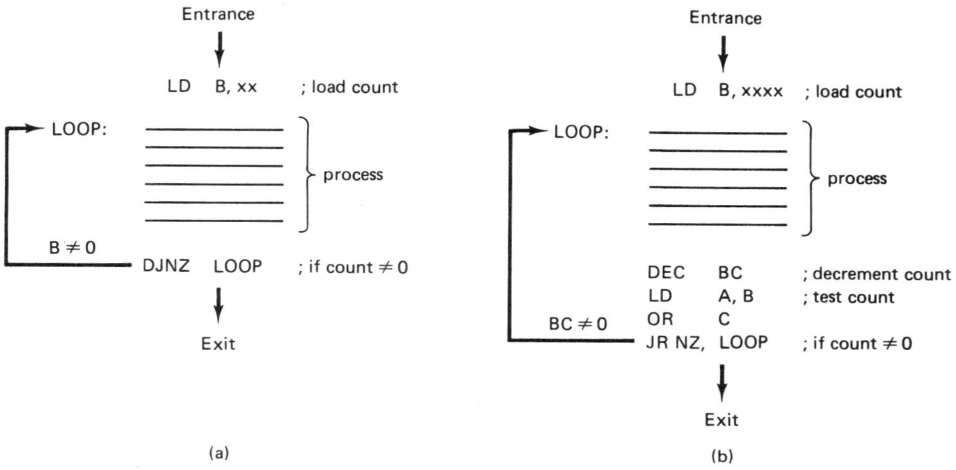

Figure 7–15   (a) The program used to go through a process up to 256 times (XX = 00) using a single register counter; (b) the program used to go through a process up to 65,536 times (XXXX = 0000) using a register pair counter.

Reading and counting the grades.   The first portion of the program must read grades until the 101 is encountered, count the number of grades entered, and store them in memory for later use (see Figure 7-16). The do–while construct or the repeat–until construct can be used to read and the store the grades. Remember the example that stored the carriage return (repeat–until) and the other example (do–while) that didn't? In this program we do not need to store the 101, so the do–while construct is selected. The process for this first structure reads a grade or the number 101 and stores it in memory and also counts how many grades are entered.

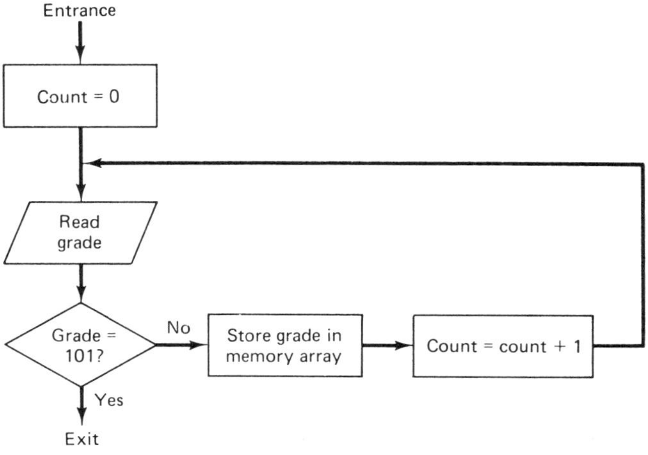

Figure 7–16   The flowchart sequence using the do-while structure to read and count grades for example one.

Computing and displaying the average.   The second part of this example, illustrated in Figure 7-17, is required to find the average of the test grades and display that average. To generate the average, the grades are added together and then the sum is divided by the total number of grades. Because the grades are counted in the first portion of the problem, it is easy to use the programmed–loop construct to add the grades together. Once they are summed, the sequence construct is used to generate the average and display the result.

A simplified flowchart of example 1.   If the prior flowcharts are examined closely, it will be seen that some of the functions can be combined to generate a new and much improved form of the flowchart. First, if the average is all that interests us, the grades do not need to be stored in the memory. If this is the case, then only one loop is required to form the sum of all of the grades. Refer to Figure 7-18 for a shortened version of the combination of the flowcharts of Figures 7-16 and 7-17.

Program Example 2

Suppose that software for a dollar–bill changer is required for your company's new bill changer, and you are assigned the task of developing the software for the changer. The

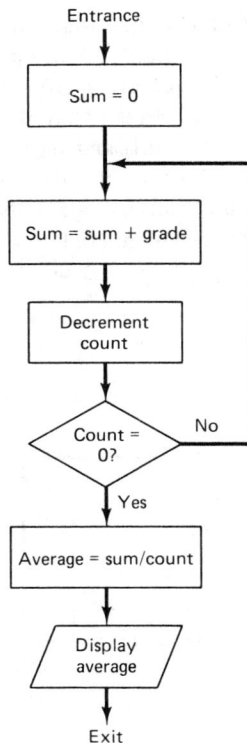

Figure **7–17** The flowchart used to determine and display the average for example one.

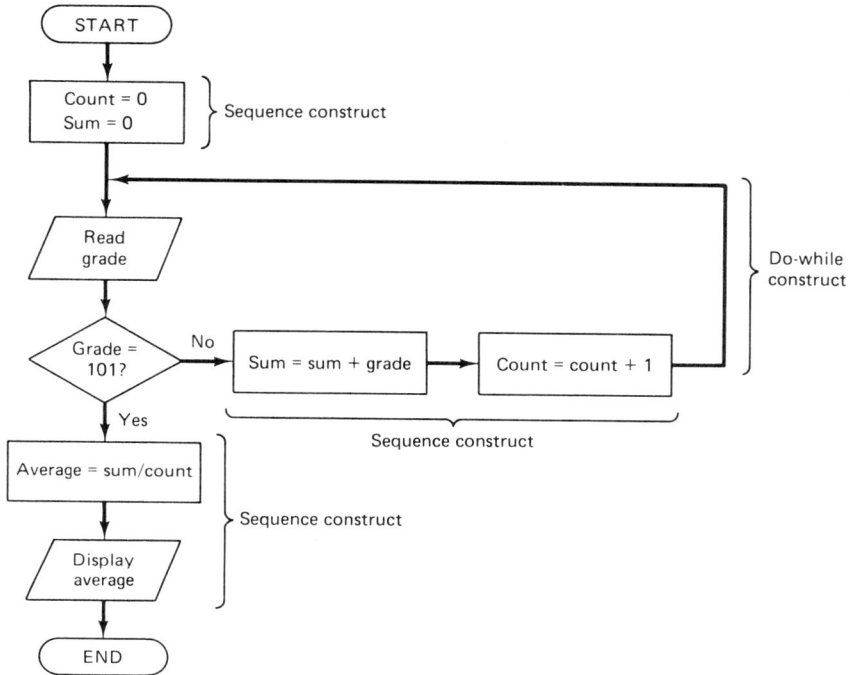

Figure 7–18   The final and most efficient flowchart for program example one.

changer mechanism contains a sensor that detects paper in the bill slot, a motor to run the bill into and out of the mechanism, another sensor to detect a valid $1 bill, and a solenoid that returns a mechanically loaded dollar's worth of change to the customer. No provision other than an idiot light is provided to indicate that the machine is out of change. Customers lose their dollars if they do not see the out–of–change light. (Most changers seem to work this way!)

The flowchart for this program is illustrated in Figure 7-19. Notice that the repeat–until, if–then, and sequence constructs are used in this flowchart. Also notice that this program never ends. A control program is normally this way and is often called an end–less loop. The first portion of the program uses the repeat–until structure to test the paper sensor—repeat–until a bill or other piece of paper is stuffed into the changer slot. Once a bill is detected it is pulled into the machinery because the motor is activated to run the bill to the position where it is tested for a valid $1 bill. Here the if–then structure is used to determine if the bill is valid or not. If it is not a valid $1 bill, the piece of paper will run out of the machine and the entire sequence is repeated. If it is a valid $1 bill, the bill is run into a collection box and the coin changers dispenses a dollar's worth of change.

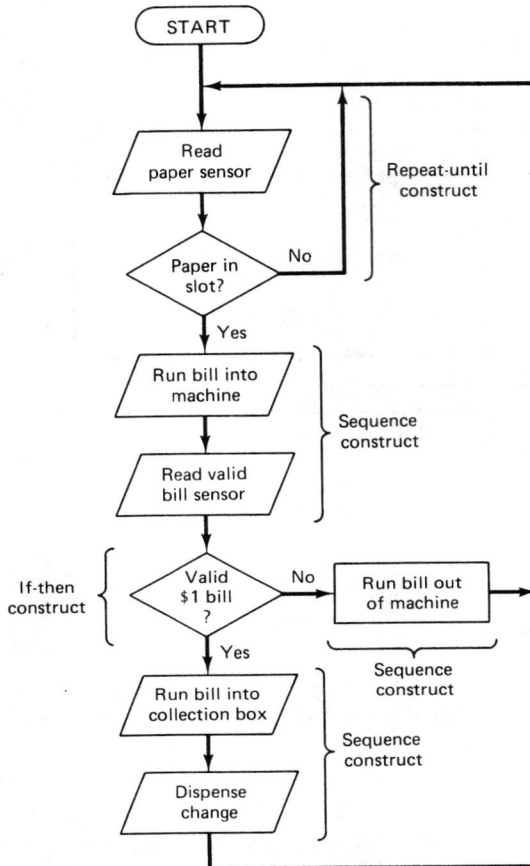

Figure 7–19 The flowchart of the program for a dollar bill changer.

Program Example 3

Suppose that 100 student test scores are stored in a memory array and a program is needed to determine how many students received an A, B, C, D, and F test score. The first construct that comes to mind is the programmed–loop construct, which allows a number of processes to be executed a fixed number of times. In this case, 100 test scores must be examined to determine how many of them are various letter grades. To count each grade category, if–then constructs are used. This program example is illustrated in Figure 7-20.

Here the programmed–loop is extremely important because 100 test scores are to be checked for a particular range of values. The scores are tested by a series of if–then statements that are used to determine if the score lies within a grade range. If the score

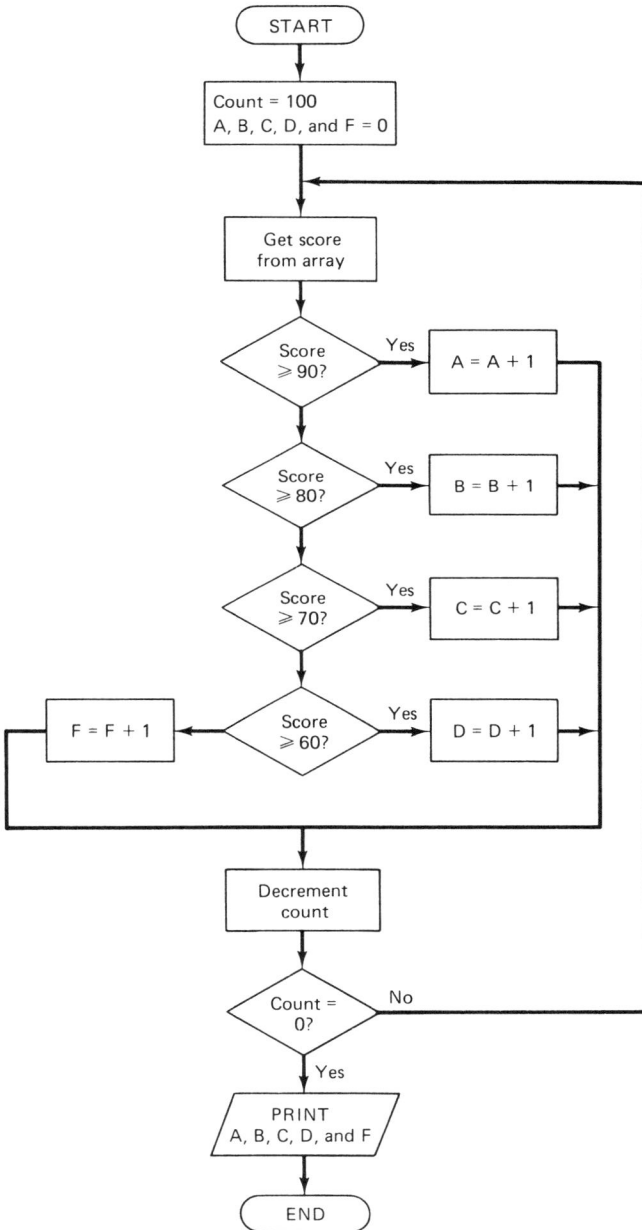

Figure 7–20 The flowchart of the program for determining how many sutdents received A, B, C, D or F grades.

is within the range, the program increments a counter so that it can be counted. Then the process is repeated 100 times, so that each and every test score can be tested and counted.

7-5 SUMMARY _____

1. Structured programming is a programming methodology that aids in the development of complex programs by using a series of standard constructs.

2. A flowchart is used to illustrate the flow of a program for the programmer and also the lay person. The flowchart is an important portion of the program's documentaton that allows later modifications to be made with ease.

3. Flowcharts are normally constructed with six standard flowcharting symbols: process, predefined process, input/output, decision, connector, and terminal.

4. The process flowcharting symbol is used to indicate a process, and the predefined process symbol is used to indicate a subroutine which is a predefined process.

5. The input/output flowcharting symbol is used to indicate any I/0 operation, such as read a keyboard, write to the printer, and so forth.

6. The decision flowcharting symbol allows the program to ask a simple question, usually with two outcomes, such as true–false, yes–no, or positive–negative.

7. The connector flowcharting symbol indicates a break in the flow of the program that is continued elsewhere at another connector. Connectors normally appear in pairs and contain either a number or a letter for identification.

8. The terminal flowcharting symbol is used to indicate the start or the end of a program or a predefined process.

9. Structured programming is accomplished via uniform flowcharting groupings called constructs. A construct is a sequence of steps that has one entrance point and one exit point.

10. There are five constructs that are used to create a flowchart to solve any problem —sequence, if–then, if–then–else, repeat–until, and do–while. In addition to these five constructs, another—the programmed–loop construct—appears so often in programming that it is also included.

11. The sequence construct is the most basic of all constructs, usually containing a series of process, predefined process, and input/output flowcharting symbols.

12. The if–then construct allows the programmer the ability to ask a question in a program. The if–true–then or if–false–then constructs are the two forms of this structure.

13. On occasion, both true and false conditions of the if–then construct occur. In this case the if–then–else construct applies.

14. The repeat–until construct allows a process to be repeated until a particular condition occurs. An example is starting your automobile. You repeat, keeping pressure

applied to the turned ignition key until the roar of the engine is heard. (Repeat until roar.)

15. The do–while construct is very similar to the repeat–until construct. In fact, the only difference is that the repeat–until construct does the process before the test and the do–while construct executes the process only after the condition is tested.

16. The programmed–loop construct is a combination of the repeat–until and the if–then constructs. It allows a process to be repeated X number of times.

7-6 GLOSSARY

Construct   A grouping of flowchart symbols that performs one of the following tasks: sequence, if–then, if–then–else, repeat–until, and do–while.

Flowchart   A grouping of symbols that are used to show the flow of a program. The flowchart is used to write a program and also document the program.

For–next   A statement found in a BASIC language program which allows a process to be repeated X number of times.

Process   A single step or group of steps in the flowchart of a program.

Programmed–loop   A construct that allows a process to be repeated a fixed number of times.

Structured programming   A programming technique that uses a small set of constructs to form the flowchart for the program.

QUESTIONS AND PROBLEMS

7-1. What is a flowchart?

7-2. Draw and label the six flowcharting symbols most often used with assembly language programming.

7-3. What is normally found inside the process flowcharting symbol?

7-4. The predefined process symbol is used most often to evoke what?

7-5. What normally appears inside the input/output flowcharting symbol?

7-6. Is there any limit to the type of question that may be asked in a decision flowcharting symbol?

7-7. What is a construct?

7-8. List the constructs that are used in structured assembly language programming.

7-9. Develop an example sequence construct that will show someone how to open up a door.

7-10. Using the if–then construct, develop a flowchart that will show someone how to check to see if a door is locked, and if it isn't, lock it.

7-11. Repeat question number 7-10 using the opposite if–then construct (i.e., if you used the if–true–then construct, use the if–false–then construct.)

7-12. Using the if–then–else construct, show someone how to decide whether to exit a bedroom through a door or through a window. (Assume that the house is on fire and the door is closed.)

7-13. Your house is being robbed and you tell your spouse (friend) to call the police. Develop a flowchart that shows how to do this by using the repeat–until construct.

7-14. Is it possible to draw a flowchart for Question 7-13 using the do–while construct? (You are not allowed to precede the do–while construct with a sequence construct.)

7-15. What is the main difference between the repeat–until construct and the do–while construct?

7-16. Develop a flowchart that will search through 100 grades to determine if any of them are a zero. If there is a zero, indicate it by setting a flag (place a logic 1 in a flag).

7-17. Why does the DEC BC instruction, in a programmed–loop, need to be followed by the LD A,B and OR C instructions?

7-18. Show another way to test a register pair for a zero condition after the DEC BC instruction.

chapter 8

Data Manipulation and Arithmetic Programming Techiniques

This chapter presents the methodology behind data transfer and arithmetic. Data are transferred, exchanged, added, subtracted, multiplied, and divided. Data transfers are extremely useful when working in some systems, as are arithmetic operations such as multiplication and division. This chapter introduces a core of these important processes in subroutine form that are used throughout the remainder of the text.

8-1 OBJECTIVES

Upon completion of this chapter, you will be able to:

1. Develop software to transfer bytes or words of data with the Z80 microprocessor.
2. Develop software that exchanges bytes or words of data.
3. Manipulate ASCII–coded data via character string transfers.
4. Use addition to sum data.
5. Use subtraction to find the difference of two lists of data.
6. Multiply and divide.

8-2 BLOCK DATA TRANSFERS AND EXCHANGES

A block of data is a grouping of bytes or words in a microprocessor's memory. This section illustrates how blocks of data, either byte (8-bits) or word (16-bits), are transferred and exchanged. In many systems it is often required that blocks of data be transferred from one place to another.

Transferring Bytes of Data

As illustrated in the chapter on data transfer instructions, the Z80 microprocessor contains an instruction that allows block transfers.

Suppose that the block of data beginning at location 1000H through 1123H is transferred into 2000H through 2123H. In order to transfer all 124H bytes of data, the block transfer instruction LDIR must be revisited.

LDIR is a complex instruction that uses BC as a counter, DE to address the destination, and HL to address the source. Example 8-1 illustrates how simple it is to write a program to accomplish this transfer using the LDIR instruction. This program uses EQU to define the addresses and count.

Example 8-1

```
                                  ORG   100H
0100 21 00 10    START:   LD    HL,BLOCK1   ;address source
0103 11 00 20             LD    DE,BLOCK2   ;address destination
0106 01 24 01             LD    BC,COUNT    ;load count
0109 ED B0               LDIR              ;transfer block
010B 18 FE      ENDP:    JR    ENDP        ;wait
                         ;
010D 00 10      BLOCK1:  EQU   1000H       ;equates
010D 00 20      BLOCK2:  EQU   2000H
010D 24 01      COUNT:   EQU   124H
```

Transferring Words of Data

Word transgers can be handled as byte transfers if the count is doubled before the transfer occurs. Figure 8-1 illustrates the flowchart used for a subroutine that transfers the words of data from one section of the memory to another.

The subroutine written from this flowchart requires that the HL, DE, and BC register pairs are preloaded with information before it is called. Here DE is the destination address, HL is the source address, and BC is the count of words to be transferred. Notice (see Example 8-2) how the count is doubled before the data are transferred by this subroutine. The reason is that the byte data transfer instruction (LDIR) is used in this subroutine.

Example 8-2

```
                         ;word transfer subroutine MWORD
                         ;
                         ;DE = Destination address
                         ;HL = Source address
                         ;BC = word count
                         ;
                                  ORG   100H
0100 CB 21      MWORD:   SLA   C           ;double BC
0102 CB 00               RLC   B
0104 EB B0               LDIR              ;transfer data
0106 C9                  RET               ;return
```

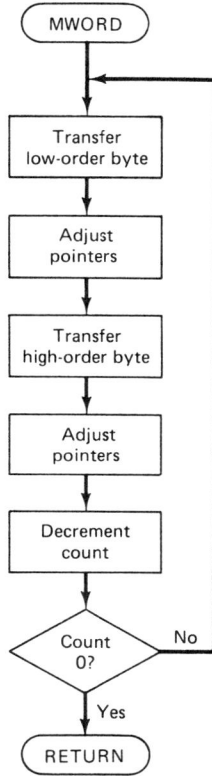

Figure 8–1 The flowchart of a subroutine that moves a block of words from one area of memory to another.

Example 8-3 illustrates the calling sequence that moves 100H words of data beginning from memory location 1200H to memory beginning at 2300H.

Example 8-3

```
                    ;calling sequence for MWORD
                    ;
                            ORG   110H
0110 21 00 12       START:  LD    HL,1200H  ;address source
0113 11 00 23               LD    DE,2300H  ;address destination
0116 01 00 01               LD    BC,100H   ;load count
0119 CD 00 01               CALL  MWORD     ;move words
011C 18 FE          ENDP:   JR    ENDP      ;wait
```

Exchanging Bytes of Data

Suppose that it is required to exchange the 80H bytes of a block of memory beginning at location 2800H with the 80H bytes beginning at memory location 2880H. Here the programmed loop construct is very helpful. The flowchart for this exchange appears in Figure 8-2.

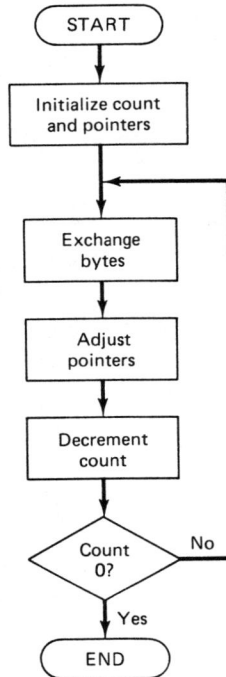

Figure 8–2 Flowchart required to exchange a block of bytes in one area of memory with another.

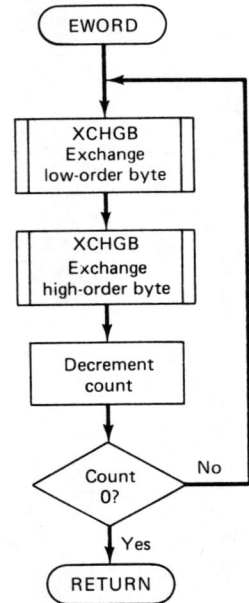

Figure 8–3 The flowchart of a subroutine that exchanges a block of words in one area of memory with another.

The program which is written from this flowchart appears in Example 8-4. Notice that to accomplish the exchange, the data are held in the C register temporarily. Also notice that the B register is used as a counter so that the DJNZ instruction can be used to control the counter loop. HL and IX are used in this program to address memory data.

Example 8-4

```
                        ;program to exchange bytes of data
                        ;
                        ORG   100H
0100 21 00 28  START:   LD    HL,2800H  ;address memory
0103 DD 21 80 28        LD    IX,2880H
0107 06 80              LD    B,80H     ;load count
0109 7E        LOOP:    LD    A,(HL)    ;exchange bytes
010A DD 4E 00           LD    C,(IX)
010D 71                 LD    (HL),C
010E DD 77 00           LD    (IX),A
0111 23                 INC   HL        ;increment pointers
0112 DD 23              INC   IX
0114 10 F3              DJNZ  LOOP      ;repeat B times
0116 18 FE     ENDP:    JR    ENDP      ;wait
```

Word Block Exchanges

Like word transfers, word exchanges are accomplished in a very similar manner. The only difference between their flowcharts is the exchange word (see Figure 8-3) instead of the transfer word. This example of exchange word software is written as a subroutine and is listed in Example 8-6 with the calling sequence illustrated in Example 8-5. This subroutine uses the HL and IX registers to address the memory data to be exchanged and the DE register as a counter. Notice how the relative jump is used here to test the DE pair for a zero.

Example 8-5

```
                        ;calling sequence for subroutine EWORD
                        ;equates
                        ;
                              ORG   100H
0100 00 28              DEST:   EQU   2800H    ;define destination
0100 00 10              SOUR:   EQU   1000H    ;define source
0100 00 02              COUNT:  EQU   200H     ;define count
                        ;
                        ;calling sequence
                        ;
0100 21 00 28           START:  LD    HL,DEST  ;address destination
0103 DD 21 00 10                LD    IX,SOUR  ;address source
0107 11 00 02                   LD    DE,COUNT
010A CD 10 01                   CALL  EWORD    ;exchange words
010D 18 FE              ENDP:   JR    ENDP     ;end program
```

Example 8-6

```
                        ;
                        ;subroutine to exchange words
                        ;addressed by IX and HL
                        ;
                        ;count is in DE
                        ;
                              ORG 110H
0110 7E                 EWORD:  LD    A,(HL)    ;exchange low byte
0111 DD 4E 00                   LD    C,(IX)
0114 71                         LD    (HL),C
0115 DD 77 00                   LD    (IX),A
0118 23                         INC   HL        ;increment pointers
0119 DD 23                      INC   IX
011B 7E                         LD    A,(HL)    ;exchange high byte
011C DD 4E 00                   LD    C,(IX)
011F 71                         LD    (HL),C
0120 DD 77 00                   LD    (IX),A
0123 23                         INC   HL        ;adjust pointers
0124 DD 23                      INC   IX
0126 1B                         DEC   DE        ;decrement count
0127 7A                         LD    A,D       ;test count
0128 B3                         OR    E
0129 20 E5                      JR    NZ,EWORD  ;if count <> 0
012B C9                         RET             ;return
```

Notice that the subroutine EWORD contains two identical sequences of instructions that exchange the low byte and the high btye of the 16-bit word. This sequence can be written as a subroutine to simplify the software and also improve the readability of the subroutine. Example 8-7 shows the EWORD subroutine rewritten so that the bytes (low and high) are each moved with a new subroutine called XCHGB.

Example 8-7

```
                        ;subroutine to exchange words
                        ;addressed by HL and IX
                        ;
                        ;count is in DE
                        ;
                        ;uses subroutine XCHGB
                        ;
                                ORG    110H
  0110  CD 1C 01        EWORD:  CALL  XCHGB      ;exchange low byte
  0113  CD 1C 01                CALL  XCHGB      ;exchange high byte
  0116  1B                      DEC   DE         ;decrement count
  0117  7A                      LD    A,D        ;test count
  0118  B3                      OR    E
  0119  20 F5                   JR    NZ,EWORD   ;if count <> 0
  011B  C9                      RET              ;return
                        ;
                        ;subroutine that exchanges bytes addressed
                        ;by HL and IX
                        ;
  011C  7E              XCHGB:  LD    A,(HL)     ;exchange byte
  011D  DD 4E 00                LD    C,(IX)
  0120  71                      LD    (HL),C
  0121  DD 77 00                LD    (IX),A
  0124  23                      INC   HL         ;adjust pointers
  0125  DD 23                   INC   IX
  0127  C9                      RET              ;return
```

8-3 CHARACTER STRING TRANSFERS

What is a character string? A character string is a grouping of ASCII-coded characters (see Appendix C for a detailed list) that are most often terminated by an ASCII carriage return code (0DH) and a line feed code (0AH). (Table 8-1 illustrates many different-length character strings.) Character strings are usually variable in length and normally contain from no characters (null string), to up to hundreds of characters. At times character strings also include a count of the number of characters stored in the string. Character strings are used in systems that deal with ASCII-coded data, which today includes most systems.

TABLE 8-1.   REPRESENTATIVE ASCII-CODED CHARACTER STRINGS

String	ASCII-coded string
WHAT	57 49 41 54 0D 0A
ABC	41 42 43 0D 0A
12	31 32 0D 0A
	0D 0A (null string)
to be	74 6F 20 62 65 0D 0A
4.9	34 2E 39 0D 0A

String Transfers

A program, or more appropriately a subroutine, that transfers a variable-length character string from one section of the memory to another is listed in the flowchart of Figure 8-4. Notice that the programmed–loop construct is not used to develop this flowchart as with the block transfer and exchanges of the last section. Instead, the repeat–until construct is used to transfer data as long as the data are not a line feed (0AH). This means that the character string length is normally limited only by the width of the CRT screen on the printer page. (A carriage return moves the print head or cursor to the left-hand margin of the CRT screen or printer page. The line feed moves the print head or cursor to a new line on the CRT or printer page.) This subroutine transfers the character string from the block of memory addressed by the HL register pair to the block of memory addressed by the DE register pair. The calling sequence is illustrated in Example 8-8 and the subroutine itself is in Example 8-9.

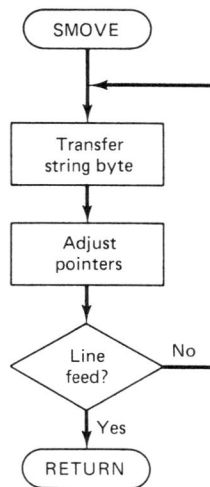

Figure 8–4 The flowchart of a subroutine used to transfer a character string from one area of memory to another.

Example 8-8

```
                              ORG  2000H
                         ;data for this example
                         ;
2000 41 42 0D 0A              DB   'AB',0DH,0AH
                         ;
                         ;equates
                         ;
                              ORG  100H
0100 00 10               DEST:    EQU  1000H    ;destination address
0100 00 20               SOUR:    EQU  2000H    ;source address
                         ;
                         ;program to transfer the character string
                         ;
0100 11 00 10            START:   LD   DE,DEST  ;address DEST
0103 21 00 20                     LD   HL,SOUR  ;address SOUR
0106 CD 50 01                     CALL SMOVE    ;move string
0109 18 FE               ENDP:    JR   ENDP     ;wait
```

Example 8-9

```
                         ;
                         ;subroutine to transfer a character string
                         ;from memory addressed by HL to memory
                         ;addressed by DE.
                         ;
                              ORG  150H
0150 7E                  SMOVE:   LD   A,(HL)   ;transfer byte
0151 12                           LD   (DE),A
0152 23                           INC  HL       ;increment pointers
0153 13                           INC  DE
0154 FE 0A                        CP   LF       ;test for line feed
0156 20 F8                        JR   NZ,SMOVE ;if not line feed
0157 C9                           RET           ;return
                         ;
                         ;equates for SMOVE
                         ;
0158 0A 00               LF:      EQU  0AH      ;define line feed
```

8-4 BINARY ADDITION AND SUBTRACTION

The programmer has a complete set of instructions for accomplishing single 8-bit addition and subtraction in the Z80 microprocessor. These instructions include immediate, register addressed, register indirect addressed, and indexed forms. (Refer to tables 4-1, 4-2, 4-5, and 4-6 for a complete list of these instructions.)

Summing Numbers

Suppose that the ten 8-bit numbers stored at memory locations 2800H through 2809H are to be added together. To accomplish this, one of the 8-bit addition instructions is

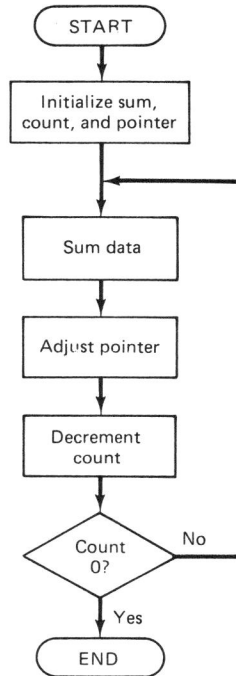

Figure 8–5   The flowchart of a program that sums a set of memory data.

selected, but which one and what structured programming construct? Whenever a set of memory data are manipulated, HL, IX, or IY is used to address the data. (HL is always the first choice because the instructions that use HL require less memory space to store in a program.) In this example the ADD A,(HL) instruction is used. Because 10 numbers are to be added the programmed–loop construct is used here. A flowchart for this program is illustrated in Figure 8-5 and the program is listed in Example 8-10.

Example 8-10

```
                        ;
                        ;example program that adds 10 bytes
                        ;of data together and leaves the 8-bit
                        ;sum in the accumulator.
                        ;
                              ORG   100H
0100 21 00 28     START:      LD    HL,2800H  ;address data
0103 06 0A                    LD    B,10      ;load count
0105 AF                       XOR   A         ;clear sum
0106 86           LOOP:       ADD   A,(HL)    ;add data
0107 23                       INC   HL        ;address next datum
0108 10 FC                    DJNZ  LOOP      ;loop B times
010A 18 FE        ENDP:       JR    ENDP      ;wait
```

What is wrong with the program listed in Example 8-10? The main problem with this program is that the largest sum can only be an FFH. This is fine if the 10 numbers are small, but programs must work with any set of data. In this case a provision must be included to handle overflows after each addition. A simple modification to this program can easily correct this omission. The C register is used to store any overflows that occur, so that the 16-bit result is stored in the C and A registers after executing the program listed in Example 8-11.

Example 8-11

```
                              ;
                              ;example program that adds 10 bytes
                              ;of data together and leaves the 16-bit
                              ;sum in C and A.
                              ;
                                      ORG   100H
      0100  21 00 28          START:  LD    HL,2800H  ;address data
      0103  06 0A                     LD    B,10      ;load count
      0105  AF                        XOR   A         ;clear sum
      0106  4F                        LD    C,A
      0107  86                LOOP:   ADD   A,(HL)    ;add data
      0108  30 01                     JR    NC,DOWN   ;if no carry
      010A  0C                        INC   C         ;add carry to C
      010B  23                DOWN:   INC   HL        ;adjust pointer
      010C  10 F9                     DJNZ  LOOP      ;repeat B times
      010E  18 FE             ENDP:   JR    ENDP      ;wait
```

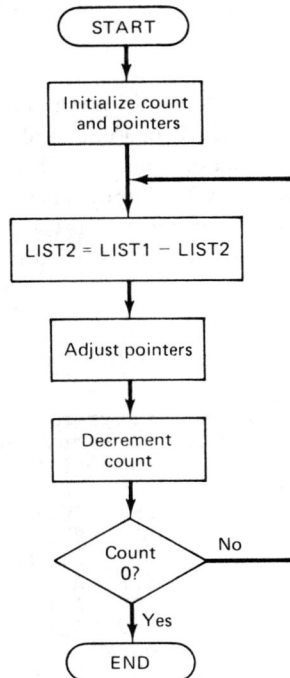

Figure 8–6 The flowchart of a program that forms the differences for two sets of numbers stored in the memory.

Binary Subtraction

Subtraction is a little different from addition because one list of numbers is not normally subtracted. Suppose that two lists of numbers, each 10H bytes long, appear in the memory: LIST1 is stored at memory locations 2800H—280FH and LIST2 is stored at 2810H—281FH.

A program is to be written that will subtract the contents of LIST2 from LIST1 and store the differences at LIST2. This operation is repeated 16 times (10H) until all 16 sets of numbers are subtracted. Again the programmed–loop construct is used to develop the flowchart (see Figure 8-6) and the program written from the flowchart in Example 8-12.

Example 8-12

```
                        ;program to subtract LIST2 data from
                        ;LIST1 data and store the difference
                        ; in LIST2
                        ;
                              ORG    100H
0100 21 10 28   START:    LD     HL,LIST2   ;address LIST2
0103 11 00 28             LD     DE,LIST1   ;address LIST1
0106 06 10               LD     B,10H      ;load count
0108 12         LOOP:    LD     A,(DE)     ;get LIST1
0109 96                   SUB    (HL)       ;subtract LIST2
010A 77                   LD     (HL),A     ;save in LIST2
010B 23                   INC    HL         ;adjust pointers
010C 13                   INC    DE
010D 10 F9               DJNZ   LOOP       ;if count <> 0
010F 18 FE     ENDP:    JR     ENDP       ;wait
                        ;
                        ;equates
                        ;
0111 00 28     LIST1:   EQU    2800H      ;define LIST1
0111 10 28     LIST2:   EQU    2810H      ;define LIST2
```

The main difference btween the addition problem and this problem is that two sets of numbers are addressed in this example where one set was addressed in the addition problem. Here the DE register pair is used to address LIST1, and the HL register pair is used to address LIST2. This order cannot be reversed because the memory data can be subtracted only by using the HL register pair to address the memory. The DE pair cannot be used to address memory and perform the subtraction required.

8-5 MULTIPLICATION AND DIVISION ──────────────────

Unfortunately, the Z80 microprocessor cannot multiply or divide without a program. This section details the algorithms for both multiplication and division so that programs can be written that use these operations. Three techniques are available for multiplication and two for division. In addition, both signed and unsigned multiplication and division are presented.

Unsigned Multiplication by Repeated Addition

Repeated addition is the simplest method of multiplication to understand and for small numbers a very useful method. The principle behind this technique is the programmed–loop construct. If two 8-bit numbers are multiplied, one of the numbers can be used as the counter and the other number can be added to a zero the number of times in the counter. Example 8-13 illustrates how the number 7 is multiplied by a 3 using repeated addition. Notice from this example that the product of 7 × 3 is generated by adding 7 three times. If the product of 6 × 4 is required, 6 is added 4 times.

$$7 \times 3 = 21$$
$$\text{or}$$
$$7 + 7 + 7 = 21$$

A subroutine that uses this technique is illustrated in the flowchart of Figure 8-7 and the subroutine for the multiplication is listed in Example 8-15 with the calling sequence listed in Example 8-14. Notice that the product, which is formed by multiplying the accumulator times the B register, is a double–length product found in the HL register pair after returning from the subroutine. The reason that a double–length product is used is so that the two numbers that are multiplied together by subroutine can result in a product that is larger than 256.

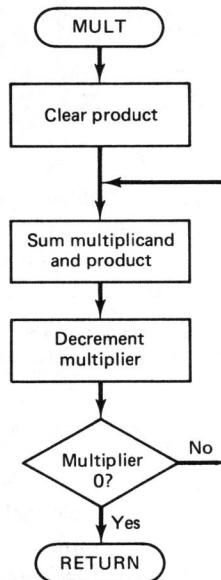

Figure 8–7 The flowchart used to multiply 2 numbers via the repeated addition technique.

Example 8-13

```
    7 X 3 = 21

        or

  7 + 7 + 7 = 21
```

Example 8-14

```
                    ;The calling sequence for MULT
                    ;
                        ORG   100H
0100 06 03      START:  LD    B,3      ;load multiplier
0102 3E 06              LD    A,6      ;load multiplicand
0104 CD 10 01           CALL  MULT     ;HL = A X B
0107 18 FE      ENDP:   JR    ENDP     ;wait
```

Example 8-15

```
                    ;subroutine that multiplies the accumulator
                    ;times B and leaves the 16-bit product
                    ;in the HL pair
                    ;
                        ORG   110H
0110 21 00 00   MULT:   LD    HL,0     ;clear product
0113 5F                 LD    E,A      ;form 16-bit multiplicand
0114 16 00              LD    D,0
0116 19         LOOP:   ADD   HL,DE    ;form partial product
0117 10 FD              DJNZ  LOOP     ;repeat until B = 0
0119 C9                 RET            ;return
```

Unsigned Constant Multiplication

In many cases the number 10 or another fixed or constant number is used as a multiplier. Rather than use the repeated addition technique presented earlier, another technique is often used that results in a much faster multiplication.

Suppose that a program requires the number in the HL register pair to be multiplied by a 4. The easiest way to accomplish this is by using the ADD HL,HL instruction. Recall that ADD HL,HL doubles the contents of the HL register pair. If HL is doubled twice, it is multiplied by a 4. (See the subroutine listed in Example 8-16.) This example is almost too simple to write as a subroutine.

Example 8-16

```
                        ORG   110H
0110 29         MULT4:  ADD   HL,HL    ;HL times 2
0111 29                 ADD   HL,HL    ;HL times 4
0112 C9                 RET            ;return
```

Suppose that it is desired to multiply the number in the HL register pair by a 10. How can this be accomplished? The first step is to convert the multiplier (10) to binary (see Example 8-17) and then use the one bit positions to form the product by adding their binary power of two values together. In this example, multiplication by 10 is formed by adding a 2 and an 8 times the original multiplicand of 6 together. If 2 times and 8 times the multiplicand are added, the result is 10 times the multiplicand. Example 8-18 shows the subroutine that multiplies the contents of the HL register pair by a 10.

Example 8-17

```
        8  4  2  1

 10 = 1  0  1  0



     12  (2 times 6)
  +  48  (8 times 6)
  ----
     60  (the product)
```

Example 8-18

```
                        ;subroutine that multiplies HL by 10
                        ;
                            ORG  110H
0110  29    MULT10:    ADD  HL,HL      ;2 times HL
0111  55              LD   D,H         ;save 2 times HL
0112  5D              LD   E,L
0113  29              ADD  HL,HL       ;4 times HL
0114  29              ADD  HL,HL       ;8 times HL
0115  19              ADD  HL,DE       ;sum 8 and 2 times HL
0116  C9              RET              ;return
```

The Multiplication Algorithm

The most flexible version of multiplication is the multiplication algorithm that shifts and adds a number to accomplish multiplication. The algorithm is developed by observing the steps required to multiply two binary numbers on a piece of paper with a pencil. If the multiplier bit is a 1, the multiplicand is added to the product, and if the multiplier bit is a 0, no addition takes place. Besides addition, the multiplication process requires that the multiplicand is shifted each time it is added to the product. Look at the binary example multiplication illustrated in Example 8-19 so that you understand how the partial products are the multiplicand shifted to the left and also notice that the product is double width.

In addition to shifting the multiplicand left to form each partial product, the multiplier must be interrogated to determine whether or not to add a partial product. On paper your finger is used to keep track of each bit in the multiplier; in the computer the multiplier is shifted right and the carry keeps track of each bit. The carry is then used

Example 8-19

```
      1001    (9)
   X  1111   (15)
   --------
      1001    (9)
     10010   (18)
    100100   (36)
   1001000   (72)
   --------
 10000111  (135)
```

to determine if the partial product is added or not. If the multiplier becomes a zero, the multiplication process is complete.

Figure 8-8 illustrates the flowchart of the multiplication algorithm. The subroutine written from this flowchart is listed in Example 8-20. This subroutine multiplies the E register by the accumulator and leaves the product in the HL register pair. A register trace appears in Table 8-2 where the numbers 9 and 5 are multiplied together.

Example 8-20

```
               ;subroutine that A X E and leaves
               ;16-bit product in HL register pair
               ;
                       ORG  110H
0110 21 00 00  MULT:   LD   HL,0      ;clear product
0113 55                LD   D,H       ;clear MSB of multiplicand
0114 B7        LOOP:   OR   A         ;test A
0115 28 09             JR   Z,ENDP    ;if zero
0117 1F                RRA            ;shift multiplier right
0118 30 01             JR   NC,LOOP1  ;if no carry
011A 19                ADD  HL,DE     ;add multiplicand
011B EB        LOOP1:  EX   DE,HL     ;shift multiplicand
011C 29                ADD  HL,HL
011D EB                EX   DE,HL
011E 18 F4             JR   LOOP      ;repeat
0120 C9        ENDP:   RET            ;return
```

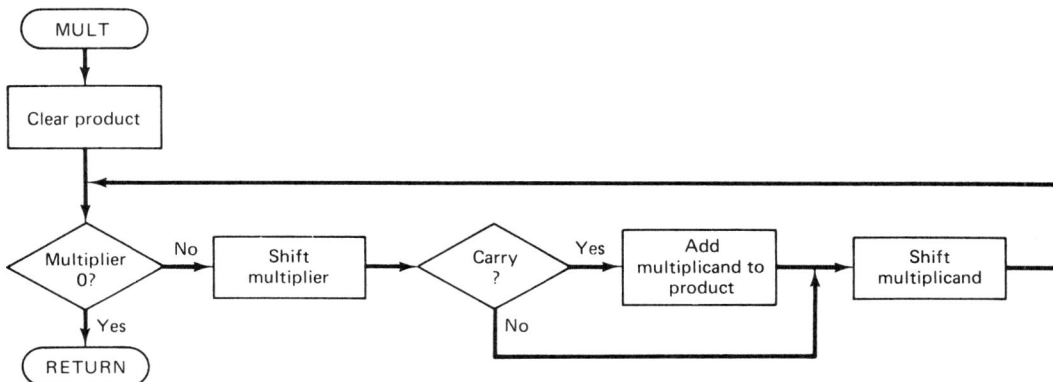

Figure 8–8 An algorithm illustrating binary multiplication using the shift and add technique.

TABLE 8-2. REGISTER TRACE OF THE MULTIPLICATION SUBROUTINE DEPICTED IN EXAMPLE 8-20 FOR THE NUMBERS 5 TIMES 9

PC	Carry	A	DE	HL	Instruction
0110	X	05	XX09	0000	LD HL,O
0113	X	05	0009	0000	LD D,H
0114	0	05	0009	0000	OR A
0115	0	05	0009	0000	JR Z,ENDS ;(0120H)
0117	1	02	0009	0000	RRA
0118	1	02	0009	0000	JR NC,LOOP1 ;(011BH)
011A	0	02	0009	0009	ADD HL,DE
011B	0	02	0009	0009	EX DE,HL
011C	0	02	0009	0012	ADD HL,HL
011D	0	02	0012	0009	EX DE,HL
011E	0	02	0012	0009	JR LOOP ;(0114H)
0114	0	02	0012	0009	OR A
0115	0	02	0012	0009	JR Z,ENDS ;(0120H)
0117	0	01	0012	0009	RRA
0118	0	01	0012	0009	JR NC,LOOP1 ;(011BH)
011B	0	01	0009	0012	EX DE,HL
011C	0	01	0009	0024	ADD HL,HL
011D	0	01	0024	0009	EX DE,HL
011E	0	01	0024	0009	JR LOOP ;(0114H)
0114	0	01	0024	0009	OR A
0115	0	01	0024	0009	JR Z,ENDS ;(0120H)
0117	1	00	0024	0009	RRA
0118	1	00	0024	0009	JR NC,LOOP1 ;(011BH)
011A	0	00	0024	002D	ADD HL,DE
011B	0	00	002D	0024	EX DE,HL
011C	0	00	002D	0048	ADD HL,HL
011D	0	00	0048	002D	EX DE,HL
011E	0	00	0048	002D	JR LOOP ;(0114H)
0114	0	00	0048	002D	OR A
0115	0	00	0048	002D	JR Z,ENDS ;(0120H)
0120	0	00	0048	002D	RET

Note: The HL register pair contains the product of 5 times 9 or a 45 (002DH) at the RET instruction.

Division by a Constant

If data are shifted left, they are multiplied by a 2 for each bit position of the shift as described earlier in this section. If data are shifted to the right, they are divided by a 2 for each bit position of the shift. Knowing this and the technique used to multiply by a constant, a technique can be developed so that a number can be divided by any power of 2. For example (see Example 8-21), if a number is to be divided by a 4, it can be shifted right two places. Each shift divides the number by a 2 so that two shifts will divide the number by a 4. Notice in this example the wrong answer resulted. If the carry is added to the answer, it is rounded up to the correct result. The carry holds 0.5 and if added to the result will round the result up to obtain a rounded result. If not added a truncated result is obtained. A subroutine that divides the accumulator register by a 4 and rounds the answer is illustrated in Example 8-22.

Example 8-21

```
Number  Carry  Value

1100110   0       102

 110011   0        51 (shifted once)

  11001   1        25 (shifted twice)
```

Example 8-22

```
                    ;subroutine to divide A by 4.
                    ;
                            ORG  110H
0110 CB 3F          DIV4:   SRL  A          ;shift right
0112 CB 3F                  SRL  A          ;shift right
0114 CE 00                  ADC  A,0        ;round result
0116 C9                     RET             ;return
```

The Division Algorithm

To divide a number by any integer value, the division algorithm is normally used to develop a subroutine. The division algorithm uses a combination of shifting left, comparing, subtracting, and setting bits to perform binary division. Before it can be understood, a review of binary division on paper is in order, as illustrated in Example 8-23.

Example 8-23

```
        01001
   11 )11011
        11
        --
         11
         11
         --
```

In this example a 27 (11011) is divided by a 3 (11) and the result is a 9 (1001). To accomplish this division, the divisor is compared with a portion of the dividend. The first comparison is 11 with 1. Because 11 is larger than 1, a 0 is placed in the quotient. Next, the 11 is compared with 11 because the first 2 bits of the dividend are now compared with the divisor. This time they are equal. If the divisor and the portion of the dividend it is compared with are equal or the portion of the dividend is larger, a subtraction occurs and a 1 is placed in the quotient. This comparison is continued until all the bits of the

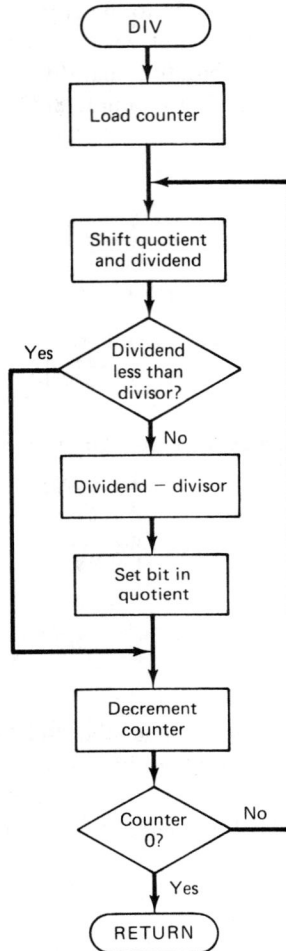

Figure 8–9 The flowchart of the divide algorithm.

dividend are compared with the divisor. The flowchart illustrating this algorithm is shown in Figure 8-9.

Using this flowchart as a guide, the subroutine listed in Example 8-24 divides the L register by the C register. The quotient is placed in the L register and the remainder is placed in the H register upon return from this subroutine. The dividend may not exceed 127 for this subroutine to function properly.

Example 8-24

```
                    ;subroutine that divides L by C
                    ;leaving the quotient in L and the
                    ;remainder in H
                    ;
                            ORG    110H
0110 06 08          DIV:    LD     B,8          ;load count
0112 26 00                  LD     H,0          ;clear quotient
0114 29             DIV1:   ADD    HL,HL        ;shift left
0115 7C                     LD     A,H          ;compare
0116 91                     SUB    C
0117 38 02                  JR     C,DIV2
0119 67                     LD     H,A
011A 2C                     INC    L
011B 10 F6          DIV2:   DJNZ   DIV1         ;if count <> 0
011D C9                     RET                 ;return
```

To assure correct operation of this subroutine, the register trace is illustrated in Table 8-3 for a 72 (1001000) divided by an 11 (1011).

Signed Multiplication and Division

With signed multiplication and division, before the DIV or MULT subroutine is called the operands are checked for a difference in the signs, and the outcome, positive or negative, is held for after the operation. After the signs are checked both numbers are tested and made positive, and then the multiplication or division subroutine is called. After the operation is completed the result is two's complemented if the result is negative.

Example 8-25 illustrates the subroutine called before multiplying and Example 8-26 shows the subroutine called after multiplication so that signed multiplication is performed. If division is required the same subroutines are used except the registers two's complemented are different.

Example 8-25

```
                    ;subroutine that test the A and E
                    ;registers before a multiplication
                    ;
                            ORG    150H
0150 F5             CHKB:   PUSH   AF           ;save A
0151 AB                     XOR    E            ;set sign of result
0152 32 63 01               LD     (FLAG),A     ;save for later
0155 F1                     POP    AF           ;restore A
0156 CD 64 01               CALL   MAKE         ;make positive
0159 F5                     PUSH   AF
015A 7B                     LD     A,E
015B CD 64 01               CALL   MAKE         ;make positive
015E 5F                     LD     E,A
015F CD 10 01               CALL   MULT         ;multiply
0162 C9                     RET                 ;return
```

(continued p. 153)

TABLE 8-3. REGISTER TRACE OF SUBROUTINE DIV (EXAMPLE 8-24) USING A 72 DIVIDED BY AN 11

PC	Carry	A	B	C	H	L	Instruction
0110	X	XX	8	0B	XX	48	LD B,8
0112	X	XX	8	0B	00	48	LD H,0
0114	0	XX	8	0B	00	90	ADD HL,HL
0115	0	00	8	0B	00	90	LD A,H
0116	1	F5	8	0B	00	90	SUB C
0117	1	F5	8	0B	00	90	JR C,DIV2 ;(011BH)
011B	1	F5	7	0B	00	90	DJNZ DIV1 ;(0114H)
0114	0	F5	7	0B	01	20	ADD HL,HL
0115	0	01	7	0B	01	20	LD A,H
0116	1	F6	7	0B	01	20	SUB C
0117	1	F6	7	0B	01	20	JR C,DIV2 ;(011BH)
011B	1	F6	6	0B	01	20	DJNZ DIV1 ;(0114H)
0114	0	F6	6	0B	02	40	ADD HL,HL
0115	0	02	6	0B	02	40	LD A,H
0116	1	F7	6	0B	02	40	SUB C
0117	1	F7	6	0B	02	40	JR C,DIV2 ;(011BH)
011B	1	F7	5	0B	02	40	DJNZ DIV1 ;(0114H)
0114	0	F7	5	0B	04	80	ADD HL,HL
0115	0	04	5	0B	04	80	LD A,H
0116	1	F9	5	0B	04	80	SUB C
0117	1	F9	5	0B	04	80	JR C,DIV2 ;(011BH)
011B	1	F9	4	0B	04	80	DJNZ DIV1 ;(0114H)
0114	0	F9	4	0B	09	00	ADD HL,HL
0115	0	09	4	0B	09	00	LD A,H
0116	1	FE	4	0B	09	00	SUB C
0117	1	FE	4	0B	09	00	JR C,DIV2 ;(011BH)
011B	1	FE	3	0B	09	00	DJNZ DIV1 ;(0114H)
0114	0	FE	3	0B	12	00	ADD HL,HL
0115	0	12	3	0B	12	00	LD A,H
0116	0	07	3	0B	12	00	SUB C
0117	0	07	3	0B	12	00	JR C,DIV2 ;(011BH)
0119	0	07	3	0B	07	00	LD H,A
011A	0	07	3	0B	07	01	INC L
011B	0	07	2	0B	07	01	DJNZ DIV1 ;(0114H)
0114	0	07	2	0B	0E	02	ADD HL,HL
0115	0	0E	2	0B	0E	02	LD A,H
0116	0	03	2	0B	0E	02	SUB C
0117	0	03	2	0B	0E	02	JR C,DIV2 ;(011BH)
0119	0	03	2	0B	03	02	LD H,A
011A	0	03	2	0B	03	03	INC L
011B	0	03	1	0B	03	03	DJNZ DIV1 ;(0114H)
0114	0	03	1	0B	06	06	ADD HL,HL
0115	0	06	1	0B	06	06	LD A,H
0116	1	FB	1	0B	06	06	SUB C
0117	1	FB	1	0B	06	06	JR C,DIV2 ;(011BH)
011B	1	FB	0	0B	06	06	DJNZ DIV1 ;(0114H)
011D	1	FB	0	0B	06	06	RET

Note: The quotient (L) is a 6 and the remainder (H) is a 6. (72/11 = 6, remainder of 6.)

(Example 8-25 continued)

```
                        ;
                        ;data definitions
                        ;
0163 00                 FLAG:    DB    0
                        ;
                        ;subroutine to make the A register
                        ;positive
                        ;
0164 B7                 MAKE:    OR    A        ;test A
0165 F0                          RET   P        ;if positive
0166 2F                          CPL            ;2's complement
0167 3C                          INC   A
0168 C9                          RET            ;return
```

Example 8-26

```
                        ;subroutine to correct the result
                        ;in HL after a multiplication
                        ;
0169 3A 63 01           TEST:    LD    A,(FLAG)   ;get flag
016C B7                          OR    A          ;test A
016D F0                          RET   P          ;if positive
016E 7C                          LD    A,H        ;change HL to negative
016F 2F                          CPL
0170 67                          LD    H,A
0171 7D                          LD    A,L
0172 2F                          CPL
0173 6F                          LD    L,A
0174 23                          INC   HL
0175 C9                          RET              ;return
```

8-6 SUMMARY ─────────────────────────────────────

1. Block data transfers are used to transfer a group of bytes or words from one area of the memory to another.

2. Block data exchanges are used to exchange the byte-wide or word-wide contents of two blocks of the memory.

3. The programmed–loop and repeat–until constructs proved useful in this chapter.

4. This chapter shows the importance of subroutines in many programming techniques.

5. A character string is a group of ASCII characters that is terminated with a carriage return (an ASCII ODH) and a line feed (an ASCII OAH).

6. Character strings may be of any length, although they are usually at most one printed line in length. If a character string contains no characters, except for a carriage return and a line feed, it is called a null string.

7. Binary addition and subtraction is accomplished via the following addressing modes: immediate, register, register indirect, and indexed.

8. Whenever 8-bit numbers are summed, it is important to leave enough room for the result. In most cases 16 bits are required to hold the sum of even just a few 8-bit numbers.

9. Binary multiplication is carried out in three different fashions: repeated addition, and two methods of shifting and adding.

10. When numbers are multiplied together the product is always a double-width product.

11. Binary division is accomplished by one of two techniques: shifting; or shifting, comparing, subtracting, and setting bits in the result.

12. The quotient and remainder are binary integers that are equal in width to the divisor.

13. For signed division and multiplication the numbers are made positive before the division or multiplication and adjust to negative if needed after the multiplication or division.

8-7 GLOSSARY

Array   See Memory array.

Block data exchange   A technique that is used to exchange the byte or word contents of one section of the memory with another.

Block data transfer   A technique that is used to transfer the bytes or words from one part of the memory to another.

Calling sequence   The group of instructions that are required to place data in registers for a subroutine and to CALL a subroutine.

Carriage return   The ASCII-coded character (0DH) that is used to return the print head or cursor to the left-hand margin of the printed page or CRT screen.

Character string   Character strings are groupings of ASCII-coded characters that terminate with a carriage return and a line feed in most systems.

Double-width product   Whenever two numbers are multiplied together the product is always twice as wide, hence, double-width product.

Line feed   The ASCII-coded character (0AH) that is used to feed paper up a line or move the CRT cursor down a line.

Memory array   A section of the memory that contains a group of similar bytes, words, or character strings is often called an array.

Null character string   A null character string contains only a carriage return and a line feed.

QUESTIONS AND PROBLEMS

8-1. Using the LD A,(mem) and the LD (mem),A instructions develop a sequence of instructions that will transfer 5 bytes of memory from locations 2800H—2804H to 2820H—2824H.

8-2. Redo the program in question 8-1 using the programmed–loop construct.

8-3. List one important feature of any subroutine.

8-4. Compare the main difference in the software for a word block data transfer and a word block data exchange.

8-5. When writing software, is readability an important consideration? Explain your answer.

8-6. Develop a flowchart and a program that will transfer 100 bytes of data from memory area 0000H—0063H to 2800H—2863H and also to 2000H—2063H.

8-7. Write hexadecimal versions of the following ASCII character strings.
(a) What are you doing?
(b) I don't know.
(c) Explain that!
(d) Well, so I can.
(e) Whom do you trust?

8-8. Is there any limit to the number of characters stored in one character string?

8-9. Explain what the carriage return and line feed codes accomplish on a printer.

8-10. What program construct is used when a character string is transferred from one area of the memory to another?

8-11. Write a sequence of instructions that will add the contents of the B register to the C register.

8-12. Write a sequence of instructions that will add the contents of the BC register pair to the DE register pair.

8-13. Using the repeated addition method of multiplication, write a subroutine that will multiply the contents of the HL register pair by the accumulator and leave the 24-bit product in EHL.

8-14. Using the unsigned constant method of multiplication, develop a subroutine that will multiply the contents of the HL register pair times 13 decimal. The result should be left in the HL register pair.

8-15. Can the accumulator be multiplied by a 3/8? If so write the software.

8-16. Write a subroutine that divided the HL register pair by the C register.

8-17. Write a multiplication subroutine that will multiply the HL pair times the DE pair and leave the product in BC and DE as a 32-bit number.

_____

chapter 9

Conversions, Table Lookup, and Time Delays

This chapter covers some very important programming techniques that are often found in control systems. Conversions are useful whenever data need be converted from one form to another. Table lookup techniques are also used to convert data from one form to another. Time delays are very useful in controlling real-time events or devices.

9-1 OBJECTIVES _____

Upon completion of this chapter, you will be able to:

1. Convert ASCII to BCD or hexadecimal and convert BCD or hexadecimal to ASCII.
2. Convert BCD as it comes from a keyboard or other device into binary.
3. Convert binary to BCD for use on numeric displays.
4. Use tables and the table-lookup technique to convert from any code to any other code.
5. Construct menu-driven software by using a jump or call table.
6. Create time delays of from a few microseconds to many hours.

9-2 ASCII CODE CONVERSION _____

At first glance ASCII code conversion seems trivial because it is rather easy to convert between ASCII-coded numbers and BCD. The ASCII-coded numbers range from 30H-

39H (see Appendix C) for the decimal numbers 0—9. To convert from BCD to ASCII, a 30H is added to the BCD number, and to convert from ASCII to BCD, a 30H is subtracted from the ASCII-coded number. It is more difficult to convert between ASCII and hexadecimal.

ASCII-to-Hexadecimal Code Conversion

Again refer to the ASCII codes listed in Appendix C and notice that the letters A—F are coded as 41H—46H. It would be much easier for code conversion if they were 3AH—3FH. If this were the case a 30H could be added or subtracted to convert between ASCII and hexadecimal. Because the ASCII-coded numbers and letters are separated by a bias of 7, the characters must be examined to determine if they are numbers or letters. If they are numbers then a 30H is subtracted to convert from ASCII to hexadecimal, and if they are letters a 37H is subtracted. This process is illustrated in the flowchart of Figure 9-1 and the subroutine listing of Example 9-1.

Example 9-1

```
                     ;subroutine to convert ASCII to hexadecimal
                     ;the A register is converted here
                     ;
                            ORG 110H
0110 D6 30    ASHEX:    SUB 30H        ;subtract 30H
0112 FE 0A              CP  0AH        ;test for letter
0114 38 02              JR  C,ASHEX1   ;if number
0116 D6 07              SUB 7          ;reduce by 7
0118 C9       ASHEX1:   RET            ;return
```

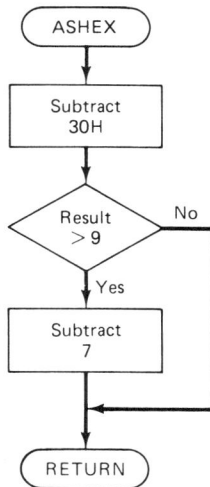

Figure 9–1   Flowchart for converting AS-CII hexadecimal data to hexadecimal data.

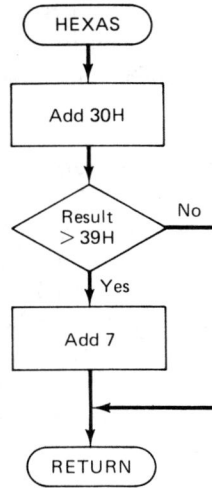

Figure 9–2 Standard flowchart for converting hexadecimal data to ASCII hexadecimal data.

Hexadecimal-to-ASCII Code Conversion

Converting to ASCII code from hexadecimal is almost identical to converting from hexadecimal to ASCII. The only difference is that instead of subtracting 30H or 37H they are added. Refer to Figure 9-2 for the flowchart of this process and to Example 9-2 for the subroutine listing that converts the accumulator from a hexadecimal code to an ASCII code.

Example 9-2

```
                        ;subroutine to convert hexadecimal to ASCII
                        ;
                                ORG  120H
0120 C6 30              HEXAS:  ADD  A,30H      ;add 30H
0122 FE 3A                      CP   3AH        ;test for letter
0124 38 02                      JR   C,HEXAS1   ;if number
0126 C6 07                      ADD  A,7        ;increase by 7
0128 C9                 HEXAS1: RET             ;return
```

9-3 BCD-TO-BINARY CONVERSION

Converting BCD numbers into binary numbers is easy if the number is between 0 and 9 because there is no conversion. It is more difficult when the number exceeds 9. The most common approach to convert from BCD to binary is to take the BCD number and multiply the ten's digit by a 10 and add it to the unit digit. This works well as long as the number is a two-digit BCD number. A three-digit number has its hundred's digit multiplied by

100, its ten's digit multiplied by 10, and then the unit's digit is added to the other two digits after they are multiplied.

The BCD-to-Binary Conversion Algorithm

From the prior description of the BCD-to-binary conversion process, it is easy to generate an algorithm for the conversion. Starting with the most significant digit of a variable-length BCD number and a value of 0 for the result, multiply the result by a 10 and add the digit. This is repeated until all the BCD digits of the number are added to the result. Example 9-3 shows a few BCD numbers converted to binary using this algorithm. (Of course, in the computer the result, multiplication by 10, and the addition are all accomplished in binary.)

Example 9-3

(a) Convert 109_{BCD} to binary:

$$0 \times 10 + 1 = 1$$
$$1 \times 10 + 0 = 10$$
$$10 \times 10 + 9 = 109$$

(b) Convert 2001_{BCD} to binary:

$$0 \times 10 + 2 = 2$$
$$2 \times 10 + 0 = 20$$
$$20 \times 10 + 0 = 200$$
$$200 \times 10 + 1 = 2001$$

The flowchart for this algorithm is illustrated in Figure 9-3 and the subroutine is listed in Example 9-4. In this example software the BCD number is assumed to be stored in the memory location indirectly addressed by the DE register pair and the result is returned (in binary) in the HL register pair. The BCD number can be anything from 0 —65,535 in value and it is assumed to end with a non-numeric code (0AH—FFH).

Example 9-4

```
                    ;subroutine to convert BCD to binary
                    ;result = HL
                    ;DE indirectly addresses BCD number
                    ;range 0--65,535
                    ;
                         ORG   200H
0200 21 00 00  BCDBIN:   LD    HL,0       ;clear result
0203 1A        BCDBIN1:  LD    A,(DE)     ;get digit
```

(Example 9-4 continued)

```
0204 FE 0A                CP    0AH          ;test for number
0206 30 0C                JR    NC,BCDBIN2   ;if not number
0208 CD 15 02             CALL  MULT10       ;multiply HL by 10
020B 85                   ADD   A,L          ;sum digit
020C 6F                   LD    L,A
020D 7C                   LD    A,H
020E CE 00                ADC   A,0
0210 67                   LD    H,A
0211 13                   INC   DE           ;address next digit
0212 18 EF                JR    BCDBIN1      ;repeat
0214 C9       BCDBIN2:    RET                ;return
              ;
              ;multiply HL by 10
              ;
0215 29       MULT10:     ADD   HL,HL        ;HL X 2
0216 44                   LD    B,H          ;save HL X 2
0217 4D                   LD    C,L
0218 29                   ADD   HL,HL        ;HL X 4
0219 29                   ADD   HL,HL        ;HL X 8
021A 09                   ADD   HL,BC        ;HL X 10
021B C9                   RET                ;return
```

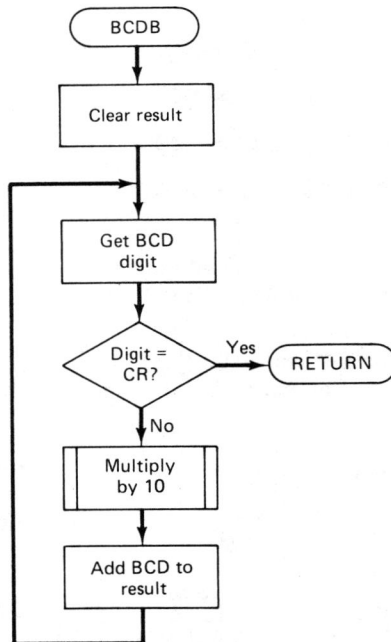

Figure 9-3 Flowchart for converting BCD integers into binary integers. The flowchart for multiply by 10 is not shown.

9-4 BINARY-TO-BCD CONVERSION

Binary-to-BCD conversions are required to output decimal data in any computer system. This type of conversion is as simple as BCD-to-binary except that the process is a little different. To convert from binary to BCD, the binary number is divided by 10 and the remainders become the BCD digits of the result.

Binary-to-BCD Conversion Algorithm

From the prior description of the binary-to-BCD conversion it is rather simple to write an algorithm for binary-to-BCD conversion. Starting with the binary number to be converted, divide by 10. The remainder becomes the least significant digit of the BCD number, and the quotient is again divided by a 10. The division process repeats until the quotient becomes a zero. Example 9-5 shows how a few binary numbers are converted with this algorithm into BCD.

Example 9-5

(a) Convert 100101_2 to BCD:

$$100101_2/1010_2 = \text{quo. } 11_2 \qquad \text{rem. } 111_2 \quad (7)$$
$$11_2/1010_2 = \text{quo. } 0 \qquad \text{rem. } 11_2 \quad (3)$$

(b) Convert 1100110_2 to BCD:

$$1100110_2/1010_2 = \text{quo. } 1010_2 \qquad \text{rem. } 10_2 \quad (2)$$
$$1010_2/1010_2 = \text{quo. } 1_2 \qquad \text{rem. } 0 \quad (0)$$
$$1_2/1010_2 = \text{quo. } 0 \qquad \text{rem } 1_2 \quad (1)$$

Figure 9-4 illustrates the flowchart written from the algorithm and Example 9-6 lists the subroutine developed from the flowchart. Notice that the subroutine converts the binary number stored in the HL register pair into a string of BCD digits stored beginning at the memory location indirectly addressed by the BC register pair. The number has its order reversed by placing it on the stack after each division by 10. Remember the first remainder is the least significant, so the order must be reversed before it is stored in the memory. The last thing that this subroutine does is store an FFH in memory following the BCD number.

Example 9-6

```
                      ;subroutine to convert the binary number
                      ;in the HL pair into a BCD string at
                      ;the memory location addressed by BC
                      ;
                             ORG   300H
   0300 3E FF         BINBCD:  LD    A,0FFH      ;load FFH
```

```
0302 F5                      PUSH  AF          ;save it
0303 7C                      LD    A,H         ;test for 0
0304 B5                      OR    L
0305 28 03                   JR    Z,BINBCD2   ;if 0
0307 CD 17 03  BINBCD1:      CALL  DIV10       ;divide by 10
030A F5        BINBCD2:      PUSH  AF
030B 7C                      LD    A,H         ;test for 0
030C B5                      OR    L
030D 20 F8                   JR    NZ,BINBCD1  ;repeat
030F F1        BINBCD3:      POP   AF          ;save number
0310 02                      LD    (BC),A
0311 03                      INC   BC
0312 FE FF                   CP    0FFH        ;test for FFH
0314 20 F9                   JR    NZ,BINBCD3  ;repeat
0316 C9                      RET               ;return
               ;
               ;subroutine to divide HL by 10 and
               ;place the remainder in A and the
               ;quotient in HL.
               ;
0317 C5        DIV10:        PUSH  BC          ;save BC
0318 06 10                   LD    B,16        ;load count
031A 11 00 00                LD    DE,0        ;clear quotient
031D EB        DIV11:        EX    DE,HL       ;shift quotient left
031E 29                      ADD   HL,HL
031F EB                      EX    DE,HL
0320 29                      ADD   HL,HL       ;shift dividend left
0321 30 01                   JR    NC,DIV12    ;if no carry
0323 1C                      INC   E
0324 D5        DIV12:        PUSH  DE
0325 7B                      LD    A,E         ;compare with 10
0326 D6 0A                   SUB   10
0328 5F                      LD    E,A
0329 7A                      LD    A,D
032A DE 00                   SBC   A,0
032C 57                      LD    D,A
032D 38 03                   JR    C,DIV13     ;if dividend smaller
032F F1                      POP   AF
0330 2C                      INC   L
0331 F5                      PUSH  AF
0332 D1        DIV3:         POP   DE
0333 10 D8                   DJNZ  DIV11       ;repeat
0335 7B                      LD    A,E         ;get remainder
0336 C1                      POP   BC          ;restore BC
0337 C9                      RET               ;return
```

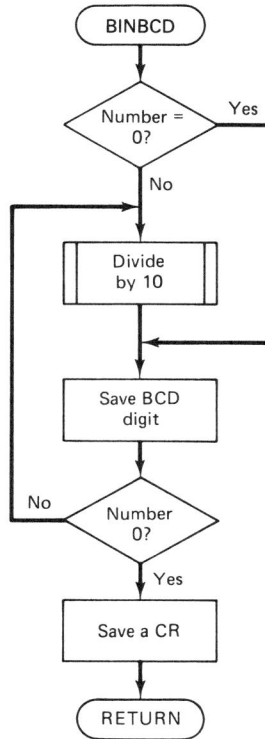

Figure 9–4 Flowchart for converting binary integers into BCD integers. The flowchart for dividing by 10 is not shown.

9-5 DIRECT TABLE LOOKUP FOR DATA CONVERSION ——————————

Table loop techniques are used to convert data from one form to another. One fairly common data conversion that uses this technique is BCD or hexadecimal-to-seven-segment code for LED, fluorescent, or LCD displays.

Hexadecimal-to-Seven-Segment Code Conversion

Figure 9-5 illustrates a seven-segment LED display device and the binary bit pattern required to light up the different lettered sections. Here the most significant bit is undefined and can be used to control the decimal point on the display if desired. There are two basic types of seven-segment LED displays available: the common-anode display and the common-cathode display. Common-anode displays are connected so that 5 V is applied to all the internal anode connections of the LEDs. Common-anode displays require a logic zero applied to a segment to light the segment. Common-cathode displays are connected so that all the cathodes are grounded internally. Common-cathode displays require the application of 5 V to a segment to light.

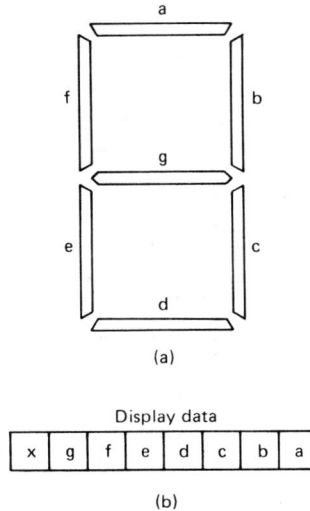

(a)

Display data

x	g	f	e	d	c	b	a

(b)

Figure 9-5 (a) The segment pattern of a 7-segment LED or LCD display device; (b) the binary bit pattern of the data used to control each segment of the 7-segment display device.

Seven-segment lookup table. Suppose that common-cathode displays are used and a table is required for coding each of the numbers 0—9 and the hexadecimal letters A—F. A table for each character is formed as illustrated in Example 9-7. This table will be used with a subroutine for converting hexadecimal code into seven-segment code for the display.

Example 9-7

```
              ;MSB = 0
              ;hexadecimal to 7-segment conversion
              ;table for use with common-cathode
              ;or common-anode display with inverters
              ;
                        ORG  300H
0300  3F      TABLE:    DB   3FH        ;0
0301  06                DB   06H        ;1
0302  5B                DB   5BH        ;2
0303  4F                DB   4FH        ;3
0304  66                DB   66H        ;4
0305  6D                DB   6DH        ;5
0306  7D                DB   7DH        ;6
0307  27                DB   27H        ;7
0308  7F                DB   7FH        ;8
0309  6F                DB   6FH        ;9
030A  77                DB   77H        ;A
030B  7C                DB   7CH        ;b
030C  39                DB   39H        ;C
030D  5E                DB   5EH        ;d
030E  79                DB   79H        ;E
030F  71                DB   71H        ;F
```

Lookup conversion subroutine.   Software that uses the table formed in Example 9-7 refers to the table by using the hexadecimal data as a portion of the memory address. Notice that the first location of the table contains the seven-segment code for a 0, the second contains the code for a 1, and so forth. If the HL register pair is loaded with the starting address of the table (0300H) and the hexadecimal data are moved into L, then HL will point to the correct seven-segment data for the hexadecimal number. A short subroutine that references the table is listed in Example 9-8. This subroutine is very useful if the table begins at a memory location that ends with a 00H. If the table begins at any other location, a bias must be added to the hexadecimal number before it is moved into the L register. Suppose that the table begins at location 2832H. The bias is 32H and it must be added to the hexadecimal number as illustrated in Example 9-9. If the table crosses a page boundary (100H), the bias must be added to the entire HL register pair. Because of this problem, it is more efficient to begin all the lookup tables at the beginning of a page boundary.

Example 9-8

```
                      ;table lookup subroutine that refers
                      ;to TABLE for the 7-segment code.
                      ;
                              ORG 500H
0500 26 03            LOOK:   LD   H,03H        ;address table
0502 6F                       LD   L,A
0503 7E                       LD   A,(HL)       ;convert
0504 C9                       RET               ;return
```

Example 9-9

```
                      ;table lookup subroutine that refers
                      ;for the 7-segment code.
                      ;this subroutine converts the contents
                      ;of the accumulator to 7-segment code
                      ;
                              ORG 500H
0500 26 03            LOOK:   LD   H,03H        ;address table
0502 C6 32                    ADD  A,32H        ;add bias
0504 6F                       LD   L,A
0505 7E                       LD   A,(HL)
0506 C9                       RET               ;return
```

Direct table lookup is a very efficient way of converting from one code to another and finds an application for converting ASCII code to EBCDIC (a code used in some large mainframe computer systems) and various other codes found in many different systems.

Using Table Lookup for Jump Tables

Today, many programs are menu driven. A menu-driven program is one in which a menu of options is presented to the operator, who chooses the option required to perform a

CORRECT, the spelling program
written by Barry B. Brey, copyright 1984

0 — Correct the spelling in a text file.
1 — Erase a word from the dictionary.
2 — Add a word to the dictionary.
3 — Print the dictionary.
4 — Set up the printer.
5 — Create a new dictionary.
6 — Delete a dictionary.

Enter your choice:

Figure 9–6   Display presented by a menu-driven spelling program. All the user does is enter the numerical choice from the menu and the function will execute.

given task. Figure 9-6 illustrates a menu that might be encountered for a program that corrects the spelling of a text file stored on a disk. The user enters the numerical choice and the computer executes the function described by the choice.

The software that handles the menu is a jump table-lookup subroutine. After the numeric choice is entered, it appears in the accumulator, and subroutine JUMP is called. JUMP, as listed in Example 9-10, refers to a jump table, which contains the address of each program for CORRECT. Once the 16-bit address is located, the HL register pair is loaded with it and the JP (HL) instruction is executed. JP (HL) is the instruction that jumps to the memory location addressed by the HL register pair. A few programming concepts are important in this example, such as the ADD A,A instruction, which doubles the contents of the accumulator. Doubling the accumulator is required because each table entry is 16 bits (two bytes) in length. Also important is the addition of the doubled lookup number to the beginning address of the jump table. This is required because no origin is specified for the table. This allows the table to be placed anywhere in the memory by the assembler. Because assemblers are used for software development, this step is very important if no origin is specified.

Example 9-10

```
              ;subroutine to reference the jump table
              ;for the address of the program that
              ;correspondes to the number in the
              ;accumulator.
              ;
              ;accumulator must equal 0--6
              ;
                       ORG 500H
0500 21 0E 05  JUMP:   LD  HL,JTAB    ;address table
0503 87                ADD A,A        ;double A
0504 5F                LD  E,A        ;save in DE
0505 16 00             LD  D,0
0507 19                ADD HL,DE      ;adjust address
0508 5E                LD  E,(HL)     ;get address
0509 23                INC HL
050A 56                LD  D,(HL)
050B E1                POP HL         ;clear return
050C EB                EX  DE,HL      ;place address in HL
050D E9                JP  (HL)       ;go execute
```

(Example 9-10 continued)

```
                                 ;
                                 ;jump table for program CORRECT
                                 ;
050E 00 29    JTAB:    DW   CORR          ;correct spelling
0510 2A 2A             DW   ERA           ;erase word
0512 63 2A             DW   ADDW          ;add word
0514 8F 2A             DW   PRI           ;print
0516 02 2B             DW   SETU          ;setup
0518 33 2B             DW   CRE           ;create
051A 03 2C             DW   DLE           ;delete
```

9-6 TIME DELAYS

Time-delay software is required for a wide variety of I/O interfacing and also for some forms of programs. Examples of some time delays that are required with I/O include keyboard contact debouncing, controlled pulse-width generation (monostable multivibrator simulation), and the generation of periodic waveforms (symmetrical or asymmetrical). Examples of time delays for programs include delays required for the operator to read a message, and allowing the operator a certain amount of time to respond to a question.

Using Appendix A to Determine Instruction Execution Time

Appendix A lists the instructions available for use with the Z80 microprocessor and the number of system clock periods required to execute them. A clock cycle is normally equal to either 500 ns (on the 2 MHz version of the Z80) or 250 ns (on the 4 MHz version). If the LD A,B instruction requires 4 clocks to execute it then takes 4×500 ns or 2 µs (on the 2 MHz Z80), or 4×250 ns or 1 µs (on the 4 MHz Z80). The execution times for all the instructions are determined in the same manner.

   Some of the branch, call, and return instructions have two times listed for execution. The longer time occurs when a jump, call, or return occurs and the shorter time when no jump, call, or return occurs. An example is The DJNZ instruction. This instruction requires 13 clocks if it jumps and only 8 clocks if no jump occurs.

Short Time Delays

Short time delays are easy to implement because a single loop and an 8-bit counter can be used for the software. Example 9-11 illustrates a simple technique for obtaining short time delays. Here the B register is loaded with the count of XX, and the program executes the DJNZ instruction XX number of times. The total amount of the time delay is equal to the time it takes to CALL the subroutine, execute it, and return from it. Example 9-12 shows how the time for this subroutine is calculated and how a value for XX can be found if the time is known. The first equation is the sum of the time it takes to CALL, RET, LD B,XX and execute DJNZ one time plus the time it takes to execute DNJZ XX-1 times. If the count is 256 (00H) it takes slightly more than 1.6 ms to execute this subroutine.

Example 9-11

```
                    ;subroutine for a short time delay
                    ;using a single 8-bit counter
                    ;
                    ;c = clocks
                    ;us = microseconds
                    ;
                    ;assumes a 2 MHz Z80
                    ;
                            ORG   200H
0200 06 XX          SDELAY:  LD   B,XX    ;7c, 3 1/2 us
0202 10 FE          SLOOP:   DJNZ SLOOP   ;8/13c, 4 or 6 1/2 us
0204 C9                      RET          ;10c, 5 us
```

Example 9-12

If XX is known:

$$time = 21 \ \mu s + (XX - 1)(6 \ 1/2 \ \mu s)$$

If time is known:

$$XX = \frac{time - 21 \ \mu s}{6 \ 1/2 \ \mu s} + 1$$

Long Time Delays

In many instances, a time delay of longer than 1.6 ms is required. This is attainable by using a register pair as a counter instead of a single register. Example 9-13 illustrates a time-delay subroutine that is able to generate delays of slightly greater than 851 ms. Example 9-14 depicts the equations required to calculate the time required to execute the delay or to calculate the count required for a particular time delay. Note that the maximum count is 65,536 when XXXX is a 0000H because the decrement occurs before the condition of the counter is tested.

Example 9-13

```
                    ;subroutine for a long time delay
                    ;using a register pair as a counter
                    ;
                    ;c = clocks
                    ;us = microseconds
```

(Example 9-13 continued)

```
                         ;
                         ;assumes a 2 MHz Z80
                         ;
                                 ORG  300H
0300 01 XX XX    LDELAY:   LD   BC,XXXX     ;10c, 5 us
0303 0B          LDELAY1:  DEC  BC          ;6c, 3 us
0304 78                    LD   A,B         ;4c, 2 us
0305 B1                    OR   C           ;4c, 2 us
0306 20 FB                 JR   NZ,LDELAY1  ;7/12c, 3 1/2 or 6 us
0308 C9                    RET              ;10c, 5 us
```

Example 9-14

```
                         ;One hour time delay
                         ;
                                 ORG  400H
0400 11 20 1C    HOUR:     LD   DE,7200     ;load counter
0403 CD 0C 04    HOUR1:    CALL LDELAY      ;wait 1/2 second
0406 1B                    DEC  DE
0407 7A                    LD   A,D
0408 B3                    OR   E
0409 20 F8                 JR   NZ,HOUR1
040B C9                    RET              ;after an hour
                         ;
                         ;subroutine for a 1/2 second delay
                         ;
040C 01 3C 96    LDELAY:   LD   BC,38460    ;load count
040F 0B          LDELAY1:  DEC  BC
0410 78                    LD   A,B
0411 B1                    OR   C
0412 20 FB                 JR   NZ,LDELAY1
0414 C9                    RET              ;after 1/2 second
```

Extremely Long Time Delays

Extremely long time delays are created by using the long time-delay subroutine LDELAY in nested loops. If LDELAY is set for a delay of 1/2 second, time delays in multiples of 1/2 second are easily created. Example 9-14 shows how a time delay of 1 hour is generated using the LDELAY subroutine and another register pair for timing.

9-7 SUMMARY _____

1. Data conversion is important because the form of the data never seems to fit the application. For example, keyboards often generate different data from those that displays may require.

2. Binary-coded decimal-to-ASCII code conversion is accomplished by adding a 30H to the BCD number. ASCII-to-BCD conversion is accomplished by subtracting 30H from the ASCII-coded data.

3. ASCII-to-hexadecimal conversion is effected by subtracting a 30H if the original ASCII character is a number or 37H if it is a letter. Hexadecimal-to-ASCII conversion is accomplished by adding 30H to a number and 37H to a letter.

4. Converting BCD to binary is accomplished by starting with a binary value of 0. After starting at 0, as each BCD digit is encountered, the binary number is multiplied by 10 and the BCD digit is added to generate the binary result.

5. Binary numbers are converted to BCD numbers by dividing the binary number by 10 and saving the remainders. This division continues until the quotient becomes a zero.

6. Table-lookup techniques are excellent for converting codes and referencing programs through jump tables.

7. The only efficient, and possibly the only method of converting from BCD or hexadecimal code to seven-segment code for use with LED or LCD displays is via direct table lookup.

8. A very efficient way to handle menu-driven software is through the jump table. A table is created that contains the addresses of various programs and the addresses are accessed via table lookup techniques.

9. Time-delay software is used in many system programs to control I/O devices and also to place time delays in software. In the Z80 microprocessor, time delays can range in value from a few microseconds to years in length.

9-8 GLOSSARY

Clock   One period of time whereby all internal and external Z80 events are timed.

Jump Table   Jump tables contain memory addresses of subprograms or subroutines stored elsewhere in the memory. Reference to these subprograms or subroutines is made through the jump table.

Menu   A selection of functions that are presented to the computer user through a numbered or lettered list of options displayed on the CRT screen.

Menu-driven   Software that is selected and executed from a menu is considered menu-driven software. An entire system can be menu-driven if all the available software options are presented on one or more menus.

Page   A computer memory page is equal to 256 bytes.

Table lookup   A programming technique that uses a table to convert data from one form to another or references a key that points to other data or programs.

Time delay software   Software that is written to execute in an accurate and predictable amount of time. This is possible because instruction execution times are known.

QUESTIONS AND PROBLEMS

9-1. Why is there a need for data conversion?

9-2. ASCII numbers are converted to BCD numbers by adding what hexadecimal value?

9-3. BCD numbers are converted to ASCII numbers by subtracting what hexadecimal value?

9-4. When converting from hexadecimal to ASCII, what problem is encountered if one number is added to accomplish the conversion?

9-5. Write a subroutine that converts the hexadecimal contents of the accumulator into two ASCII-coded characters stored in the BC register pair. (B should hold the most significant character and C the least.)

9-6. Whenever a BCD number is converted to binary, it is added to a binary number that is first multiplied by a _____ .

9-7. Binary numbers are converted to BCD by dividing by _____ and saving the _____ after each division.

9-8. Modify the lookup table presented in Example 9-7 so that it contains entries for codes 10H—13H, which contain the following characters: 10H = n, 11H = U, 12H = H, and 13H = r.

9-9. Write a subroutine that uses the subroutine of Example 9-8 to convert the contents of the accumulator into two seven-segment codes that are stored in the BC register pair.

9-10. If the POP instruction is removed from Example 9-10 can each subprogram be ended with a return, converting them into subroutines?

9-11. How much time is required to execute the following instructions if a 2 MHz clock is used?
  (a) LD A,(HL)
  (b) EX DE,HL
  (c) JR LOOP
  (d) JP LOOP
  (e) LD HL,1234H

9-12. Repeat question number 9-11 using a 4 MHz clock.

9-13. What count is used in Example 9-11 to cause a 1.2 ms $\pm$ 2 percent time delay?

9-14. How much time delay is generated by Example 9-11 if a count of 12H is used?

9-15. What count is used in Example 9-13 to cause a 100 ms $\pm$ 2 percent time delay?

9-16. If a count of 1000H is used in Example 9-13 what amount of time delay is generated?

chapter 10 _____

Introduction to the Z80 System Architecture

Before the Z80 microprocessor's hardware and interfacing can be studied, it is important to have a basic understanding of the Z80 microprocessor and the basic architecture of the system. In this chapter you are given the information that you will need to interface the microprocessor to memory and I/O devices in the remainder of this text.

10-1 OBJECTIVES _____

Upon completion of this chapter, you will be able to:

1. Understand the basic function of each pin of the Z80 microprocessor.
2. Explain how the system timing relates to the operation of the basic system components such as memory and I/O.
3. Describe the operation of the buses during the execution of instructions.

10-2 THE Z80 PINOUT _____

The pinout of the Z80 is important because it illustrates which pin connections are available for interfacing and also the function of each pin. This section details the purpose of each pin, describes the characteristics of each pin, and discusses power supply requirements and decoupling.

Pinout

Figure 10-1 illustrates the pinout of the Z80 microprocessor, which is packaged in a 40-pin dual-in-line package (DIP). Pins 11 and 29 are used for the application of +5.0 V and ground (0 V), respectively. This power supply arrangement is unique to the Z80 because most 40-pin integrated circuits have pins 40 and 20 used to DC power. In most

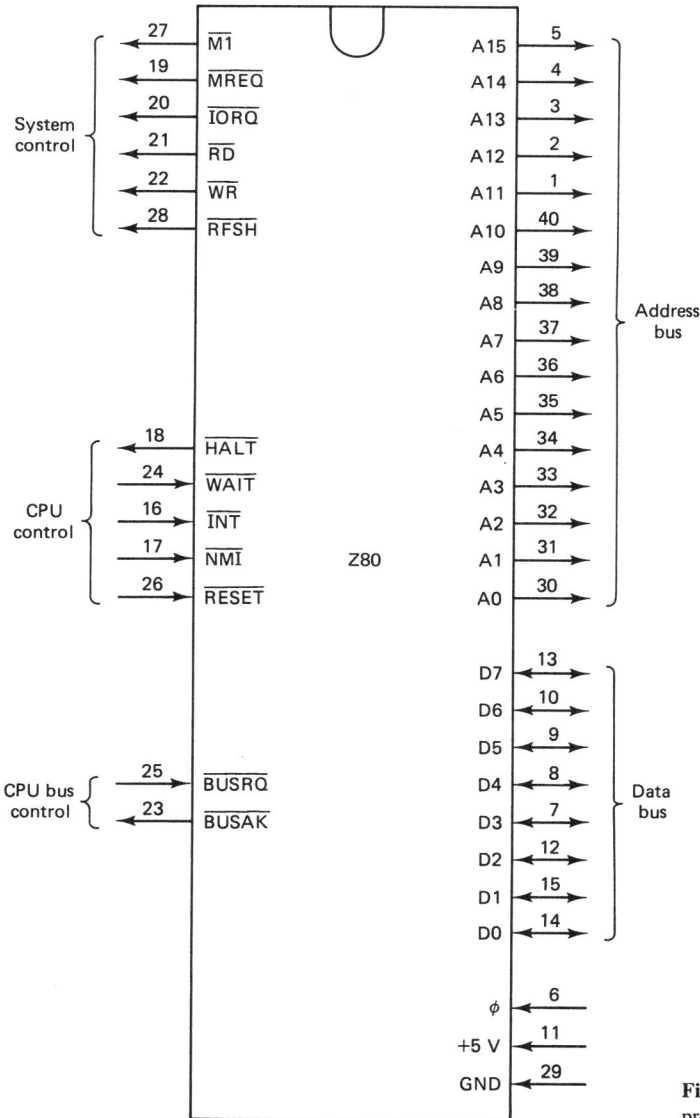

Figure 10–1 The pinout of the Z80 micro-processor.

TABLE 10-1. FANOUT CHARACTERISTICS OF THE Z80 MICROPROCESSOR

Logic type	Part number	Fanout
TTL	74XXX	1
TTL	74SXXX	1[a]
TTL	74LSXXX	4
CMOS	CD4XXX	10[b]
HCMOS	74HCXXX	10[b]
MOS	Various	10[b]

[a]Only if the noise immunity is derated to 350 mV.

[b]A fanout of 10 is limited by the maximum recommended bus capacitance of 150 pF. If the capacitive load is greater, all the timing is degraded.

circuitry it is common practice to connect a capacitor (0.1 μF) across pins 11 and 29 (or 40 and 20) to decouple the chip from the power supply. Without a decoupling capacitor, transients might be generated that could destroy data in the Z80 or other components connected to the power supply.

The Z80 requires a maximum power supply current of approximately 200 mA with a voltage that must be ±5 percent for proper operation. If the supply voltage falls outside of this range, the microprocessor will not function properly. If the voltage exceeds 7.0 V the circuit will become damaged.

Pin characteristics in general. The Z80 microprocessor can directly drive a wide variety of TTL and MOSFET digital integrated circuits. Table 10-1 illustrates the fanout (number of inputs that may be connected to an output) of the Z80 to various other logic circuits.

The input pins represent a very light current load of only ±10 μA at a very low capacitance of about 5 pF. This means that the input connections may be connected to other logic families (TTL and MOSFET) without any special interfacing circuitry.

The noise immunity for the Z80 microprocessor is 400 mV, which is identical to standard TTL digital circuitry. With this noise immunity figure it is possible to drive a bus of a maximum length of about 15 inches with a bus capacitance of 150 pF.

Clock Pin

The Z80 clock input pin (φ) is TTL compatible if it is pulled up to +5 V through a 330 Ω resistor. Otherwise any squarewave generator that provides a fairly symmetrical square-wave at 2 MHz. Figure 10-2 depicts a simple circuit that allows the clock to be generated from a crystal. Here a 4 MHz crystal is connected to function in a ring oscillator whose output is fed to a D flip-flop. The D flip-flop is used to generate a symmetrical squarewave of 2 MHz for the Z80.

The output of the D flip-flop is tied to a driver that provides the Z80 with its clock. Here a pullup and pulldown transistor are used to drive the clock input high and low.

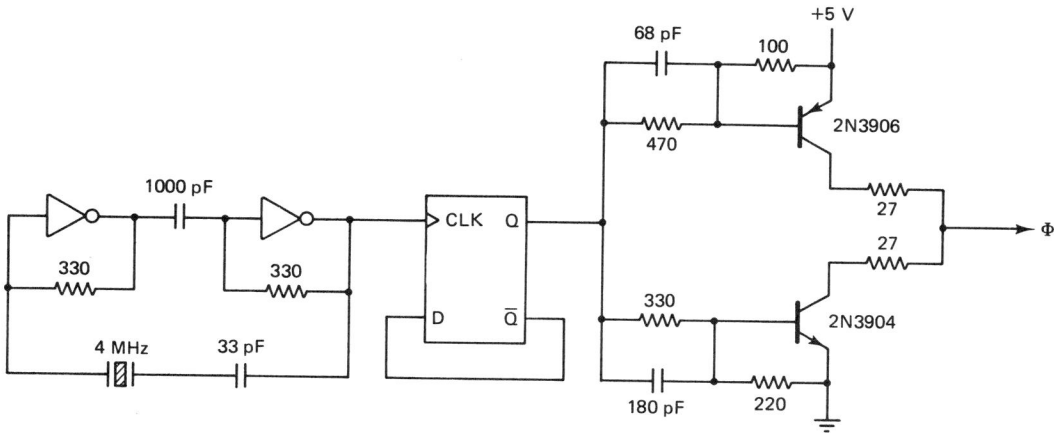

Figure 10–2 Z80 clock generation circuitry.

Machine Status Bits

Several of the pins on the Z80 indicate control or status information to the system. These pins are M1, MREQ, RFSH, and HALT. During the normal operation of the microprocessor these pins may be tested to determine what type of operation the Z80 is executing.

HALT—The HALT pin becomes a logic 0 whenever the HALT instruction is executed. HALT remains a logic 0 until the microprocessor is either interrupted or reset where it continues to execute instructions.

M1—The M1 pin becomes a logic zero whenever the Z80 fetches an opcode from the memory. M1 also goes low during an interrupt acknowledge along with the IORQ pin.

RFSH—The RFSH (refresh) pin becomes a logic zero to indicate that the lower 7 bits of the address bus contain a refresh address from the R register. RFSH and the refresh address are always presented to refresh dynamic RAM during the second half of an opcode fetch.

MREQ—The MREQ signal indicates that the address bus contains a valid memory address for a memory read or write operation.

IORQ—The IORQ signal indicates that the address bus contains a valid I/O port number for an IN or an OUT instruction. It also goes low during the M1 cycle of an interrupt acknowledge sequence.

Read and Write Control

The RD (read) and WR (write) control signals are used in conjunction with the IORQ and MREQ signals to enable the memory or I/O for read and write operations. Figure

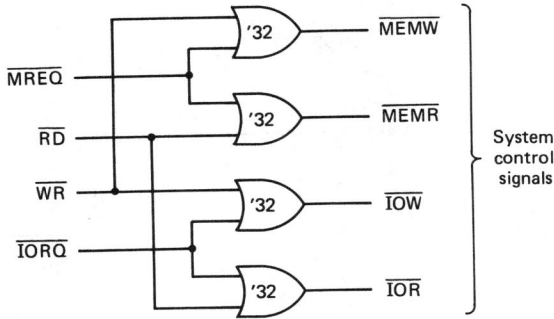

Figure 10–3 Generation of the Z80 system control signals $\overline{\text{MEMW}}$, $\overline{\text{MEMR}}$, $\overline{\text{IOW}}$, and $\overline{\text{IOR}}$.

10-3 illustrates a simple circuit that is used to generate a $\overline{\text{RD}}$ signal for the memory ($\overline{\text{MEMR}}$) and I/O ($\overline{\text{IOR}}$) and a $\overline{\text{WR}}$ signal for the memory ($\overline{\text{MEMW}}$) and the I/O ($\overline{\text{IOW}}$).

Address and Data Bus Connections

The Z80 has 16 pins that are dedicated to function as the address bus and 8 pins that are dedicated to function as the data bus.

Address bus connections. The address bus (A0—A15) is a 16-bit bus that is used for three purposes in the Z80 microprocessor. It is used for addressing memory ($\overline{\text{MREQ}}$ active), addressing an I/O device ($\overline{\text{IORQ}}$ active), and addressing memory for a refresh ($\overline{\text{RFSH}}$ active). When used to address the memory the address bus contains a 16-bit address which allows any of 64K different memory locations to be read from or written to by the Z80. In the I/O mode, the address bus contains an 8-bit I/O address (port number) that is used to address one of 256 different I/O devices. The I/O port number appears on the least significant 8 address bits (A0—A7). During a refresh operation, the address bus contains a 7-bit refresh address on address pins A0—A6.

Data bus connections. The data bus connections (D0—D7) are used to transfer data between the Z80 and the memory or I/O. This is a bidirectional bus that contains information for the memory or I/O during a write operation and accepts information during a read operation. At other times (between a read or write) the data bus is at its high impedance state.

Resetting the Z80

The $\overline{\text{RESET}}$ input to the Z80 microprocessor is used to initialize the Z80 after power is applied and also to reinitialize it if a $\overline{\text{HALT}}$ occurs or some other catastrophic event. When the Z80 is reset it begins executing software from memory location 0000H because its program counter is cleared to zero. In addition, the $\overline{\text{RESET}}$ input also disables interrupts by clearing the interrupt enable flip-flop, places a NOP instruction in the instruction register, clears the refresh register, and selects interrupt mode 0.

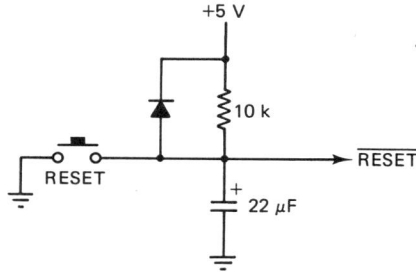

Figure 10–4 Resetting the Z80 microprocessor.

Figure 10-4 illustrates a simple circuit that is used to assure that the Z80 is reset
upon the application of the DC power. Here an RC circuit is used to hold the RESET
pin at a logic 0 level for a short period of time after +5.0 V is applied. The push-button
is used to manually reset the Z80 at the operator's leisure. Notice that this circuit provides
an active low reset pulse for the microprocessor and also an active high reset pulse for
initializing system components when required.

Interrupt Control Pins

The Z80 system has two interrupt control inputs (NMI and INT) and an output that is
hidden in the operation of the IORQ and M1 pins. An interrupt is a hardware signal that
interrupts the normal execution of software by calling an interrupt service subroutine.
You could say that an interrupt is a hardware-initiated subroutine CALL.

If the NMI (nonmaskable interrupt) input is placed at a logic 0 level it calls the
subroutine that begins at memory location 0066H. This pin is a negative edge-triggered
input that must be brought back to a logic 1 level and then held low before it is recognized
by the Z80. The NMI pin is nonmaskable, which means that it is always active—it
always calls the subroutine which starts at memory location 0066H.

The INT input is a level-sensitive input that must be held low until it is recognized.
Once recognized, it may be returned to its logic 1 level. The INT input is maskable, that
is, it can be turned on and off by the EI (enable interrupt) and DI (disable interrupt)
instructions. Its operation depends on which mode has been selected—0, 1, or 2.

Figure 10-5 shows how the interrupt acknowledge signal is generated by combining
the IORQ, M1 and RD signals. When the INT input is acknowledged, the Z80 expects
the opcode for a restart instruction (mode 1) or the least significant portion of the interrupt
vector address (mode 2) to be placed on the data bus. This signal is used to accomplish
that.

The WAIT Input

The WAIT input is used to indicate that external memory or I/O is ready to transfer data
when high and not ready when low. By controlling this pin, the Z80 can be made to wait
for slow memory or I/O. A slow memory device is one that requires an access time that

+5 V

1 k

(74LS244)

1 — D7

1 — D6

1 — D5

0 — D4

0 — D3

1 — D2

1 — D1

1 — D0

(E7H)

To data bus

$\overline{\text{IOR}}$*

$\overline{\text{M1}}$

'32 $\overline{\text{INTA}}$

* $\overline{\text{IOR}}$ is the combination of $\overline{\text{IORQ}}$ and $\overline{\text{RD}}$

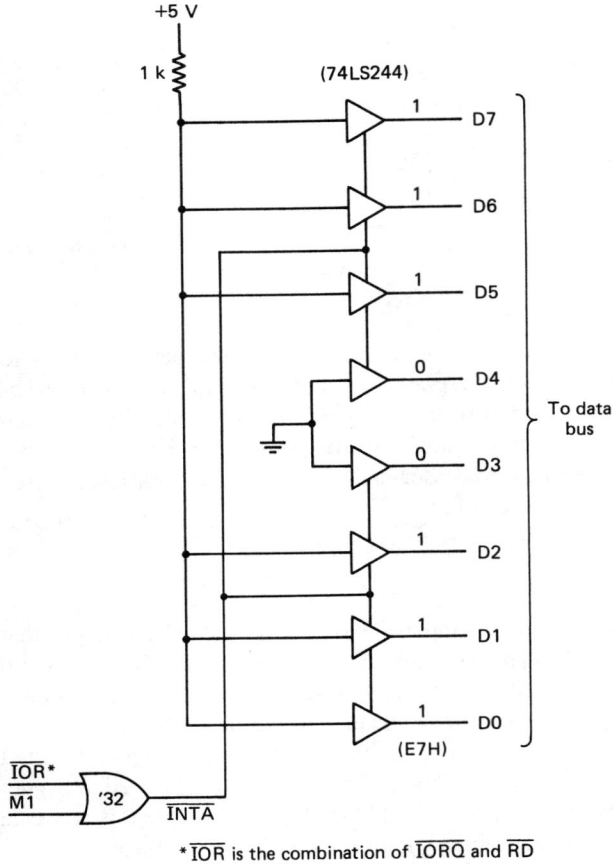

Figure 10–5 Generating an $\overline{\text{INTA}}$ signal that applies an E7H to the data bus in response to an interrupt ($\overline{\text{INT}}$). This causes an RST 4 instruction to execute.

is too long for the Z80. More discussion of this is presented in the section on memory interface.

Another use for the $\overline{\text{WAIT}}$ input is the RUN/$\overline{\text{STOP}}$ function (see Figure 10-6). By connecting a simple switch to the $\overline{\text{WAIT}}$ input, the Z80 can be made to run a program or stop running a program. Here the Z80 stops executing software whenever the switch is closed.

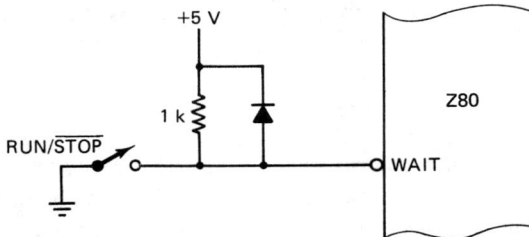

+5 V

1 k

Z80

RUN/$\overline{\text{STOP}}$

$\overline{\text{WAIT}}$

Figure 10–6 The RUN/$\overline{\text{STOP}}$ function using the $\overline{\text{WAIT}}$ input.

Direct Memory Access (DMA)

The last two pins on the Z80 microprocessor are the $\overline{\text{BUSRQ}}$ (bus request) and the $\overline{\text{BUSAK}}$ (bus acknowledge) pins. The $\overline{\text{BUSRQ}}$ pin is used by an external device to gain access to the Z80 system address, data, and control buses. If $\overline{\text{BUSRQ}}$ is placed at a logic 0 level the Z80 open-circuits the address, data, and control bus pins. It does this so that an external (direct memory access) device can directly address the memory and I/O. The $\overline{\text{BUSAK}}$ signal is an indicator to the external device that the Z80 has indeed open-circuited its buses.

DMA (direct memory access) is an important I/O technique that allows data to be placed into or removed from the memory at a very high rate of speed. DMA accesses can often occur at the rate of millions of bytes per second and are very useful for interfacing CRTs and disk memory to a microprocessor.

10-3 BUFFERING THE Z80 FOR LARGE SYSTEMS

Because of the limited drive capability of the Z80 microprocessor, often in a larger system the address and data buses are buffered. This section of the text discusses buffering both buses. Each bus is buffered in a different manner because the address bus is unidirectional and the data bus is bidirectional.

Buffering the Address Bus

The address bus is rather simple to buffer because it is unidirectional and the buffers may be left enabled at all times unless a DMA system is in use. Figure 10-7 illustrates the pinout of the 74LS244 octal bus-buffer. This device is actually 2 separate quad buffers in one package. If the output enable pin ($\overline{\text{G}}$) is grounded, the device functions as a non-inverting buffer. The output provides 32 mA of current at a logic 0 and 5.2 mA of current at a logic 1 output. This device will drive the largest of Z80 systems. If $\overline{\text{G}}$ is tied high (logic 1) then the output connections are at their high impedance (open-circuited) state.

Figure 10-8 illustrates a pair of 74LS244 bus buffers that are used to buffer the address bus of the Z80. Notice that the four $\overline{\text{G}}$ pins are tied common and connected to the active low $\overline{\text{BUSAK}}$ pin through an inverter. $\overline{\text{BUSAK}}$ is a logic 1 during normal microprocessor operation so that the $\overline{\text{G}}$ pins are grounded and the buffers are actively buffering the address bus. If a DMA occurs ($\overline{\text{BUSRQ}} = 0$), the $\overline{\text{BUSAK}}$ output becomes a logic 0 which places a logic 1 on the $\overline{\text{G}}$ pins of the buffers, disabling them.

Buffering the Data Bus

To buffer the data bus, a bidirectional bus-buffer is required. The 74LS245 is an octal bidirectional bus-buffer that is illustrated in Figure 10-9. The 74LS245 has two control inputs: $\overline{\text{G}}$ (output enable) and DIR (direction). The $\overline{\text{G}}$ pin functions in the same manner

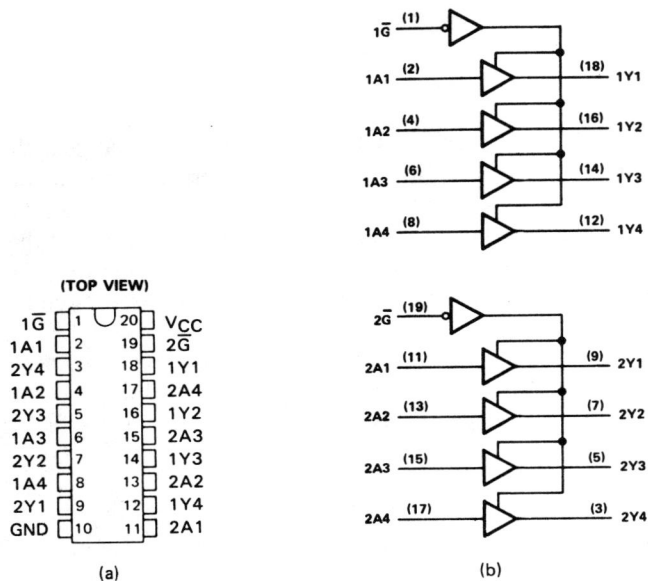

Figure 10–7 The 74LS244 octal buffer. (a) Pinout; and (b) logic diagram. (Courtesy of Texas Instruments, Inc.)

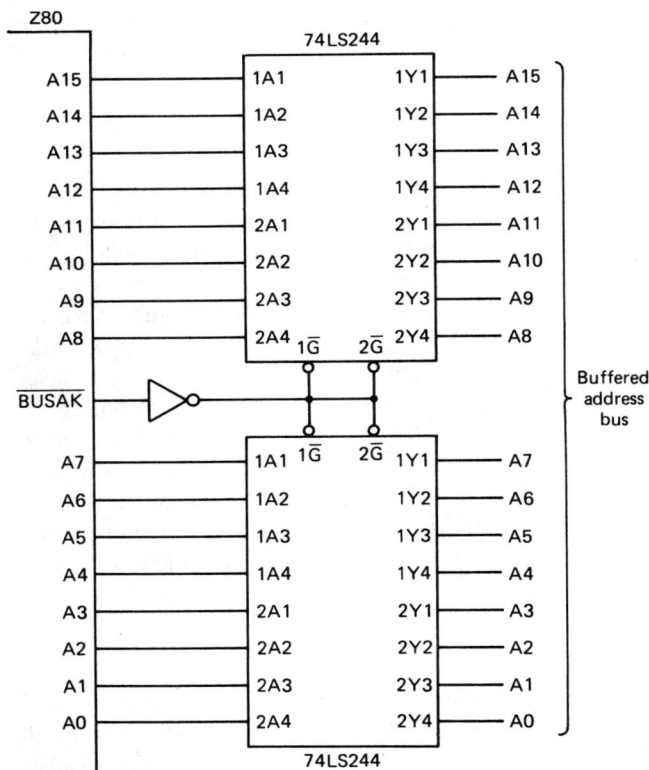

Figure 10–8 A Z80 with a fully buffered address bus.

180

(TOP VIEW)

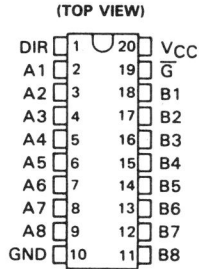

(a)

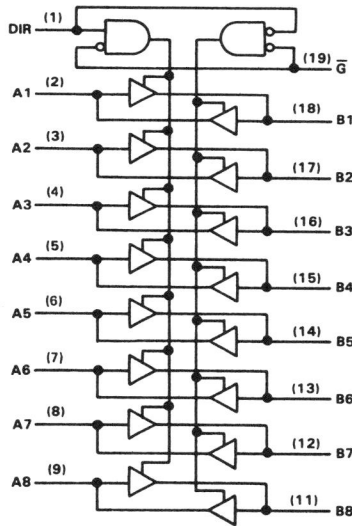

(b)

FUNCTION TABLE

ENABLE $\overline{G}$	DIRECTION CONTROL DIR	OPERATION
L	L	B data to A bus
L	H	A data to B bus
H	X	Isolation

(c)

Figure 10–9 The 74LS245 bidirectional bus buffer. (a) Pinout; (b) logic diagram; and (c) function table. (Courtesy of Texas Instruments, Inc.)

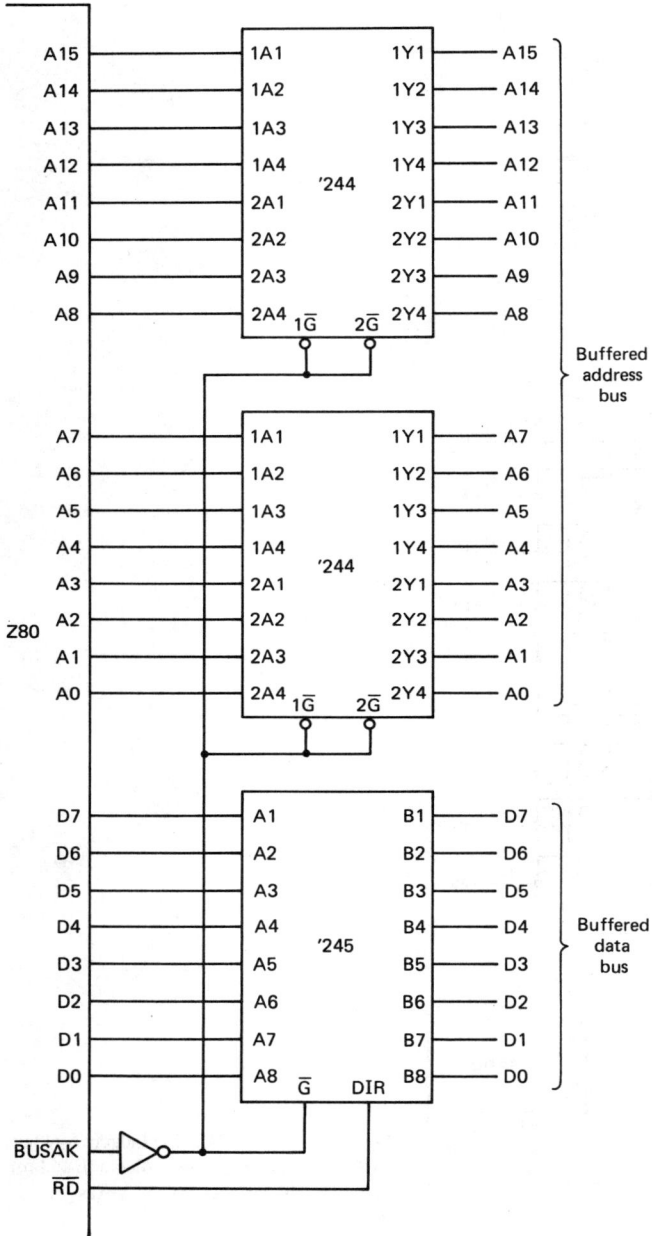

Figure 10–10 A fully buffered Z80 microprocessor.

as it did on the 74LS244. If $\overline{G}$ is a logic 1, the buffer is disabled (high impedance on all I/O pins), and if a logic 0, the buffer is enabled and drives the bus.

The DIR pin controls the direction of data flow through the bidirectional bus-buffer. If the DIR pin is grounded, data flow from the B connections to the A connections, and if DIR is connected to a logic 1, data flow from the A connections to the B connections.

Figure 10-10 illustrates a fully buffered Z80 microprocessor. Here both the address bus and the data bus have been buffered. Notice that the $\overline{RD}$ signal is connected to the DIR pin of the 74LS245 to control the direction of the data flow. When read becomes a logic zero the buffer's direction is switched so that the data flow into the microprocessor from the memory or I/O through the system bus. Also notice that the $\overline{G}$ input is connected to the inverted output of the $\overline{BUSAK}$ signal.

10-4 *THE Z80 READ AND WRITE TIMING*

The timing of the microprocessor is important if the external memory and I/O operation are to be understood with the execution of instructions. Timing also plays an important part in the selection of compatible memory and I/O components.

Basic Read Timing

The Z80 microprocessor has two memory read cycles: (1) the opcode fetch (see Figure 10-11) and (2) the memory or I/O read (see Figure 10-12). If the timing of both are compared it is noticed that the data are read from the memory at different points. In the M1 or opcode fetch timing diagram, the data are read at the raising edge of the clock (↑) at the start of T3. In the memory or I/O read timing diagram the data are read at the falling edge of the clock (↓) in the middle of T3. Since memory must be able to function in both the M1 cycle and also the memory or I/O read cycle, the one with the least amount of access time is chosen for study (M1).

The amount of access time allowed by the Z80 microprocessor is from the point where the address appears on the address bus (about the midpoint of T1) to where it is sampled by the microprocessor (at the start of T3). Notice that this is less than two complete clocking periods of time.

The address delay time (time required for the address to appear after the start of T1) is 145 ns for the Z80 (2 MHz version) and 110 ns for the Z80 (4 MHz version). The only other time that needs to be discussed for memory read is the required setup time before the (↑) edge of the clock at the start of T3. This setup time is 60 ns (Z80) or 50 ns (Z80A). To calculate the access time the setup time and address delay times are subtracted from 2 clocking periods. If the clock is 2 MHz the access time allowed by the Z80 is 795 ns (1000 ns – 145 ns – 60 ns), or for the Z80A operating with a 4MHz clock, 340 ns (500 ns – 110 ns – 50 ns).

Most modern memory devices require a maximum of 450 ns for ROM and 250 ns for the RAM to accomplish a read. If the Z80A microprocessor is used with a 4MHz clock, the microprocessor does not allow enough access time. It only allows the memory

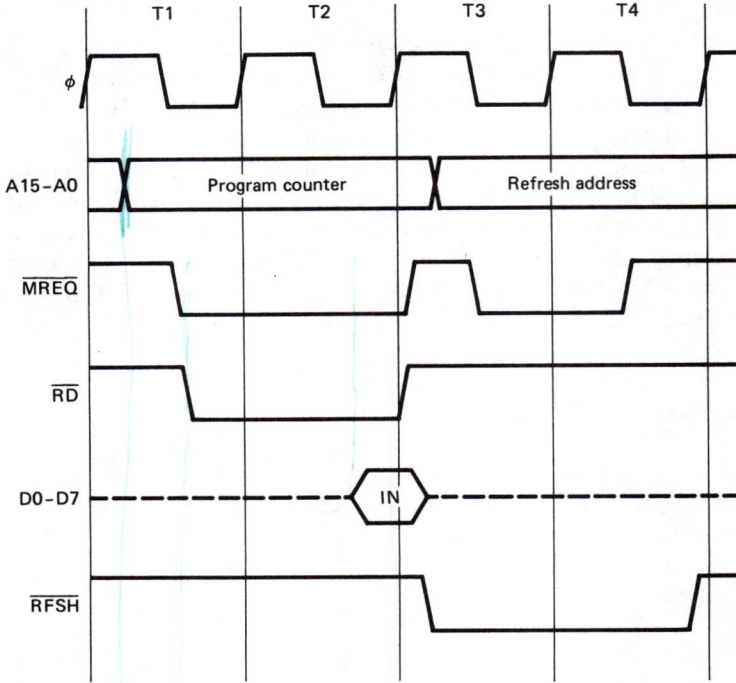

Figure 10–11 The opcode fetch (M1) timing for the Z80 microprocessor.

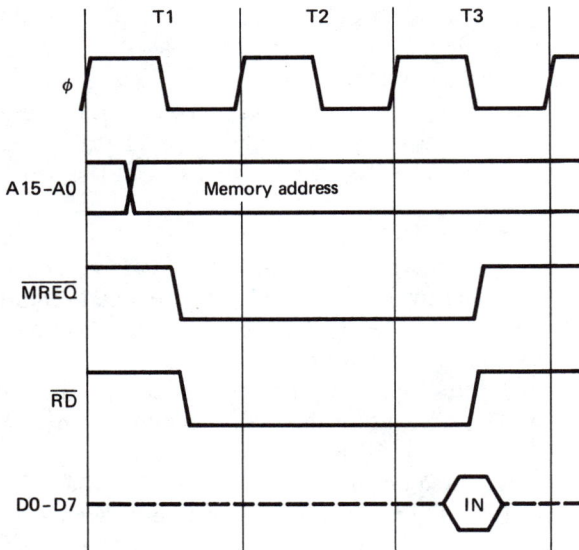

Figure 10–12 A memory read cycle in the Z80 system.

340 ns. Later, in the chapter on memory interface, a solution to this problem is presented. Again it is very important to remember the amount of access time allowed by the microprocessor so that a memory device can be chosen that will function properly.

Basic Write Timing

Figure 10-13 illustrates the basic write timing of the Z80 microprocessor. Notice how similar this timing is to the read timing presented in Figure 10-12. Writing timing differs from the read timing in only two respects, the microprocessor asserts the $\overline{WR}$ signal in place of the $\overline{RD}$ signal, and sends data out of the data bus connections instead of reading data from them. Data are written into a memory device or an I/O device when the $\overline{WR}$ signal returns to a logic 1 level (↑). Observe in the timing that this occurs after the middle of the T3 clocking cycle. There is actually slightly more time allowed the memory to do a write than to do a read.

Refresh Timing

Notice in Figure 10-11 that the last two clocking periods have nothing to do with a memory read. They are set aside so that any dynamic RAM in the system can be refreshed. During the last two clocking periods of the M1 (opcode fetch) machine cycle, the Z80 outputs the refresh counter on the least significant 7 address bits (A0—A6) so that a 16K (or larger) dynamic RAM can be easily refreshed.

  If you look at the last two clocking periods of M1 you notice that it looks like a regular memory read sequence, but in place of the $\overline{RD}$ signal the $\overline{RFSH}$ signal occurs.

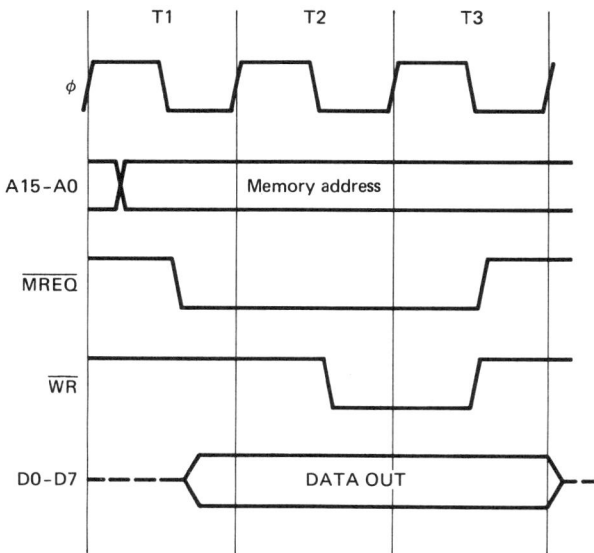

Figure 10–13 Write cycle timing for the Z80.

In the Chapter on memory interface, dynamic RAMS are connected to the Z80 and this refresh address and RFSH signal are used to refresh the memory during each M1 cycle.

10-5 SUMMARY

1. The Z80 microprocessor is packaged in a 40-pin dual-in-line package (DIP) that requires $+5.0$ V at $+-5$ percent tolerance to operate properly. The Z80 requires a maximum of 200 mA of current and the supply voltage may never exceed $+7.0$ V.

2. The fanout from the Z80 microprocessor is 10 MOS or CMOS devices. If TTL is connected, the fanout is four 74LSXXX or one 74XXX device.

3. The clock input to the Z80 is a standard TTL signal at 2 MHz for most applications.

4. The machine status signals include $\overline{\text{HALT}}$, $\overline{\text{M1}}$, $\overline{\text{RFSH}}$, $\overline{\text{MREQ}}$, and $\overline{\text{IORQ}}$. These signals indicate a halt instruction is executed (HALT), an opcode fetch (M1), a refresh operation (RFSH), a memory operation (MREQ), and an I/O operation (IORQ).

5. The microprocessor controls the operation of the memory through the $\overline{\text{RD}}$ and $\overline{\text{WR}}$ signals which are combined with $\overline{\text{MREQ}}$ to generate the memory signals $\overline{\text{MEMR}}$ and $\overline{\text{MEMW}}$, and the I/O through $\overline{\text{IOR}}$ and $\overline{\text{IOW}}$.

6. The Z80 communicates to the memory and I/O through an address bus (A0—A15), which contains 16 pins and addresses 64K bytes of memory and 256 bytes of I/O, and through the data bus (DO—D7), which contains 8 pins.

7. Whenever the Z80 is reset it begins executing software from memory location 0000H.

8. The interrupt structure of the Z80 is accessed via two input pins: $\overline{\text{NMI}}$ and $\overline{\text{INT}}$. The NMI input calls the subroutine that begins at memory location 0066H, and the INT pin functions in three modes: 0, 1, and 2.

9. The $\overline{\text{WAIT}}$ input is used to cause the Z80 to wait for slow memory.

10. Direct memory access (DMA) is accomplished through the $\overline{\text{BUSRQ}}$ input pin. If BUSRQ is placed at a logic 0 level, the address, data, and control buses to their high-impedance state. This allows an external controller to gain access to the memory and I/O.

11. The Z80 is buffered with 74LS244 bus-buffers for the address bus and with 74LS245 bidirectional bus-buffers for the data bus.

12. The Z80 actually allows two times for memory access. One, during M1, is shorter than the other, during a read operattion. During M1, the Z80 allows 795 ns of time for the memory to access data if it is operated with a 2 MHz clock.

13. Data written to memory or I/O are normally transferred to these devices on the zero-to-one transition of the $\overline{\text{WR}}$ signal.

14. During the second half of the M1 machine cycle, the address bus contains the

refresh address for dynamic RAM. In addition, the Z80 sends the system the $\overline{\text{RFSH}}$ signal to indicate that the address bus contains the refresh address.

10-6 GLOSSARY

Address bus   A set of connections used to address the memory and I/O.

Data bus   A microprocessor bus that is used to transfer data between the microprocessor, and the memory, and I/O.

DMA   Direct memory access is an I/O technique where an external device turns the Z80 off and gains access to its address, data, and control buses.

Interrupt   A hardware-initiated subroutine call.

IORQ   A signal that indicates the Z80 is executing an I/O instruction.

Memory access time   This is the time allowed to the memory device to present the data to the data bus. It is measured from when the microprocessor outputs the address until the point where the data is read from the data bus.

MREQ   The memory request signal indicates that the Z80 is accessing memory.

RD   The read signal is used to notify the memory or I/O that it is time to place data on the data bus for a read operation.

T-State   A T-state is one Z80 clocking period. T-states are used to explain the operation of the microprocessor.

Wait state   A special mode of operation where the microprocessor waits for slow memory or I/O. Wait states are inserted by grounding the WAIT pin.

WR   The write signal is used to notify the memory or I/O that it is time to remove the data from the data bus. Data are normally extracted at the zero-to-one transition of the WR signal.

QUESTIONS AND PROBLEMS

10-1. The Z80 microprocessor is packaged in a _____ -pin DIP.

10-2. A _____ μF capacitor is normally used to decouple the microprocessor from the system power supply.

10-3. How many 74LSXXX unit loads can be driven by the Z80 without buffers?

10-4. What limits the number of MOS loads connected to a Z80 output pin?

10-5. What is indicated by the $\overline{\text{HALT}}$ pin when it is a logic 0?

10-6. What new system signal is generated when the $\overline{\text{IORQ}}$ and $\overline{\text{RD}}$ signals are combined?

10-7. RFSH indicates that the Z80 has placed the _____ address on the address bus.

10-8. The M1 pin goes to a logic zero for what type of Z80 operation?

10-9. A memory read operation occurs when $\overline{\text{MREQ}}$ = _____ and $\overline{\text{RD}}$ = _____ .

10-10. A memory write operation occurs when $\overline{\text{MREQ}}$ = _____ and $\overline{\text{WR}}$ = _____ .

10-11. Whenever the Z80 is reset through the $\overline{\text{RESET}}$ pin, it begins executing software at memory location _____ .

10-12. If a one-to-zero transition occurs on the $\overline{\text{NMI}}$ input, the Z80 calls the subroutine that begins at memory location _____ .

10-13. An interrupt acknowledge is indicated by what?

10-14. How many modes of operation are available for the $\overline{\text{INT}}$ interrupt input?

10-15. If the $\overline{\text{WAIT}}$ pin is placed at a logic 0 level, the Z80 microprocessor will _____ .

10-16. DMA is an acronym for what?

10-17. Describe what occurs when the $\overline{\text{BUSRQ}}$ input is placed at a logic 0 level.

10-18. The $\overline{\text{BUSAK}}$ signal is placed at a logic 0 by the microprocessor in response to what event?

10-19. A T-state is equal to what?

10-20. How much time does the Z80 microprocessor allow the memory to access data if operated with a 2 MHz clock?

10-21. How much time does the Z80 microprocessor allow the memory to access data if operated with a 1.5 MHz clock?

10-22. During an M1 machine cycle, data are read from memory during T1 and T2. What occurs during T3 and T4?

chapter 11

Memory Interface

Before the Z80 microprocessor can execute a program or do anything, it must have memory. This chapter presents techniques that are used to interface memory to the microprocessor. The types of memory interfaced to the microprocessor include EPROM, SRAM (static RAM), and DRAM (dynamic RAM).

11-1 OBJECTIVES

Upon completion of this chapter, you will be able to:

1. Describe the purpose of the $\overline{\text{MEMR}}$ and $\overline{\text{MEMW}}$ control signals.
2. Explain how an area of the memory is decoded and design the decoder circuit.
3. Populate the memory with ROM and RAM memory devices at various locations.
4. Connect dynamic RAM to the Z80 microprocessor.
5. Describe bank selection as it applies to the microprocessor's memory.

11-2 MEMORY

Before a memory device can be connected to the microprocessor it must first of all be understood. The purpose of this section of the text is to introduce the three common forms of memory and explain their operation. Memory is normally found as ROM, static RAM (SRAM), and dynamic RAM (DRAM).

ROM Memory

Read-only memory (ROM) is available in many different forms: ROM is programmed at the factory for a mask setup fee; PROM is programmed by the user; EPROM is programmed and erased (if needed) by the user; and EEPROM or NOVRAM is programmed and erased electrically by the user.

ROM.   The read-only memory is used whenever a system is put into mass production. The reason is that the manufacturer charges a $3,000—$5,000 setup charge to design the last mask in the fabrication process. These ROMs are programmed at the factory as they are constructed. Because of the mask setup charge, the ROM is not used unless there will be at least 5,000—10,000 units sold.

PROM.   A PROM is a programmable read-only memory that is programmed in the field by the user. The PROM is constructed with tiny silicon oxide or nichrome fuses that are burned open in a device called a PROM programmer (burner). When a fuse is burned open, the bit position being programmed is usually set to a logic 0 level. The PROM is a TTL device that contains a small number of high-speed memory locations. For this reason, its use has fallen off in recent times except when high speed is an important consideration. Access times for PROMs are normally 25 ns.

EPROM.   The EPROM is an erasable, programmable read-only memory that can be programmed in the field and erased in the field. As with the PROM, the EPROM is programmed in a device called an EPROM programmer. The EPROM programmer applies a 25 V pulse to the memory location being programmed and traps charges in a special MOSFET transistor. This trapped charge remains there until it is erased by ultra-violet light, or until it bleeds off through the insulator. The manufacturers of this device claim it will retain a charge for over 20 years.

EEPROM or NOVRAM.   The EEPROM or electrically erasable, programmable read-only memory is a device that is programmed and erased in the system. No special programmer is needed for this type of read-only memory. Cost and reliability seem to at the present retard the application of this device. It lasts for only 10,000 programmings and costs considerably more than an equivalent EPROM.

The 27XX Family of EPROMs

Today, if an EPROM is required it is most often one of the 27XX series EPROM. This type of EPROM is a byte-wide memory device which contains memory that is 8-bits in width. Memory is listed by the manufacturer as so many words by so many bytes. For example, a 2K X 8 memory device is one that has 2K (2048) memory locations, each of which is 8 bits wide. The 27XX family has the following part numbers: 2704 (512 X 8), 2708 (1K X 8), 2716 (2K X 8), 2732 (4K X 8), 2764 (8K X 8), 27128 (16K X 8), 27256 (32K X 8), and the 27512 (64K X 8).

TMS2732A. . . JL Package
(top view)

A7	1		24	V$_{CC}$
A6	2		23	A8
A5	3		22	A9
A4	4		21	A11
A3	5		20	$\overline{G}$/V$_{PP}$
A2	6		19	A10
A1	7		18	$\overline{E}$
A0	8		17	Q8
Q1	9		16	Q7
Q2	10		15	Q6
Q3	11		14	Q5
GND	12		13	Q4

Pin nomenclature	
A0–A11	Addresses
$\overline{E}$	Chip enable
$\overline{G}$/V$_{PP}$	Output enable/+21 V
Q1–Q8	Outputs
V$_{CC}$	+5 V power supply

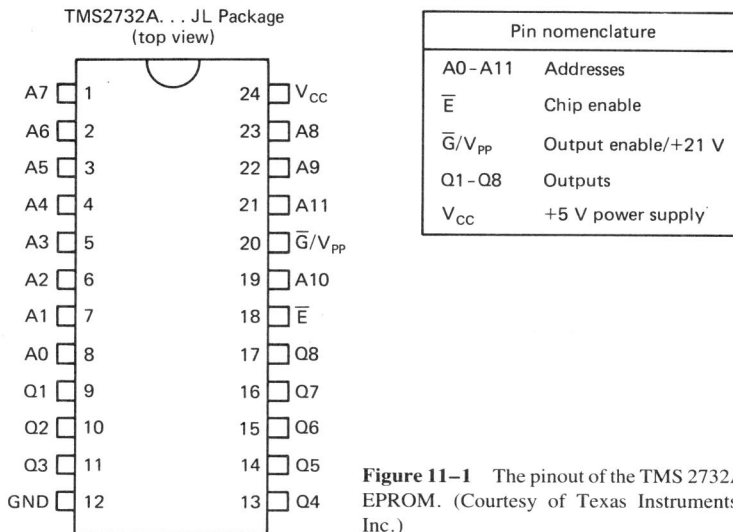

Figure 11–1   The pinout of the TMS 2732A EPROM. (Courtesy of Texas Instruments, Inc.)

Figure 11-1 depicts the pinout of the 2732 (4K X 8) EPROM. Notice that this device has 12 address input connections because it takes 12 pins to address 4K bytes of memory. Also notice that it has 8 data output connects so that a byte of data can be read at a time.

Controlling the EPROM during a read operation is a rather simple task. The EPROM has two control inputs: $\overline{G}$ (output enable), which is used to connect the output of the memory to the data bus, and $\overline{E}$ (chip enable), which is used to enable the memory device. For data to appear at the outputs both the $\overline{E}$ and $\overline{G}$ connections must be a logic 0, otherwise the output pins remain at their high-impedance state.

To read information from an EPROM, the address of the location is applied to the address pins, the $\overline{G}$ pin is grounded, and then the $\overline{G}$ pin is grounded (see the timing diagram of the 2732 in Figure 11-2). Within 450 ns or less after the address is applied, for standard 2732 EPROMs, the data appear at the output pins provided $\overline{E}$ and $\overline{G}$ are also grounded.

Static RAM

Figure 11-3 illustrates the pinout of the TMS4016 (6116 is also a common part number) static RAM. This device has 2048 bytes of memory (2K X 8) and is very common. Notice it comes in a 24-pin integrated circuit as did the 2732 EPROM.

The TMS4016 has 11 address pins (A0—A10) and 8 data input/output connects. It is controlled by three pins: $\overline{G}$, $\overline{W}$, and $\overline{S}$. The $\overline{S}$ (select) pin is used to select the memory device for a particular area of the memory, the $\overline{G}$ (gate or output enable) pin is used to enable the output buffers during a read operation, and the $\overline{W}$ (write) is used to write data into the read/write memory.

Read cycle timing

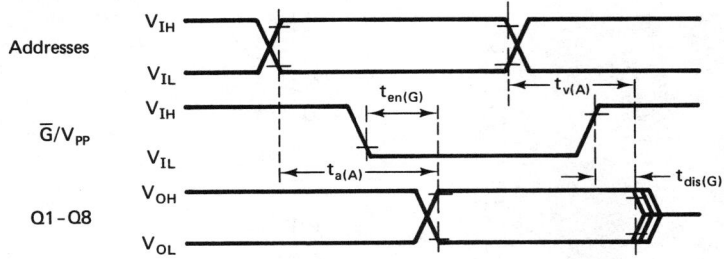

Standby mode

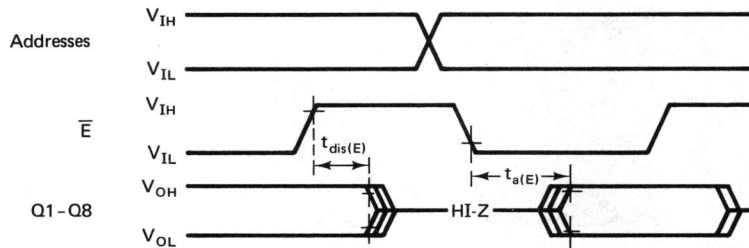

Program cycle timing

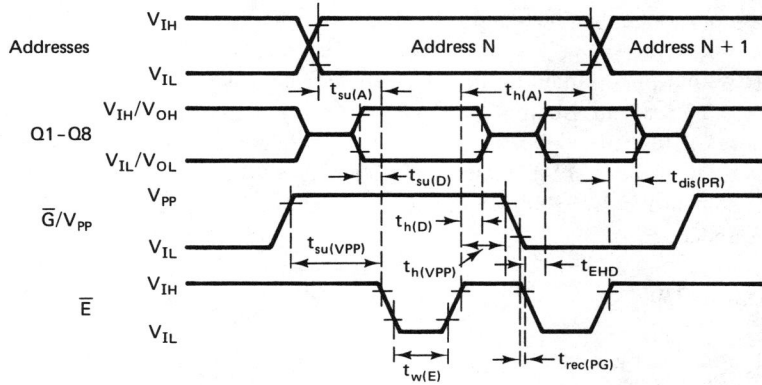

Timing measurement reference levels: Inputs 0.8 V and 2 V
Outputs 0.8 V and 2 V

Figure 11–2 The timing diagrams for the 2732A EPROM. (Courtesy of Texas Instruments, Inc.)

TMS4016 24-Pin plastic
dual-in-line package
(top view)

A7	1	24	V_{CC}
A6	2	23	A8
A5	3	22	A9
A4	4	21	$\overline{W}$
A3	5	20	$\overline{G}$
A2	6	19	A10
A1	7	18	$\overline{S}$
A0	8	17	DQ8
DQ1	9	16	DQ7
DQ2	10	15	DQ6
DQ3	11	14	DQ5
V_{SS}	12	13	DQ4

Pin nomenclature	
A0–A10	Addresses
DQ1–DQ8	Data in/data out
$\overline{S}$	Chip select
$\overline{G}$	Output enable
$\overline{W}$	Write enable
V_{SS}	Ground
V_{CC}	+5 V supply

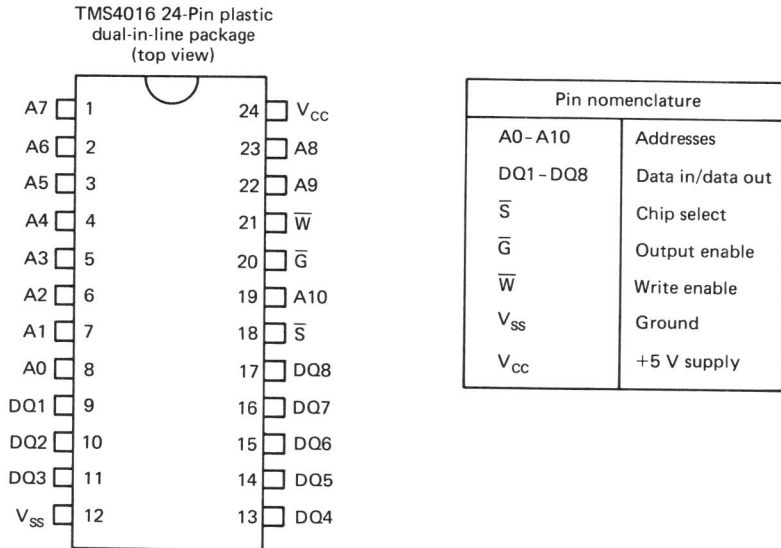

Figure 11–3 The pinout of the TMS4016 2kx8 SRAM. (Courtesy of Texas Instruments, Inc.)

Figure 11-4 illustrates the timing diagram for the TMS4016. Here the address is applied, then $\overline{S}$ is grounded, and either a $\overline{G}$ is applied to read data or a $\overline{W}$ is applied to write the data. Access times for this memory device are 250 ns. This is short enough to allow any version of the Z80 microprocessor to be interfaced without any special wait states.

Dynamic RAM

Dynamic RAM devices are memory that retain data for a small amount of time (typically 2—4 ms). After this short period of time the data in the memory must be read and rewritten (refreshed). Refreshing is accomplished by the Z80 microprocessor after each opcode fetch cycle. Luckily, when the DRAM (dynamic RAM) is refreshed many internal locations are refreshed together.

Figure 11-5 illustrates the pinout of the TMS4116 DRAM. This is a 16K X 1 memory device that is packaged in an 18-pin integrated circuit. The DRAM has 7 address inputs that are used to access any of the 16K memory locations. How can 7 address pins be used to address 16K of memory? This is accomplished by multiplexing the address into these 7 pins one half at a time. The column address (A0—A6) is entered in coincidence

(a)

(b)

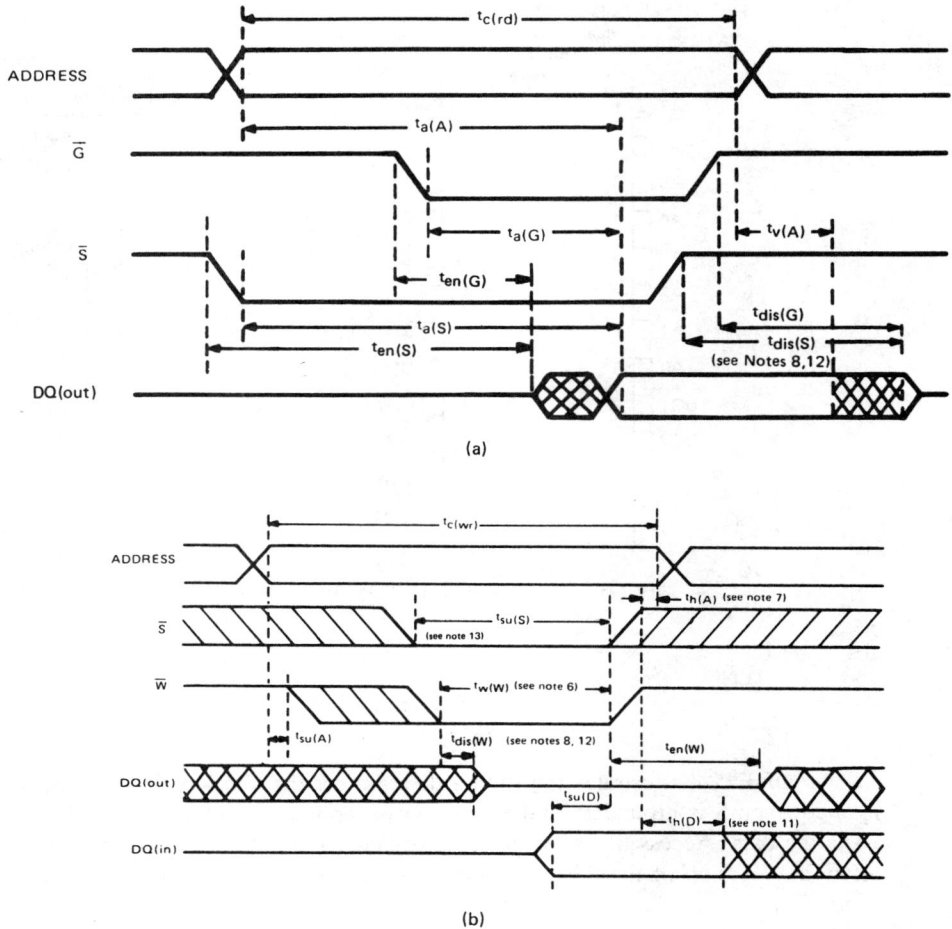

Figure 11–4 (a) Read cycle timing for the TMS4016 and (b) write cycle timing. (Courtesy of Texas Instruments, Inc.)

with the column address strobe ($\overline{\text{CAS}}$), and the row address (A7—A13) is entered in coincidence with the row address strobe ($\overline{\text{RAS}}$). This operation is illustrated in the timing diagram presented in Figure 11-6.

To refresh the TMS4116, the $\overline{\text{RAS}}$ signal is applied along with the refresh address. The refresh address is a 7-bit address that is used to refresh 128 memory locations at one time. With the TMS4116, 128 refresh cycles are required in each 2 ms increment of time to completely refresh the memory. Because the Z80 outputs the refresh address and a $\overline{\text{RFSH}}$ signal, refreshing DRAM is a rather simple task for the Z80.

16-Pin plastic
dual-in-line package
(top view)

V_{BB}	1	16	V_{SS}
D	2	15	$\overline{CAS}$
$\overline{W}$	3	14	Q
$\overline{RAS}$	4	13	A6
A0	5	12	A3
A2	6	11	A4
A1	7	10	A5
V_{DD}	8	9	V_{CC}

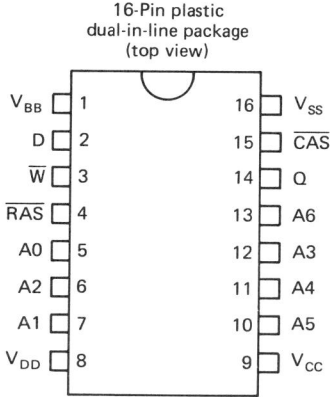

Pin nomenclature				
A0 – A6	Address inputs		$\overline{W}$	Write enable
$\overline{CAS}$	Column address strobe		V_{BB}	−5 V power supply
D	Data input		V_{CC}	+5 V power supply
Q	Data output		V_{DD}	+12 V power supply
$\overline{RAS}$	Row address strobe		V_{SS}	0 V ground

Figure 11–5   The pinout of the TMS4116 DRAM. (Courtesy of Texas Instruments, Inc.)

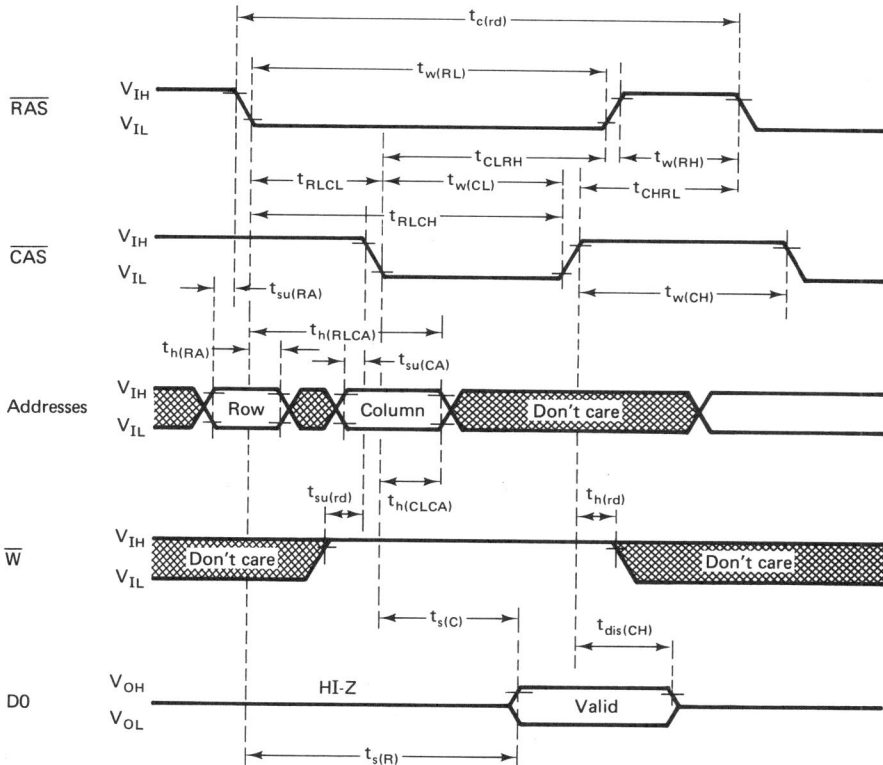

Figure 11–6   Read cycle timing for the 4116. (Courtesy of Texas Instruments, Inc.)

11-3 DECODING THE MEMORY

In order to place a memory device in the memory at a unique location, the memory address, as it comes from the Z80, must be decoded. This is most often accomplished with a medium-scale TTL decoder. This text will use the 74LS138 3-to-8 line decoder because of its extreme popularity in the industry. It also presents the 74LS139, which also finds fairly widespread application.

The Z80 as Seen by the Memory

Before decoders are discussed, the Z80, from the memory's viewpoint, must be discussed. Figure 11-7 illustrates how the Z80 microprocessor appears to the memory. Notice that only the address, data, and some of the control pins are illustrated. The reason for this is that the memory only uses these pins. The remaining Z80 pins are used for other than memory purposes. As far as the memory is concerned, the Z80 is a 16-bit address bus (A0—A15), an 8-Bit data bus (D0—D7), and the $\overline{\text{MEMR}}$ and $\overline{\text{MEMW}}$ control signals. The $\overline{\text{RFSH}}$ signal is only used for dynamic RAM interface and is presented with dynamic RAM in Section 11-5. Likewise the $\overline{\text{WAIT}}$ input is only used if the memory is very slow, and slow memory is discussed in Section 11-4 on memory systems.

Decoding the Address

Before any type of memory can be connected to the Z80, the memory address must be decoded to select the memory. Often the 74LS138 or 74LS139 is used to accomplish address decoding.

The 74LS138 3-to-8 line decoder.   Figure 11-8 illustrates the pinout of the Z80 and truth-table of the 74LS138 3-to-8 line decoder. This device has 6 input connections and 8 outputs. Three of the inputs (A, B, and C) are used to select one of the 8 outputs, and the other three are used to enable the decoder. If the decoder is not enabled, all the output connections are a logic 1, and if the decoder is enabled, the output addressed by A, B, and C is a logic 0. The enable inputs ($\overline{\text{G2A}}$, $\overline{\text{G2B}}$, and G1) must all be active to cause an output to become a logic 0. This means that $\overline{\text{G2A}}$ and $\overline{\text{G2B}}$ must be a logic 0 and G1 must be a logic 1.

The 74LS139 dual 2-to-4 line decoder.   This circuit is similar to the 74LS138 except that it is a dual 2-to-4 line decoder. If the pinout, block diagram, and truth-table of Figure 11-9 are viewed it is noticed that this device is actually two separate components in one package. Each half had 2 address inputs (A and B) that select which of the 4 outputs becomes a logic 0, and an $\overline{\text{G}}$ input that must be true (0) for any of the outputs to become a logic 0. The 74LS139 is not as popular as the 74LS138, but it still finds application.

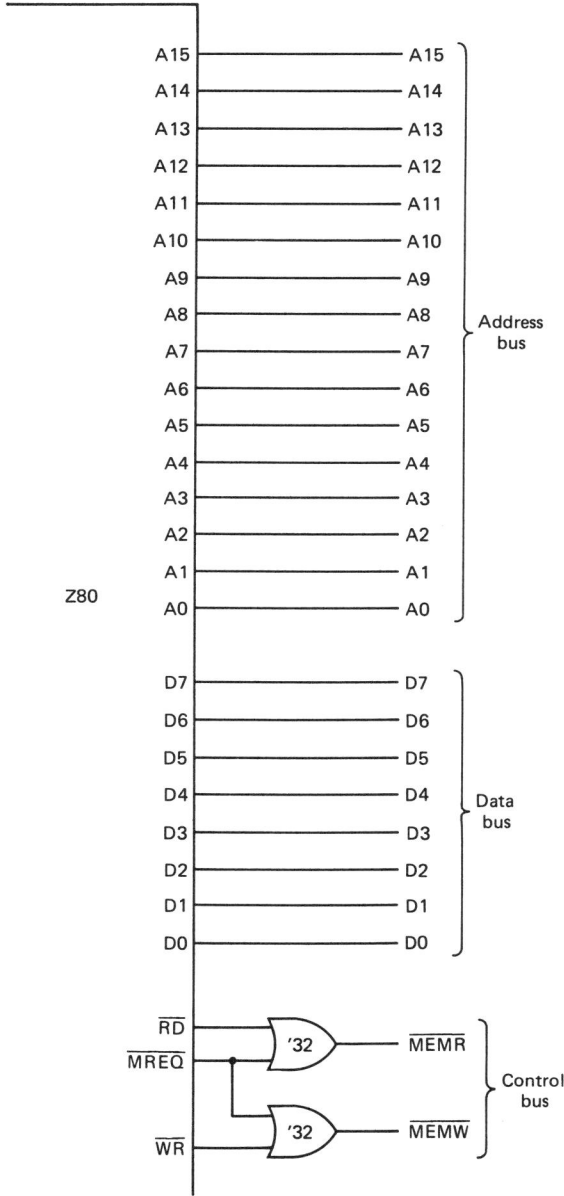

Figure 11–7 The Z80 as seen by the system memory components.

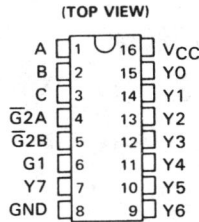

(TOP VIEW)

```
         ┌──┬──┬──┐
    A  ┤1  U  16├ Vcc
    B  ┤2     15├ Y0
    C  ┤3     14├ Y1
  G2A  ┤4     13├ Y2
  G2B  ┤5     12├ Y3
   G1  ┤6     11├ Y4
   Y7  ┤7     10├ Y5
  GND  ┤8      9├ Y6
         └─────────┘
```

(a)

FUNCTION TABLE

ENABLE INPUTS		SELECT INPUTS			OUTPUTS							
G1	G2*	C	B	A	Y0	Y1	Y2	Y3	Y4	Y5	Y6	Y7
X	H	X	X	X	H	H	H	H	H	H	H	H
L	X	X	X	X	H	H	H	H	H	H	H	H
H	L	L	L	L	L	H·	H	H	H	H	H	H
H	L	L	L	H	H	L	H	H	H	H	H	H
H	L	L	H	L	H	H	L	H	H	H	H	H
H	L	L	H	H	H	H	H	L	H	H	H	H
H	L	H	L	L	H	H	H	H	L	H	H	H
H	L	H	L	H	H	H	H	H	H	L	H	H
H	L	H	H	L	H	H	H	H	H	H	L	H
H	L	H	H	H	H	H	H	H	H	H	H	L

*$\overline{G2} = \overline{G2A} + \overline{G2B}$

(b)

Figure 11–8 (a) The pinout and (b) function table of the 74LS138 3-to-8 line decoder. (Courtesy of Texas Instruments, Inc.)

Using the 74LS138 to decode an address.   Suppose that you have purchased a 2732 EPROM and you wish to have it function at memory locations 1000H—1FFFH, a 4K byte segment of the 64K memory. How is this accomplished?

The first step is to write the first memory location on a piece of paper in binary as illustrated in Example 11-1. Here the number is written so that it appears in groups of 4 (binary-coded hexadecimal). Next the least significant 12 address bits are crossed out because they are decoded by the memory component. (The 2732 has 12 address inputs.) Example 11-2 illustrates this. What remains are 4 address connects (A15—A12). These address connections are unique to this section of the memory.

Example 11-1

0 0 0 1   0 0 0 0   0 0 0 0   0 0 0 0

Example 11-2

0 0 0 1   X X X X   X X X X   X X X X

How are A15—A12 connected to the decoder? This is accomplished by connecting the remaining bits to the inputs of the decoder. Example 11-3 illustrates the recommended connection to the 74LS138.

(TOP VIEW)

1Ḡ	1	16	V_CC
1A	2	15	2Ḡ
1B	3	14	2A
1Y0	4	13	2B
1Y1	5	12	2Y0
1Y2	6	11	2Y1
1Y3	7	10	2Y2
GND	8	9	2Y3

(a)

FUNCTION TABLE

INPUTS		OUTPUTS			
ENABLE	SELECT				
Ḡ	B	A	Y0	Y1	Y2	Y3
H	X	X	H	H	H	H
L	L	L	L	H	H	H
L	L	H	H	L	H	H
L	H	L	H	H	L	H
L	H	H	H	H	H	L

(b)

(c)

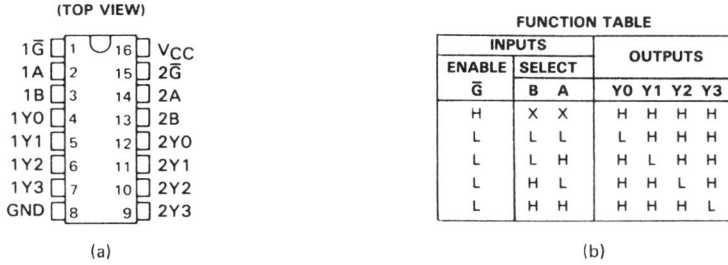

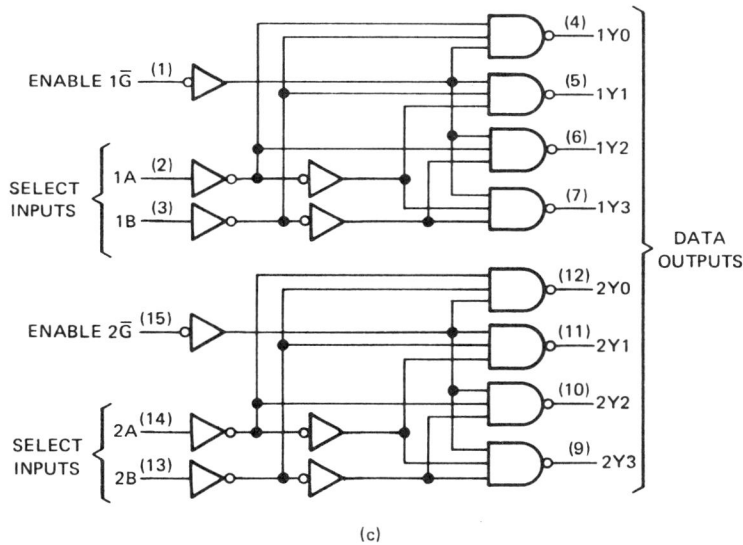

Figure 11–9   The (a) pinout, (b) function table, and (c) block diagram of the 74LS139 dual 2-to-4 line decoder. (Courtesy of Texas Instruments, Inc.)

Example 11-3

```
G2A  C B A
 0   0 0 1    X X X X    X X X X    X X X X
```

Notice in this example that $\overline{G2A}$ is connected to address bit A15, C to A14, B to A13, and A to A12. This means that if A15 is a logic zero the 74LS138 is enabled. The C, B, and A inputs select output 1. The schematic of this connection is illustrated in Figure 11-10. Only one of the 8 outputs (output 1) is connected to anything.

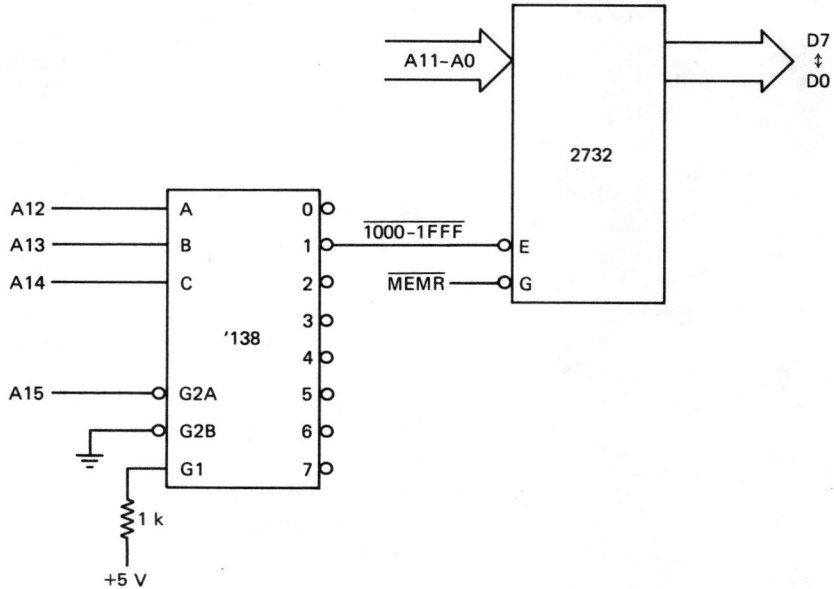

Figure 11–10   A single 2732 interfaced to the Z80 microprocessor using a 74LS138 to decode the memory location.

Example 32K X 8 Memory System

Figure 11-11 illustrates a 32K X 8 memory system that uses eight 2732 EPROMs. Here a single 74LS138 is used to select the eight EPROMs. Also notice that the A15 connection is made to the G1 input of the 74LS138. The memory is only selected when A15 is a logic 1 or for memory locations 8000H—FFFFH. By placing the A15 signal on G2A or G2B, the memory is decoded at locations 0000H—7FFFH.

11-4 MEMORY SYSTEMS

This section of the text concentrates on developing complete memory systems that consist of both ROM and RAM. This allows for a thorough discussion of decoding and also selecting different size memory components.

Example System 1

Suppose that it is desired to populate a memory with 8K of EPROM beginning at memory location 0000H and 2K of RAM beginning at memory location 6000H. The memory

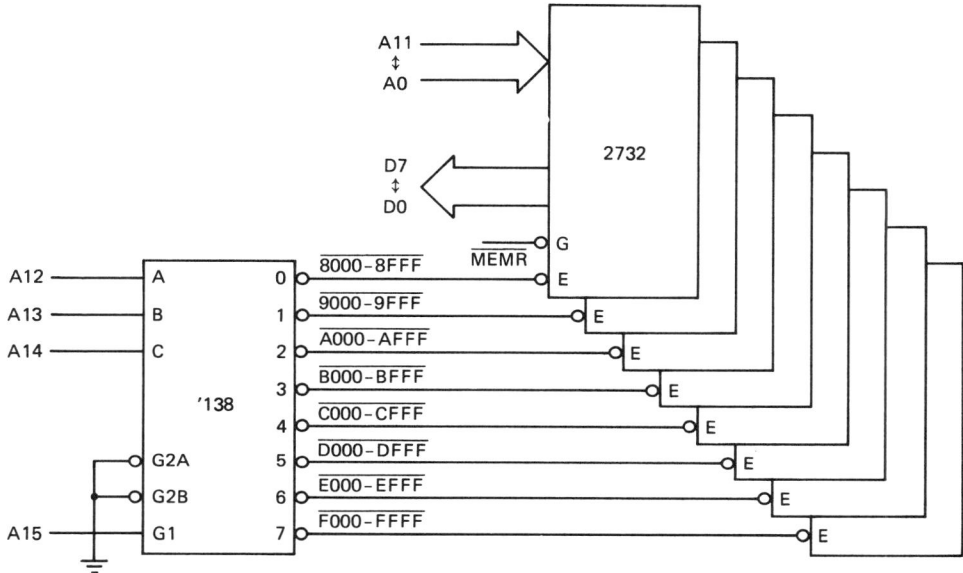

Figure 11–11   An array of eight 2732 EPROMs interfaced to the Z80 microprocessor through a 74LS138 decoder.

system is for a dedicated application that will never have additional memory added at a future date.

The first step in interfacing memory for this example is to note that no additional memory will ever be added to the system. This simplifies the task of interfacing, because the memory address does not need to be completely decoded. In fact, the output of the decoder need only select memory for location 0000H, 1000H, and 6000H. Location 0000H—0FFFH is on the first EPROM, 1000H—1FFFH is on the second EPROM, and location 6000H—67FFH is on the RAM.

Figure 11-12 illustrates the decoder and memory devices as they are connected to function for this example. Notice that no special treatment is given to the RAM even though it only contains half as much memory as the EPROM device. How can this circuit function? It is basically the same decoder presented in the last section (see Figure 11-11) that selects 4K blocks of the memory except that output 6 is connected to a RAM that has 2K of memory.

The RAM is enable for memory location 6000H—6FFFH even though it only contains half that much memory. What happens in a system? Nothing really happens except that the 2K RAM overlays a 4K block of memory. If data are written to memory location 6000H they also will appear to be written at location 6800H. You might say that the memory has a shadow from location 6800H—6FFFH. Although data appear to be in this part of the memory, they are actually the same data as in 6000H—67FFH. No problem occurs because of this situation because no data would be stored in the overlaid

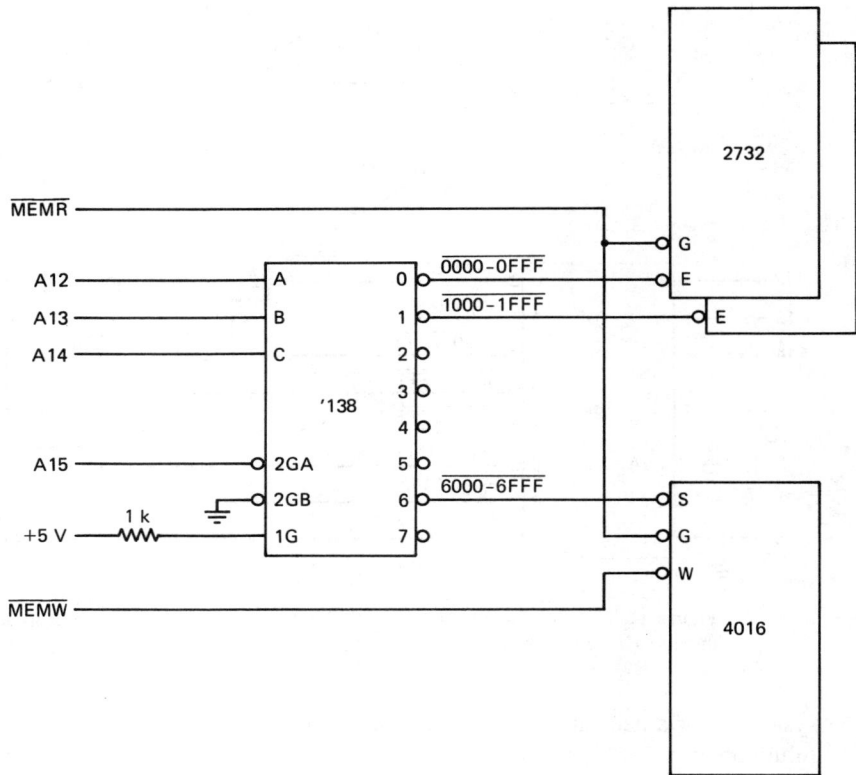

Figure 11–12 The selection logic for a memory system that consists of 2kx8 SRAM and 8kx8 EPROM.

or shadowed area of the memory. The person writing the software would be told the ROM is at location 0000H—1FFFH and the RAM is at location 6000H—67FFH.

Example System 2

Figure 11-13 illustrates a larger memory system that contains 16K of EPROM (locations 0000H—3FFFH) and 4K of RAM (locations C000H—CFFFH). Here a different tack is taken in decoding the memory addresses. The 74LS139 decoder is used so that one-half is used to decode the EPROM, and the other half is used to decode the RAM.

Example System 3

This third example (see Figure 11-14) shows a RAM card that contains 32K bytes of RAM stored on 16 different TMS4016 RAMs. Here two decoders, 74LS138s, are used

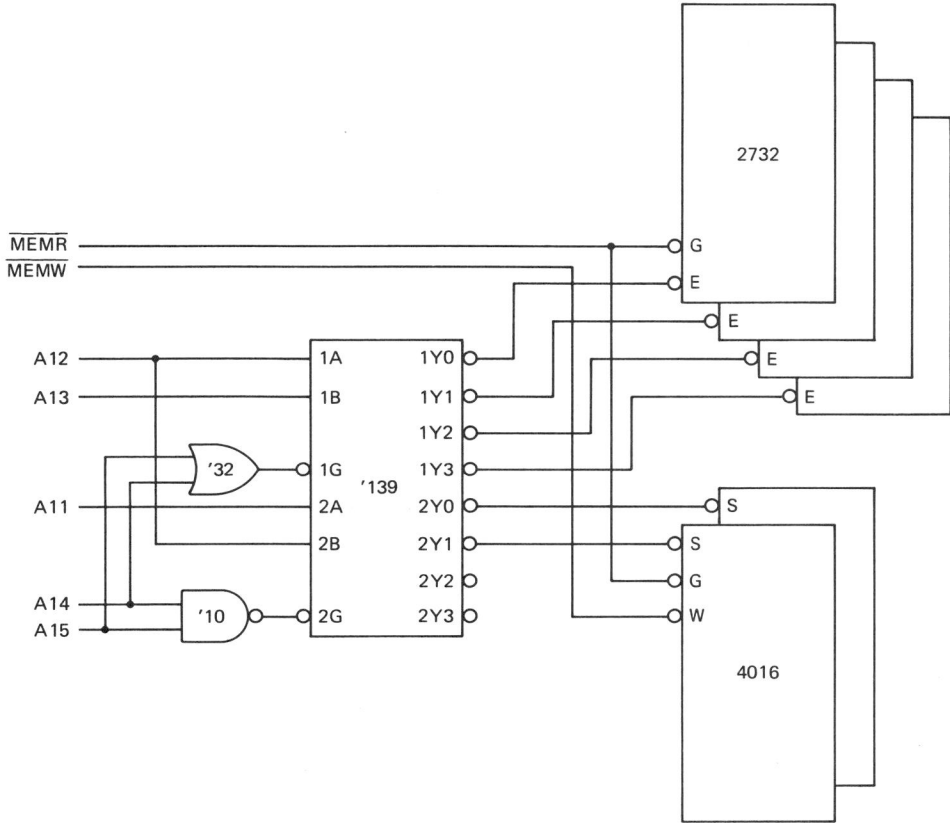

Figure 11–13 The selection logic for a memory system that contains a 16kx8 EPROM and a 4kx8 SRAM.

to select the 16 RAMs. The addresses that have been chosen for this example problem begin at location 8000H and extend to location FFFFH—the entire top half of the memory.

Notice in this example that the memory is buffered because it exceeds the loading rules discussed in Chapter 10. The buffers are placed on each input to this board so that the microprocessor need not be buffered. In practice, as in this illustration, each input connection from the Z80 has been buffered to represent one 74LSXXX TTL unit load.

Slow Memory

Some memory components (EPROMs) require 450 ns of time to access the data. If they are used with the Z80 microprocessor, no problem exists. If they are used with the Z80A running with a 4MHz crystal, then a problem does exist. The Z80A operating with a

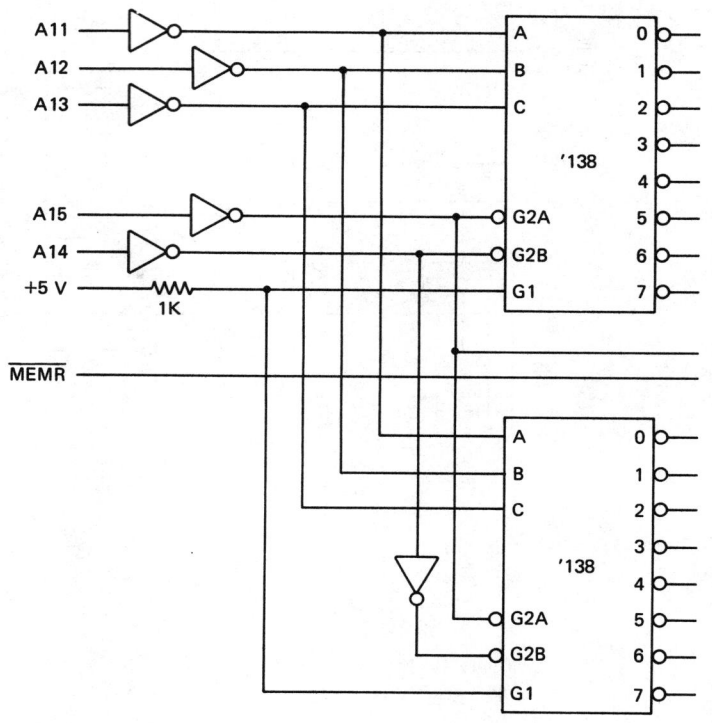

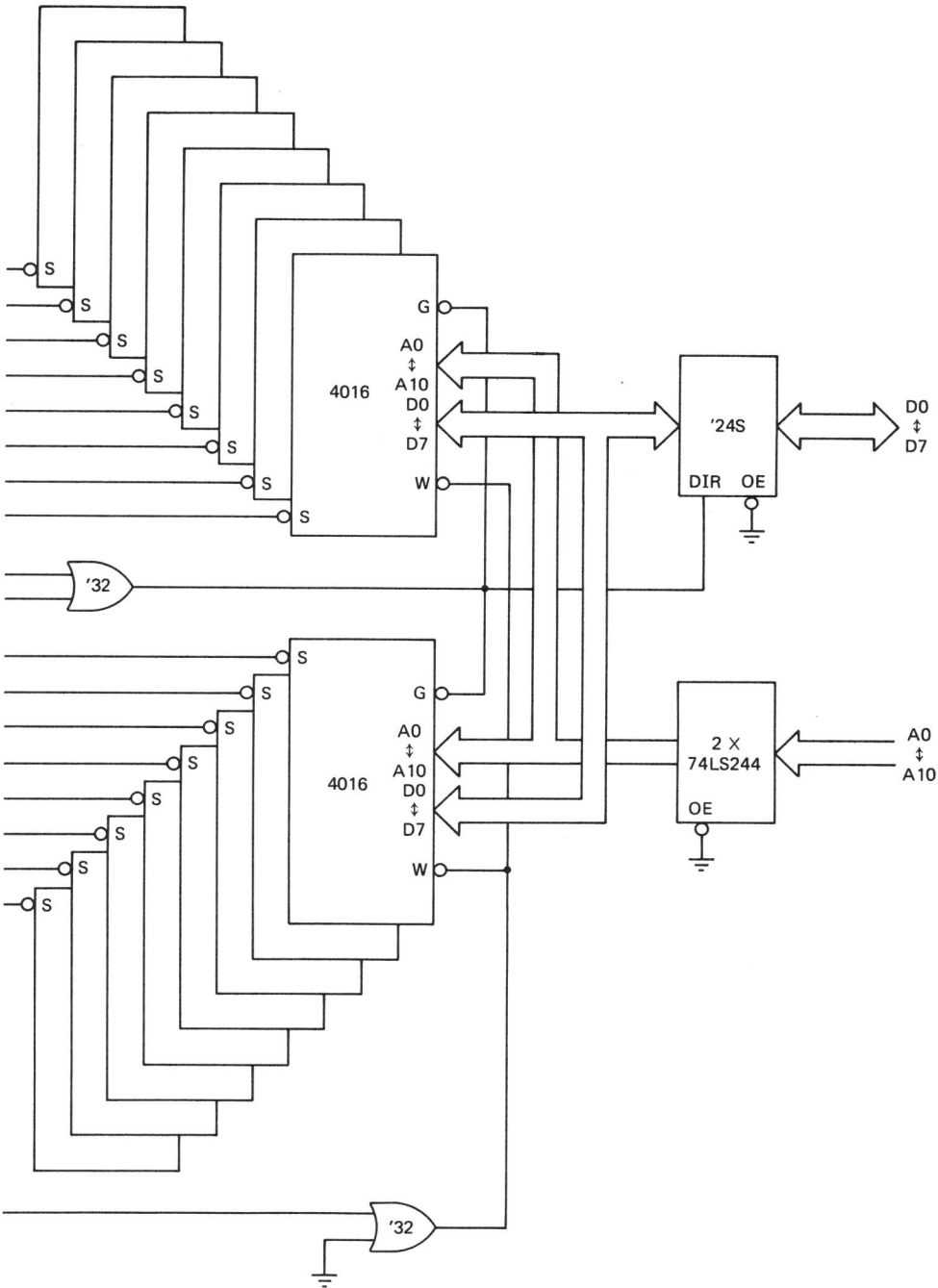

Figure 11–14 A 32kx8 SRAM memory array that is fully buffered.

4MHz crystal allows the memory less than 450 ns of time to access the data. If a 450 ns EPROM is connected, then the data will never be presented to the microprocessor in time.

To circumvent the problem of the slow memory device, Zilog has added a $\overline{\text{WAIT}}$ pin to the Z80. If $\overline{\text{WAIT}}$ is a logic zero, the microprocessor waits for the slow memory. By controlling the $\overline{\text{WAIT}}$ pin, it is possible to extend the access time by multiples of the system clock. If one wait state is inserted, then the access time is stretched by one clocking period.

The $\overline{\text{WAIT}}$ input is tested by the Z80 at the one-to-zero transition of the clock. If $\overline{\text{WAIT}}$ is a logic zero at this edge in T2 the next state is Tw (wait state) instead of T3. This delays the point at which data are read from the data bus increasing the access time allowed the memory.

The next sample point is during Tw where $\overline{\text{WAIT}}$ is again tested to determine if an additional Tw is entered or T3. If, during Tw, $\overline{\text{WAIT}}$ is a logic one then the next state is T3. Figure 11-15 illustrates a simple circuit used to insert one Tw and the waveform

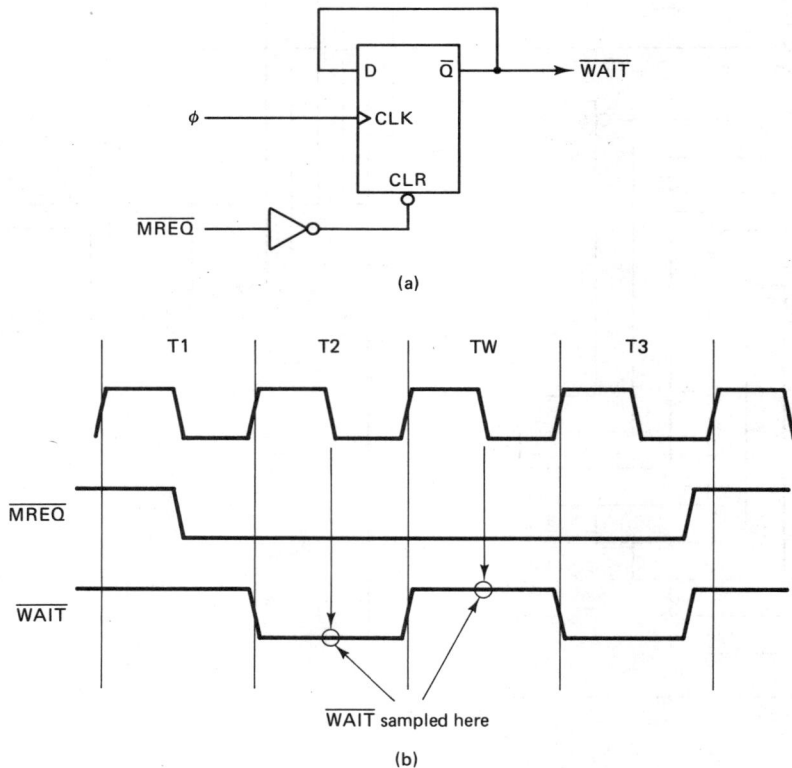

Figure 11–15 Wait state generation. (a) The circuit used to insert one wait state and (b) the timing generated by the circuit.

obtained at $\overline{\text{WAIT}}$. Here a simple D-type flip-flop is connected so that it toggles on the zero-to-one transition of the clock whenever $\overline{\text{MREQ}}$ is a logic zero. This effectively inserts one wait state into the timing diagram.

11-5 DYNAMIC RAM

Dynamic RAM (DRAM) is a little more complicated to interface to the Z80 than static RAM. The reason is that dynamic RAM must be periodically refreshed, and this requires some additional circuitry. DRAM also requires a multiplexer because it has multiplexed input pins. Luckily the Z80 provides the refresh address and a signal called $\overline{\text{RFSH}}$ or additional circuitry would be required to interface the DRAM.

Connecting the Address Connections to the DRAM

As mentioned at the start of this chapter, the 4116 DRAM has 7 address inputs that are used to accept the 14 address bits and also the refresh address. In order to pass this information to the 4116 at the proper time, an address multiplexer is attached to the 7 address pins as illustrated in Figure 11-16.

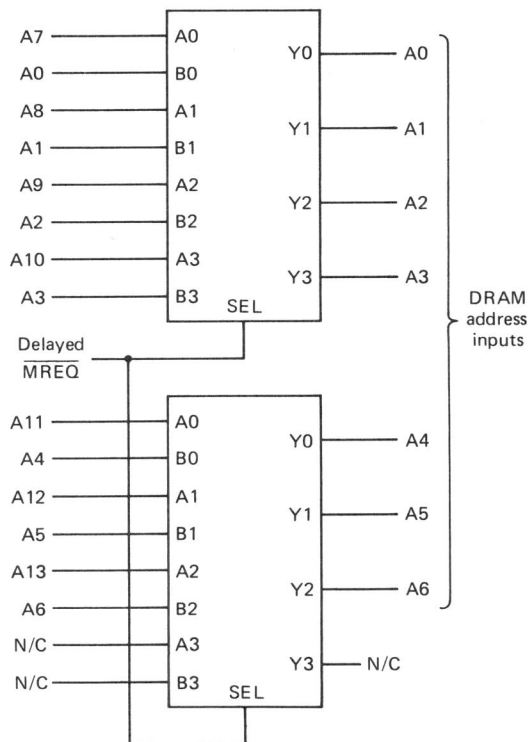

Figure 11–16   Multiplexing the address bus for the multiplexed address inputs of a DRAM.

This Figure shows how two 74157 quad 2 line-to-1 line multiplexers can be used to pass the proper address bits through to the DRAM. The 74157 connects the A input to the output whenever the SEL pin is at a logic zero level and the B inputs whenever the SEL pin is a logic one. Here the B inputs are wired to address bits (A0—A6) and the A inputs to (A7—A13). The MREQ signal is used, after being delayed, to select A0—A6 when high, and A7—A13 when low. The refresh address is passed through from address bits A0—A6 during a refresh cycle.

The 32K X 8 DRAM Memory

Figure 11-17 illustrates the complete DRAM system for 32K X 8 bytes of memory. Here sixteen 4116 memory devices are set up in an array so that a byte of data is written to each location. The memory is activated each time that a MREQ signal occurs or for a RFSH.

Figure 11-18 illustrates the timing for this DRAM memory array so that it may be understood. Notice how MREQ causes a cycle to begin. The MREQ signal generates the RAS signal which clocks the row address into the memory. Shortly after this, the MREQ signal reaches the 74157 multiplexers and connects the address bits A7—A13 to the memory device and the CAS signal occurs to strobe this address into the DRAM column address latches.

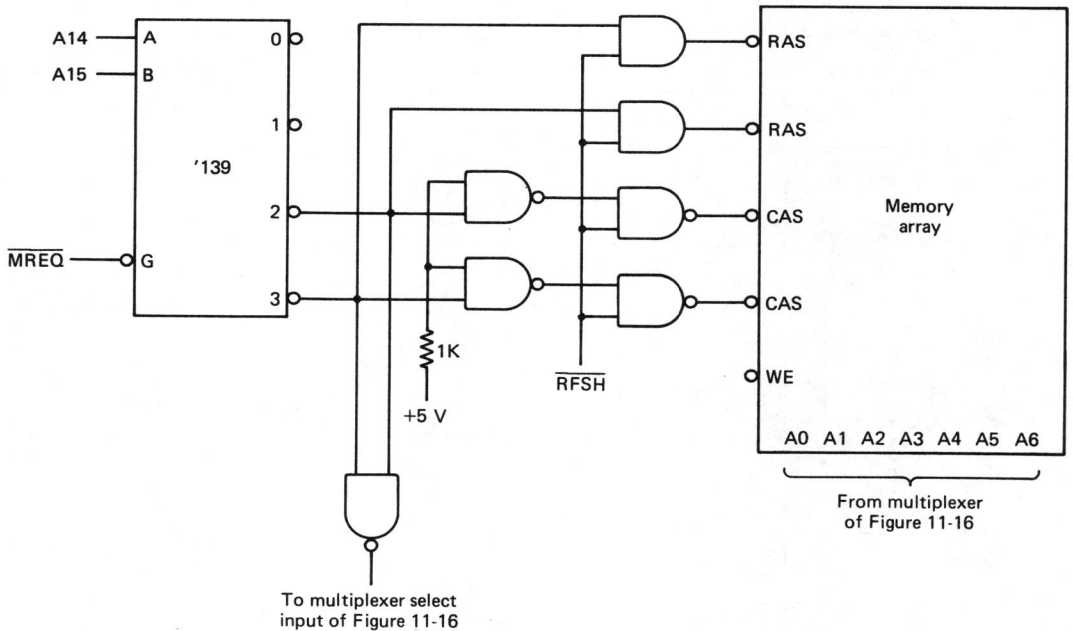

Figure 11–17 A 32kx8 DRAM memory.

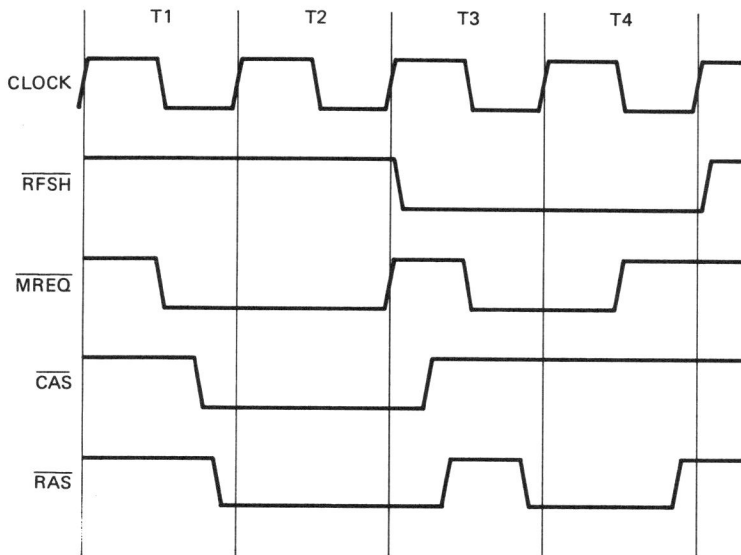

Figure 11–18   The timing for the DRAM memory of Figure 11–17.

Refreshing the memory.   When the $\overline{RFSH}$ signal becomes a logic zero, it grounds $\overline{RAS}$ of both banks causing the DRAM to refresh a row (128 bits) of memory. The DRAM refreshes a new row everytime that the Z80 fetches an opcode, because it sends out a new refresh address. This means that the entire DRAM is refreshed every 128 instructions. One problem can occur for this type of refresh. If the HALT instruction is executed, no additional opcode fetches occur and hence no more refreshes. If DRAM is connected to the Z80 the HALT instruction may not be used.

Selection.   A 74LS139 decoder is used to steer the $\overline{CAS}$ signal to the appropriate DRAM bank of the memory for a read or write operation. The $\overline{CAS}$ signal not only strobes the column address into the column address latch, it also selects the DRAM. Here DRAM bank 0 is selected for memory locations 8000H—BFFFH, and DRAM bank 1 is selected for memory locations C000H—FFFFH.

11-6 SUMMARY

1. Many forms of memory are connected to the microprocessor with ROM, static RAM, and dynamic RAM being the most common forms.
2. ROM memory is available in many forms: factory programmed ROM, field programmable PROM, programmable and erasable EPROM, and the EEPROM or NOVRAM which is programmable and erasable electrically.

3. All memory devices have address inputs that are used to select a memory location; data inputs and/or outputs that are used to transfer the data between the memory and microprocessor; and control inputs that control the reading and writing of data to the memory and also selection.

4. Dynamic RAM (DRAM) is a type of RAM that requires that the contents of the memory are periodically refreshed. A refresh operation consists of reading the data from the memory and rewriting it. DRAMs typically refresh many memory locations at a time.

5. Memory devices must be enabled to function at a particular area of memory. This is accomplished by decoding the memory address to produce a signal that enables the memory, applying the RD signal to enable the outputs, and applying the WR signal to cause a write.

6. The 74LS138 and 74LS139 are two very popular address decoders. The 74LS138 is a 3-to-8 line decoder and the 74LS139 is a dual 2-to-4 line decoder.

7. The WAIT pin is used to cause the Z80 to pause and wait for slower memory to access data. In most cases, if waits are needed, only one is required. The WAIT input is sample on the one-to-zero transition of the clock during T2 and Tw.

8. The address inputs of a dynamic RAM are multiplexed to save pins on the integrated circuit. The RAS signal is used to strobe the row address into the DRAM, and the CAS signal strobes the column address into the DRAM.

9. To refresh a DRAM, the refresh address is applied to the address inputs, and the RAS signal is activated. To read or write to a DRAM, the row and column addresses are entered through the address pins by applying the RAS and CAS signals. CAS also performs the chip select function on the DRAM.

10. DRAM memory is typically selected by steering the CAS signal to the appropriate bank of memory.

11-7 GLOSSARY

Address multiplexer   A device that takes the memory address and passes one half or the other to the address pins of the DRAM.

Chip enable   An input to an EPROM that enables or allows the EPROM to read data provided the OE input is also active.

Column address strobe (CAS)   An input to a DRAM that strobes the column address into the column address latch and also serves as the chip selection input.

Decoder   A device that converts one input code to another. In the case of memory address decoders, it converts the address to a code that selects a memory device.

Dynamic RAM (DRAM)   A memory component that allows data to be read or written and retains data for about 2 ms.

EPROM   Erasable programmable read-only memory which is erased by exposing it to a high-intensity ultra-violet light.

EEPROM   Electrically erasable programmable read-only memory is a device that is both programmable and erasable with an electrical signal.

Output enable   An input to an EPROM that enables the data to appear at the output connections provided the CE input is also active.

PROM   Programmable read-only memory which is programmed by burning open nichrome or silicon oxide fuses.

Refresh   The act of reading a DRAM in a special way that causes 128 bits to be read and rewritten. This is usually caused by activating the RAS pin.

Row address strobe (RAS)   An input to a DRAM that strobes the row address into the row address latch and also serves as a pin that causes a refresh to occur.

Static RAM (SRAM)   A memory component that allows data to be read or written and also retains that data for as long as the power is applied.

WAIT input   An input to the Z80 that causes the microprocessor to enter into wait states.

Wait state   A state of the Z80 microprocessor where it waits for a slower memory component to access data.

QUESTIONS AND PROBLEMS

11-1. What are the three common types of memory connected to microprocessors?

11-2. The ROM is a device that is programmed in what manner?

11-3. The PROM is programmed in what manner?

11-4. The EPROM is a programmable read-only memory that can be erased by what method?

11-5. How many times can an EEPROM be erased?

11-6. Select a 27XX EPROM that contains 32K bytes of memory.

11-7. What is the purpose of the output enable (OE) pin on an EPROM?

11-8. True or false: Both the OE and CE pins must be at a logic 0 level to read data from an EPROM.

11-9. How much time is required by the standard EPROM to access data?

11-10. How many address inputs are present on the TMS4016 SRAM?

11-11. What is the purpose of the G input to the TMS4016 memory?

11-12. True or false: If the S input and the W input are both connected to a logic 0 on the TMS4016, a read operation is performed.

11-13. What two pins are used for sending the address into the TMS4116 DRAM?

11-14. What is the purpose of the RFSH signal from the Z80?

11-15. The 74LS138 has _____ input connections and _____ output connections.

11-16. The memory sees the Z80 microprocessor as which signals?

11-17. The 74LS138 is enabled only if which pins are grounded and which are pulled up to 5 V?

11-18. Design a decoder that will select a memory device so that it functions at memory locations 9000H—97FFH.

11-19. Design a decoder so that it selects four memory devices starting at memory location 4000H. (Each device is a 4K memory component.)

11-20. Design a memory system that contains two 8K ROMs at memory location 0000H—3FFFH and two 2K RAMs at memory location 4000H—4FFFH.

11-21. Repeat question 11-20 but place the ROM at location 2000H—5FFFH and the RAM at location A000—AFFFH.

11-22. When is the $\overline{\text{WAIT}}$ input to the Z80 sampled?

11-23. A wait state is equal to one _____.

11-24. What is the purpose of the address multiplexer in a DRAM memory?

11-25. Which Z80 signal indicates that the refresh address is present on the address bus?

11-26. What Z80 signal is used to start a normal access to the DRAM?

11-27. Which DRAM pin is activated to accomplish a refresh?

11-28. Modify the circuit of Figure 11-18 so that it addresses memory at locations 4000H—BFFFH.

11-29. What occurs when a HALT instruction is executed with DRAM interfaced to the Z80?

chapter 12

Input/Output Interfacing
Using Parallel Ports

This chapter presents the basic design methodology behind parallel data interfacing. It also discusses port decoding and the 8255A parallel interface adapter. Applications are an important part of this presentation, with a keyboard and multiple-digit seven-segment numeric display used as illustrative examples of interfacing the Z80 microprocessor to external devices.

12-1 OBJECTIVES

Upon completion of this chapter, you will be able to:

1. Explain the operation of the basic input and output ports.
2. Decode an I/O port number to produce enable signals and I/O strobes.
3. Explain the operation of the 8255A parallel interface adapter.
4. Use the 8255A to control external I/O devices.

12-2 THE BASIC INPUT/OUTPUT PORT

This section develops the basic input and output ports for the Z80 microprocessor. It also discusses the control signals required for I/O and the instructions used to accomplish I/O.

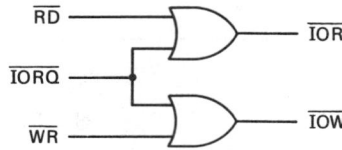

Figure 12–1 Circuit that generates $\overline{IOR}$ and $\overline{IOW}$ from IORQ, RD, and WR.

The Basic I/O Instructions and Control Signals

The Z80 microprocessor uses 2 instructions for I/O: IN and OUT. The IN instruction inputs data to the accumulator from an external I/O device whose 8-bit address appears on the address bus connections A0—A7. The Z80 addresses 256 different input devices. The OUT instruction sends a copy of the accumulator to an external I/O device that is also addressed through address connections A0–A7. Likewise the Z80 addresses 256 output devices. In both instructions the accumulator data are transferred via the system data bus.

In order to control an input or output device, two additional control signals are discussed: $\overline{IOR}$ and $\overline{IOW}$. These new control signals are generated by combining the $\overline{IORQ}$ signal with the $\overline{RD}$ and $\overline{WR}$ signals from the Z80. Figure 12-1 illustrates a simple circuit that generates these control signals.

The Z80 microprocessor issues the $\overline{IORQ}$ signal whenever the IN or OUT instruction is executed. If the IN instruction is executed, the $\overline{RD}$ signal also goes low, and if the OUT instruction is executed, the $\overline{WR}$ signal goes low. When $\overline{RD}$ is combined with $\overline{IORQ}$ the $\overline{IOR}$ signal, which is active for an IN, is generated. Likewise, when the $\overline{WR}$ signal is combined with the $\overline{IORQ}$ signal, the $\overline{IOW}$ signal is generated for each OUT instruction.

The Basic Input Port

Figure 12-2 illustrates the basic Z80 input port. Here a 74LS244 three-state buffer is used to apply the input data to the data bus during an input instruction. With this circuit any TTL data can be input to the microprocessor. If non-TTL data are to be input, they can be conditioned by the use of an analog-to-digital converter or other level shifting device.

The circuit illustrated decodes I/O port number 12H as it appears on the address bus (A0—A7) during the execution of the IN 12H instruction. It combines the decoded address with the $\overline{IOR}$ signal discussed in the previous segment of the section of the text. The output of this decoder circuit generates an enable signal to the 74LS244 so that the TTL compatible input data are applied to the data bus during the IN 12H instruction. As mentioned, the IN 12H instruction inputs data to the accumulator so that the TTL compatible data are found in the accumulator after this instruction's execution.

The basic input port is found in applications where switches are read or other simple external devices are read. This circuit is always found for an input device, but it may be incorporated within a programmable device as will be discussed later in this chapter.

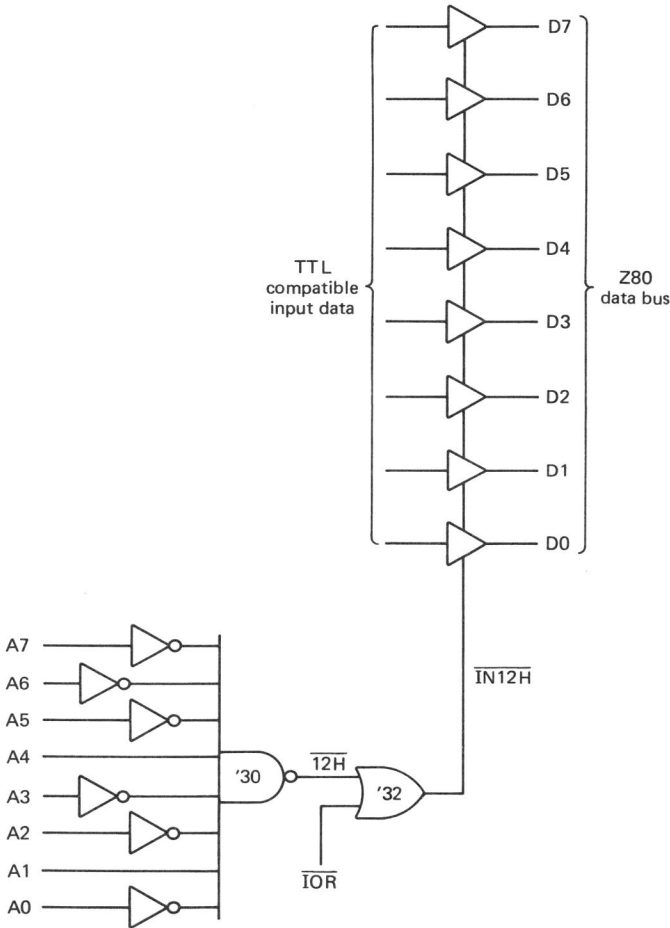

Figure 12–2   Simple input port that accepts TTL data at I/O port number 12H.

The Basic Output Port

The basic output port is used to output TTL data to some external device from the accumulator of the Z80. In all cases the output port consists of a latch to capture the accumulator data from the data bus and hold them for the output device. If the data are to be analog information, they can be converted with a digital-to-analog converter.

Figure 12-3 illustrates the basic output port that responds to I/O port number 2FH. Whenever the OUT 2FH instruction is executed, the address (port number) is decoded with a NAND gate and the output of the NAND gate is combined with the $\overline{\text{IOW}}$ signal to generate a clock pulse for the 74LS374 octal latch. Each time the OUT 2FH instruction

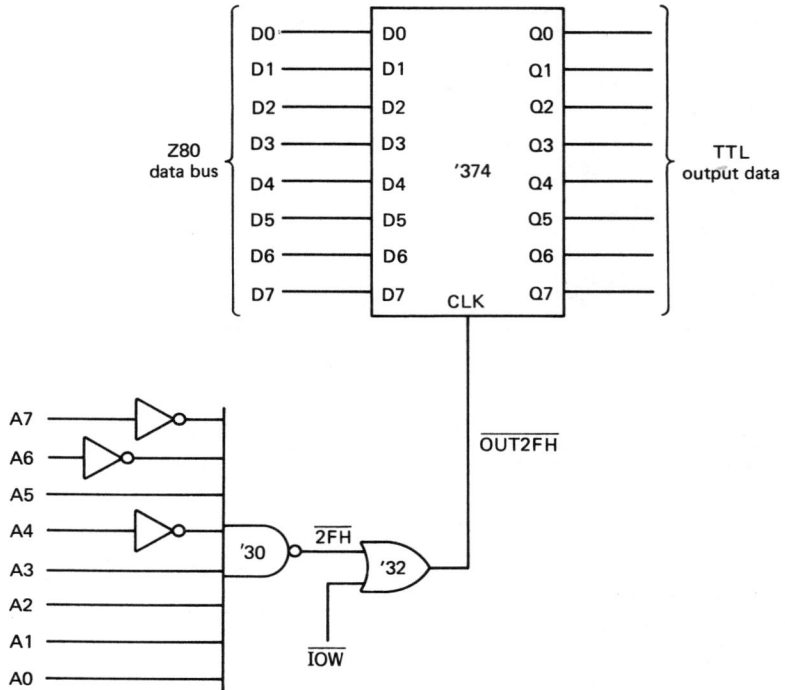

Figure 12-3   Simple output port that holds data at I/O port number 2FH.

is executed, it clocks the data into the latch. As mentioned, the OUT instruction applies the contents of the accumulator to the data bus during its operations so that this circuit captures accumulator data and holds them for some external device.

Virtually all output devices contain this latch, and the latch may be inside of an external device or it may be separate, but in almost every case the external device will contain the latch. Without a latch, output data appear on the data bus for only a microsecond or so, which means that, without the latch, the data are compatible with very few output devices.

12-3 INTRODUCTION TO THE 8255A PROGRAMMABLE INTERFACE ADAPTER

The 8255A programmable peripheral interface adapter (PPIA) is a very popular low-cost component found in many applications today. It has 24 pins for I/O which are programmable in groups of 12 pins. Each group operates in three separate modes from simple I/O to strobed I/O to bidirectional I/O. The 8255A is able to interface any TTL-compatible parallel I/O device to the Z80 microprocessor with ease.

8255A BLOCK DIAGRAM

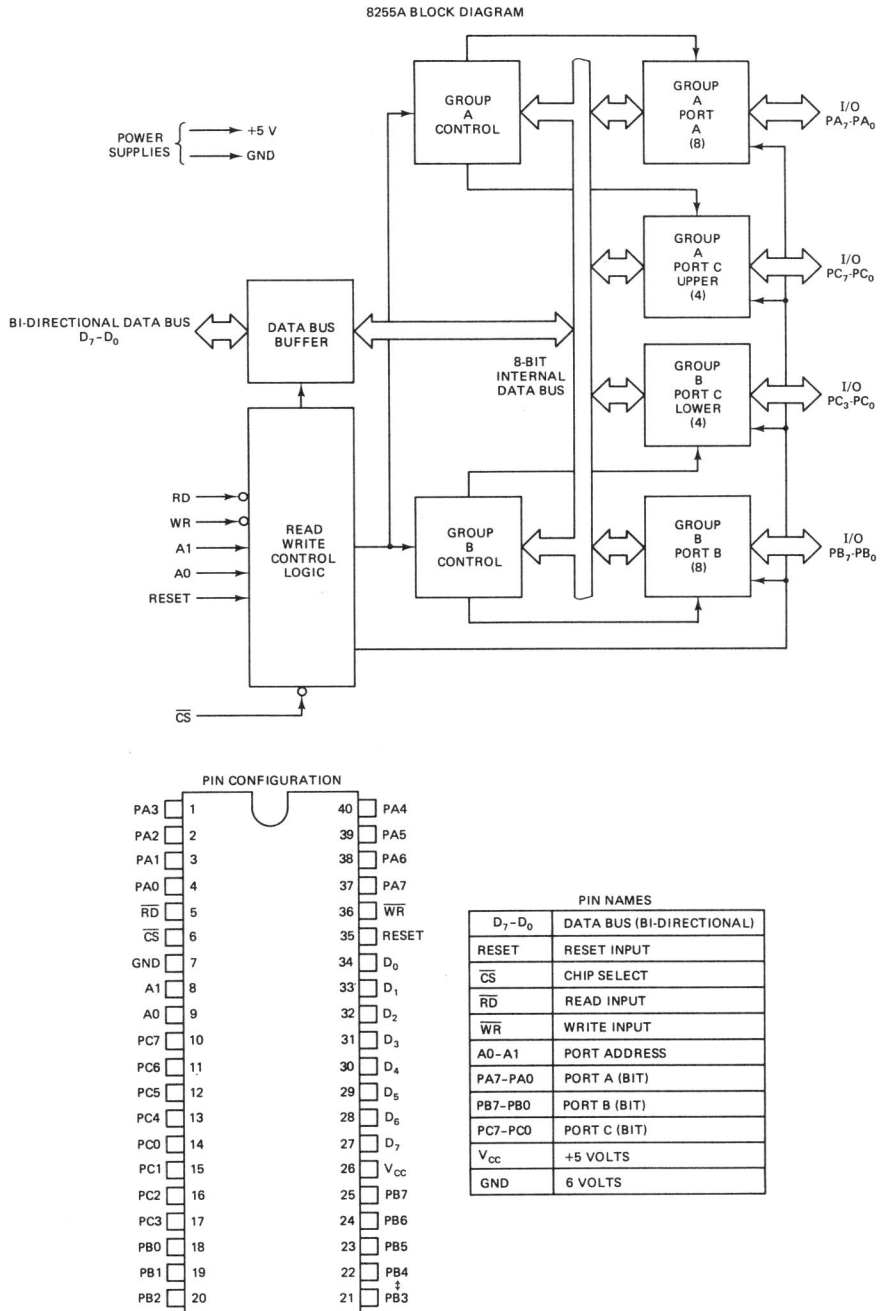

Figure 12–4   Pinout and block diagram of the 8255A.

TABLE 12-1.   I/O PORT ASSIGNMENTS FOR THE 8255A

A7	A6	A5	A4	A3	A2	A1	A0	Function
X	X	X	X	X	X	0	0	port A
X	X	X	X	X	X	0	1	port B
X	X	X	X	X	X	1	0	port C
X	X	X	X	X	X	1	1	command

Note: the Xs (don't cares) are chosen by the decoder attached to the $\overline{CS}$ input pin.

Basic Description of the 8255A

Figure 12-4 illustrates the pinout and block diagram of the 8255A. The pinout depicts that the 8255A has three I/O ports (A, B, and C) which are programmed in two groups of 12 pins. Group A consists of port A (PAO—PA7) and the upper half of port C (PC4—PC7), and group B consists of port B (PB0—PB7) and the lower half of port C (PCO—PC3). Port selection is accomplished via the $\overline{CS}$ input pin and address pins A0 and A1 which together internally choose an I/O port or the command register. Table 12-1 illustrates the I/O ports assignments for programming.

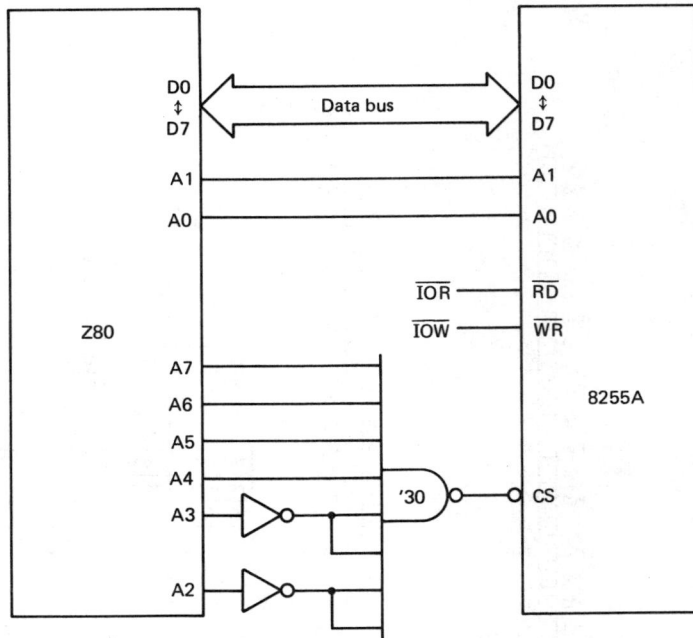

Figure 12–5   The Z80 connected to the 8255A.

The 8255A is a simple device to connect to the Z80 microprocessor (see Figure 12-5). As seen in this illustration, the pins from the Z80 are connected directly to the 8255A without much intervention of logic circuitry. The only logic circuit required is a decoder attached to the $\overline{CS}$ input of the 8255A. Here the 8255A is decoded so that it responds to I/O ports F0H (port A), F1H (port B), F2H (port C), and F3H (command). The other pins are all directly connected to the Z80.

The RESET input causes the I/O ports to be programmed as input ports so that no damage occurs to the circuitry attached to the port pins. If these ports are to be used as output ports, then the 8255A must be programmed through the command port (F3H in this example) to function as outputs.

Programming the 8255A

The 8255A is a rather simple device to program because it only has two internal command registers that are programmed, as depicted in Figure 12-6. Figure 12-6 (a) shows the main command register, which allows the user to program I/O port groups A and B separately. This command register is selected whenever a 1 is output to the leftmost bit position of this command register.

The group B pins are programmable either as input pins or as output pins. Group B also allows the selection of either mode 0 or 1 operation. Mode 0 operation is basic input/output, and mode 1 operation is strobed input/output. Basic I/O operation programs the 8255A to function as a basic input or output port (see Section 12-2). Strobed I/O operation programs the 8255A to operate port B as either input or output with handshaking (polling) for port B supplied by Port C.

The group A pins are programmable as either input or output pins that operate in modes 0, 1, or 2. In all cases, except mode 0, port A is programmed as the input or output port with port C acting as handshaking signals for port A. Modes 0 and 1 are identical in operation as group B, and mode 2 sets up port A as a bidirectional I/O port with port C supplying the handshaking signals.

If a 0 is placed in the leftmost bit position of the command register (see Figure 12-6 [b]), then the bits of port C are individually addressable so that they can be set or cleared if operated in modes 1 or 2. If operated in mode 0, the data are directly output to port C. This command register and the pins of port C are useful for generating control strobe signals.

Mode 0 Operation

Figure 12-7 illustrates the 8255A (port A) connected to a set of LED indicators. Mode 0 operation allows data to be sent to port A (or B or C) where they are held until next output instruction. Also illustrated in Figure 12-7 is a single push-button switch connected to port B. Port B is programmed to function as a simple input port (mode 0).

Example 12-1 illustrates how the command register is programmed so that the circuit of Figure 12-7 functions as described.

CONTROL WORD

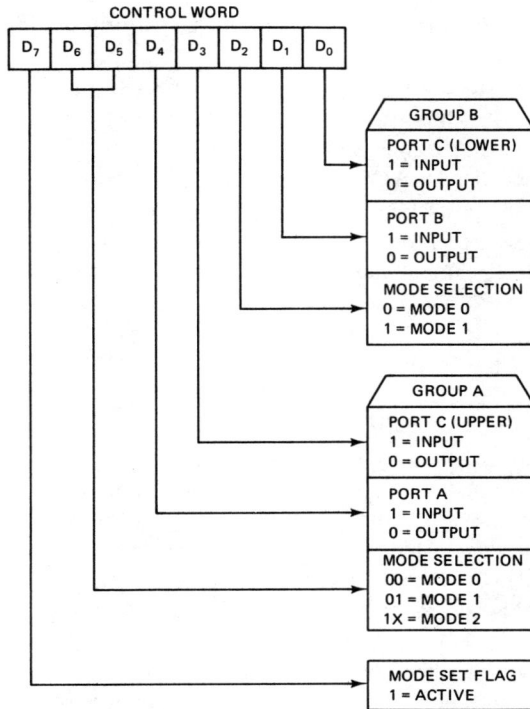

(a)

CONTROL WORD

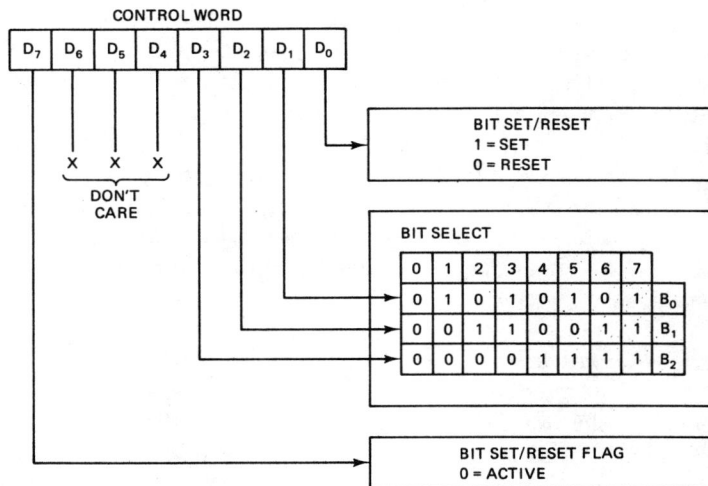

(b)

Figure 12–6 (a) The control register for the 8255A and (b) the bit set and reset control word. (Courtesy of Intel Corporation.)

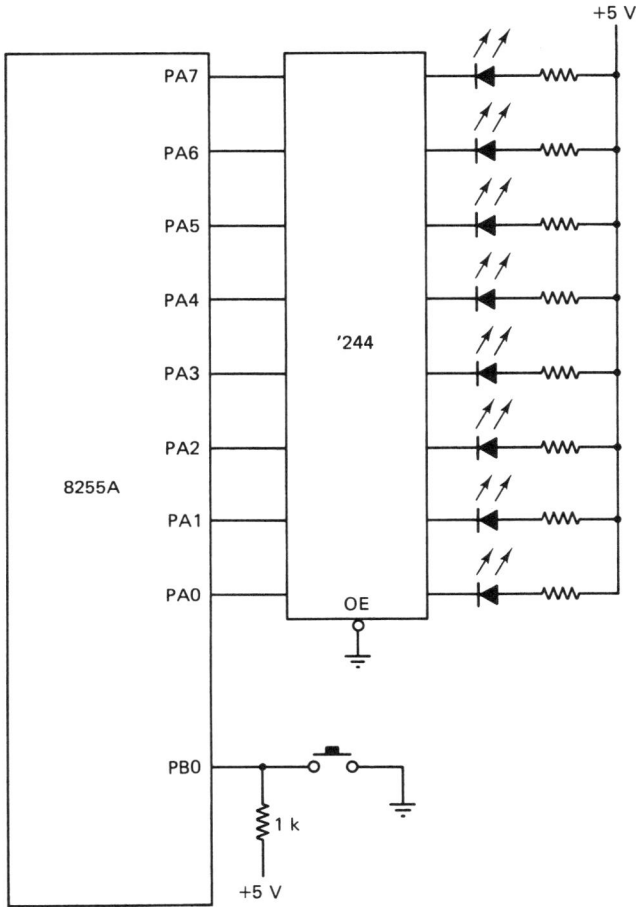

Figure 12-7 Circuit that interfaces eight LED indicators and a push-button switch to the 8255A.

Example 12-1

```
;
;software to initialize the 8255A
;
          LD  A,10000010B    ;set up command
          OUT (COMMAND),A    ;program 8255A
```

A program written to illustrate the operation of the 8255A in this mode is listed in Example 12-2. Here the program checks the push-button switch, and if the switch is pressed, the number displayed on the LED displays is incremented in binary. The flowchart for this program is illustrated in Figure 12-8. Notice that the switch is debounced and when it stops bouncing the number on the LED displays is read from port A, incremented, and output back to port A. A switch must be debounced whenever it is read because all

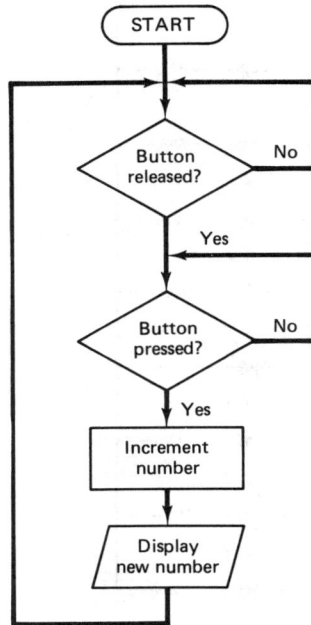

Figure 12–8 The flowchart for the software depicted in Example 12–1.

mechanical switches bounce. To debounce a switch, a time delay is used to wait until it stops bouncing. This program contains the software for such a time delay.

Example 12-2

```
;
;software to read the push-button switch, debounce it,
;and increment the binary number appearing on the LED
;displays
;
;wait for release
;
START:    IN   A,(PORTB)        ;read switch
          RRCA                  ;switch to carry
          JR   NC,START         ;if active
          CALL BOUNCE           ;debounce switch
          IN   A,(PORTB)        ;read switch
          RRCA                  ;switch to carry
          JR   NC,START         ;if active
;
;wait for depression of switch
;
START1:   IN   A,(PORTB)        ;read switch
          RRCA                  ;switch to carry
          JR   C,START1         ;if inactive
          CALL BOUNCE           ;debounce switch
          IN   A,(PORTB)        ;read switch
          RRCA                  ;switch to carry
          JR   C,START1         ;if inactive
```

(Example 12-2 continued)

```
;
;increment binary number on LEDs
;
              IN    A,(PORTA)       ;read port A
              INC   A               ;increment number
              OUT   (PORTA),A       ;write port A
              JR    START           ;repeat operation
;
;time delay subroutine
;
BOUNCE:       LD    BC,700H         ;load count
BOUNCE1:      DEC   BC              ;decrement count
              LD    A,B             ;test BC
              OR    C
              JR    NZ,BOUNCE1      ;if not zero
              RET
```

Strobed Input Operation (Mode 1)

Mode 1 operation of the 8255A selects handshaking for port A or port B by using the port C pins as handshaking control signals. Figure 12-9 illustrates the internal structure of the 8255A for strobed input operation and also the mode 1 strobed input timing diagram.

Port C definitions for mode 1 strobed input

$\overline{STB}$—Strobe: an input used to load data into the port A or B latch, which holds the information until it is input to the microprocessor via an IN instruction.

IBF—Input Buffer Full: an output that indicates the input latch contains data for the microprocessor. The $\overline{STB}$ signal causes IBF to set, and the IN instruction causes IBF to clear.

INTR—Interrupt Request: an output used to request an interrupt. INTR becomes a logic 1 when the $\overline{STB}$ signal becomes a logic 1 and is cleared when the IN instruction is executed.

INTE—Interrupt Enable: neither an input nor an output, but an internal bit programmed via the bit set and reset command register. INTE A is programmed as bit position PC4, and INTE B is programmed as bit position PC2.

PC7, PC6—Port Pins 7 and 6: general purpose I/O pins in mode 1 strobed input operation. These pins are controlled with the bit set and reset command register when used as output pins and read via port C when used as input pins.

Strobed input example.   An excellent example of a strobed input device is a keyboard. If a keyboard encoder integrated circuit is used, it scans the keyboard and debounces the keyswitches. Whenever the encoder detects a keystroke it provides a strobe and also the ASCII coded equivalent of the keyswitch pressed. Figure 12-10 illustrates a keyboard encoder connected to function with the 8255A in the strobed input mode (1).

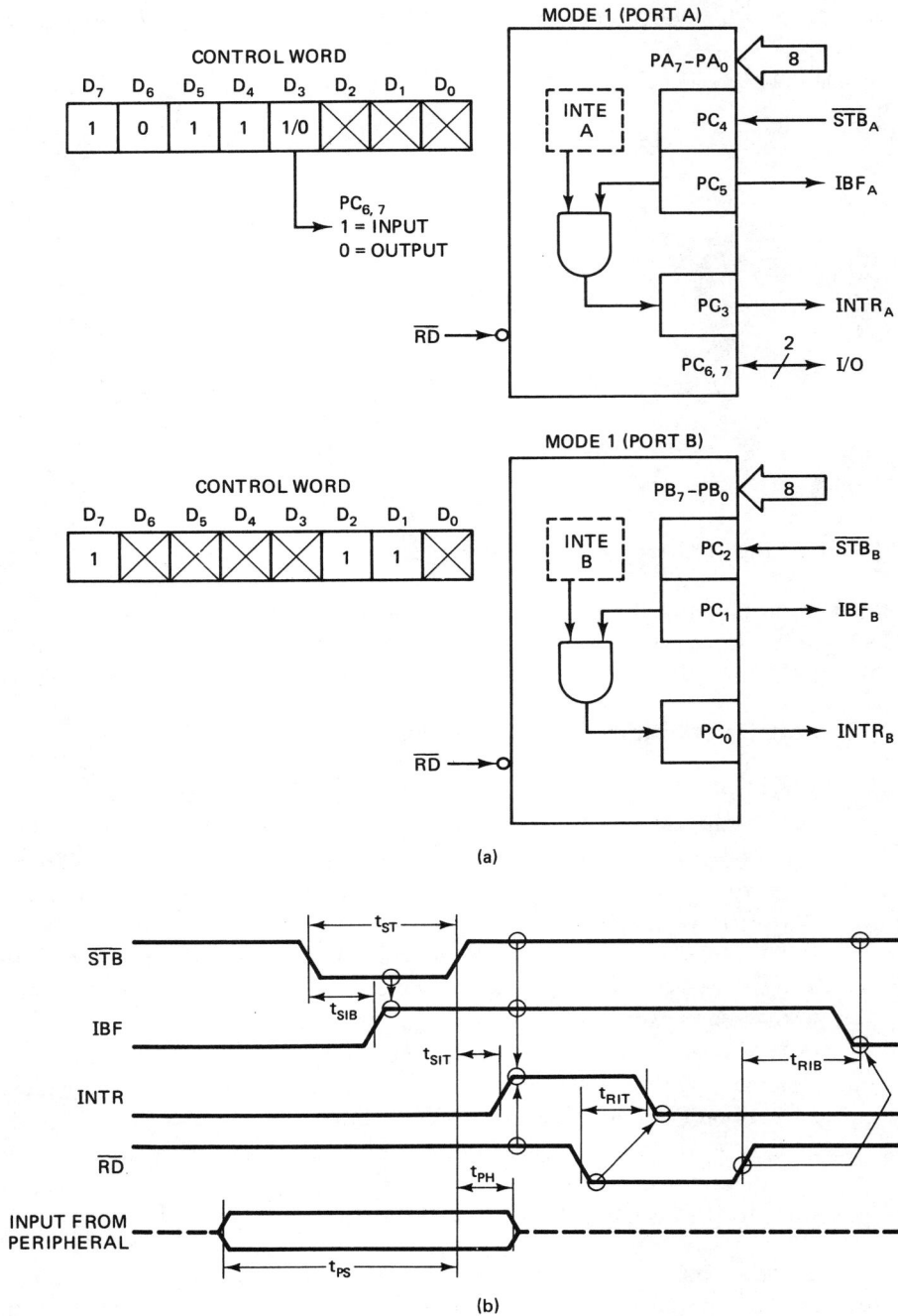

Figure 12–9 Mode 1 strobed input operation of the 8255A. (a) Internal structure. (b) Timing diagram. (Courtesy of Intel Corporation.)

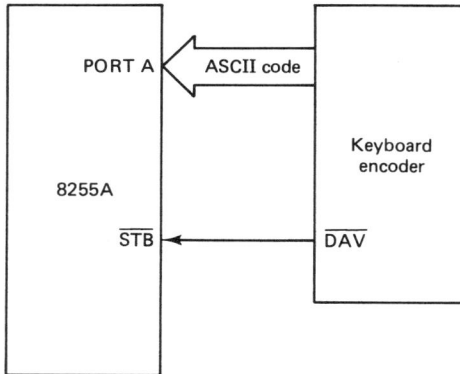

Figure 12–10 A keyboard encoder interfaced to the 8255A.

Here the data output pins from the encoder are connected to port A, and the $\overline{DAV}$ (data available) signal is connected to the $\overline{STB}$ input. If a keystroke occurs the encoder places the ASCII character on the port A input pins and activates the $\overline{DAV}$ pin for 1 μs. Because $\overline{DAV}$ is attached to the $\overline{STB}$ pin this clocks the ASCII data into the port A latch and also sets the IBF signal. IBF is tested by the software to determine if a key is pressed.

A subroutine that is used to read the keyboard and return with the keyboard ASCII data in the accumulator appears in Example 12-3.

Example 12-3

```
;
;subroutine that reads an ASCII character from the
;keyboard via port A.
;
BIT5:      EQU   20H               ;mask for PC5
;
READ_KEY:  IN    A,(PORTC)         ;input IBF
           AND   BIT5              ;check IBF
           JR    Z,READ_KEY        ;if IBF = 0
           IN    A,(PORTA)         ;input ASCII data
           RET
```

Strobed Output Operation (Mode 1)

Figure 12-11 illustrates the internal structure of the 8255A for strobed output operation and also the timing diagram.

Port C definitions for mode 1 strobed output

$\overline{OBF}$—Output Buffer Full: an output that goes low whenever data are output to the port A or port B latch. This signal is set whenever the $\overline{ACK}$ pulse returns from the external device and cleared when data are written to the port with an OUT instruction.

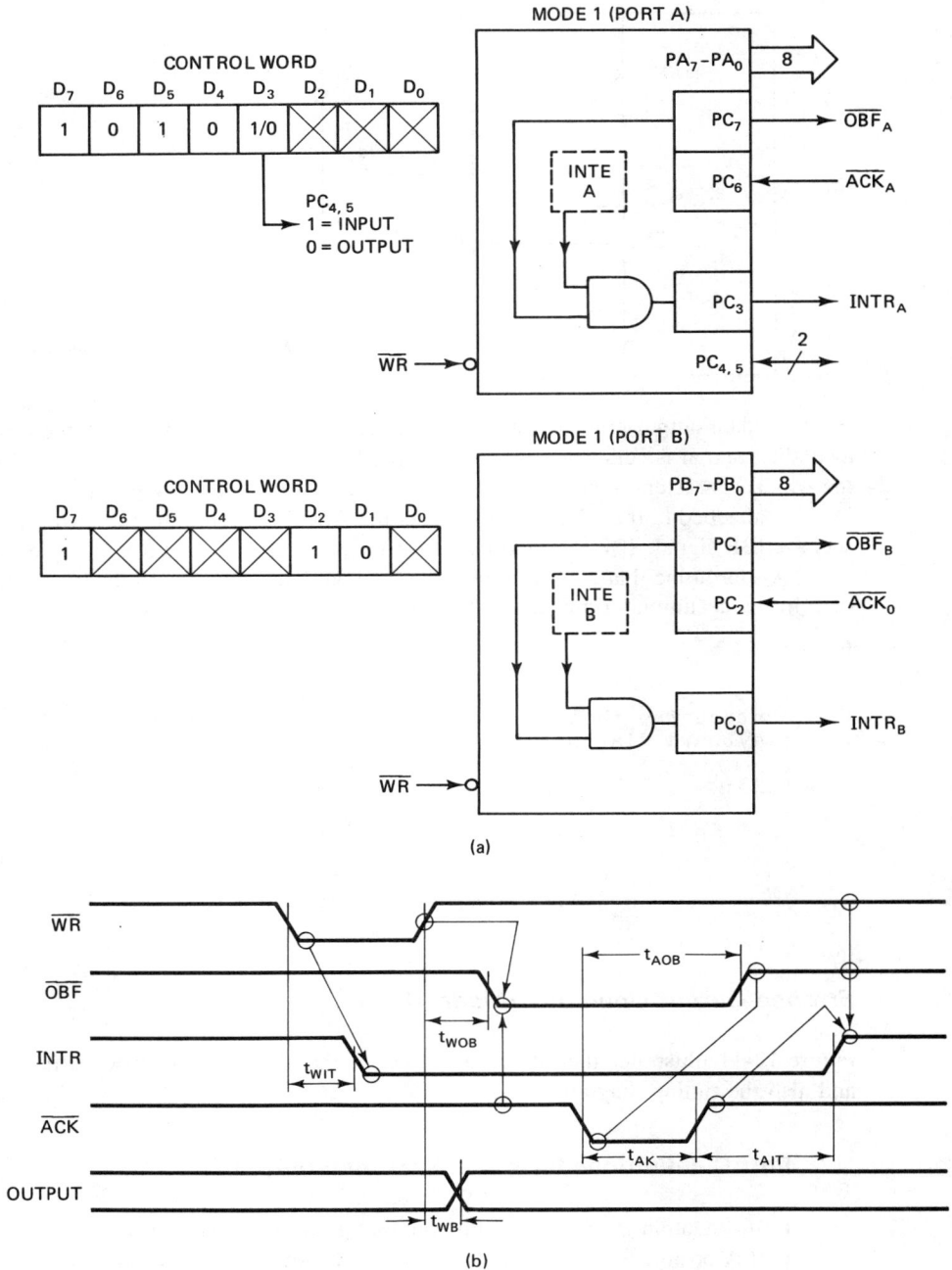

Figure 12–11 Strobed output operation of the 8255A. (a) Internal structure. (b) Timing diagram. (Courtesy of Intel Corporation.)

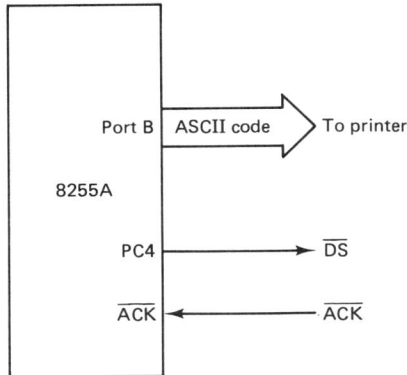

Figure 12–12 The 8255A connected to a parallel printer.

$\overline{\text{ACK}}$—Acknowledge Input: a signal that causes the $\overline{\text{OBF}}$ pin to return to a logic 1 level. $\overline{\text{ACK}}$ is a response from an external device that indicates it has received the data from the 8255A.

INTR—Interrupt Request: a signal that can be used to interrupt the microprocessor whenever the external device acknowledges ($\overline{\text{ACK}}$) the output data.

INTE—Interrupt Enable: neither an input nor an output, but an internal bit programmed via the bit set and reset command register. INTE A is programmed as bit PC6 and INTE B as bit PC2.

PC5, PC4—Port Pins 4 and 5: general purpose I/O pins that are controlled with the set and reset command register or input via the IN port C instruction.

Strobed output example.   A good example of a strobed output device is the parallel printer interface. Figure 12-12 depicts how port B is connected to a parallel printer. Here the ASCII inputs to the printer are connected to the port B output pins, a $\overline{\text{DS}}$ (data strobe) is connected to port C, and the $\overline{\text{ACK}}$ signal from the printer is connected to the $\overline{\text{ACK}}$ input of port C.

In this circuit, there is no signal to generate the $\overline{\text{DS}}$ strobe to the printer, so PC4 is used along with software to generate the $\overline{\text{DS}}$ signal. The $\overline{\text{ACK}}$ signal that is returned to the 8255A indicates that the printer has received the ASCII character from port B and is ready to receive another. The software to transmit an ASCII character to the printer is listed in Example 12-4. This subroutine first tests the $\overline{\text{OBF}}$ signal to determine if the printer has removed the data from port B. If it has, the subroutine then sends the ASCII character located in the B register to the printer via port B and also sends the $\overline{\text{DS}}$ signal.

Example 12-4

```
;
;subroutine that transmits the contents of the B
;register to the printer.
;
BIT1:     EQU   2
;
```

(Example 12-4 continued)

```
;check printer ready
;
PRINT:      IN    A,(PORTC)        ;get OBF
            AND   BIT1             ;test OBF
            JR    Z,PRINT          ;if OBF = 0
;
;send character
;
            LD    A,B              ;get ASCII character
            OUT   (PORTB),A        ;send it
;
;send DS
;
            LD    A,00001000B      ;clear DS
            OUT   (COMMAND),A
            LD    A,00001001B      ;set DS
            OUT   (COMMAND),A
            RET
```

Bidirectional Operation (Mode 2)

Mode 2, bidirectional operation, functions only for the group A pins. Port A becomes a bidirectional port allowing data to be transmitted and received over the same eight wires. Bidirectional data are useful when interfacing two computers. Figure 12-13 shows the internal configuration and the timing diagram for mode 2 bidirectional operation of port A.

Port C definitions for bidirectional mode 2 operation

INTR—Interrupt Request: an output used to interrupt the microprocessor for both input and output conditions.

$\overline{\text{OBF}}$—Output Buffer Full: an output that indicates that the output buffer contains data for the microprocessor from the bidirectional bus.

$\overline{\text{ACK}}$—Acknowledge: an input that enables the three-state output connections of the bidirectional bus to send data. If $\overline{\text{ACK}}$ is a logic 1, the bus is at its high impedance state.

$\overline{\text{STB}}$—Strobe: an input used to load data into the input bus from the bidirectional bus.

IBF—Input Buffer Full: an output that indicates that data are stored in the input buffer and awaiting action from the microprocessor.

INTE—Interrupt Enable: an internal bit that allows the INTR pin to function. INTE 1 is controlled by bit PC6 and INTE 2 is controlled by PC4.

PC2, PC1, and PC0—general purpose I/O pins in mode 2 controlled by the bit set and reset command register or input as port C.

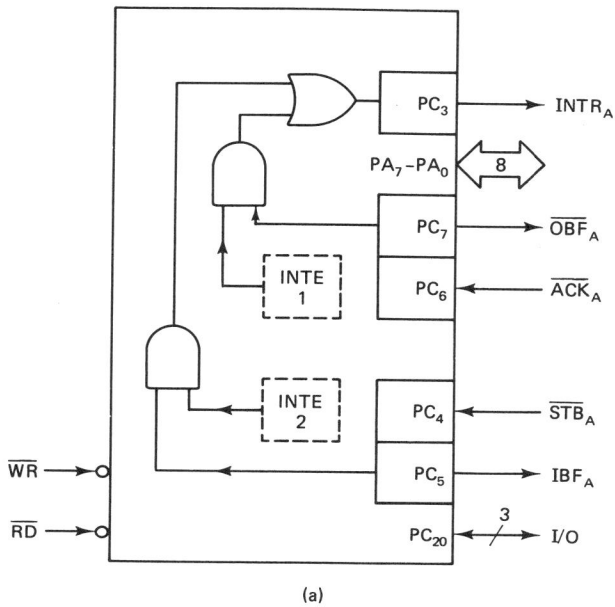

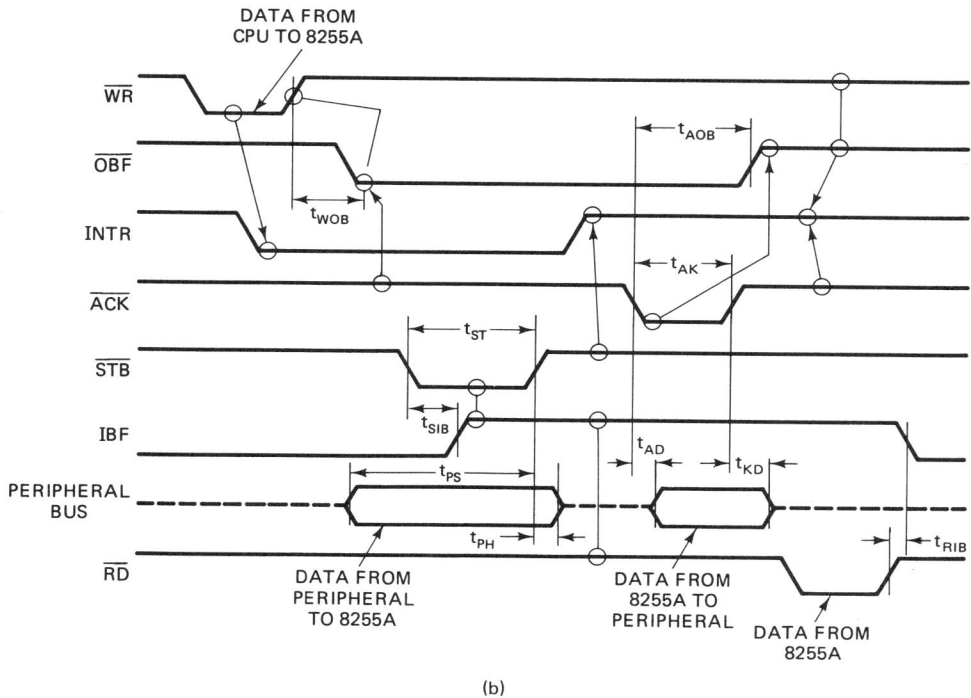

Figure 12–13 Mode 2 bidirectional operation of the 8255A. (a) Internal structure. (b) Timing diagrams. (Courtesy of Intel Corporation.)

The bidirectional bus.   The bidirectional bus can be used only if all input (IN) and output (OUT) instructions reference port A. To transmit data through the bidirectional bus, the program checks the $\overline{\text{OBF}}$ signal to determine if the output buffer is empty. If the buffer is empty, then data are sent to the buffer with an OUT instruction. The external circuitry also monitors the $\overline{\text{OBF}}$ signal to determine if data are being sent. If data are detected, the circuit exerts the $\overline{\text{ACK}}$ signal to extract the data from the output buffer. The $\overline{\text{ACK}}$ signal turns on the three-state buffers so that the external device can see the data, and it also places the $\overline{\text{OBF}}$ signal back at its logic 1 level. Example 12-5 lists the software that is used to transmit data from the B register through the bidirectional bus.

Example 12-5

```
;
;subroutine that transmits the B register through
;the bidirectional bus.
;
BIT7:      EQU  80H                ;OBF test bit
;
;test OBF
;
SEND:      IN   A,(PORTC)          ;get OBF
           AND  BIT7               ;test OBF
           JR   Z,SEND             ;if OBF = 0
;
;send data
;
           LD   A,B                ;get data
           OUT  (PORTA),A          ;send data
           RET
```

To receive data through the bidirectional bus of port A, the IBF bit is tested with the software to determine if data are available in port A. These data are then input with an IN instruction. The external interface sends data into the bidirectional bus by activating the $\overline{\text{STB}}$ signal, which latches the data into port A and causes IBF to go high. When IBF is a logic 1, it indicates that the port contains data for the microprocessor. Example 12-6 lists the subroutine that inputs data from the bidirectional bus and returns with them in the accumulator register.

Example 12-6

```
;
;subroutine that inputs data from the bidirectional
;bus and returns with it in the accumulator.
;
BIT5:      EQU  20H                ;test bit for IBF
;
;check IBF
;
READ:      IN   A,(PORTC)          ;get IBF
           AND  BIT5               ;test IBF
           JR   Z,READ             ;if IBF = 0
;
;read data
;
           IN   A,(PORTA)          ;get data
           RET
```

	MODE 0		MODE 1		MODE 2
	IN	OUT	IN	OUT	GROUP A ONLY
PA_0	IN	OUT	IN	OUT	←——→
PA_1	IN	OUT	IN	OUT	←——→
PA_2	IN	OUT	IN	OUT	←——→
PA_3	IN	OUT	IN	OUT	←——→
PA_4	IN	OUT	IN	OUT	←——→
PA_5	IN	OUT	IN	OUT	←——→
PA_6	IN	OUT	IN	OUT	←——→
PA_7	IN	OUT	IN	OUT	←——→
PB_0	IN	OUT	IN	OUT	———
PB_1	IN	OUT	IN	OUT	———
PB_2	IN	OUT	IN	OUT	———
PB_3	IN	OUT	IN	OUT	———
PB_4	IN	OUT	IN	OUT	———
PB_5	IN	OUT	IN	OUT	———
PB_6	IN	OUT	IN	OUT	———
PB_7	IN	OUT	IN	OUT	———
PC_0	IN	OUT	$INTR_B$	$INTR_B$	I/O
PC_1	IN	OUT	IBF_B	$\overline{OBF}_B$	I/O
PC_2	IN	OUT	$\overline{STB}_B$	$\overline{ACK}_B$	I/O
PC_3	IN	OUT	$INTR_A$	$INTR_A$	$INTR_A$
PC_4	IN	OUT	$\overline{STB}_A$	I/O	$\overline{STB}_A$
PC_5	IN	OUT	IBF_A	I/O	IBF_A
PC_6	IN	OUT	I/O	$\overline{ACK}_A$	$\overline{ACK}_A$
PC_7	IN	OUT	I/O	$\overline{OBF}_A$	$\overline{OBF}_A$

(MODE 0 OR MODE 1 ONLY — applies to the PB rows in the MODE 2 column)

Figure 12–14 The mode summary of the 8255A. (Courtesy of Intel Corporation.)

Mode Summary

As the preceding section indicates, the 8255A is a very flexible peripheral interfacing component. It can be used in applications that range from simple I/O to complex I/O requiring handshaking and bidirectional buses. Figure 12-14 provides a summary of the three operating modes of the 8255A.

12-4 A KEYBOARD

One very important interface to any computer system and many control systems is the keyboard. Keyboards come in a wide variety of sizes and shapes, but this section makes no attempt to cover all of them. It does attempt to provide a strategy that allows any keyboard of any size to be attached to the microprocessor.

The Keyswitch

The switch on a keyboard is a normally open push-button switch that mechanically bounces when it is closed and opened. Figure 12-15 shows the effect of keyswitch bouncing whenever it is closed and opened. As can be seen from this illustration, bouncing causes problems. A bounce is seen as multiple closures of the keyswitch.

In order to eliminate problems from a bouncing key a time delay is commonly used. If one waits for 10—15 ms after the switch is closed or opened it will stop bouncing and reach its steady state condition. Software is normally used to cause this time delay whenever a keyswitch is read.

The Keyboard

Most keyboards are set up as a matrix of rows and columns. Whenever a keyswitch is closed (pressed) it makes a connection between a row and a column. Today some commonly found keyboard matrixes are 4 × 4, 4 × 5, and larger versions of up to 4 × 16 for a full ASCII keyboard.

The Keyboard Interface

This example uses a 4 × 5 key matrix interfaced to an 8255A. Here (see Figure 12-16) the keyboard is connected so that port A provides output signals to the columns (5 of them), and port B inputs data from the rows (4 of them). This arrangement allows any column to be selected by outputting a logic zero to the selected column. Once a column of 4 keys is selected the rows are input and tested to see if a logic 0 appears on a row. If a zero appears, a keyswitch is closed, and if none appears the keyswitch is open.

Figure 12-17 depicts the flowchart used to read the keyboard. Notice that the first section of the flowchart checks to see if a key is released. This is done so that it is certain that no key is pressed when the software is entered, and it prevents multiple keystrokes from occurring. The next segment of the flowchart tests to see if a key is closed. Once it is detected, and debounced, the position of the closed keyswitch is calculated and returned as a number between 00H and 13H.

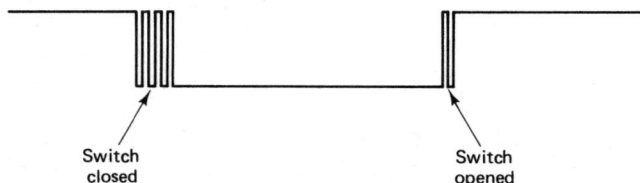

Switch
closed

Switch
opened

Figure 12–15 The timing diagram generated by opening and closing a switch.

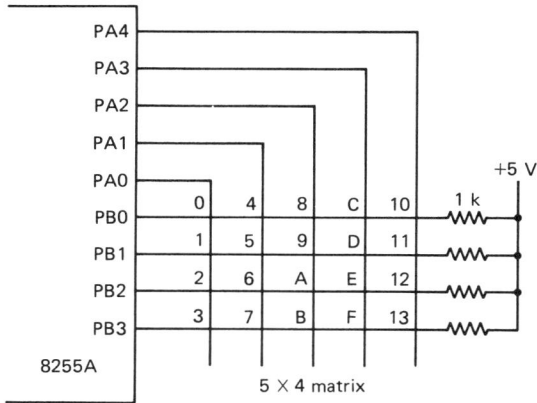

Figure 12–16 A 5×4 matrix interfaced to the 8255A.

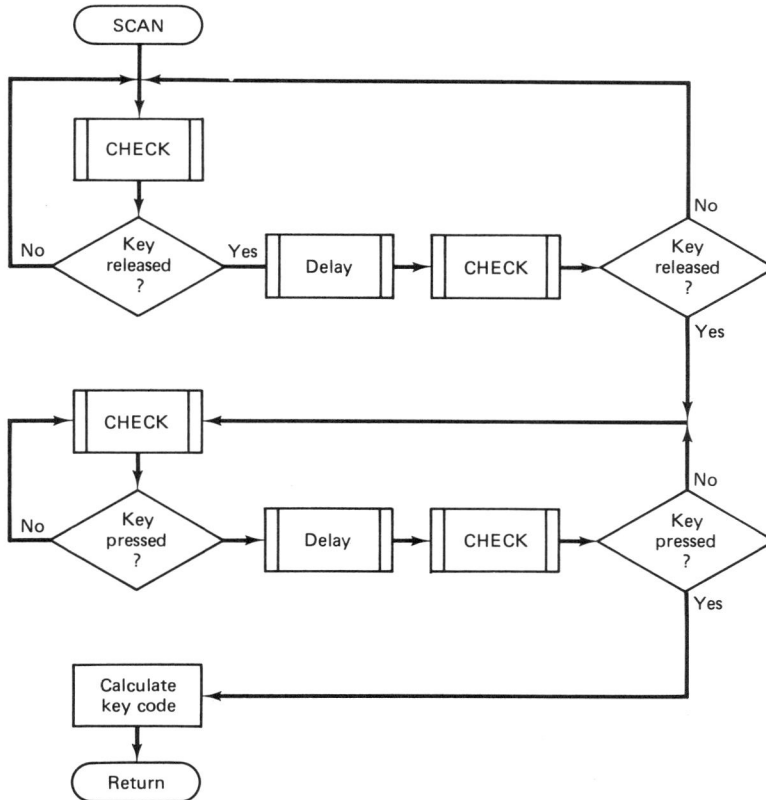

Figure 12–17 Flowchart that scans the keyboard illustrated in Figure 12–16 and returns with the number of the depressed key.

The subroutine written from this flowchart appears in the listing of Example 12-7. Notice that subroutine CHECK tests to see if a key is closed in any column. The return from CHECK occurs with the zero flag set or cleared. A return zero indicates that none of the keys on the entire keyboard are closed, and a return non-zero indicates that a key switch is closed. The C register indicates which column number (1-5) has the closed keyswitch upon a return.

Example 12-7

```
;
;subroutine that scans the keyboard and returns with
;the position of the closed key in the accumulator.
;
;wait for release
;
SCAN:       CALL  CHECK           ;check switches
            JR    NZ,SCAN         ;if switch closed
            CALL  DELAY           ;debounce
            CALL  CHECK           ;check switches
            JR    NZ,SCAN         ;if switch closed
;
;wait for closed switch
;
SCAN1:      CALL  CHECK           ;check switches
            JR    Z,SCAN1         ;if switches open
            CALL  DELAY           ;debounce
            CALL  CHECK           ;check switches
            JR    Z,SCAN1         ;if switches open
;
;calulate key position
;
            DEC   C               ;adjust C to 0--4
            LD    A,C             ;C x 4
            ADD   A,A
            ADD   A,A
            LD    C,A
            LD    B,OFFH          ;load count
SCAN2:      IN    A,(PORTB)       ;get row
            RRCA                  ;shift right
            INC   B               ;increment count
            JR    C,SCAN2         ;if no switch
            LD    A,B             ;form key code
            ADD   A,C
            RET
;
;scan key subroutine
;
CHECK:      LD    C,5             ;load count
            LD    B,OFEH          ;load select pattern
CHECK1:     LD    A,B             ;select column
            OUT   (PORTA),A
            RLCA
            LD    B,A
            IN    A,(PORTB)       ;check for a key
            INC   A               ;test keys
            RET   NZ              ;return if a key closed
```

(Example 12-7 continued)

```
                DEC   C                ;decrement count
                JR    NZ,CHECK1        ;check more columns
                RET
        ;
        ;time delay
        ;
        DELAY:  LD    DE,600H          ;set count
        DELAY1: DEC   DE               ;decrement count
                LD    A,D              ;test for 0
                OR    E
                JR    NZ,DELAY1        ;if not zero
                RET
```

SCAN takes the data from CHECK as passed in register C and subtracts a one from them so that the column numbers 0-4 are represented in C. C is then multiplied by a 4 so that the starting position of each column (0, 4, 8, C, or 10H) is indicated by the C register. Port B is then input so that a rotate instruction can count the exact row number of the key switch. This row number is added to the C register to locate the exact key switch.

12-5 A NUMERIC DISPLAY

Numeric displays are an integral part of many microprocessor-based systems. This section of the text interfaces a series of four 7-segment numeric displays to the Z80 microprocessor using the NMI interrupt input to drive the software.

The 7-Segment LED Display

Seven-segment displays are available in two basic types: the common anode and common cathode displays. Common anode displays are constructed so that +5 V is applied to the anodes of all the internal LEDs, and each cathode is grounded through a current limiting resistor to cause a segment to light. The common cathode display functions in basically the same manner except the cathodes are all tied to ground and +5 V is applied to a segment through a current limiting resistor to light it.

Figure 12-18 illustrates the standard schematic symbol for a 7-segment display. The segments are lettered from a-g, and either one or two decimal points may be present. Most LED displays require a current of 10 mA to fully illuminate a segment.

The Multiplexed 4-Digit Display

Figure 12-19 depicts four 7-segment displays that are multiplexed and connected to a single 8255A. The 8255A provides the 7-segment code for all digits from port A (mode 0, output operation) and the pattern to select a digit from port B (mode 0, output operation).

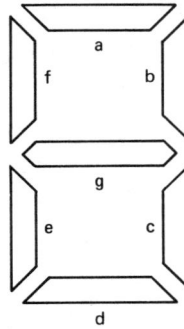

Figure 12–18 The 7-segment LED display.

Each segment and each anode connection (common anode displays) connect to a driver circuit because the 8255A cannot provide the required current. In use, each digit is turned on for one-fourth of the time which means that the segment current must be increased so that the average power per display remains the same. In this case, the segment current is 40 mA (4 times 10 mA) and each anode may draw up to 280 mA (7 times 40 mA). Hence, the segment drive must pass 40 mA of current and the anode driver 280 mA.

The anode driver. Figure 12-20 illustrates the anode driver. Here a PNP transistor is used to apply $+5$ V to the anode of a display whenever the input to the base is lowered below $+5$ V. The base resistor is chosen by using $+0.4$ V as a logic zero input and a voltage drop of 0.7 V across the emitter-base junction. This leaves 3.9 V

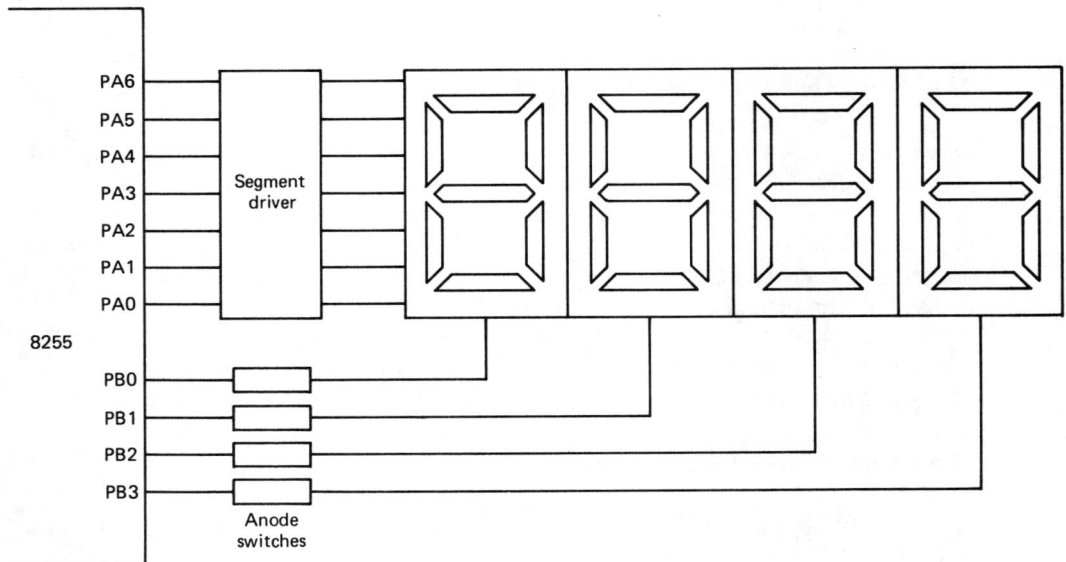

Figure 12–19 A multiplexed display.

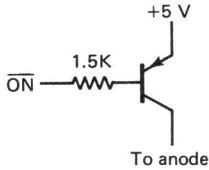

Figure 12–20   The anode switch.

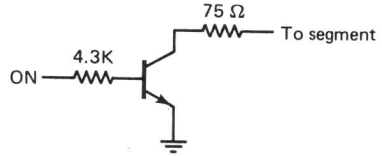

Figure 12–21   The segment driver.

across the base resistor. The base current is 1/100 (minimum gain of this transistor) of the emitter current of 270 mA. or 2.7 mA. The value of the base resistor is approximately 1.5 K.

The segment driver.   Figure 12-21 illustrates the segment driver. Here the current is limited by R1 and is chosen so that 40 mA of current flows in this example. The voltage across this resistor is $+5$ V minus the drop across the LED inside of the display (about 1.8 V typically) minus the drop across both the anode transistor and the segment driver transistor (about 0.2 V). The value of R1 is therefore 3 V divided by 40 mA or 75 ohms.

The base resistor Rb is determined by using the minimum logic 1 input voltage of 2.4 V minus the base-emitter voltage drop of 0.7 V or 1.7 V. The base resistor current is 1/100 (assumes minimum transistor gain of 100) the emitter current of 40 mA or a base current of 400 μA. Here the resistor is about 4.3 K.

The software.   Example 12-8 lists the initialization dialog and the subroutine that is called by a NMI interrupt input and is stored at memory location 0066H. The circuit (not shown) that is connected to the NMI input, causes an interrupt once per millisecond. Each time this subroutine is called, it displays a 7-segment character on a new digit. The 7-segment characters are stored in a four-byte section of the memory called the display RAM. This means that once the Z80 is turned on, this subroutine is called from that point forward once per millisecond.

Example 12-8

```
;
;initialization dialog for the 4-digit multiplexed
;display.
;
INIT:       LD    HL,RAM           ;blank displays
            LD    C,4
INIT1:      LD    (HL),00H
            INC   HL
            DEC   C
            JR    NZ,INIT1
            LD    A,0EEH            ;setup display pointer
            LD    (POINT),A
            LD    A,0               ;setup display position
            LD    (POS),A
             .     .
             .     .
```

(Example 12-8 continued)

```
;
;subroutine called by the NMI interrupt input, once
;per millisecond.
;
            ORG   66H
DISPLAY:    PUSH  AF              ;save registers
            PUSH  HL
            LD    A,(POINT)       ;select a new digit
            OUT   (PORTB),A
            RLC
            LD    (POINT),A
            LD    A,(POS)         ;send 7-segment code
            LD    HL,RAM
            LD    L,A
            LD    A,(HL)
            OUT   (PORTA),A
            LD    A,L             ;adjust position
            INC   A
            LD    (POS),A
            SUB   A,4             ;check for last
            JR    NZ,DISPLAY1
            LD    (POS),A
DISPLAY1:   POP   HL
            POP   AF
            RET
;
;display RAM
;
            ORG   2000H
RAM:        DS    4
```

12-6 INTERRUPTS AND THE 8255A

The 8255A is capable of interrupting the Z80 when it is operated in mode 1 or mode 2. This section of the text illustrates the use of the 8255A to implement a parallel printer interface. This interface was implemented earlier in this chapter, but as a strobed output with handshaking rather than an interrupting I/O port.

The Hardware

Figure 12-22 illustrates the 8255A and the interconnections to the printer and also to the Z80 microprocessor. Notice that the INTR output for port A is attached to the NMI interrupt input of the Z80. This means that whenever the $\overline{ACK}$ pulse returns from the printer, the INTR pin goes to a logic 1 level requesting an interrupt. This circuit is different from the one presented earlier in this chapter because the $\overline{OBF}$ signal is not checked.

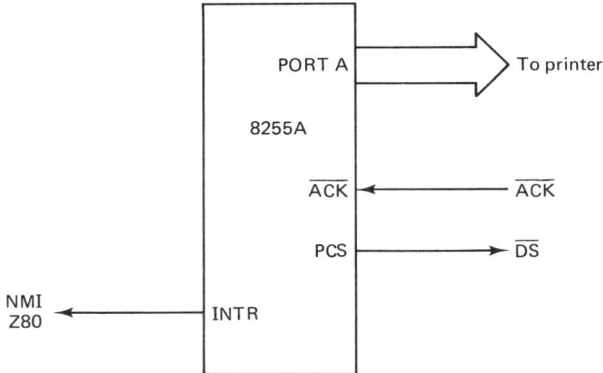

Figure 12–22   The 8255A interfaced to a printer as an interrupting port.

The Software

The software for this interface is in two parts: the first initializes and starts the transfer, and the second is the interrupt service subroutine. Example 12-9 lists the subroutine that begins to print a block of data addressed by the contents of the HL register pair, whose length is stored in the BC register pair. In addition to starting the transfer, which is a matter of enabling the port A interrupt, this subroutine also stores a 1 in memory location FLAG. FLAG indicates that the printer is busy printing a block of data and is cleared at the end of the transfer.

Example 12-9

```
;
;subroutine called to start printing a block of data
;addressed by the HL register pair whose length is
;is stored  in the BC register pair.
;
TRANS:    LD    (ADDR),HL      ;store address
          LD    H,B            ;store count
          LD    L,C
          LD    (COUNT),HL
          LD    A,1            ;1 to FLAG
          LD    (FLAG),A
          LD    A,0DH          ;enable interrupt
          OUT   (COMMAND),A
          RET
```

The interrupt service subroutine is listed in Example 12-10. This subroutine is called each time that the print buffer (port A) is emptied by the printer via the $\overline{ACK}$ pulse. The subroutine transfers a byte of data from the memory location addressed by ADDR and transfers COUNT number of bytes. After each byte is output to port A, the $\overline{DS}$ signal is generated via the bit set and reset command register and PC5. At the completion of transferring the COUNT number of bytes, the FLAG is cleared to 00H and future interrupts are disabled.

Example 12-10

```
;
;interrupt service subroutine that transfers a byte
;to the printer via port A.
;
INTER:      PUSH AF                 ;save registers
            PUSH HL
            PUSH DE
            LD   HL,(COUNT)         ;get count
            EX   DE,HL
            LD   HL,(ADDR)          ;get address
            LD   A,(HL)             ;get data
            OUT  (PORTA),A          ;send data
            LD   A,OAH              ;send DS
            OUT  (COMMAND),A
            LD   A,OBH
            OUT  (COMMAND),A
            INC  HL                 ;increment address
            LD   (ADDR),HL          ;save address
            EX   DE,HL
            DEC  HL                 ;decrement count
            LD   (COUNT),HL         ;save count
            LD   A,H                ;test count for zero
            OR   L
            JR   NZ,INTER1          ;if not zero
            LD   A,OEH              ;disable interrupts
            OUT  (COMMAND),A
INTER1:     POP  DE
            POP  HL
            POP  AF
            RET
```

12-7 SUMMARY

1. The IN and OUT instructions transfer data between the accumulator of the Z80 and an I/O device via the data bus. The address (I/O port number) appears on the address bus in bit positions A0—A7.

2. I/O control signals $\overline{IOR}$ and $\overline{IOW}$ are generated by combining the $\overline{IORQ}$ signal with the $\overline{RD}$ signal to generate $\overline{IOR}$ and the $\overline{WR}$ signal to generate $\overline{IOW}$.

3. The basic input port consists of an octal three-state buffer that applies the input data to the data bus during an IN instruction.

4. The basic output port consists of an octal latch that captures data bus information during an OUT instruction for an external output device.

5. The 8255A is a programmable peripheral interface adapter that contains three 8-bit I/O ports. These ports are operated in basic I/O (mode 0), strobed I/O (mode 1), or bidirectional I/O (mode 2) modes of operation.

6. The 8255A command registers control how I/O ports A, B, and C are programmed and also control the bits of register C when it is operated in mode 1 or mode 2.

7. Whenever the 8255A is reset it selects the simple input mode of operation for all three I/O ports.

8. For modes 1 and 2 operation, the 8255A uses port C to provide handshaking for port A and/or port B.

9. Keyswitches mechanically bounce for 10—15 ms. This bounce must be removed, or the system attached to the switch will see more than one stroke per closure.

10. Keyboards are often in the form of a matrix of keys. The columns are connected to an output port, and the rows are connected to an input port. With this connection it is possible to read any key on the keyboard.

11. Keystrokes are debounced with a time delay subroutine which waits until the key stops bouncing before it is actually sampled.

12. Two types of 7-segment displays are available: common anode and common cathode.

13. The multiplexed display uses a scheme where one display is on at a time, but since the displays are scanned at a fairly high rate of speed it appears that they are all on at all times.

14. The anode driver, for a multiplexed common anode display, is a transistor switch that applies $+5$ V to the anode of the selected display.

15. The segment driver, for a multiplexed common anode display, is a transistor switch that applies ground to a segment of the multiplexed display.

12-8 GLOSSARY

Common anode-display   An LED display that has all of the anode connections tied common so that a segment is illuminated by grounding a cathode.

Common cathode display   An LED display that has all the cathode connections tied common so that a segment is illuminated by applying $+5$ V to an anode.

Debounce   The act of removing the bounce from a switch.

Handshaking   The act of two systems synchronizing through the use of two or more control lines.

I/O port   The I/O device is often called an I/O port.

Input port   An I/O device that collects data for the microprocessor.

Keyboard encoder   A device that scans a keyboard and checks for a key closure; debounces the closure; provides an ASCII code for the key; and provides handshaking signals that indicate the key is closed.

Keyboard matrix   A keyboard arranged in a series of columns and rows so that when a switch is closed, it connects one column and one row.

Latch   A device that holds data. Whenever a clock pulse is provided, the latch catches the data at its inputs and retains them until the next clock.

Multiplexed display   A multiple digit display that shares the segment drivers with all the display digits.

Output port   An I/O device that accepts and holds data from the microprocessor.

Port address   The address of the I/O device which is found on the Z80 address bus on bits A7-A0.

Scan   The act of looking through all the rows or columns of a matrixed keyboard for a closed switch.

Seven-segment LED display   A device constructed of 7 LED diodes. The 7-segment display is designed so that it can display numbers.

Strobed input   Whenever data are clocked and held in an input port for the microprocessor, the port is called a strobed input port.

Strobed output   Whenever data are sent out of the microprocessor and held in a latch until an external device strobes (removes) them from the latch.

Switch bounce   Switches mechanically bounce when closed. This bouncing causes the switch to output more than one pulse each time it is closed.

Three-state buffer   A device that functions as either a buffer, when active, or an open circuit, when inactive.

QUESTIONS AND PROBLEMS

12-1. How many different input ports are available in the Z80?

12-2. On which Z80 pins does the I/O port number appear during an IN or an OUT instruction?

12-3. The $\overline{\text{IOR}}$ signal is generated by logically combining _____ with _____.

12-4. The $\overline{\text{IOW}}$ signal is generated by logically combining _____ with _____.

12-5. The basic input port always consists of what component?

12-6. The basic output port always consists of what component?

12-7. Briefly describe the 8255A.

12-8. 8255A programming group A consists of which ports lines?

12-9. Given an 8255A, connect it to the Z80 so that it functions at I/O ports 20H-23H.

12-10. Given an 8255A, connect it to the Z80 so that it functions at I/O ports 54H-57H.

12-11. Describe what the RESET input to the 8255A accomplishes when it is activated.

12-12. Develop the software required to program the 8255A so that the group A pins function as simple inputs (mode 0) and the group B pins function as simple outputs (mode 0). (Assume that the I/O port is 43H.)

12-13. Develop the software required to program the 8255A so that the group A pins function as strobed inputs and the group B pins function as strobed outputs. (Assume that the I/O port is 97H.)

12-14. Connect a push-button switch to port A pin PA3 and another to port A pin PA2. Write software so that these switches are read, debounced, and cause the contents of memory location 2000H to be cleared to zero if PA3 is active and set it to all ones if PA2 is active. (Assume the I/O ports are 38H-3BH.)

12-15. Explain the purpose of the $\overline{\text{STB}}$ input for strobed input operation of the 8255A.

12-16. Explain the function of the IBF input for strobed input operation of the 8255A.

12-17. Describe how the set reset instruction is used to control the port C pins.

12-18. Explain the relationship between the $\overline{OBF}$ and $\overline{ACK}$ signals for strobed output operation of the 8255A.

12-19. Develop software that inputs data from port B using the strobed input mode of operation. (Assume that the I/O ports are A4H-A7H.)

12-20. Which port is bidirectional when the 8255A is operated in mode 2?

12-21. Which port C pins are general purpose I/O pins in mode 2 operation of the 8255A?

12-22. Explain the effect of the OUT instruction during mode 2 operation of the 8255A.

12-23. Describe the signal found at a push-button switch when it is closed or opened.

12-24. How long will a switch normally bounce?

12-25. In a matrix keyboard, what happens when a switch is closed?

12-26. Explain how the CHECK subroutine functions in Example 12-7.

12-27. Compare the common anode 7-segment display with the common cathode version.

12-28. Modify the anode driver circuit of Figure 12-20 so that it will drive a 7-digit display. (Assume the normal current per segment is 10 mA before multiplexing.)

12-29. Modify the circuit of Figure 12-21 so that it functions for an 8-digit display. (Assume that the normal current per segment is 10 mA before multiplexing.)

12-30. The 8255A will operate with interrupts in which modes?

12-31. When does the INTR pin become a logic one in the strobed input mode of operation?

12-32. When does the INTR pin become a logic one in the strobed output mode of operation?

chapter 13

Serial Communications

Today, serial communications play an extremely important part in many microprocessor based systems. Serial data transfer is the method used to transfer data through the telephone lines and also in the industrial environment for machine control. This chapter is meant as an introduction to serial data. Until this point this text has concentrated on parallel data transfer.

One of the more commonly found devices for serial data transfer is the USART (universal synchronous/asynchronous receiver/transmitter). The 8251A is presented in this text because of its wide application in the field of digital data communications.

13-1 OBJECTIVES

Upon completion of this chapter, you will be able to:

1. Compare asynchronous and synchronous serial data.
2. Define the term Baud.
3. Compare FSK and PSK data transmissions.
4. Program the 8251A so that it sends and receives either asynchronous or synchronous data.
5. Explain how the modem functions in a data communications system.
6. Describe the RS-232C signals used for modem control.

13-2 INTRODUCTION TO SERIAL DATA COMMUNICATIONS _____

This section of the text describes asynchronous data, synchronous data, baud, and various other factors in the data communications environment. It also presents an overview of both FSK and PSK data so that an understanding of these two important methods of serial data communications are understood.

Asynchronous Serial Data

Figure 13-1 illustrates the typical asynchronous serial data stream. Here three ASCII characters are transmitted with even parity, one stop bit, and one start bit for a total of 10 bits. Notice that not all bits contain information; in fact only seven of the ten do. The parity bit indicates whether the data are received correctly. The start and stop bits are used in lieu of the clocking signal which is not transmitted with the data. Instead it is assumed that the data are transmitted within 10% of some predefined frequency.

Receiving asynchronous serial data.   Because no clock is sent with the asynchronous data, they must be detected with some semblance of accuracy. In order to accomplish this, the data are transmitted with a start bit and then followed by the data, the parity bit, and finally the stop bit. The receiver synchronizes to the data by searching for the start bit in a stream of stop bits.

Figure 13-2 shows the way that this is accomplished. Here the data stream is sampled until it becomes a logic zero, after which one-half of one bit of time elapses until it is sampled again. Once it is sampled in the center of the start bit, the data are then sampled nine additional times at one-bit time increments. The sampled data are collected in an internal serial shift register where they are shifted into a parallel byte of data. After parity is tested and errors tested for, the stop bit is tested. If a stop bit is present then the data are valid; if it isn't then a framing error is indicated. A framing error usually occurs if the data are received at the wrong Baud rate, and it should not occur under normal circumstances.

Baud rate.   The data are said to be transmitted at a particular baud rate. In the case of the asynchronous transmission, this is the reciprocal of the bit time. For example, if the bit time is 3.33 ms, then the Baud rate is 1/3.33 ms or 300 Baud. Notice that 300 Baud does not mean that 300 bits of information are sent per second. It means that 300 bits are sent including starts, stops, data, and parity. If there are one start, one parity, and one stop bit per ASCII character (a 7 bit code), then the 300 Baud rate means that 30 ASCII characters per second are transferred. (300 ÷ 10)

Table 13-1 lists some common asynchronous data transmission rates along with other valuable information. Notice that the only noncomforming Baud rate is 110. This is normally used in either Baudot (5 data bits) or ASCII (7 data bits) systems. Systems using 110 Baud were often electro-mechanical printers or teletypewriters. (Note that these are not the only rates in use, but a representative example of the most common.)

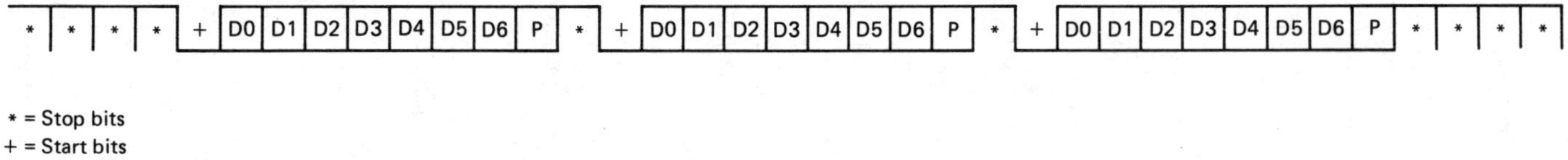

Figure 13–1 Asynchronous serial data showing 3 ASCII characters.

* = Stop bits
\+ = Start bits

| + | D0 | D1 | D2 | D3 | D4 | D5 | D6 | P | * | * | * |

Sample

Found
start
bit

Begin searching
for next
start bit

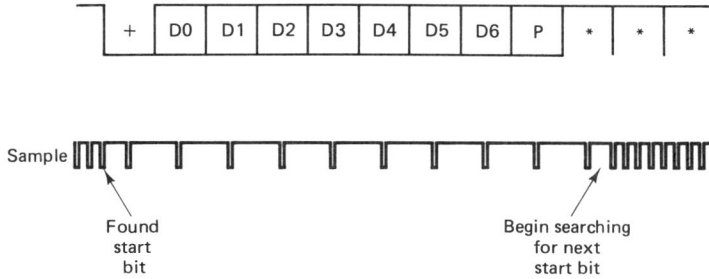

Figure 13–2   Sample intervals for each data bit.

Synchronous Serial Data

Synchronous data, unlike asynchronous data, are transmitted with a clock pulse. This eliminates the need for the start and stop bits which effectively increases the data transmission rate. For example, suppose that data are transmitted at 300 Baud. If data are sent asynchronously then 30 characters are transmitted per second, but if sent synchronously, about 42.9 characters are sent per second ($300 \div 7$), a much more efficient system. Notice that with synchronous transmission the Baud rate and data bit rate can be equal if no parity is sent.

Synchronous data are normally used with high data rates. Table 13-2 illustrates some of the more common data rates used in synchronous data communications systems.

Figure 13-3 illustrates synchronous data and also the clock signal that is transmitted with them. Notice that the positive edge (zero-to-one transition) is at the center of each of the data bits.

FSK

A method of transmitting data over the telephone wires, often employed at lower Baud rates, is FSK (frequency shift keying). As the name implies, FSK is actually a way of

TABLE 13-1. COMMON ASYNCHRONOUS DATA TRANSMISSION RATES*

Baud	Stops	Application
110	1-1/2 or 2	Electro-mechanical teleprinters
300	1	Telephone data communications
600	1	Telephone data communications
900	1	(rarely used)

*Note that in all cases 7 bits of data appear plus parity and stop. The only exception is for 110, which is often 5 bits of data, parity, 1-1/2 stops, and a start bit.

TABLE 13-2.   COMMON SYNCHRONOUS DATA TRANSMISSION RATES

Baud	Application
1200	General purpose telephone data communications over a normal voice line
2400	Dedicated data communications over compensated leased lines
4800	Dedicated data communications over compensated leased lines
9600	Dedicated data communications over compensated leased lines

Note: A compensated line is one that is adjusted for a wider frequency response by the telephone company.

converting the digital data into a signal that is easily passed by the telephone wires, frequency modulation.

Why aren't digital TTL data sent directly across the telephone lines? TTL data are a non-sinusoidal signal that is distorted by the amplifiers found in the telephone system. The telephone system is designed to pass sinewaves and distorts squarewaves to the point where the data would be lost if sent as a TTL signal. Think of 30 minutes of stop pulses before any data are sent. This is essentially a DC signal, and the phone system is designed to pass a 300–3000Hz AC signal. With FSK, the serial digital pulses are converted into two audio tones: one tone for a logic zero and the other for a one.

Figure 13-4 illustrates an FSK signal and the digital signal that generates it. Notice that the logic one data bit is converted to the higher frequency signal. It is a standard to use 2025 Hz (logic 0) and 2225 Hz (logic 1) or 1075 HZ (logic 0) and 1275 Hz (logic 1). Because two separate bands of frequencies are available, data communications often take place in both directions simultaneously on the telephone lines. This type of communication has the sender use one band then the receiver use the other band of frequencies. Simultaneous two-way communications is called full-duplex operation. If data are transmitted in one direction at a time it is called half-duplex operation; and if only transmitted in one direction at all times it is called simplex operation.

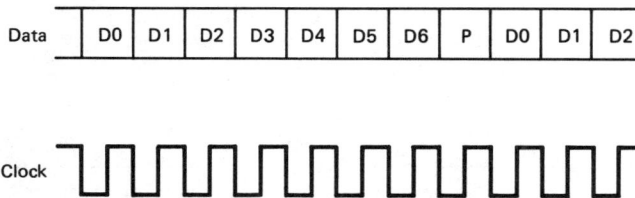

Figure 13–3 Synchronous data showing the clock signal used to synchronize the data.

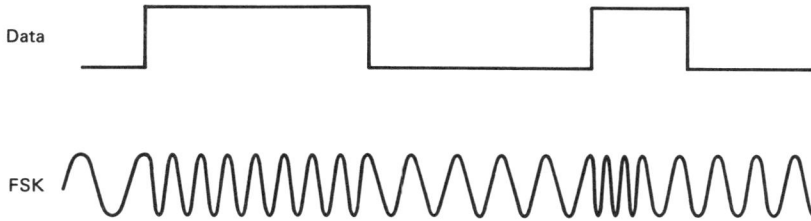

Figure 13–4   Digital data and the FSK signal that it generates in an FSK modem.

PSK

Another method of transmitting data over the telephone lines is via phase shift keying (PSK). PSK is normally used for transferring data at higher rates of speed than FSK because of the way that the data are encoded for transmission.

Figure 13-5 illustrates PSK data and also the digital data used to create it. One method of sending PSK is by sending a carrier (clock) along with the data in synchronous communications environments. The data are encoded as a phase difference between the carrier and the clock. Today either 4 or 8 phases are sent in this manner.

Figure 13-5 shows how the different dibits (2 bits) of data are encoded as a phase angle. In this Figure, a 00 is 0°, a 01 is 90°, a 10 is 180° and an 11 is 270°. PSK allows 2 bits (or 3) of data to be transmitted in the same time it takes for one bit in the FSK system. If three bits are encoded they are called a tribit.

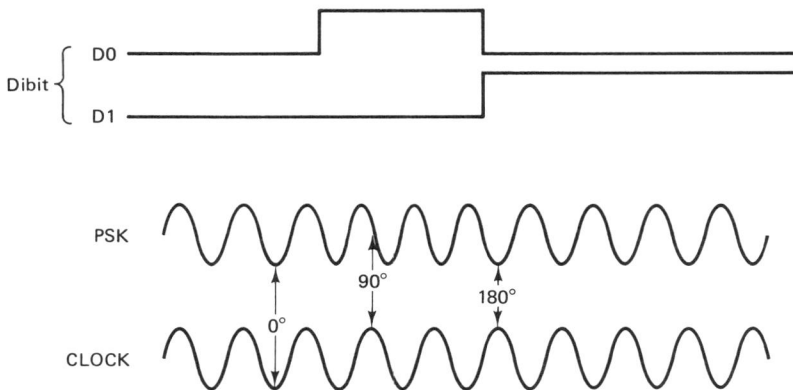

Figure 13–5   PSK and the phase relationship between it and the synchronizing clock.

Modems

Modems are devices that convert TTL digital serial data into either FSK or PSK. They also convert received data in either FSK or PSK back to TTL. The word modem is a conjunction of MOdulator/DEModulator. More information on modems and their control appears later in this chapter.

13-3 THE 8251A USART

The 8251A universal synchronous/asynchronous receiver/transmitter (USART) is a device that converts parallel digital data from the Z80 into serial TTL digital data. It also provides control signals to a modem, error detection, and handshaking data to the Z80.

The 8251A is capable of transmitting and receiving data at rates of between DC–64K Baud for synchronous data and DC–19.2K Baud for asynchronous data. The receiver and transmitter are separate which allows data to be received or transmitted at different Baud rates, but both must operate in synchronous or asynchronous mode because the receiver and transmitter are programmed together.

Description of the 8251A

Figure 13-6 illustrates the pinout and block diagram of the 8251A. The 8251A is packaged in a 28 pin integrated circuit that requires a single $+5$ V power supply for operation. It also requires an external timing signal that is used to set the Baud rate of the transmitter and receiver sections.

Pin functions.

RESET—Reset Input: a pin that clears the internal circuitry that is normally connected to the same circuit that clears or resets the Z80.

CLK—Clock Input: a pin used to generate internal timing for that 8251A that is connected to the Z80 clocking source. It in no way generates the Baud rate of the 8251A.

$\overline{WR}$—Write Input: a pin used to send data into the internal command register during programming or into the internal data register for transmission.

$\overline{RD}$—Read Input: a pin used to read the status word or read the internal data register.

$C/\overline{D}$—Command/Data Input: a pin that is used to select either data or command. If this input is a logic one, data are written into the internal command register or read from the internal status register. If a logic zero, data are either transmitted or received by the USART.

$\overline{CS}$—Chip Select Input: an active low input that selects the 8251A for programming or for data transfer.

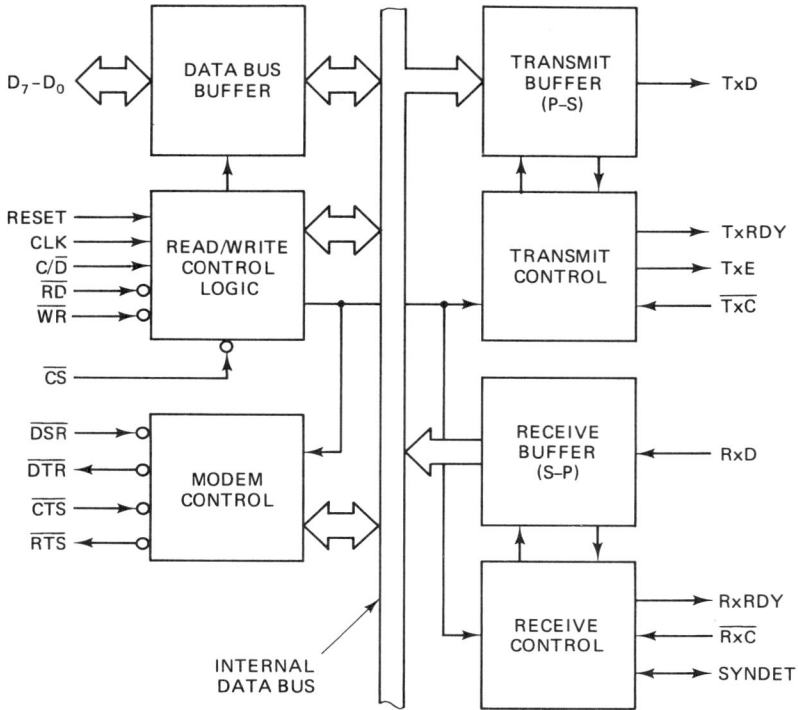

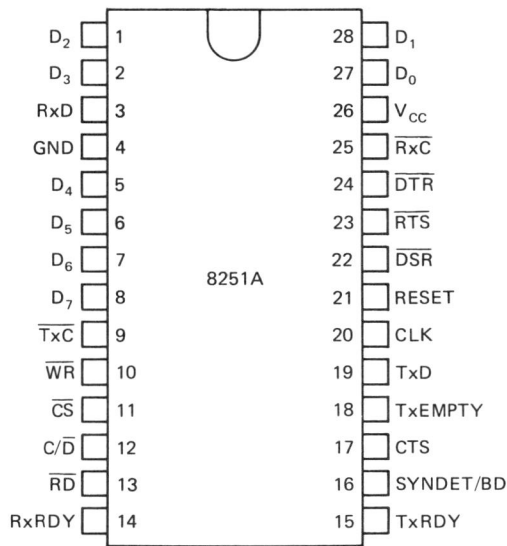

Figure 13–6 The pinout and functional block diagram of the 8251A communications interface adapter. (Courtesy of Intel Corporation.)

$\overline{\text{DSR}}$—Data Set Ready Input: an inverting input bit that is used to test the status of the data set (modem). $\overline{\text{DSR}}$, when active, indicates that the data set is operational.

$\overline{\text{DTR}}$—Data Terminal Ready Output: an output that is programmable to indicate that the data terminal (Z80 and the 8251A) is operational.

$\overline{\text{RTS}}$—Request-to-Send Output: an output that is used in the half-duplex mode of operation to request that the modem set up for data transmission.

$\overline{\text{CTS}}$—Clear-to-Send Input: used to indicate to the 8251A that the modem is clear to transmit data. In order for the 8251A to transmit anything this input must be at its logic zero level.

D0—D7—Data Bus: a series of pins connected to the Z80 data bus.

TxD—Transmit Data Output: The serial output data pin from the USART.

TxRDY—Transmitter Ready Output: a pin that indicates the transmitter section of the 8251A is ready to receive another byte for conversion to serial by the USART.

TxEMPTY—Transmitter Empty Output: indicates that the transmitter section of the 8251A is completely empty.

$\overline{\text{TxC}}$—Transmitter Clock Input: an input that supplies the transmitter section with its timing element.

RxD—Received Data Input: serial data input to the USART.

RxRDY—Receiver Ready Output: a signal that indicates that the receiver section of the 8251A has received a byte of data.

$\overline{\text{RxC}}$—Receiver Clock Input: an input that supplies the receiver section with its timing element.

SYNDET/BD—Sync Detect/Break Detect Output: Indicates that the sync or sync characters are detected in synchronous operation or that the break character is detected in asynchronous operation. A break character is two complete frames of start bits.

Programming the 8251A

Programming the 8251A is fairly simple. It requires two basic steps to complete: programming the mode set register and programming the operational command register. The mode set register is used to initialize the 8251A, and the operational command register is used to control the operation of the 8251A after it is initialized.

Programming the mode set register.   Before the mode set register is programmed, the 8251A must be reset. Resetting the 8251A does not occur from the RESET input because of an apparent design flaw; instead it must be reset by sending out a 00H to the command register followed by a 04H. The three 00H outputs clear the internal command register and the 04H resets the 8251A.

Once the 8251A is reset, it can now be sent the mode set command which directs it to function in either the asynchronous or synchronous mode. Figure 13-7 illustrates both of these mode set control words. Both mode set words specify the number of data

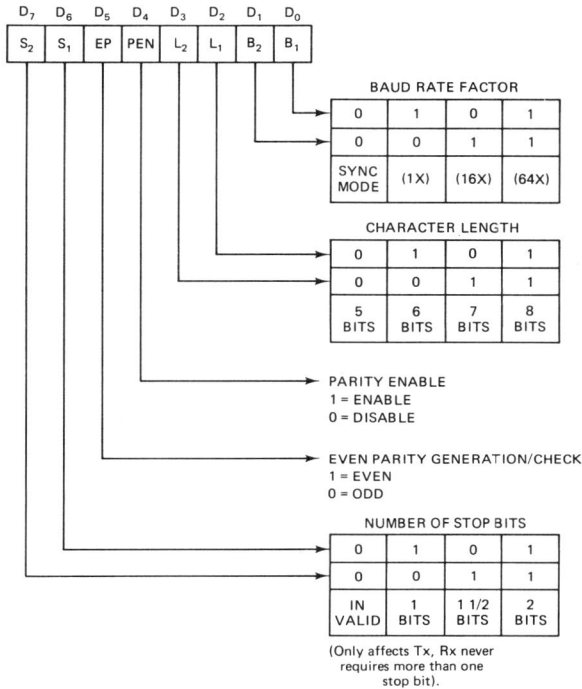

D₇	D₆	D₅	D₄	D₃	D₂	D₁	D₀
S₂	S₁	EP	PEN	L₂	L₁	B₂	B₁

BAUD RATE FACTOR

0	1	0	1
0	0	1	1
SYNC MODE	(1X)	(16X)	(64X)

CHARACTER LENGTH

0	1	0	1
0	0	1	1
5 BITS	6 BITS	7 BITS	8 BITS

PARITY ENABLE
1 = ENABLE
0 = DISABLE

EVEN PARITY GENERATION/CHECK
1 = EVEN
0 = ODD

NUMBER OF STOP BITS

0	1	0	1
0	0	1	1
IN VALID	1 BITS	1 1/2 BITS	2 BITS

(Only affects Tx, Rx never requires more than one stop bit).

(a)

D₇	D₆	D₅	D₄	D₃	D₂	D₁	D₀
SCS	ESD	EP	PEN	L₂	L₁	0	0

CHARACTER LENGTH

0	1	0	1
0	0	1	1
5 BITS	6 BITS	7 BITS	8 BITS

PARITY ENABLE
(1 = ENABLE)
(0 = DISABLE)

EVEN PARITY GENERATION/CHECK
1 = EVEN
0 = ODD

EXTERNAL SYNC DEFECT
1 = SYNDET IS AN INPUT
0 = SYNDET IS AN OUTPUT

SINGLE CHARACTER SYNC
1 = SINGLE SYNC CHARACTER
0 = DOUBLE SYNC CHARACTER

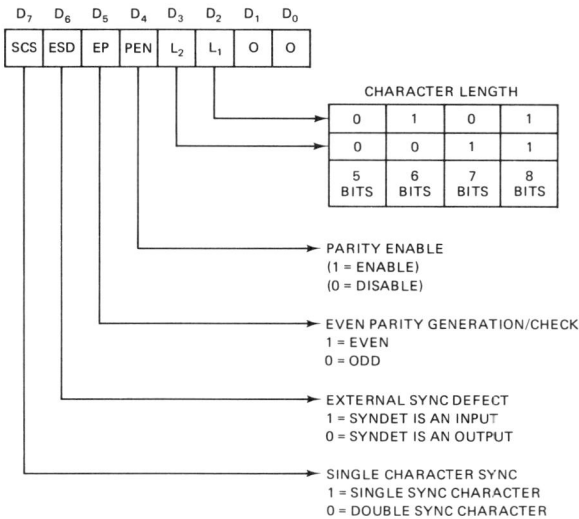

Note: in external sync mode programming double character sync will affect only the Tx

(b)

Figure 13-7 Mode set control words. (a) Asynchronous. (b) Synchronous. (Courtesy of Intel Corporation.)

bits and parity, but nothing else is similar. In the asynchronous mode set word, the number of stop bits and the clock divider are programmed. In the synchronous mode set register, the number of sync characters and the function of the SYNDET pin is programmed. SYNDET is programmed as either an input or as an output. When SYNDET is programmed as an input, it causes sync characters to be transmitted when active; as an output, it indicates that sync characters are being transmitted by the 8251A.

When the mode set register is programmed it is sent one byte of data to program it for asynchronous operation and two or three bytes for synchronous operation. Synchronous operation requires that the sync characters (one or two) are sent to the 8251A immediately after the mode set register is programmed.

Programming for asynchronous operation.   Suppose that the 8251A is to be operated in the asynchronous mode with 7 data bits, even parity, and one stop bit. It also requires a clock divider of 16. The clock divider of 16 causes the transmitted and received Baud rates to be equal to the frequency placed on the $\overline{TxC}$ and $\overline{RxC}$ pins to be divided by 16. The subsequent Baud rate is then $\overline{TxC} \div 16$ and $\overline{RxC} \div 16$. Figure 13-8 illustrates how the 8251A is interfaced to the Z80 so that it operates at I/O ports 80H and 81H. In this example 81H is the command port and 80H is the data port.

Example 13-1 illustrates the software required to program the 8251A to operate as indicated. The first part of the software is used to reset the 8251A. Once programmed in the reset mode, the 8251A is sent the mode set command. The last portion of the software enables both the transmitter and receiver by controlling the operational command register. The operational command register and the bit patterns that command the 8251A are illustrated in Figure 13-9. This register enables the transmitter and receiver, and it

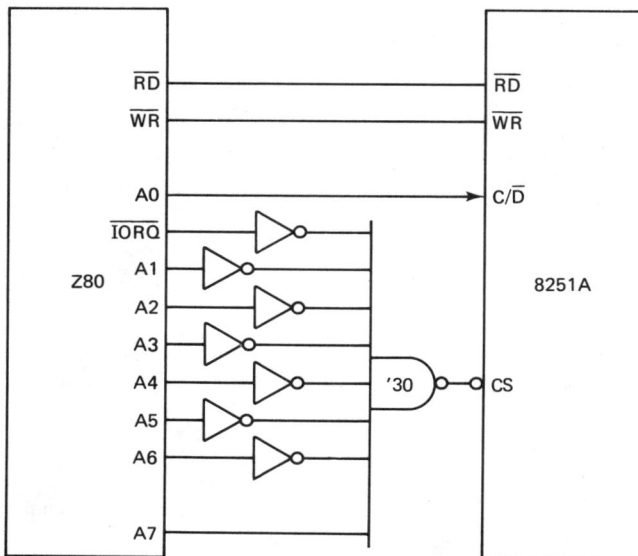

Figure 13-8 The 8251A decoded so that it operates at I/O ports 80H and 81H.

D$_7$	D$_6$	D$_5$	D$_4$	D$_3$	D$_2$	D$_1$	D$_0$
EH	IR	RTS	ER	SBRK	RxE	DTR	TxEN

TRANSMIT ENABLE
1 = ENABLE
0 = DISABLE

DATA TERMINAL READY
"High" will force $\overline{DTR}$ output
to zero

RECEIVE ENABLE
1 = ENABLE
0 = DISABLE

SEND BREAK CHARACTER
1 = forces TxD low
0 = normal operation

ERROR RESET
1 = reset error flags
      PE, OE, FE

REQUEST TO SEND
"High" will force RTS
output to zero

INTERNAL RESET
"High" return 8251A to
mode instruction format

ENTER HUNT MODE
1 = enable search for
      sync characters

(Has no effect
in async mode)

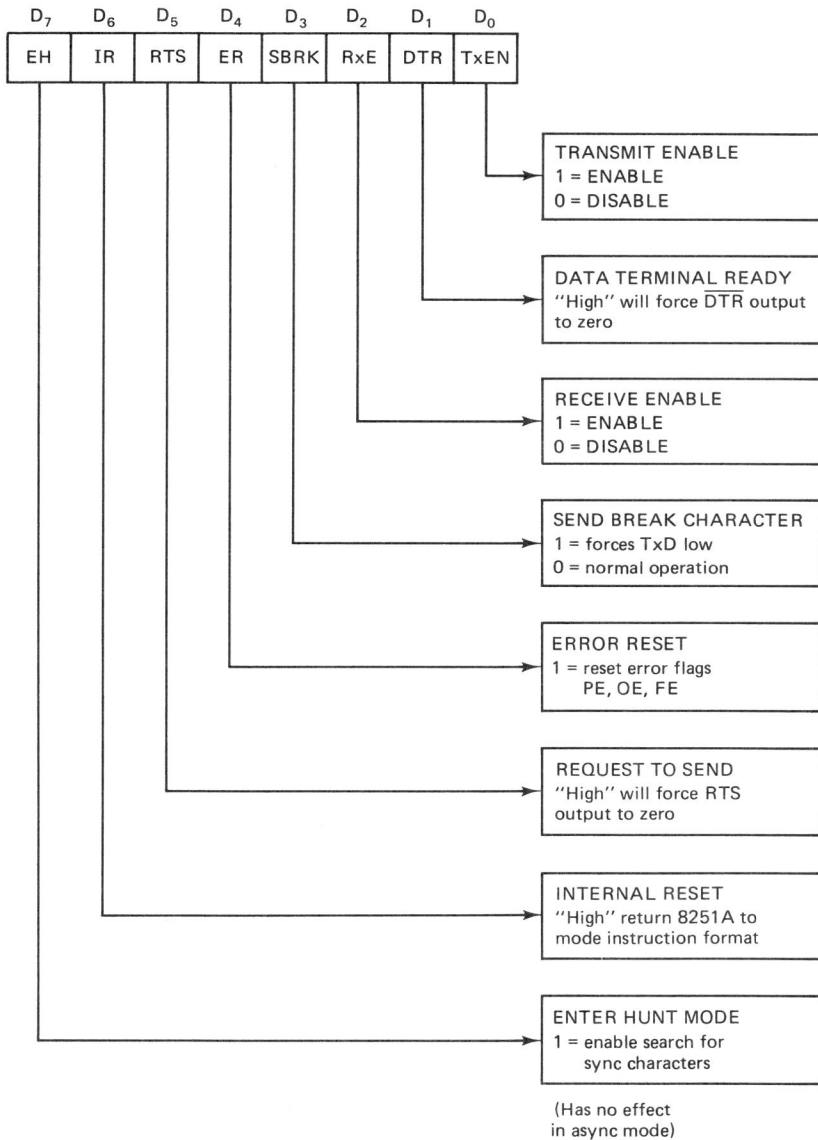

Note: Error reset must be performed whenever
       RxEnable and enter hunt are programmed.

Figure 13–9   The command register of the 8251A. (Courtesy of Intel Corporation.)

also controls the DTR and RTS pins on the 8251A, sends a break character in asynchronous mode, resets errors, resets the 8251A, and enters into the hunt mode for synchronous operation.

Example 13-1

```
;
;software to program the 8251A so that it functions
;in the asynchronous mode.
;
COMMAND:   EQU   81H          ;declare the command port
;
;reset the 8251A
;
INIT:      LD    A,0
           OUT   (COMMAND),A
           OUT   (COMMAND),A
           OUT   (COMMAND),A
           LD    A,40H
           OUT   (COMMAND),A
;
;program mode set register
;
           LD    A,01111010B
           OUT   (COMMAND),A
;
;program operational command register
;
           LD    A,00010101B
           OUT   (COMMAND),A
```

Programming for synchronous operation.   Synchronous operation requires that the 8251A is programmed differently from the way it is for asynchronous operation. The main difference is that after the mode set register is programmed the one or two sync characters are programmed before the command register. In synchronous operation, the sync characters are used to allow the receiver to start receiving data bits.

Example 13-2 shows how the 8251A is programmed for synchronous operation with 7 data bits, even parity, the SYNDET pin programmed as an output, and two sync characters. Here the sync characters are a 7EH and a 7FH, which are not normally sent for ASCII transmissions so that they are unique. These are often used as sync characters in synchronous data communications.

Example 13-2

```
;
;software to program the 8251A for synchronous
;operation.
;
COMMAND:   EQU   81H          ;declare the command port
;
;reset the 8251A
;
```

(Example 13-2 continued)

```
SETUP:      LD   A,O
            OUT  (COMMAND),A
            OUT  (COMMAND),A
            OUT  (COMMAND),A
            LD   A,40H
            OUT  (COMMAND),A
;
;program mode set register
;
            LD   A,10111000B
            OUT  (COMMAND),A
;
;program sync characters
;
            LD   A,7EH
            OUT  (COMMAND),A
            LD   A,7FH
            OUT  (COMMAND),A
;
;program command register
;
            LD   A,00010101B
            OUT  (COMMAND),A
```

Using the 8251A for Serial Communications

Once the 8251A is programmed it is ready to use for serial data communications. Before we can develop software to transmit or receive data, the structure of the status register of the 8251A must be understood.

Figure 13-10 depicts the bit pattern of the 8251A status register. The status register contains the status of the modem control pin (DSR); the condition of the transmitter and receiver via the TxRDY, TXEMPTY, and RxRDY status bits; errors that have occurred through the FE, OE, and PE bits; and the logic level of the SYNDET/BD pin.

Transmitter software.   The transmitter can be used if the $\overline{\text{CTS}}$ pin is at a logic zero level and the transmitter enable bit, in the command register, is active. If both conditions are met then the transmitter can function. The transmitter has two status bits associated with it: TxRDY and TxEMPTY. The TxRDY status bit indicates that the transmitter is ready to receive another character for transmission, and the TxEMPTY status bit indicates that the transmitter has completely transmitted all data.

The software, see Example 13-3, for transmitting a byte of data first tests the TxRDY bit to determine if it is all right to send another character to the 8251A for transmission. If the 8251A is ready, the subroutine continues and sends the contents of the B register to the 8251A.

D_7	D_6	D_5	D_4	D_3	D_2	D_1	D_0
DSR	SYNDET BRKDET	FE	OE	PE	TxEMPTY	RxRDY	TxRDY

Note 1

Same definitions as I/O pins

PARITY ERROR
The PE flag is set when a parity error is detected. It is reset by the ER bit of the command instruction. PE does not inhibit operation of the 8251A.

OVERRUN ERROR
The OE flag is set when the CPU does not read a character before the next one becomes available. It is reset by the ER bit of the command instruction. OE does not inhibit operation of the 8251A; however, the previously overrun character is lost.

FRAMING ERROR (Async only)
The FE flag is set when a valid stop bit is not detected at the end of every character. It is reset by the ER bit of the command instruction. FE does not inhibit the operation of the 8251A.

DATA SET READY
Indicates that the DSR is at a zero level.

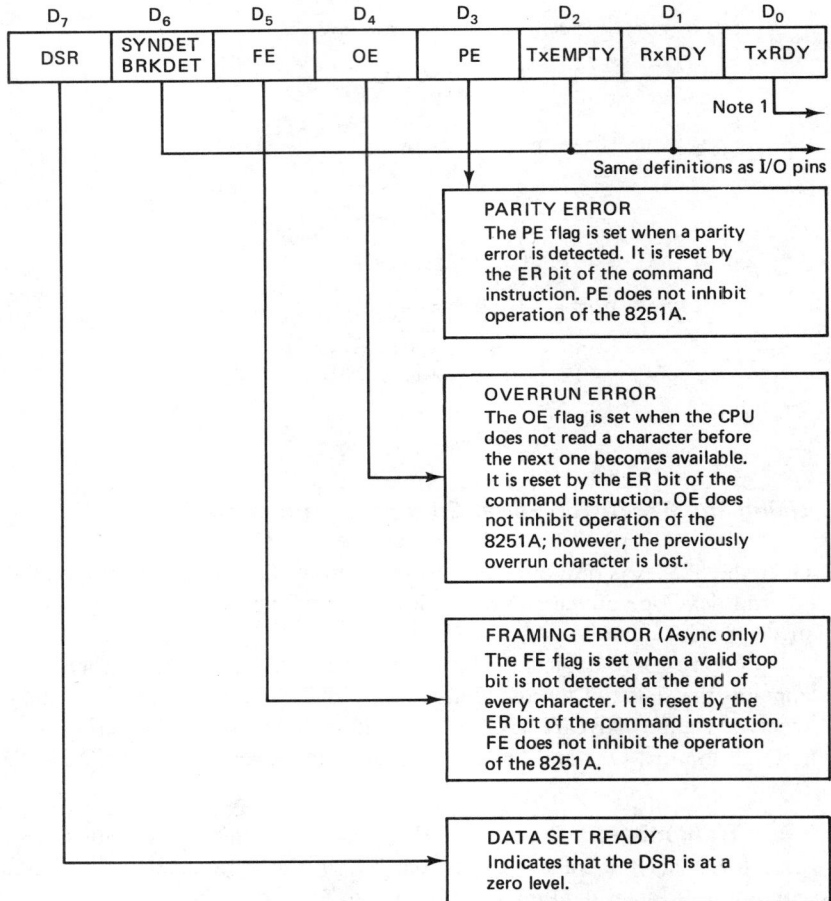

Note 1: TxRDY status bit has different meanings from the TxRDY output pin. The former is not conditioned by $\overline{CTS}$ and TxEN; the latter is conditioned by both $\overline{CTS}$ and TxEN.

i.e. TxRDY status bit = DB buffer empty

TxRDY pin out. DB buffer empty = ($\overline{CTS}$ 0) = (TxEN 1)

Figure 13–10   Status register of the 8251A. (Courtesy of the Intel Corporation.)

Example 13-3

```
;
;subroutine to transmit the contents of the
;B register
;
COMMAND:    EQU    81H           ;declare command port
DATA:       EQU    80H           ;declare data port
;
;test status of transmitter
;
SEND:       IN     A,(COMMAND)   ;get status
            RRCA                 ;move TxRDY to carry
            JR     NC,SEND       ;if not ready
;
;send data
;
            LD     A,B           ;get data
            OUT    (DATA),A
            RET
```

Receiver software.   The software to control the reception of data from the 8251A is very similar to the transmitter software. The only main difference is that the receiver can detect three error conditions: parity error (PE), overrun error (OE), and framing error (FE).

A parity error is indicative of a received character whose parity was odd if the 8251A is programmed to receive parity or even if programmed to receive old parity. Parity errors are mainly due to noise that is picked up on the serial signal during transmission through the telephone lines.

An overrun error should not normally occur. Overruns indicate that the data received by the 8251A are lost because the software failed to receive or detect them before the next data byte is received. If this type of error occurs the system software must be rewritten so that data are accepted from the USART at a higher rate.

The framing error should also not occur during normal operation. A framing error occurs whenever the stop bit or bits are missing during data reception. The most common cause for this is receiving data at the wrong Baud rate.

Example 13-4 lists the subroutine used to receive data through the 8251A. Here, as with the SEND subroutine of Example 13-3, the first portion of the subroutine tests the receiver (RxRDY) to see if it has received a byte of data. If data are received, the next portion tests to see if any errors are present. If errors are present then the data received are ignored and instead an ASCII question mark is returned as the received data. Notice that the errors must be reset by the command register if any are detected.

Example 13-4

```
;
;subroutine to receive data via the 8251A.
;The recieved data are returned in the B register
;
```

(Example 13-4 continued)

```
COMMAND:   EQU    81H          ;declare command port
DATA:      EQU    80H          ;declare data port
;
;test RxRDY
;
RECV:      IN     A,(COMMAND)  ;get status
           RRCA                ;RxRDY to carry
           RRCA
           JR     NC,RECV      ;if not ready
;
;get data
;
           IN     A,(DATA)
           LD     B,A
;
;test for errors
;
           IN     A,(COMMAND)  ;get data
           AND    38H          ;test error bits
           JR     Z,NEXT       ;if no errors
           LD     B,'?'        ;get ASCII ?
           LD     A,15H        ;reset errors
           OUT    (COMMAND),A
NEXT:      RET
```

13-4 INTERFACE STANDARDS

This section of the text explains how the modem is controlled and also describes the EIA* RS-232C and 20 mA current loop interfaces. Current loops are used in older electro-mechanical interfaces and also in control systems, and the RS-232C standard is used with modems, printers, and plotters.

The 20 mA Current Loop

The 20 mA current loop is used to transfer serial data at low Baud rates. Usually the maximum transfer rate for this type of interface is 2400 Baud. This interface is very immune to noise problems and also can be used to control machinery at fairly great distances. Distances for this standard can be up to a mile from the source of the serial data which, along with the high noise immunity, makes it ideal for industrial control environments.

Unlike most digital data, data through the current loop are in the form of current flow. The unipolar 20 mA loop has current flowing for a logic one level and no current flowing for a logic zero level. The bipolar 20 mA loop has current flowing in one direction for a logic one and in the opposite direction for a logic zero. Because the logic signals are represented by current flows, noise has little effect on the operation of this interface.

*EIA (Electronics Industries Association) is an organization of American and Japanese electronics manufacturers that proposes standards that all members must follow.

Figure 13-11 illustrates both the receiving and transmitting end of a unipolar 20 mA current loop. Notice that in this system, optical isolators are used to isolate each end of the system from the other. This is common practice to reduce noise problems due to current paths through the AC power lines between the receiver and the transmitter.

In this circuit, a logic one into the transmitter causes 20 mA of current to flow in the loop, and a logic zero causes no current flow. The receiver is sensitive to the current flow because the current flows through the LED in an optical isolator. When current flows through the LED the output of the isolator becomes a logic zero, and after passing through an invert, a logic one.

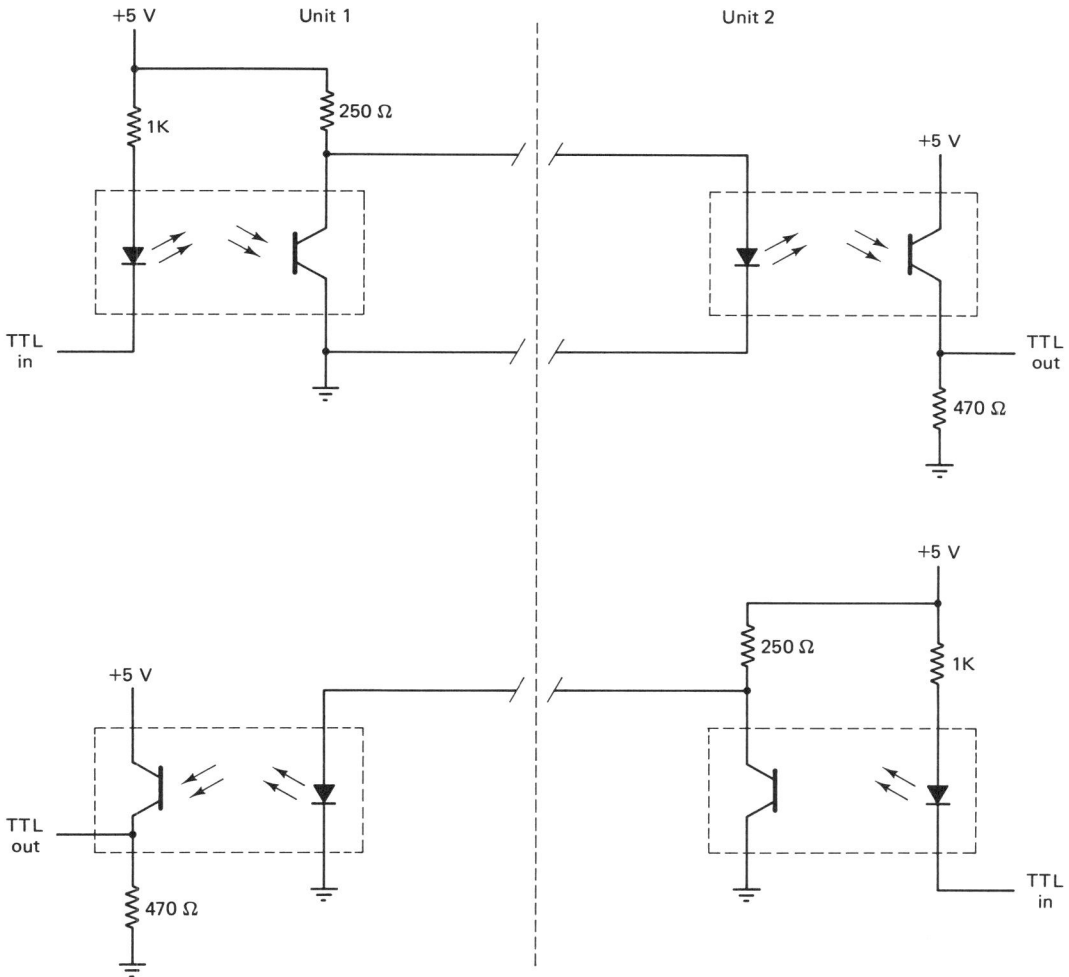

Figure 13–11   20 mA current loop interconnecting 2 units in a data communications system.

As you can see from this circuit, the current loop is a rather simple and effective way to send serial data over fairly large distances where noise immunity is important. The amount of current used may vary in practice. If a greater distance is required a 60 mA current loop is often used.

RS-232C

The RS-232C interface standard is often used for interfacing the data terminal equipment (DTE), the computer, to the data set or data communications equipment (DCE), the modem. RS-232C is a serial standard that specifies such things as the connector, logic levels, cabling distances, etc. In addition to interfacing the computer to modems, RS-232C is also used to interface to printers and plotters.

Connector and pin functions.   This standard employs a 25 pin D-shaped connector (DB-25), and in some cases a 9 pin D-shaped connector is also being used in very recent equipment. The 25-pin connector most often used, but not specified in the standard, is illustrated in Figure 13-12. As can be seen it consists of two rows of pins with the top row containing pins 1—13 and the bottom row containing pins 14—15. This arrangement (13 pins on the top and 12 on the bottom) give the connector its characteristic D-shape.

Table 13-3 lists the function of each pin of this standard. Notice that there are two possible data channels available in this standard: a primary channel and a secondary channel. In most cases only the primary channel is used.

Electrical characteristics.   The RS-232C standard allows for data distances of 50 feet with reports of distances to 1200 feet. It has a maximum usable bandwidth of from 0—19.2K Baud. This standard is not TTL compatible and uses voltage levels of +3 V minimum to +25 V maximum for a logic 0 level and −3 V minimum to −25 V maximum for the logic 1 level. (See Figure 13-13 for a graphic illustration of these logic levels.) Notice that none of the logic levels are at the ground potential. This is done to help eliminate problems from ground loops in systems. (A ground loop causes current flows between the equipment's ground terminals.) By removing the logic levels from ground, this standard prevents ground loops from causing problems to the logic signals. Figure 13-14 illustrates the pinouts of the MC1488 line driver and the MC1489 line receiver. The line driver converts TTL level signals into RS-232C signals, and the line receiver converts RS-232C signals into TTL signals. Notice that each device contains four converters. The line driver has two power supply connections: +VCC and −VCC. In most applications ± 12 V is connected to these two supply inputs so that the logic 0 and logic 1 signals are +12 V and −12 V respectively. In some computer equipment

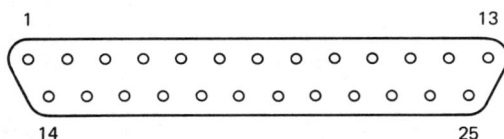

1   13

Figure 13–12   25 pin D-type connector commonly used with RS-232C.

14   25

TABLE 13-3. THE PIN FUNCTIONS OF THE RS-232C INTERFACE STANDARD

Pin	Name	Comment
1	Protective ground	Earth ground used to interconnect chasis
2	SO	Serial output is data transmitted from the data terminal to the data set
3	SI	Serial input is data received from the data set
4	$\overline{\text{RTS}}$	The request-to-send signal request that the data set sends data
5	$\overline{\text{CTS}}$	Clear-to-send tells the data terminal it can send data to the data set
6	$\overline{\text{DSR}}$	Data set ready indicates that the data set is operational
7	Signal ground	The return path for the signal
8	$\overline{\text{DCD}}$	Data carrier detect indicates that the data set has detected a carrier
9	Reserved	
10	Reserved	
11	Unassigned	
12	Secondary $\overline{\text{DCD}}$	
13	Secondary CTS	
14	Secondary transmit data	
15	TSE	Transmit signal clock
16	Secondary receive data	
17	RSE	Receive signal clock
18	Unassigned	
19	Secondary RTS	
20	DTR	Data terminal ready indicates that the data terminal is operational
21	Signal-quality	Indicates the quality of the received signal from the data set
22	RI	Ring indicator indicates that the data set is detecting a telephone ring
23	DRS	Data rate select is used to select one of two different Baud rates
24	Unassigned	
25	Unassigned	

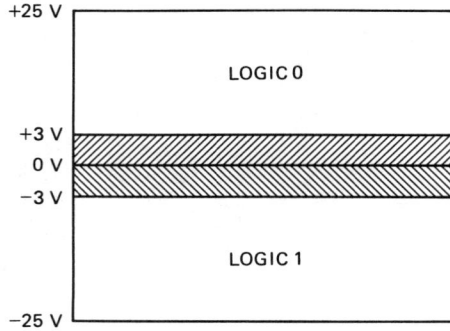

Figure 13–13 Standard RS-232C logic levels.

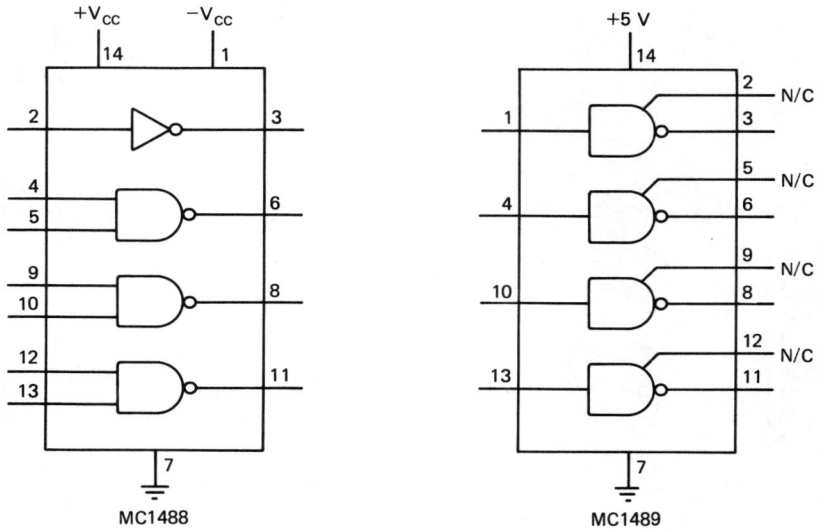

Figure 13–14 The MC1488 line driver and the MC1489 line receiver.

+5 V and −12 V are also used for these two voltage levels because of the additional cost of the +12 V supply.

The typical DCE/DTE connection.   Figure 13-15 illustrates the interconnection between the data terminal and the data set. Here line drivers and line receivers are used to buffer and convert the signals between TTL levels and RS-232C levels.

The lines that interconnect the DCE and DTE are SI, SO, $\overline{CTS}$, $\overline{DCD}$, $\overline{DSR}$, $\overline{DTR}$, RI, and $\overline{RTS}$. The function of each line is listed below:

SI—Serial input data are data that are received by the DTE from the DCE.

SO—Serial output data are data transmitted from the DTE to the DCE.

$\overline{\text{CTS}}$—Clear-to-send is a signal sent from the DCE to the DTE to indicate that data may be transmitted through the DCE. (This is normally used in half duplex operation only to indicate that the line is turned around for transmission.)

$\overline{\text{DCD}}$—Data carrier detect indicates that a valid carrier is detected by the data set. This is used on modems that automatically dial the phone number of another system. If the other system has answered, the carrier is detected and indicated by this signal.

$\overline{\text{DSR}}$—Data set ready is a signal that indicates the DCE is operational and ready to function with the DTE.

$\overline{\text{DTR}}$—Data terminal ready is a signal to the DCE that indicates the DTE is operational and ready to function.

RI—Ring indicator is only used in an auto-answer modem so that a ringing phone can be detected and answered.

$\overline{\text{RTS}}$—Request-to-send is a signal that is used to ask the DCE to turn the line around for transmission in a half duplex system.

If the modem (DCE) is operated in half duplex mode then the $\overline{\text{RTS}}$ and $\overline{\text{CTS}}$ signals are used along with the remaining signals. In a full duplex system only the $\overline{\text{DSR}}$ and $\overline{\text{DCD}}$ signals may be used.

For full duplex operation the DTE tests the $\overline{\text{DSR}}$ signal to determine if it is ready to function. If it is ready to function, the $\overline{\text{DCD}}$ signal is next poled to determine if the

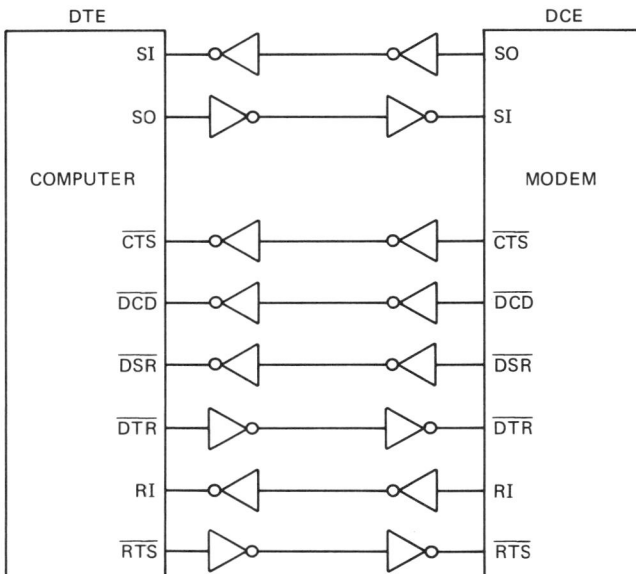

Figure 13–15 Interconnection of the DTE and DCE.

DCE is connected to a carrier. If a carrier is present communications may begin, and if it is not, then the DTE must dial up the distant computer.

For half duplex operation the initial handshaking is essentially the same except now the data may only be sent or received at one time. If the DTE wishes to transmit data it must request transmission by activating the $\overline{RTS}$ input to the DCE. Once the DCE is ready to transmit data it returns the $\overline{CTS}$ signal back to the DTE.

The RI is used in a system that has an auto-answer DCE. When the RI signal is detected by the DCE it activates RI. The DTE then lifts the hook (the receiver on the telephone), sends a carrier, and waits for the $\overline{DCD}$ signal. Once $\overline{DCD}$ is detected communications may begin.

If a synchronous DCE is connected to the DTE the receive and transmit timing elements are also connected. The received timing element is used to receive the synchronous data, and the transmit timing element is used to generate the synchronous data and it is transmitted with the data. Without these two elements synchronous communications cannot exist.

13-5 SUMMARY

1. Asynchronous data are data that are sent without any clocking pulses; instead they are sent with a start bit and one or two stops that are used for synchronization.

2. Asynchronous data are sent with either even or odd parity for error detection at the receiving end of the data communications system.

3. A framing error occurs if data are received and they do not contain a start and one or two stop bits in the proper place.

4. The Baud rate is the number of bits of information transmitted per second and includes start, data, parity, and stop bits.

5. Synchronous data are sent with a clock pulse and no start or stop bits which increases the amount of information transmitted per unit of time.

6. The FSK (frequency shift keyed) modem converts between TTL serial data and two audio tones that represent the serial TTL data. The reason is that the telephone system will not pass TTL level squarewaves.

7. Data transmission types include simplex, half duplex, and full duplex. Simplex is one-way; half duplex is two-way, but one-way at a time; and full duplex is two-way communications with both directions occurring at the same time.

8. The PSK (phase shift keyed) modem is used to convert between TTL serial data and phase shifted sinewaves. The value of the data transmitted is determined by the phase relationship between the carrier and the clock. Data are encoded in either 2 bit increments (dibits) or in three bit increments (tribits).

9. A modem (modulator/demodulator) is a device that converts between TTL serial data and either FSK or PSK.

10. The 8251A USART is a device that converts between parallel data from the Z80 into asynchronous or synchronous data.

11. The 8251A is programmed for synchronous operation by programming the mode set register followed by the command register.

12. The 8251A is programmed for synchronous operation by programming the mode set register, followed by one or two sync characters, followed by the command register.

13. The 20 mA current loop is used to interface data communications equipment and control systems in high noise environments.

14. EIA RS-232C is an interface standard that specifies the signal lines between the DTE (data terminal equipment) and the DCE (data communications equipment).

15. Modem control is allowed by the RS-232C standard via the $\overline{\text{RTS}}$ (request-to-send), $\overline{\text{CTS}}$ (clear-to-send), $\overline{\text{DTR}}$ (data terminal ready), $\overline{\text{DSR}}$ (data set ready), and the $\overline{\text{DCD}}$ (data carrier detect signals).

13-6 GLOSSARY

Asynchronous serial data   Data that are sent without clocking information; instead a start and one or two stop bits accomplish synchronization.

Baud rate   The number of bits of information transferred per second. This includes start, stops, data, and parity.

Bipolar current loop   A current loop where current flows in one direction for a logic one and the other for a logic zero.

Break character   A break in asynchronous data signified by a series of at least two frames worth of start bits.

DCE   Data communications equipment.

Dibit   Two bits that are encoded as one of four different phase angles between the carrier and the data in a PSK system.

DTE   Data terminal equipment.

Framing-error   An error that occurs when asynchronous data are received without the stop bit in the proper place. (Usually occurs due to the wrong Baud rate.)

FSK   Frequency shift keying is a communications data transfer technique that converts between TTL serial data and one audio tone for a logic zero and another for a logic one.

Line driver   A device that is designed to drive a long wire and change the data from TTL to some other form.

Line receiver   A device that is designed to receive a signal over a long wire and convert it back to a TTL signal.

Modem   A modulator/demodulator is a device that converts serial TTL data into either FSK or PSK.

Overrun error   When data are not extracted from the 8251A before the next datum is received an overrun error occurs.

Parity   The count of the number of ones in a number expressed as even or odd.

PSK   Phase shift keying is a data communications technique that converts between serial TTL data and a signal that varies in phase dependent upon the data being transmitted.

Synchronous data   Data that are transferred with a timing or clock signal.

Tribit   Three bits that are encoded to produce one of eight different phase angles between the carrier and the data in a PSK system.

Unipolar current loop   A current loop when data only flow for a logic one.

USART   Universal synchronous/asynchronous receiver/transmitter.

QUESTIONS AND PROBLEMS

13-1. Draw the serial asynchronous data stream if a 7 bit ASCII 3 (33H) is transmitted with even parity and one stop bit.

13-2. Describe how the receiver synchronizes to the asynchronous data and detects it in an asynchronous data communications system.

13-3. What is a framing error and what might cause it?

13-4. If the bit time is 100 ms, what is the Baud rate in an asynchronous system?

13-5. How many bytes of data are transmitted if the Baud rate is 1200 and there are 7 data bits, 1 start bit, 1 stop bit, and even parity?

13-6. Is a clock signal sent with synchronous data?

13-7. If 7-bit ASCII code is sent synchronously without parity at 1200 Baud, how many ASCII characters are sent per second?

13-8. What transition of the clock is at the center of each synchronous data bit?

13-9. Why isn't TTL serial data transmitted directly across the telephone lines?

13-10. What is the bandwidth of the telephone line?

13-11. FSK is _____ shift keying.

13-12. Describe the appearance of FSK serial data.

13-13. What are the standard frequencies used with the FSK system?

13-14. Explain the difference between half and full duplex.

13-15. PSK is _____ shift keying.

13-16. If two bits are used to generate PSK they are called a _____.

13-17. If three bits are used to generate PSK they are called a _____.

13-18. In a PSK system, what four phase angles are generated with a dibit?

13-19. A modulator/demodulator is more commonly called a _____.

13-20. What is a USART?

13-21. The 8251A is capable of sending and receiving asynchronous serial data at Baud rates of up to _____.

13-22. What input determines the Baud rate of the 8251A transmitter?

13-23. What is the purpose of the C/$\overline{\text{D}}$ input to the 8251A?

13-24. Explain how the 8251A must be reset after DC power is applied.

13-25. The mode set register is programmed after a _____.

13-26. Develop the software required to reset and program the 8251A so that it operates asynchronously with 6 data bits, odd parity, two stops, and a clock divider of 64. After the mode is programmed, enable only the receiver. (Use I/O port 13H as the command port.)

13-27. Develop the software required to reset and program the 8251A so that it operates synchronously with 8 data bits and two sync characters (FEH and FFH). After the mode and sync characters are programmed, enable only the transmitter. (Use I/O port 55H as the command port.)

13-28. Interface the 8251A to the Z80 so that it operates at data port number 10H and command port number 11H.

13-29. Must errors be reset if detected when the 8251A is read?

13-30. What is an overrun error?

13-31. Explain the difference between TxRDY and TxEMPTY.

13-32. When does the RxRDY signal become active?

13-33. What is a 20 mA unipolar current loop?

13-34. What is a DCE?

13-35. What is a DTE?

13-36. What is RS-232C?

13-37. What size connectors are commonly used for RS-232C?

13-38. How many feet is RS-232C able to receive and transmit data?

13-39. With RS-232C, a logic one is a _____ voltage and a logic zero is a _____ voltage.

13-40. What is the function of the $\overline{\text{DSR}}$ signal?

13-41. Explain what both the $\overline{\text{CTS}}$ and $\overline{\text{RTS}}$ signals are used to accomplish.

13-42. What is the purpose of the $\overline{\text{DCD}}$ signal?

chapter 14

The 8254 Programmable Timer

This chapter presents and uses the 8254 programmable timer, which contains three 16 bit programmable modulus counters or timers. A programmable modulus counter is a counter that counts through the same sequence of counts over and over again. For example, if a count of 4 is programmed, the counter counts from 4 down to 1 and then repeats the count.

Each timer is used to generate 6 different functions in either binary or binary-coded decimal. As will be demonstrated with examples, timers are an important portion of many microprocessor systems. They are used to generate waveforms, to time events, to develop pulses, to keep time, to control stepper motors, etc.

14-1 OBJECTIVES

Upon completion of this chapter, you will be able to:

1. Describe the function of each pin of the 8254 programmable timer.
2. Interface the 8254 to the Z80 microprocessor.
3. Develop software to program the 8254 so that it operates in any mode.
4. Use the 8254 to control a stepper motor.
5. Implement a real time clock using the 8254.

14-2 THE 8254 ARCHITECTURE

The 8254 contains three 16-bit fully programmable independent timers. Each timer (counter) is capable of counting in either binary or in binary-coded decimal (BCD). The timer itself is a modulus counter that can be programmed to count from any count of 1 to 64K. Each timer has its own input which can accept a counting frequency of between DC—10 MHz. Timers are very useful for timing real-time events, generating waveforms, controlling control systems, etc.

The 8254 Pinout

Figure 14-1 illustrate the pinout and block diagram of the 8254 timer. The 8254 is packaged in a 24 pin DIP that requires +5 V for proper operation. Notice from the block diagram that there are three timers located within the 8254. Each of these timers contains a CLK (clock) input, a GATE input, and an OUT (output). The CLK input is used to provide the timer with its basic operating frequency or count; the GATE input is used, in some modes, to start and stop the timer; and the OUT pin is where the output waveform is obtained.

Pin description.

Vcc—Power: the pin connected to the + 5 V power supply.

$\overline{WR}$—Write Input: is connected to the system $\overline{IOW}$ signal so that data can be written to the 8254 for programming.

$\overline{RD}$—Read Input: is connected to the system $\overline{IOR}$ signal so that data are read from the 8254.

$\overline{CS}$—Chip Select Input: selects the 8254 for programming or for reading the contents of the counter.

A1, A0—Address Input: is used to select timer 1, 2, or 3 or to select the control register. (See Table 14-1 for the function of these address connections.)

CLK 2, CLK 1, and CLK 0—Clock Inputs: are used to provide the timers with their basic operating frequencies. These inputs may be clocked by any TTL compatible clocking source with any frequency of between DC and 10MHz.

TABLE 14-1.   ADDRESS SELECTION FOR THE 8254 DURING CHIP SELECTION

A1	A0	Selected register
0	0	timer 0
0	1	timer 1
1	0	timer 2
1	1	control register

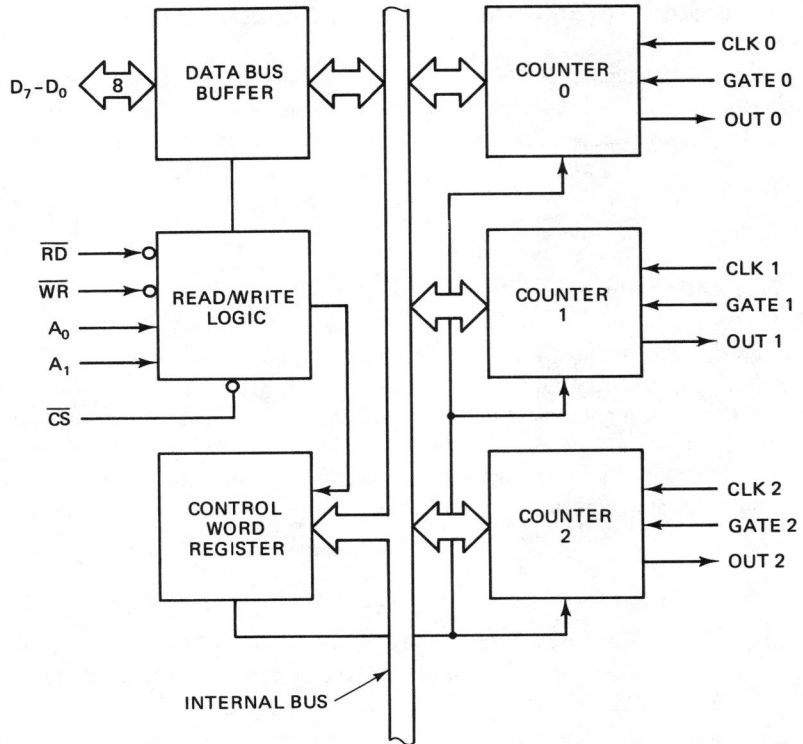

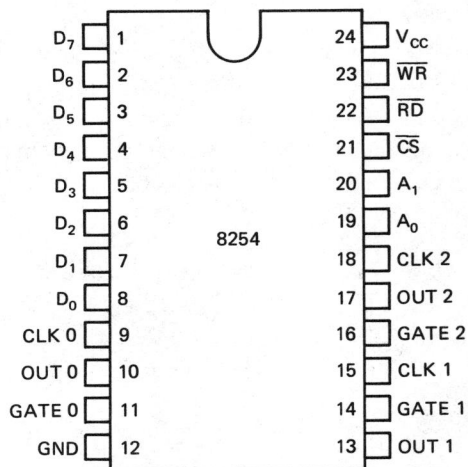

Figure 14–1 The functional block diagram and pinout of the 8254 timer. (Courtesy of Intel Corporation.)

OUT 2, OUT 1, and OUT 0—Outputs: are the output pins of the timers which are programmed to provide either a squarewave or a pulse.

GATE 2, GATE 1, and GATE 0—Gate Inputs: are used to enable (when a logic 1) or disable (when a logic 0) the timer.

GND—Ground: is connected to the system ground bus.

14-3 PROGRAMMING THE 8254

Programming the 8254 is a rather simple task because each timer is separate from the other and programmed independently. To program any timer, a control word is written to the control register followed by the initial count for the timer. The count may be written either with the LSB first followed by the MSB or in any order.

The Control Register

Figure 14-2 illustrates the control register and the purpose of each of its bits. The control register allows the programmer to select the timer, choose the mode of operation for the timer, and pick the type of operation for programming (read or write). The programmer can also select either binary or BCD operation with a bit in the control register. Each 16-bit timer may be programmed with a binary count of 0000H—FFFFH. (A binary count of 0 is 64K in the 8254.) A timer may also be programmed in BCD with a BCD count of 0000—9999. (A BCD count of 0 is 10,000.) The minimum count of 1 applies to all modes of operation except modes 2 and 3, which have a minimum count of 2.

RW1 and RW0 determine how data are read from or written to the timer. The program is able to select a write to either the most significant or least significant halves of the timer or both halves. If both halves are used, the least significant byte must be programmed before the most significant byte.

Each internal timer has its own control register that is used to select the way that the timer is programmed. If 2 bytes are programmed in a timer, the first byte (LSB) will stop the timer, and the second byte (MSB) will start the timer with the new count. The order of programming a timer is important, but the programming of different timers may be interleaved for better control. For example, the control registers may be sent to each timer for programming, and then the counts may be programmed in any order. (The order of programming the counts for different timers does not matter except for LSB followed by MSB.) Table 14-2 illustrates a method of programming the 8254.

Timer Modes of Operation

Six different modes of operation are available for each timer inside the 8254. Figure 14-3 depicts the waveforms obtained at the OUT pin for each of these six timer modes of operation, and a description of each of the models follows on page 276.

D$_7$	D$_6$	D$_5$	D$_4$	D$_3$	D$_2$	D$_1$	D$_0$
SC1	SC0	RW1	RW0	M2	M1	M0	BCD

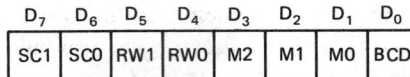

SC — Select counter:

SC1	SC0	
0	0	Select counter 0
0	1	Select counter 1
1	0	Select counter 2
1	1	Read-back command (see read operations)

M — Mode:

M2	M1	M0	
0	0	0	Mode 0
0	0	1	Mode 1
X	1	0	Mode 2
X	1	1	Mode 3
1	0	0	Mode 4
1	0	1	Mode 5

RW — Read/write:

RW1	RW0	
0	0	Counter latch command (see read operations)
0	1	Read/write least significant byte only
1	0	Read/write most significant byte only
1	1	Read/write least significant byte first, then most significant byte

BCD:

0	Binary counter 16-bits
1	Binary coded decimal (BCD) counter (4 decades)

Note: Don't care bits (X) should be 0 to insure compatibility with future Intel products.

Figure 14–2   The 8254 control register. (Courtesy of Intel Corporation.)

TABLE 14-2.   AN EXAMPLE SEQUENCE FOR PROGRAMMING TIMERS 0 AND 1

Programmed register	Timer	Comment
Control	0	program
Control	1	program
Count (LSB)	0	stop and set count
Count (LSB)	1	stop and set count
Count (MSB)	0	finish count and start
Count (MSB)	1	finish count and start

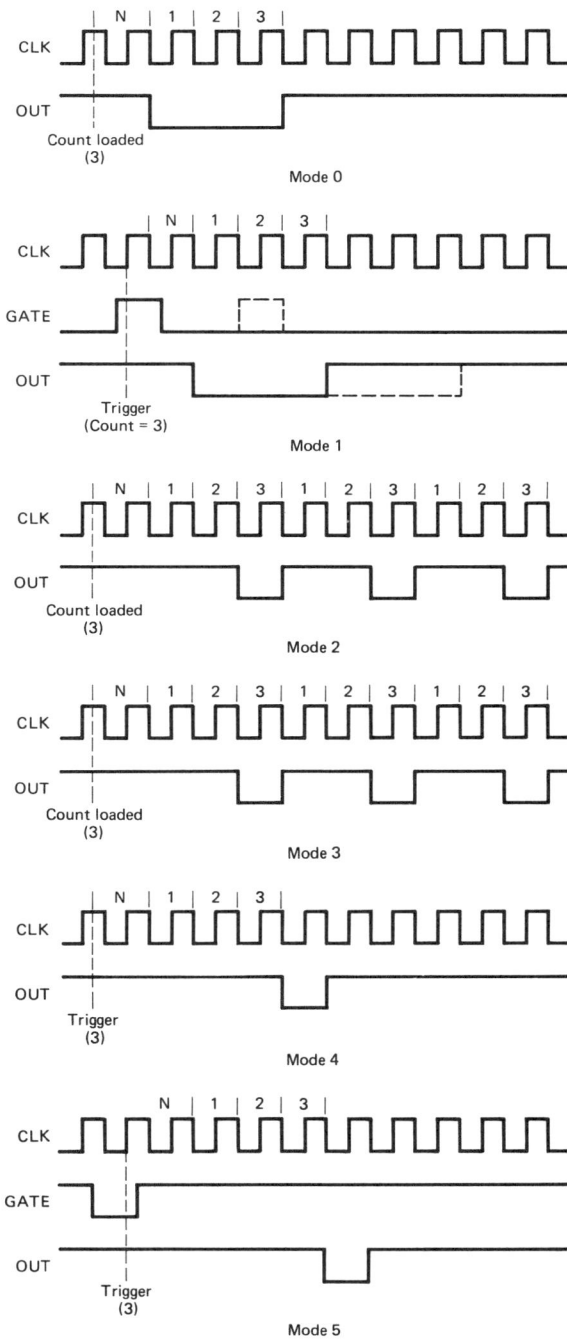

Figure 14–3 The 6 modes of operation of the 8254 timer.

Mode 0.   Mode 0 operation causes the timer to function as an events counter. In this mode, the output (OUT) becomes a logic 0 when the control register for the timer is written and remains a 0 until N + 1 input clock pulses (CLK) have occurred. (N = the programmed count.) Suppose that the timer is to count 200 input pulses at the CLK input. In order for the timer to do this, it is programmed in mode 0 for a count of 199. After 200 input pulses have been applied to the CLK input, the output pin (OUT) returns to a logic 1 level. Note that the GATE pin must be a logic 1 for the timer to count the input pulses. This mode of operation is very useful for counting external events.

Mode 1.   Mode 1 operation causes the timer to operate as a retriggerable monostable multivibrator (one-shot). In this mode, the GATE input is used to trigger or fire the one-shot. If the timer is programmed for a count of 100, and a logic 1 is applied (trigger) to the GATE, the OUT connection will become a logic 0 for 100 input CLK pulses. If a second trigger occurs before the 100 clock pulses, then the output will be extended for an additional 100 clocking periods. This mode of operation is useful in control environments.

Mode 2.   Mode 2 causes the timer to generate a series of continuous pulses from the OUT pin. Each of the output pulses is one input CLK period wide. The separation between each output pulse is determined by the count that is programmed into the timer. For example, if a count of 10 is selected, the output will be a logic 1 for 9 clocking periods and a logic 0 for 1 clocking period. This cycle is repeated until the timer is reprogrammed with a new count or a different mode of operation. The GATE input may be used to start the output pulse train (GATE = 1) or stop the output (GATE = 0).

Mode 3.   Mode 3 operation is used to generate a continuous squarewave at the OUT pin. If the count is an even number then the output high and low times will be equal to one half the count. If the count is an odd number, the low time is one count less than the high time. For example, if a count of 11 is chosen, the output will be low for 5 input clocks and high for 6 clocks. If the count is a 10, the output will be high for 5 and low for 5 clocks. As with the other modes of operation, the GATE input may be used to start and stop the timer.

Mode 4.   Mode 4 is used to cause the timer to produce one pulse. It is similar to mode 2 operation except that instead of producing a continuous stream of pulses, it produces only one pulse. For example, if a count of 100 is programmed, the output will be high for 100 clocks and then go low for one clock. After the pulse, the output returns to a logic 1 until the counter is reprogrammed. This mode of operation causes the timer to function as a software-controlled one-shot. The GATE input is used to inhibit the count if required.

Mode 5.   Mode 5 operation also causes the timer to function as a one-shot. This mode is very similar to mode 4 except that instead of triggering the timer with software, it is triggered with the GATE input. For example, if a count of 10 is programmed, the

$A_1, A_0 = 11; \ CS = 0; \ RD = 1; \ WR = 0$

D_7	D_6	D_5	D_4	D_3	D_2	D_1	D_0
SC1	SC0	0	0	X	X	X	X

SC1, SC0 — specify counter to be latched

SC1	SC0	Counter
0	0	0
0	1	1
1	0	2
1	1	Read-back command

D5, D4 — 00 designates counter latch command

X — don't care

Note: Don't care bits (X) should be 0 to insure compatibility with future INTEL products.

Figure 14–4   Counter latch control word. (Courtesy of Intel Corporation.)

output will remain high for 10 clocks after the trigger pulse (a logic 1 on the GATE pin) and then go low for one clock. Like mode 1, this mode is retriggerable.

Reading a Counter

Each internal timer has a latch that is read with the read counter operation. These latches will normally follow the count. If the contents of a timer are required at a particular time, the timer can be programmed so that the count is latched and saved for reading. Latching is accomplished by programming the counter latch control word (see Figure 14-4), which causes the contents of the timer to be held in the latch until it is read. Whenever the count is read from the latch or whenever the time is reprogrammed, the latch returns to following the timer.

When it is necessary for the contents of more than one timer to be read at the same time, it is desirable to latch more than one timer. This is accomplished with the read-back control word illustrated in Figure 14-5. Here the $\overline{COUNT}$ bit is a 0 if the contents of counter CNT 2, CNT 1, and/or CNT 0 are to be latched. If the status of the counters

$A0, A1 = 11 \quad \overline{CS} = 0 \quad \overline{RD} = 1 \quad \overline{WR} = 0$

D_7	D_6	D_5	D_4	D_3	D_2	D_1	D_0
1	1	$\overline{COUNT}$	$\overline{STATUS}$	CNT 2	CNT 1	CNT 0	0

D_5: 0 = latch count of selected counter(s)
D_4: 0 = latch status of selected counter(s)
D_3: 1 = select counter 2
D_2: 1 = select counter 1
D_1: 1 = select counter 0
D_0: reserved for future expansion; must be 0

Figure 14–5   The read-back control word. (Courtesy of Intel Corporation.)

D$_7$	D$_6$	D$_5$	D$_4$	D$_3$	D$_2$	D$_1$	D$_0$
OUTPUT	NULL COUNT	RW1	RW0	M2	M1	M0	BCD

D$_7$: 1 = out pin is 1
       0 = out pin is 0
D$_6$: 1 = null count
       0 = count available for reading
D$_5$–D$_0$: counter programmed mode

Figure 14–6 The 8254 status register. (Courtesy of Intel Corporation.)

is latched, then the $\overline{\text{STATUS}}$ bit is a 0. Figure 14-6 illustrates the status word, which allows the programmer to determine the state of the OUT pin, if the count is a 0 (null count), and how the counter is programmed (RW1, RW0, M2, M1, M0, and BCD). Note that each timer contains its own status register.

Using the Timer as a Solenoid Driver

In many control systems solenoids are used to accomplish work. A solenoid is an electromechanical device that must be energized for a specific period of time in order to accomplish work.

Figure 14-7 illustrates the 8254, the Z80, and a solenoid and the transistor driver used to provide it with enough current to operate. Here the 8254 is decoded to operate at I/O ports 10H—13H. Notice that OUT 0 is connected to the transistor driver. Here timer 0 is programmed in mode zero so that the OUT 0 pin becomes a logic zero, energizing the solenoid, for 10 ms. Why 10 ms? In this application, it is required that the solenoid is energized for 10 ms. This time will vary greatly and is totally dependent on the application.

Example 14-1 illustrates the subroutine that is called whenever the solenoid is energized. Here timer 0 is programmed so that it counts 19,999. When the timer starts, its output becomes a logic zero for 20,000 clocks which means it becomes a logic 0 for 100 ms. Here the control register is programmed so that timer 0 is programmed in mode 0 to accept a 16-bit count of 4E1FH (19,999). After the MSB of the count is output the timer begins and energizes the solenoid for 100 ms.

Example 14-1

```
;
;subroutine that programs timer 0 in mode 0 for
;a count of 19,999.  This generates a 100 ms pulse
;to energize the solenoid for 100 ms.
;
FIRE:      LD     A,00110000B      ;program control
           OUT    (13H),A
           LD     A,1FH            ;program count LSB
           OUT    (10H),A
           LD     A,4EH            ;program count MSB
           RET
```

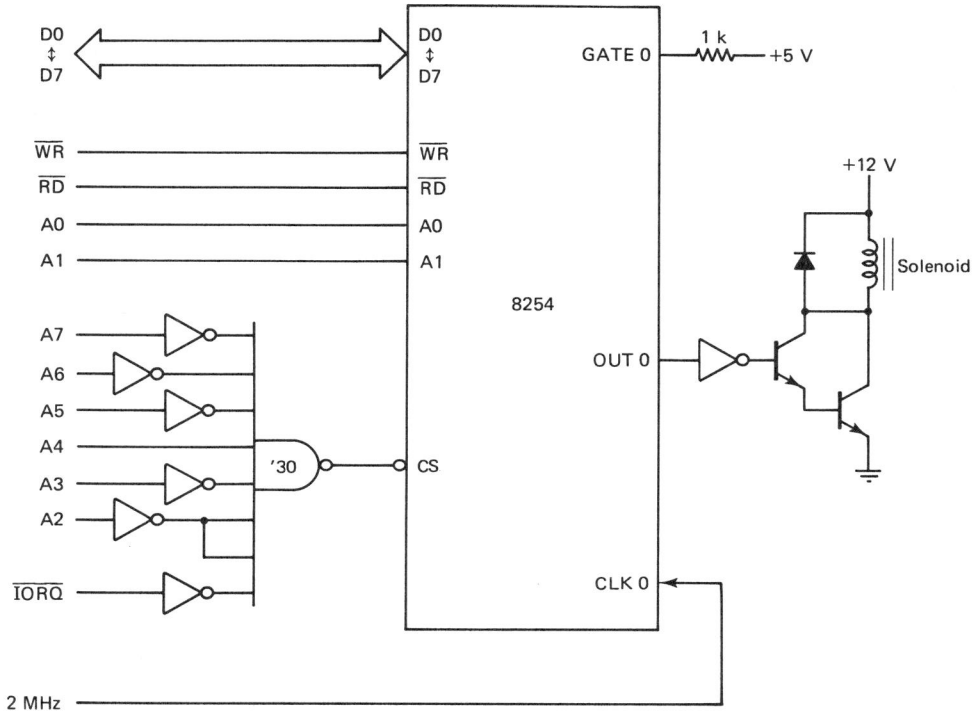

Figure 14–7   Driving a solenoid with the 8254 timer.

Using the Timer to Generate FSK

The timer can be used to generate FSK by programming it for mode 3 operation, which generates continuous squarewaves. Suppose that FSK is to be generated using 2025 Hz (logic 0) and 2225 (Hz (logic 1). This means, assuming a 2 MHz clock from the Z80, that a count of 989 is used to generate 2025 Hz and a count of 899 is used to generate a 2225 Hz output.

Figure 14-8 illustrates the 8254 interfaced to the Z80 so that it operates at I/O ports 60H—63H. Software for this circuit consists of four subroutines: send a 0, send a 1, time delay, and transmit a byte. Three of the four subroutines are listed in Example 14-2. (The time delay subroutine is not listed here.) Two of the subroutines reprogram timer 0 so that it generates either a 2025 Hz or 2225 Hz tone. The time delay subroutine is used to generate a 3.33 ms time delay so that the data are transmitted at 300 Baud. The main subroutine transmits a byte of data so that it has a start bit, 8 data bits, no parity, and 1 stop bit. The contents of the accumulator are transmitted through the timer with the TRANS subroutine.

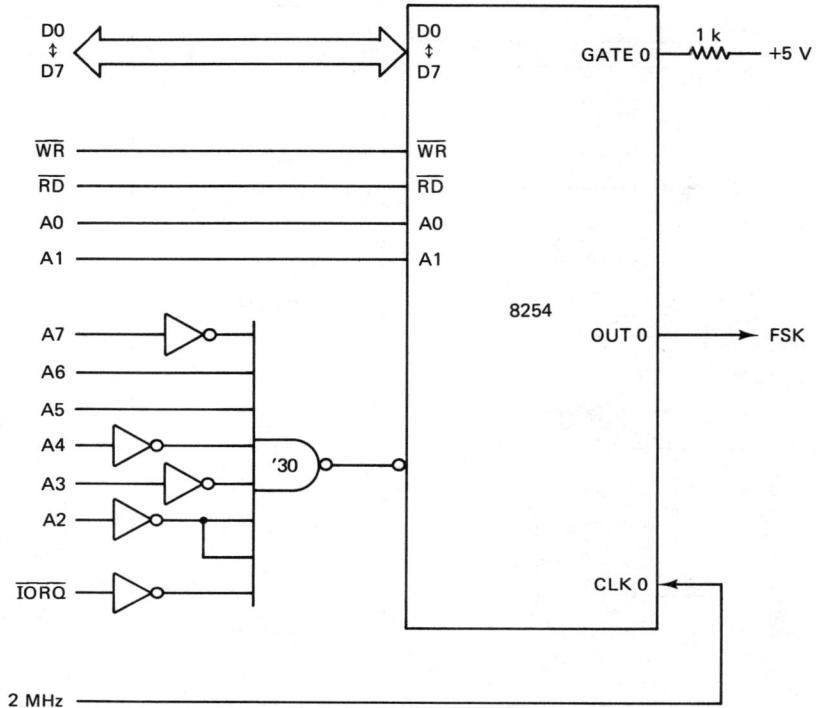

Figure 14–8 Using the 8254 to generate FSK.

Example 14-2

```
;
;subroutine to transmit a logic 0   (2025 Hz tone)
;
SENDO:      PUSH  AF                ;save A
            LD    A,00110110B       ;program control
            OUT   (63H),A
            LD    A,0DDH            ;program count LSB
            OUT   (60H),A
            LD    A,03H             ;program count MSB
            OUT   (60H),A
            CALL  DELAY             ;wait 3.33 ms
            POP   AF                ;restore A
            RET
;
;subroutine to transmit a logic 1   (2225 Hz tone)
;
SEND1:      PUSH  AF                ;save A
            LD    A,00110110B       ;program control
            OUT   (63H),A
            LD    A,83H             ;program count LSB
            OUT   (60H),A
            LD    A,03H             ;program count MSB
```

(Example 14-2 continued)

```
                OUT   (60H),A
                CALL DELAY          ;wait 3.33 msec
                POP   AF
                RET
        ;
        ;transmit a byte from the accumulator
        ;
        TRANS:  LD    B,8           ;load counter
                CALL SENDO          ;send start bit
        LOOP:   RRCA                ;get data bit
                CALL NC,SENDO       ;if 0
                CALL C,SEND1        ;if 1
                DJNZ LOOP           ;repeat for 8 bits
                CALL SEND1          ;send stop bit
                RET
```

14-4 CONTROLLING A STEPPER MOTOR

Many control applications require the use of some form of motor to position things. In many cases today, stepper motors are used to position smaller mechanical loads. This section of the text explains the operation of the stepper motor and depicts a stepper motor interface. The 8254 is used to time the operation of the motor so that it steps to the next position.

Stepper Motor Operation

The stepper motor is similar to a DC motor except that the armature of the stepper motor is a permanent magnet while the field of the DC motor is a permanent magnet. Figure 14-9 illustrates the internal construction of the stepper motor. Notice that this stepper motor has 4 field coils that are used to position the permanent magnet armature.

There are two major modes of operation for the stepper motor. The full step and the half step mode. Figure 14-10 (a) illustrates the magnetic polarities for a full step, and Figure 14-10 (b) illustrates the half step. Another technique called a microstep is also available, but beyond the scope of this text at this point. The microstep uses pulse width modulation to position the armature at any point between the steps. Microstepping allows

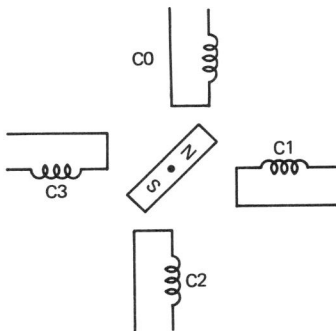

Figure 14–9 The internal construction of a stepper motor illustrating the 4 field coils and the permanent magnet armature.

(a)

(b)

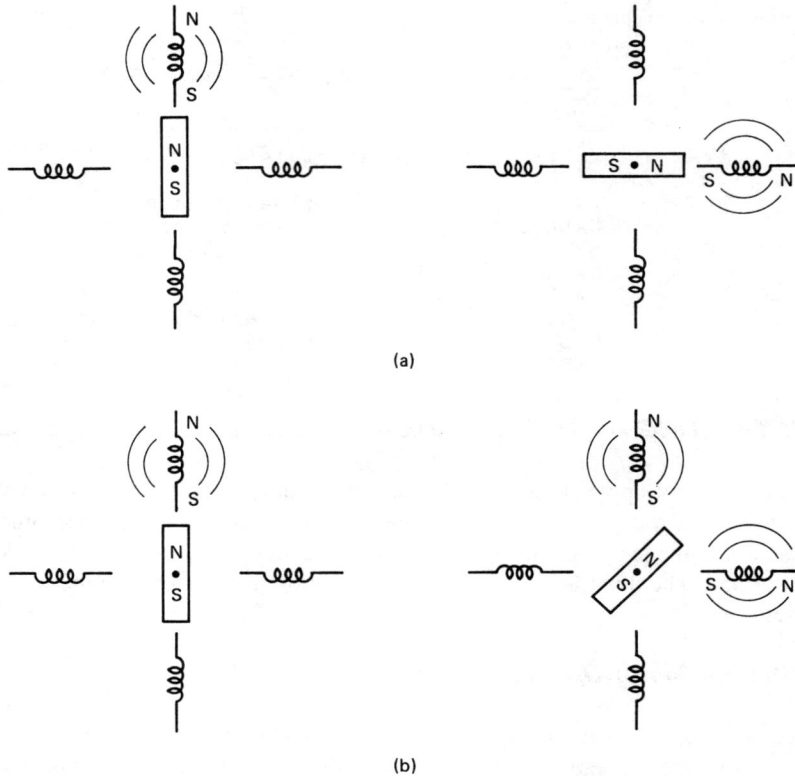

Figure 14–10   (a) The full step. (b) The half step.

the motor to be controlled with tremendous precision, but at this time still suffers from linearity in most applications.

The Stepper Motor Interface

Figure 14-11 illustrates the stepper motor interface. Notice that each field coil has its own transistor driver whose base is connected to the Z80 through an I/O port. Four bits of information are required from the Z80 in order to move or step the motor to any position. A fifth input to the interface is also provided called STEP. The STEP input is used to cause the DC voltage to the stepper coils to be changed from $+5$ V to $+12$ V for a step. When $+5$ V is applied the stepper motor holds its position, and when $+12$ V is applied it moves to a new position, because of the increased current flow, provided the 4 bit code is changed.

   Table 14-3 shows the binary code output to the four driver transistors (Q1—Q4) so that the motor moves in a full step and a half step in the clockwise and counter-

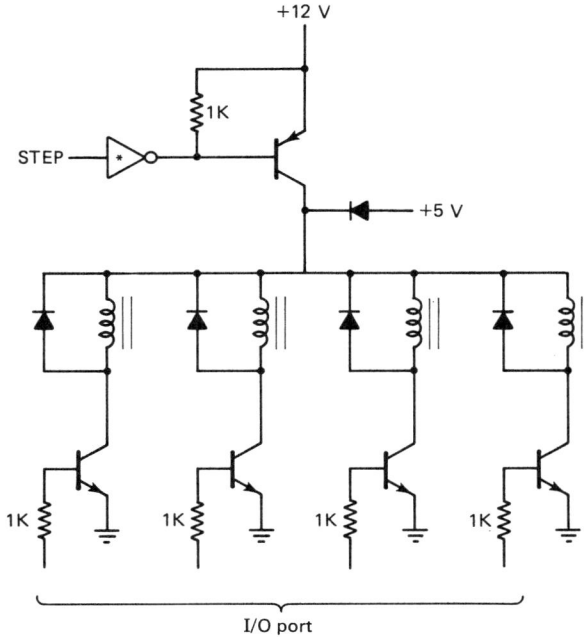

*Open collector inverter   **Figure 14–11**   Stepper motor interface.

clockwise directions. Notice that the number of steps required to move the armature one complete revolution is doubled for the half step. Also notice that in the half step mode one or two coils are active at one time. If two coils are active the armature moves to a midposition between the coils, and if one coil is active the armature lines up with the coil. In practice, the armature of the stepper is geared so that one revolution of the internal armature may produce a movement of only a few degrees in the mechanical output shaft of the motor.

Software to Move the Stepper Motor

The software to move the stepper motor is listed in Example 14-3. Here the contents of memory location POS contain the current stepper motor bit pattern. The subroutine itself causes the motor to move full steps by the number of steps found in the B register. The direction of the movement is determined by the value of the carry bit when the subroutine is called from the main program. Each step is activated by outputting a new bit pattern to the four transistors followed by the STEP pulse generated by the 8254 timer. Here the amount of time required to step the motor is 1 ms. This time varies dependent upon the size of the stepper motor.

TABLE 14-3.   FULL AND HALF STEP BIT PATTERNS FOR THE STEPPER MOTOR

		Clockwise patterns						
Full step						Half step		
Q1	Q2	Q3	Q4		Q1	Q2	Q3	Q4
1	0	0	0		1	0	0	0
0	1	0	0		1	1	0	0
0	0	1	0		0	1	0	0
0	0	0	1		0	1	1	0
					0	0	1	0
					0	0	1	1
					0	0	0	1
					1	0	0	1

		Counter-clockwise patterns						
Full step						Half step		
Q1	Q2	Q3	Q4		Q1	Q2	Q3	Q4
1	0	0	0		1	0	0	0
0	0	0	1		1	0	0	1
0	0	1	0		0	0	0	1
0	1	0	0		0	0	1	1
					0	0	1	0
					0	1	1	0
					0	1	0	0
					1	1	0	0

Example 14-3

```
        ;
        ;subroutine to full step a stepper motor in either
        ;the clockwise (carry set) or counter-clockwise
        ;(carry cleared) direction.  The B register
        ;contains the number of steps.
        ;
MOVE:       LD   A,(POS)           ;get position
            PUSH AF                ;save direction
            JR   NC,MOVE1          ;if counter-clockwise
            RRCA                   ;move clockwise
            JR   MOVE2
MOVE1:      RLCA                   ;move counter-clockwise
MOVE2:      LD   (POS),A           ;save position
        ;
        ;pulse STEP for 1 ms
        ;
            LD   A,00110000B       ;program timer 0
            OUT  (13H),A
            LD   A,0D0H            ;program count LSB
            OUT  (10H),A
            LD   A,07H             ;program count MSB
            OUT  (10H),A
            POP  AF                ;get direction
            DJNZ MOVE              ;if not done
            RET
```

14-5 A REAL-TIME CLOCK

The 8254 is an ideal device to use for a real-time clock. A real-time clock is a device that keeps time in minutes and hours or in other units. This section of the text deals with a time-of-day clock.

The Interface

Figure 14-12 illustrates the 8254 connected to the Z80 at I/O ports 20H—23H. All three timers are used for this clock. Timer 0 is used to divide (by 3600) the 60 Hz signal,

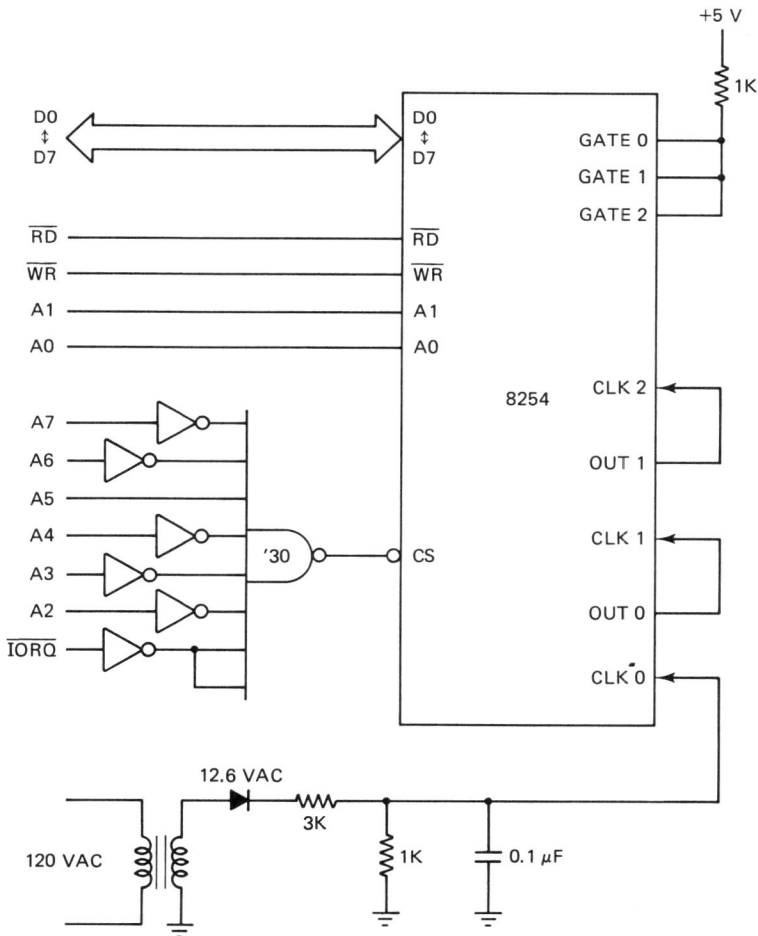

Figure 14–12 The circuit for a real time clock.

derived from the AC powerline, to produce 1 minute pulses for timer 1. Timer 1, which divides by 60, counts the 1 minute pulses and produces 1 hour pulses for timer 2. Timer 2, which divides by 24, counts the 1 hour pulses for a 24 hour count. Once the timer is programmed, the only software required to operate the system is a subroutine that reads the time from timers 1 and 2.

The Software

Example 14-4 lists a subroutine that is used to program the 8254 timer so that it functions as a real-time clock. This subroutine assumes that the current correct time of day is passed to it through the HL register pair. H contains the correct number of hours and L contains the correct number of minutes to be placed into timers 1 and 2.

Example 14-4

```
;
;subroutine to intialize the 8254 so that it
;functions as a real time clock.
;
;HL = current time of day.  (H = Hours) (L = Minutes)
;
SET:        LD      A,00110111B     ;program control 0
            OUT     (13H),A
            LD      A,01110111B     ;program control 1
            OUT     (13H),A
            LD      A,10110111B     ;program control 2
            OUT     (13H),A
            LD      A,00H           ;program timer 0 (3600)
            OUT     (10H),A
            LD      A,36H
            OUT     (10H),A
            LD      A,60H           ;program timer 1 (60)
            OUT     (11H),A
            LD      A,0
            OUT     (11H),A
            LD      A,24            ;program timer 2 (24)
            OUT     (12H),A
            LD      A,0
            OUT     (12H),A
            LD      (TIME),HL       ;save current time
            RET
```

Example 14-5 lists the subroutine that reads the time of day from the timers and returns it in the HL register pair with the H register containing the hour and the L register containing the minutes. The actual time returned is a combination of the count found in the timers and the time that is stored in memory location TIME and TIME+1. In order to read back the correct number of hours, the contents of the timer 2 must be subtracted from a 24H and then added, in BCD, to the contents of memory location TIME+1. The result of this addition must be modulo 24. Likewise, to obtain the correct number of minutes, the contents of timer 1 must be subtracted from 60H and added, in BCD, to the contents of memory location TIME. The result of this addition must be modulo 60. After all of this arithmetic the correct time of day is returned in the HL register pair.

Example 14-5

```
;
;subroutine to read the time of day.
;
;HL = time of day on return (H = Hours) (L = Minutes)
;
READ:       PUSH BC
            LD   A,11011100B        ;latch timers 1 and 2
            OUT  (13H),A
            IN   A,(11H)            ;read timer 1 (minutes)
            LD   B,A
            IN   A,(11H)
            LD   A,60H              ;adjust timer 1 count
            SUB  B
            LD   B,A
            LD   A,(TIME)           ;get minutes
            ADD  A,B
            CP   60H
            JR   C,READ1            ;if less than 60
            SUB  60H                ;adjust
READ1:      LD   L,A                ;save minutes
            IN   A,(12H)            ;read timer 2 (hours)
            LD   B,A
            IN   A,(12H)
            LD   A,24H              ;adjust timer 2 count
            SUB  B
            LD   B,A
            LD   A,(TIME+1)         ;get hours
            ADD  A,B
            CP   24H
            JR   C,READ2            ;if less than 24
            SUB  24H
READ2:      LD   H,A                ;save hours
            POP  BC
            RET
```

14-6 SUMMARY

1. The 8254 is a programmable timer that contains three, 16-bit programmable modulus counters. Each counter is programmable in 6 different modes of operation in either binary or binary-coded decimal.

2. Each timer has three hardware pins: CLK (clock input), GATE (enable input), and OUT (the timer output pin). The clock input frequency may be anything from DC to 10 MHz.

3. The 8254 has four I/O ports selected by address input pins A0 and A1. One of the four I/O ports is used to read the status register or write the control register, and the remaining three ports are used to program and read the three counters.

4. The program any of the three timers, the control register is first written followed by the count to be programmed in the timer. The control register allows any of the 6 modes to be selected and also allows the timer to operate in either binary or binary-coded decimal.

5. Various timer modes allow a timer to function as an events counter, a single-shot, pulse generator, or a squarewave generator.

6. Each timer can be read on the fly (while counting) or in the latched mode. To read it in the latched mode the counter is sent the read-back control word which latches the count so that it can be read at the leisure of the programmer.

7. Whenever the count is programmed into a timer, the programming of the least significant byte of the count stops the timer and the programming of the most significant byte starts the timer with the new count.

8. A stepper motor is a device that has a permanent magnet armature and usually four field coils.

9. Stepper motors can be stepped, or positioned, by using full steps, half steps, or microsteps.

14-7 GLOSSARY

Gate   A signal that is used to turn on (gate) a device.

Microstep   A technique that uses pulse width modulation to move the armature of a stepper motor to an infinite number of positions between poles.

Modulus   The number of states that a counter or similar device goes through. For example, a counter that counts 3, 2, 1, and 0 has four states so it is a modulo 4 counter.

Monostable multivibrator   A device that has one stable state. In most cases it changes states for a period of time and then returns to its stable state producing a pulse of known duration.

One-shot   See monostable multivibrator.

Real-time   Time measured via a clock in time of day or smaller units such as milliseconds.

Solenoid   An electro-mechanical device that provides movement when energized electrically. A current flow through the coil of the solenoid causes a magnetic field that provides motion.

Stepper motor   A motor that moves in steps because it contains multiple fields that cause a magnetized armature to move from one field pole to another.

Timer   A device that develops various output waveforms with adjustable output periods.

QUESTIONS AND PROBLEMS

14-1. How many timers are located within the 8254?

14-2. Each 8254 timer is able to operate with an input clock of from DC to _____ MHz.

14-3. What are the three pins that connect directly to each of the timers in the 8254?

14-4. What is the range of the binary count for a timer?

14-5. What is the range of the binary-coded decimal count for a timer?

14-6. Which two 8254 pins determine the internal I/O port that is selected for programming?

14-7. What is the purpose of the RW1 and RW0 bits in the 8254 control register?

14-8. Normally the control register is programmed for a timer, and then the count is output with the _____ byte first.

14-9. Whenever the _____ part of the count is programmed the timer stops counting, and whenever the _____ part of the count is programmed the counting starts.

14-10. How many different modes of operation are available for each of the 8254 timers?

14-11. What mode of operation allows the timer to generate a continuous squarewave output?

14-12. If an odd count is programmed in a timer that is operated to generate a continuous squarewave the OUT pin is a logic _____ for a longer time.

14-13. What mode of operation allows the timer to operate as an events counter?

14-14. What mode of operation allows the timer to operate as a retriggerable one-shot?

14-15. When the 8254 timer is operated to produce one pulse, explain the effect of grounding the GATE pin.

14-16. What mode of operation allows a timer to operate as a hardware triggered one-shot?

14-17. Develop software that will program timer 1 so that it operates in mode 3 with a count of 1000H. (Assume that the I/O ports are 34H-37H.)

14-18. Develop software that will program timer 2 so that it operates in mode 5 with a count of 100H. (Assume that the I/O ports are F8H-FBH.)

14-19. Explain how a timer is read by first of all latching the count.

14-20. Develop software that latches the count in timer 0, reads the timer, and stores the count in the HL register pair.

14-21. How many counters may be latched with the latch control word?

14-22. What is a null count?

14-23. What is a solenoid?

14-24. Explain the difference between the stepper motor and the DC motor.

14-25. How many field coils are found in many stepper motors?

14-26. Describe the difference between a half step and a full step as it applies to the stepper motor.

14-27. Why does the interface to the stepper motor in Figure 14-11 apply +5 V or +12 V to the motor?

14-28. Could a full step be accomplished by activating two coils at the same time? If so, explain how.

14-29. What is a real-time clock?

14-30. Explain how the software listed in Example 14-4 calculates the time of day.

chapter **15**

Analog-to-Digital and Digital-to-Analog Conversions

Many applications require either that analog data be monitored or that analog data be generated by the microprocessor. This chapter provides the detail required to sample or generate analog data using the analog-to-digital (ADC) and digital-to-analog (DAC) converters. It also provides several examples of the use of both of these devices.

15-1 OBJECTIVES

Upon completion of this chapter, you will be able to:

1. Describe the operation of the ADC and DAC explaining specifications such as resolution, accuracy, etc.
2. Interface both the ADC and the DAC to the Z80 microprocessor.
3. Describe how the ADC is used to measure temperature.
4. Describe how the DAC is used to control the speed of a DC motor.

15-2 THE DAC

This section of the text presents the DAC0830 digital-to-analog converter. This device is microprocessor compatible and quite easily interfaced to the Z80 microprocessor. The DAC is a microprocessor compatible, 8-bit converter. The digital-to-analog converter is used to convert digital microprocessor data to analog voltage to control such systems as DC motors.

The DAC0830 Pinout

The DAC0830 is an 8-bit digital-to-analog converter that functions from a single power supply with a range of supply voltages of from $+5$ V to $+15$ V. It is designed to interface with a microprocessor and converts from digital to analog in 1 μs. Figure 15-1 illustrates the pinout of the DAC0830 and the functional block diagram.

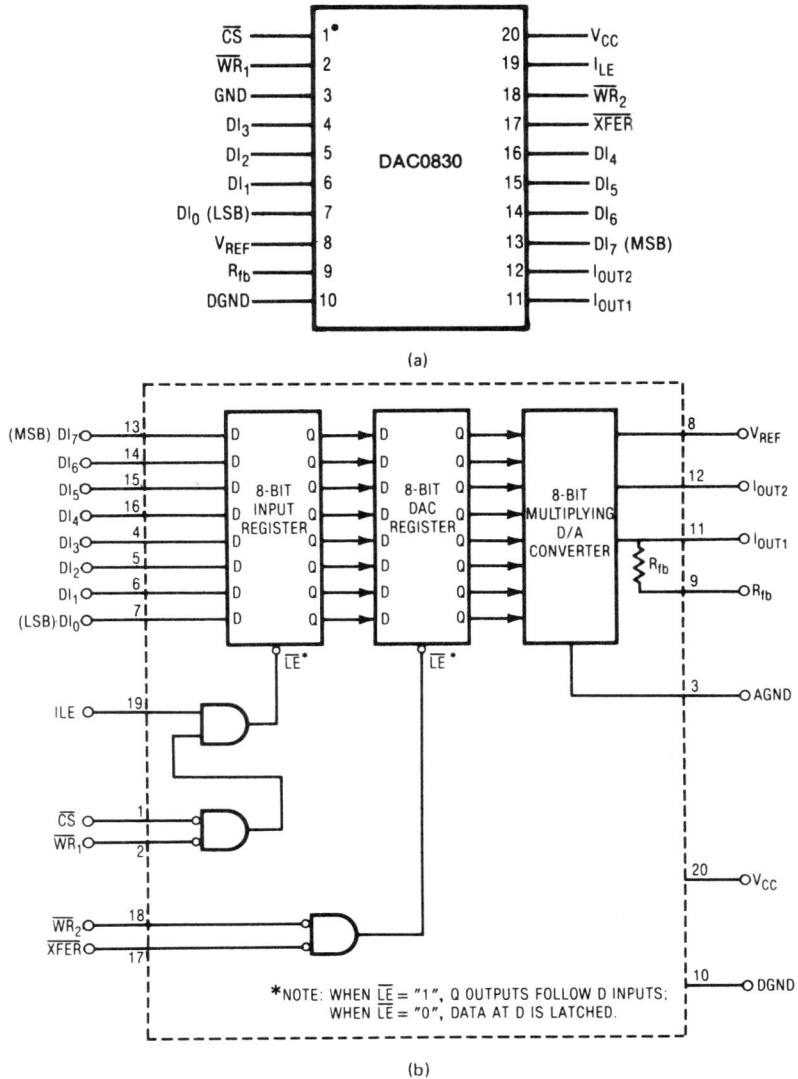

Figure 15-1   Pinout of the DAC0830 8-bit digital-to-analog converter and functional block diagram of the DAC0830. (Courtesy of National Semiconductor.)

Pin functions.   VCC—Supply Voltage Input: is where a $+5$ V to $+15$ V DC signal is applied.

AGND—Analog Ground: is normally connected to the ground terminal of the analog system.

DGND—Digital Ground: is connected to the ground terminal of the digital system.

DIO—DI7—Digital Inputs: are where the digital data is applied and are connected to the data bus in a microprocessor system.

Vref—Voltage Reference: is the voltage reference for the internal R-2R ladder network.

Rfb—Feedback Resistor: is provided for the external operational amplifier to set its gain.

IOUT (1)—Output Terminal 1: provides an output current that is proportional to the input digital number.

IOUT (2)—Output Terminal 2: provides an output current that is equal to the current generated by the voltage reference minus the current available at IOUT (1).

$\overline{\text{XFER}}$—Transfer Input: is used to enable or gate the $\overline{\text{WR2}}$ input to the DAC.

$\overline{\text{CS}}$—Chip Select Input: is used to enable or gate the $\overline{\text{WR1}}$ input to the DAC.

$\overline{\text{WR1}}$—Write Input (1): strobes the digital data into an internal holding register.

$\overline{\text{WR2}}$—Write Input (2): strobes the data from the internal latch into the digital-to-analog converter for conversion.

ILE—Internal Latch Enable: allows the $\overline{\text{WR1}}$ input to strobe data into the internal holding register.

Operation of the Analog Output of the DAC0830

There are 4 pins that determine the final output voltage of the DAC0830: Rfb, IOUT (1), IOUT (2), and Vref. The Vref input sets the reference for the internal R-2R DAC ladder network and is a negative voltage if the output is to be positive. For example, if Vref is -5 V then the full scale output voltage (1111 1111) is $+5$ V. Figure 15-2 illustrates

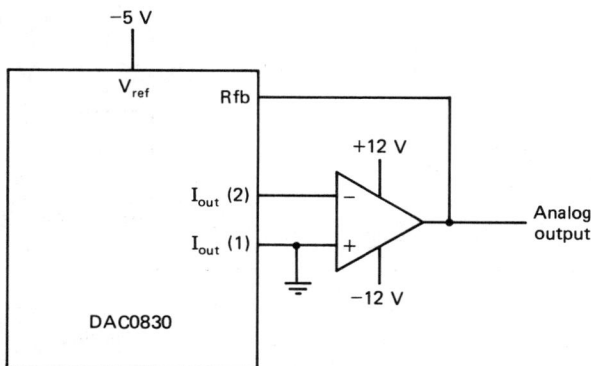

Figure 15–2   The output network of the DAC0830.

the output network required to produce a 0 to $+5$ V signal, in 255 steps, that is proportional to the digital input bit pattern. The operational amplifier (741) is connected so that the supply voltages to it are at least 3 V above the Vref voltage. Here the supply to the operational amplifier is ± 12 V, which is well above the -5 V applied to the Vref input.

Interface to the Z80 Microprocessor

Figure 15-3 illustrates the DAC0830 interfaced to the Z80 microprocessor. Here the I/O port is decoded as 28H, and the output of the port decoder is connected to the $\overline{\text{XFER}}$ input to the DAC. The $\overline{\text{IOW}}$ signal from the Z80 is connected to the $\overline{\text{WR2}}$ input. $\overline{\text{WR1}}$ and $\overline{\text{CS}}$ are at a logic 0, and ILE is at a logic one level so that the outputs internal holding register follow the information applied from the data bus of the Z80. Whenever the Z80 executes an OUT 28H,A instruction, the $\overline{\text{WR2}}$ and $\overline{\text{XFER}}$ pins both become a logic 0. This causes the DAC register to capture the data bus data at the end of the $\overline{\text{IOW}}$ strobe where it is then converted to an analog voltage by the DAC.

    The software to cause the converter to function is a simple OUT instruction. No other software is required because the converter converts to analog in just 1 μs.

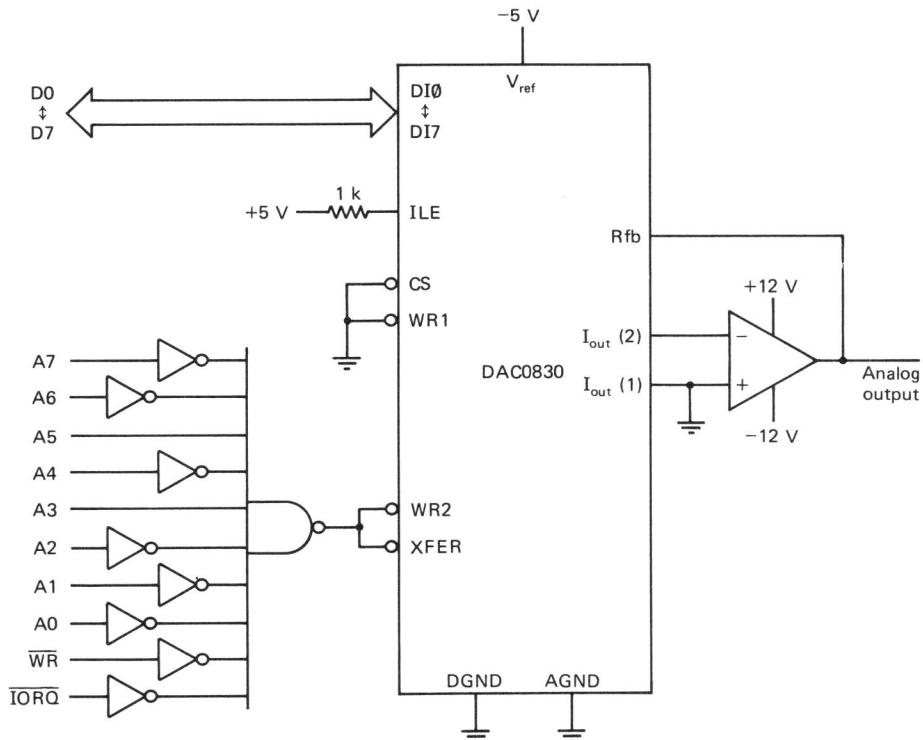

Figure 15–3   The DAC0830 interfaced to the Z80 microprocessor.

15-3 THE ADC

The analog-to-digital convert (ADC) is most often found today in integrated circuit form. Most integrated circuit converters are microprocessor compatible and are interfaced to the Z80 microprocessor with a relative ease. This section of the chapter explains the operation of the ADC0805 and illustrates how to interface it to the Z80.

The ADC0805 Pinout

Figure 15-4 illustrates the pinout of the ADC0805 analog-to-digital converter. The ADC0805 is an 8-bit microprocessor compatible converter that converts from an analog input voltage to a digital output voltage in just 100 μs.

The ADC0805 starts converting from analog to digital by pulsing the $\overline{\text{WR}}$ input while the $\overline{\text{CS}}$ input is a logic 0. The $\overline{\text{INTR}}$ output pin indicates, after up to 100 μs, that the converter has converted the input to a digital number available at the data output pins (DB0—DB7). Once $\overline{\text{INTR}}$ returns to a logic 0 level, this is after the converter is started, the data are removed from the DB pins by applying a logic 0 to both the $\overline{\text{CS}}$ and $\overline{\text{RD}}$ pins.

Pin functions. DB0—DB7—Data Bus Connections: are pins that convey the digital data to the microprocessor whenever the $\overline{\text{RD}}$ and $\overline{\text{CS}}$ inputs are at a logic 0 level.

DGND—Digital Ground: is connected to the digital system ground bus.

AGND—Analog Ground: is connected to the analog ground, which is often kept separate from the digital ground in a system.

VCC—Power Supply Input: is connected to the +5 V digital system power supply.

Vref/2—Voltage Reference: is not normally connected.

VIN(+)—Analog Input (+): is connected to the unknown analog input signal.

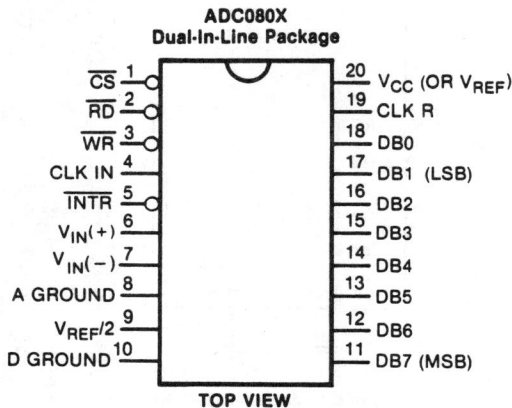

ADC080X
Dual-In-Line Package

Pin	Signal	Pin	Signal
1	$\overline{\text{CS}}$	20	V_{CC} (OR V_{REF})
2	$\overline{\text{RD}}$	19	CLK R
3	$\overline{\text{WR}}$	18	DB0
4	CLK IN	17	DB1 (LSB)
5	$\overline{\text{INTR}}$	16	DB2
6	$V_{IN}(+)$	15	DB3
7	$V_{IN}(-)$	14	DB4
8	A GROUND	13	DB5
9	$V_{REF}/2$	12	DB6
10	D GROUND	11	DB7 (MSB)

TOP VIEW

Figure 15–4 The pinout of the ADC0805 8-bit analog-to-digital converter. (Courtesy of National Semiconductor.)

VIN(−)—Analog Input (−): is often connected to ground or to another reference voltage in a system.

CLK IN—Clock Input: is connected to an external TTL level clock or used for clock generation in conjunction with the CLK R pin. (see text).

CLK R—Clock Resistor: is used as a clock feedback path.

$\overline{CS}$—Chip Select: enables both the $\overline{RD}$ and $\overline{WR}$ pins to the ADC.

$\overline{RD}$—Read Input: is used to enable the data bus output connection provided the $\overline{CS}$ input is also active.

$\overline{WR}$—Write Input: is used to start the analog-to-digital conversion process on its negative edge provided the $\overline{CS}$ input is active.

$\overline{INTR}$—Interrupt Request Output: indicates that the ADC has completed its conversion process when $\overline{INTR}$ becomes a logic 0.

The Analog Inputs

There are two analog inputs on the ADC0805: VIN (+) and VIN (−). These inputs are inputs to an internal operational amplifier and are differential inputs as illustrated in Figure 15-5. Differential inputs are inputs whose voltages are summed to produce an internal voltage to the analog-to-digital converter. For example, if a + 2 V signal is applied to the VIN (+) terminal and a − 3 V signal is applied to the VIN (−) terminal, a − 1 V signal is applied to the ADC. In many cases the VIN (−) terminal is grounded and the analog signal is applied to the VIN (+) terminal. If this is the connection, the permissible range of input voltage is 0 to + 5 V if the VCC input is at + 5 V.

In certain cases it is desired to offset the input voltage. This is accomplished by raising the VIN (−) terminal up off of ground as illustrated in Figure 15-6. Here a

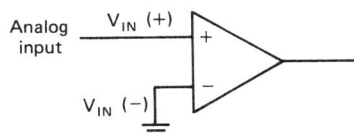

Figure 15–5 The analog input to the ADC0805.

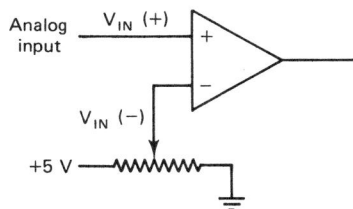

Figure 15–6 Raising the analog reference above ground.

potentiometer is used to elevate the VIN ($-$) terminal at a point above ground. This allows the user to adjust the zero reference for the converter.

Generating the Clock

The ADC0805 can be operated from an external clock input, or it can generate its own clock. When used with an external clock, the permissible range of input frequencies applied to the CLK IN pin is 100 KHz to 1460 KHz.

  If the clock is to be generated internally then the ADC will operate with an RC circuit. Figure 15-7 illustrates the RC circuit connected to the CLK IN and the CLK R pins of the ADC. Whenever this connection is used, the clock frequency is determined by the following equation:

$$\text{Fclk} \ = \ \frac{1}{1.1 \ \text{RC}}$$

Controlling the ADC0805

The ADC0805 is designed to function with the microprocessor and is easily interfaced to the Z80. Four pins—$\overline{\text{CS}}$, $\overline{\text{RD}}$, $\overline{\text{WR}}$, and $\overline{\text{INTR}}$—are used along with the three-state data bus connections (DB0—DB7) for this interface.

  The $\overline{\text{CS}}$ input is connected to the I/O port decoder, the $\overline{\text{RD}}$ input to the $\overline{\text{IOR}}$ signal, the $\overline{\text{WR}}$ input to the $\overline{\text{IOW}}$ signal, and the $\overline{\text{INTR}}$ pin is connected to either an interrupt input or to an input port bit. If connected in this manner a write to the ADC port will start the conversion and the interrupt (if connected) will cause an interrupt service subroutine to be called that reads the data from the ADC.

  Figure 15-8 illustrates the timing diagram for the ADC0805. Notice that the first event that occurs is a $\overline{\text{WR}}$ which starts the conversion process and also forces the $\overline{\text{INTR}}$ output to a logic 1. After a period of up to 100 μs, the $\overline{\text{INTR}}$ pin goes to a logic zero indicating that the converter has completed the conversion process. The final event that

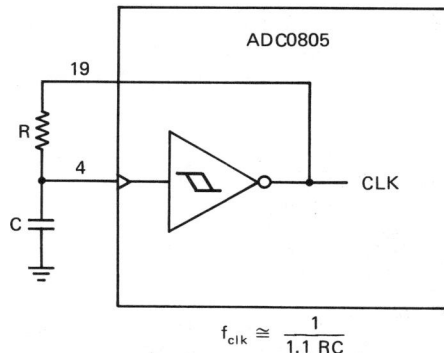

$$f_{clk} \cong \frac{1}{1.1 \ \text{RC}}$$

Figure 15–7 Generating the CLK in the ADC0805.

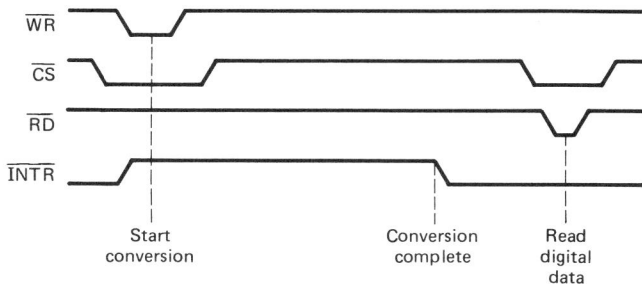

Figure 15–8   The timing diagram of the ADC0805.

occurs is a $\overline{RD}$ from the DB connections. In this interface, I/O port 10H is used to start the converter with an OUT(10H),A and to read the data from the converter with an IN A,(10H). IN A,(11H) is used to read the status of the $\overline{INTR}$ pin so that the software listed in Example 15-1 can read the data from the converter.

Example 15-1

```
;
;subroutine to start and read the ADC0805
;
;the digital data is returned in the A register
;
ADC:       OUT   (10H),A         ;start the converter
ADC1:      IN    A,(11H)         ;read INTR
           RRCA
           JR    C,ADC1          ;if not finished
           IN    A,(10H)         ;read data
           RET
```

15-4 USING THE ADC TO MEASURE TEMPERATURE

One example of using an analog-to-digital converter is a digital thermometer. There are many methods for sensing temperature changes. Some systems use a thermistor, which is a resistor that changes in value with temperature. Some use a transistor or a diode biased at just the point of conduction. This means that as the temperature changes so does the dynamic resistance of the device and hence the current flow through it. In this manner a voltage is developed that is proportional to a change in temperature. This voltage can be converted to digital data via an ADC and sampled by the microprocessor.

The Temperature Probe

The temperature probe that is most often used is a diode or a transistor. If a transistor or a diode is biased just below the normal forward bias voltage, it can act as a temperature sensor. Figure 15-9 illustrates the characteristic curve for a diode with the region between 0 V and +1 V emphasized. If the diode is biased at 0.3 V, which is below the normal

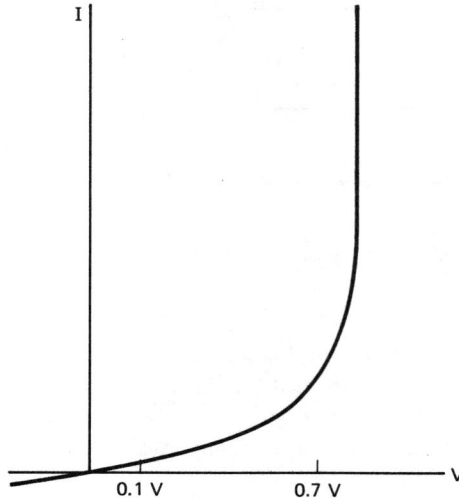

Figure 15–9 The characteristic curve of a diode.

forward bias voltage of 0.6 V or 0.7 V, then a small change in temperature will vary the conduction point on this curve. The change in diode voltage drop over a 100°F is about 0.1 V which can be amplified and applied to the input of an ADC.

The Interface to the Z80

Figure 15-10 illustrates the diode connected to the + input of an operational amplifier. Here a potentiometer is connected to the — input of the op-amp so that it can be adjusted to allow a maximum change at the output of the amplifier. The ideal voltage on the — input is approximately 0.2 V so that the amplifier, which has a gain of 10, will produce a + 1.0 V output at a normal temperature and change from 0 V to + 2.0 V over the full range of temperatures. The output of the amplifier is connected to the ADC so that its voltage can be sampled by the microprocessor.

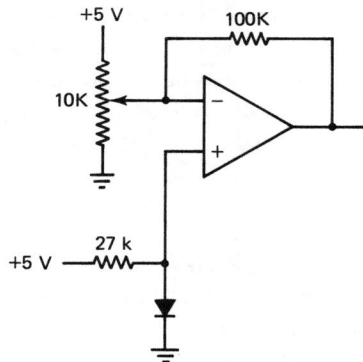

Figure 15–10 Amplifying the output from the diode temperature sensor.

15-5 *USING THE DAC TO CONTROL A DC MOTOR* _____

A DC motor is a device that is controlled by varying the amplitude and polarity of the DC voltage applied to its armature winding. If the polarity of the voltage is changed, the direction changes, and if the amplitude is changed, the speed changes. If the DC motor is to be driven in one direction, the control is often as simple as using the DAC and the operational amplifier connected to its output as described in Section 15-2. A small motor can be driven directly from the amplifier's output. A large motor requires the addition of a driver transistor.

Transistor Driver

Figure 15-11 illustrates the DAC, its operational amplifier, and a driver transistor that is used to provide a large current for a large DC motor. The transistor amplifier is used to provide a current gain so that enough current exists to spin the large motor. As the voltage at the output of the DAC and its amplifier increases, so does the voltage applied to the driver transistor's base. This increases the conduction of the transistor and allows a larger current to flow through the motor increasing its speed.

Bidirectional Motor Control

Bidirectional motor control isn't quite as simple as unidirectional control because the polarity of the voltage applied to the motor must be changed. If the DAC is used, this presents no major problem. Figure 15-12 illustrates a circuit that allows the polarity of the voltage applied to the voltage reference input (Vref) of the DAC to be changed. Changing the Vref voltage changes the polarity of the output voltage of the DAC and hence the direction of the motor connected to the operational amplifier. If Vref is $+10$ V the output voltage is somewhere between 0 V and -10 V, and if Vref is -10 V the output voltage is between 0V and $+10$ V. The level of this output voltage is determined by the digital code applied to the DAC from the microprocessor.

If a larger DC motor is controlled with this circuit, the operational amplifier is

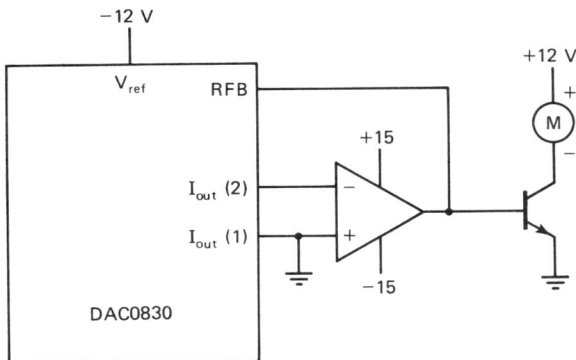

Figure 15–11   Driving a DC motor with the DAC0830.

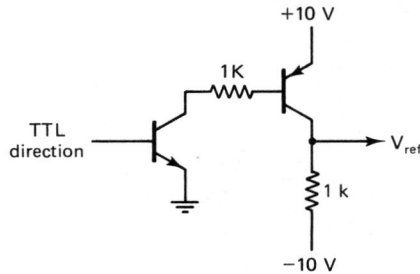

Figure 15–12 Circuit to apply $\pm 10v$ to the Vref input of the ADC0805.

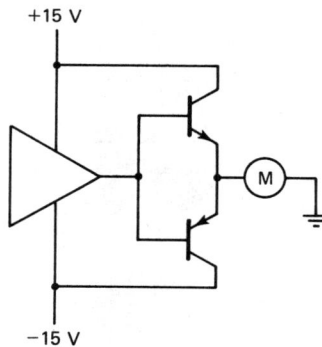

Figure 15–13 Circuit to increase the drive current to the motor.

connected to a pair of transistors that increase or boost the amount of current available to drive the motor. The circuit used to increase bidirectional drive is illustrated in Figure 15-13. In this circuit, if the output voltage is 0 V, then neither transistor is on and the motor receives no voltage. If the output of the operational amplifier becomes positive (0 to $+10$ V), the NPN transistor conducts and drives current through the armature of the motor toward ground. If the output of the operational amplifier is negative (0 to -10 V), the PNP transistor conducts and allows current to flow from ground through the motor and through the PNP transistor to -15 V.

15-6 SUMMARY

1. The DAC0830 is an 8-bit microprocessor compatible digital-to-analog converter that converts from a digital code to an analog voltage in just 1.0 µs.

2. The DAC0830 contains a holding register and the converter register. The holding register is clocked by the combination of ILE, $\overline{WR1}$, and $\overline{CS}$ and the converter register is clocked by the combination of $\overline{WR2}$ and $\overline{XFER}$.

3. The ADC0805 is an 8-bit analog-to-digital converter that requires 100 µs of time to convert an analog voltage into a digital code.

4. The ADC0805 is operated in the following fashion: $\overline{WR}$ is activated, while $\overline{CS}$ is active, to start the conversion process; next, the $\overline{INTR}$ pin is tested for a change from a logic 0 to a logic 0, which indicates that the conversion process is complete; finally, the $\overline{RD}$ pin is activated, while $\overline{CS}$ is active, to read the digital code from the output pins.

5. The ADC0805 clock is operated at between 100 KHz and 1460 KHz. This operation is achieved by an external clock applied to CLK IN or by an RC circuit attached to the CLK IN and CLK R pins.

6. Temperature is sensed by using either a thermistor or a diode junction. The diode is biased at a point where it barely conducts. When biased this way, the output voltage changes with the ambient temperature.

7. A DC motor is controlled by varying the amplitude of the applied voltage to change its speed and the polarity to change its direction.

15-7 GLOSSARY

ADC   Analog-to-digital converters convert analog voltages into digital codes.

Analog voltage   A voltage that can be an infinite number of levels.

Characteristic curve   A plot that indicates how a transistor or diode operates with applied voltages.

DAC   Digital-to-analog converters convert a digital code into an analog voltage.

Differential inputs   Inputs that are summed inside of an operational amplifier. (The summing actually subtracts the two voltages.)

Forward bias voltage   The voltage found across a diode junction when it is conducting.

Thermistor   A resistor that changes its resistance whenever the temperature changes.

QUESTIONS AND PROBLEMS

15-1. Describe the purpose of the DAC.

15-2. With the DAC0830, where is the digital code applied for conversion to analog?

15-3. What is the purpose of the Vref input to the DAC0830?

15-4. What 4 pins on the DAC0830 determine the final analog output voltage?

15-5. Explain how data are stored in the internal holding register of the DAC0830.

15-6. Explain how data are transferred into the converter of the DAC030.

15-7. If the $\overline{IOW}$ signal is used to store data in the DAC0830, at what part of $\overline{IOW}$ are the data stored?

15-8. How long does it take the DAC0830 to convert a digital code into an analog voltage?

15-9. Describe the purpose of the ADC.

15-10. With the ADC0805, where are the digital data removed after a conversion?

15-11. How much time is required for the ADC0805 to convert an analog voltage to a digital code?

15-12. How is the ADC0805 started?

15-13. What ADC0805 signal indicates that the conversion process is complete?

15-14. How are the data read from the ADC0805?

15-15. Explain how an external clock is applied to the ADC0805.

15-16. Choose R and C components so that the ADC0805 operates at 1 MHz.

15-17. Describe the effect of a change in temperature on the characteristics of a diode.

chapter 16

Introduction to Advanced Microprocessors

This chapter presents an introduction to some of the most common 16- and 32-bit microprocessors. Because Intel and Motorola appear to have the largest share of the 16- and 32-bit market, only the Intel 8086 family and the Motorola 68000 family are discussed.

Sixteen- and 32-bit microprocessors are used in many of the more modern control and computer applications because of their expanded instruction sets and also advances in the memory and I/O interface. The instruction sets contain instructions that allow multiplication and division and also allow memory data to be addressed in more diverse ways. The memory system is expanded so that these advanced microprocessors can address at least 1M bytes of memory.

16-1 OBJECTIVES

Upon completion of this chapter, you will be able to:

1. Contrast the features of some of the most common 16- and 32-bit microprocessors with the Z80 microprocessor.
2. Describe the programming model of the 8086 and 68000 microprocessors.
3. List the purpose of each of the internal registers of the 8086 and the 68000.
4. Detail the memory and/or I/O maps of the 8086 and the 68000.
5. Compare the 8- and 16-bit bus versions of the 8086/8088 and the 68000/68008.
6. Compare the 32-bit 68020 with the 16-bit 68000 and the 32-bit 80386 with the 16-bit 8086.

16-2 THE 16-BIT 8086 MICROPROCESSOR

The 8086 microprocessor is a general purpose 16-bit microprocessor that addresses 1M bytes of memory. When compared to the Z80 microprocessor, the 8086 is much more powerful because data are directly addressed as either 8- or 16-bit words, there are 1M bytes of memory, the instruction set includes multiplication and division, and the execution speed is much higher. Overall the 8086 is a powerful microprocessor which can execute larger programs and operate at a very high rate of speed in comparison to the Z80 microprocessor.

Pinout

The pinout of the 8086 microprocessor is illustrated in Figure 16-1. Notice that the 8086 is contained in a 40-pin DIP—the same size integrated circuit as the Z80 microprocessor. This is possible because Intel has multiplexed the address and data bus connections together on the address/data bus pins (AD15—AD0) of the 8086. The 8086 contains a 20-bit address bus and a 16-bit data bus which allows it to address 1M bytes of memory and transfer 8- or 16-bits of data at a time.

Memory Map

Figure 16-2 illustrates the logical and physical memory maps of the 8086 microprocessor. The logical memory map is a view of the memory as seen by the programmer, and it

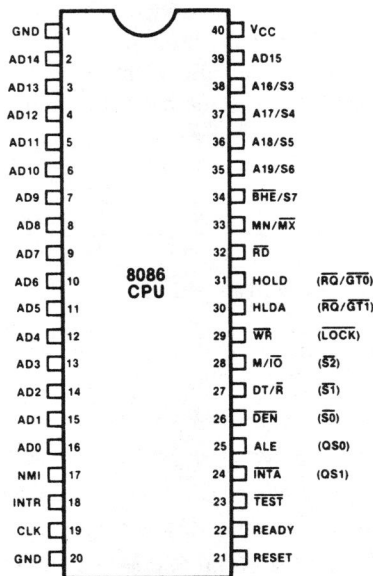

GND — 1	40 — V_{CC}	
AD14 — 2	39 — AD15	
AD13 — 3	38 — A16/S3	
AD12 — 4	37 — A17/S4	
AD11 — 5	36 — A18/S5	
AD10 — 6	35 — A19/S6	
AD9 — 7	34 — $\overline{BHE}$/S7	
AD8 — 8	33 — MN/$\overline{MX}$	
AD7 — 9	32 — $\overline{RD}$	
AD6 — 10 8086 CPU	31 — HOLD	($\overline{RQ}$/$\overline{GT0}$)
AD5 — 11	30 — HLDA	($\overline{RQ}$/$\overline{GT1}$)
AD4 — 12	29 — $\overline{WR}$	($\overline{LOCK}$)
AD3 — 13	28 — M/$\overline{IO}$	($\overline{S2}$)
AD2 — 14	27 — DT/$\overline{R}$	($\overline{S1}$)
AD1 — 15	26 — $\overline{DEN}$	($\overline{S0}$)
AD0 — 16	25 — ALE	(QS0)
NMI — 17	24 — $\overline{INTA}$	(QS1)
INTR — 18	23 — $\overline{TEST}$	
CLK — 19	22 — READY	
GND — 20	21 — RESET	

Figure 16-1 The pinout of the 8086 microprocessor. (Courtesy of Intel Corporation.)

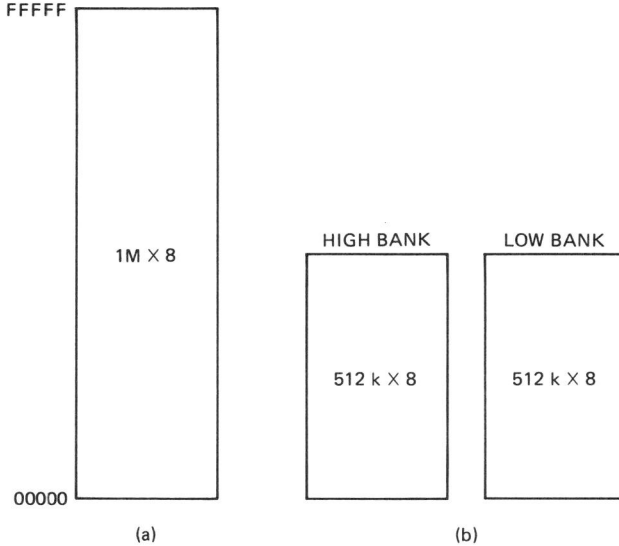

Figure 16–2 The (a) logical and (b) physical memory maps of the 8086 microprocessor.

contains 1M bytes of 8-bit wide memory. The physical memory map is the memory structure as it actually exists. In the physical map the memory consists of a set of two 8-bit wide banks with each bank containing 512K bytes of memory. These memory locations are addressed as bytes or as 16-bit words. (A word is one byte from each of the two banks of memory).

Figure 16-3 illustrates the 8086 connected to its memory. Notice that 74LS373 latches are used to demultiplex the address information from the address/data bus. The ALE signal from the 8086 is a logic one whenever the address/data bus contains memory addressing information. ALE is used as a clock signal so that the 74LS373 latches capture the address each time that ALE is active.

Memory is addressed in banks that are selected by the $\overline{BHE}$ signal (bank high enable) and the A0 address signal. If $\overline{BHE}$ is a logic 0 then the upper memory bank is selected, and if A0 is a logic 0 the lower memory bank is selected. The upper memory bank contains all of the odd-number memory bytes and the lower memory bank contains all of the even-numbered memory bytes. This arrangement allows any 8- or 16-bit data to be read or written between the microprocessor and the memory. Again, as far as the programmer is concerned, the memory is 8-bits in width.

In this circuit, memory is selected by a separate upper and a lower bank decoder (two 74LS138s). The upper memory bank is selected whenever $\overline{BHE}$ is a logic 0, and the lower bank is selected whenever A0 is a logic 0. Memory is addressed at locations 00000H—07FFFH by these two decoders.

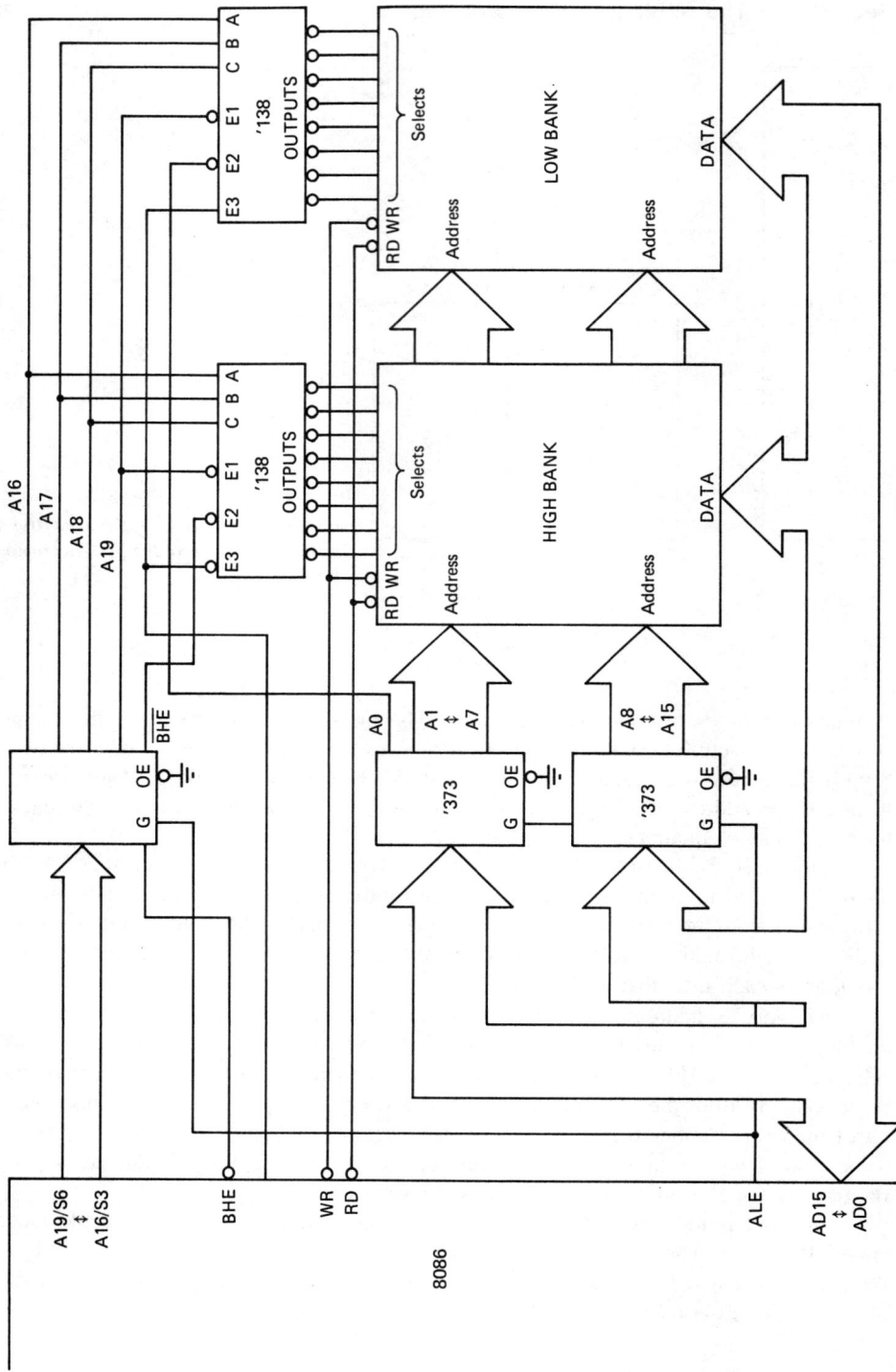

Figure 16–3 Example of an 8086 memory interface.

Programming Model

Figure 16-4 illustrates the programming model of the 8086 microprocessor. The model contains four sections of registers that are all 16-bits in width:

1. General Purpose Registers. The general purpose registers are used as either four 16-bit registers or eight 8-bit registers or any combination of 8- and 16-bit registers. The 16-bit general purpose registers are AX (accumulator), BX (base index), CX (count), and DX (data). The 8-bit general purpose registers are AH, AL, BH, BL, CH, CL, DH, and DL.

2. Segment Registers. The segment registers include CS (code segment), DS (data segment), SS (stack segment), and ES (extra segment). Each segment register is 16 bits in width and addresses a 64K byte segment of the memory. If the data segment is to be located at address 10000H—1FFFFH, then the DS register is loaded with a 1000H. The microprocessor supplies the right-most hexadecimal digit for the segment so that the 64K byte data segment begins at address 10000H if a 1000H is loaded into the DS register. If a 1234H is loaded into the CS register, the code segment begins at memory address 12340H and extends 64K bytes to address 2233FH. The code segment is where the program must be located, the stack

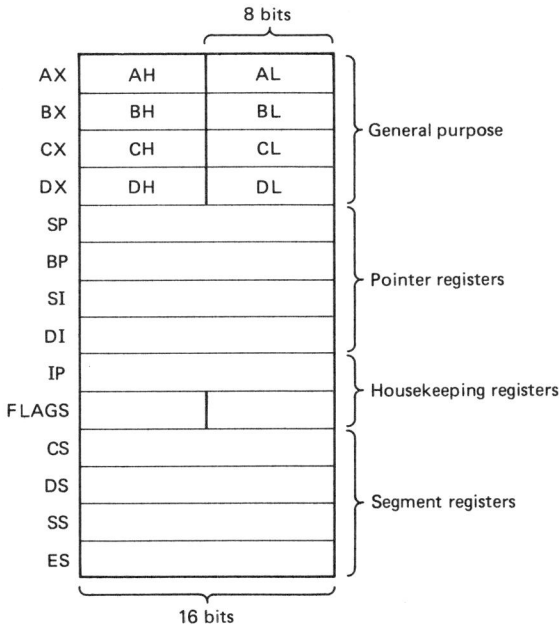

Figure 16–4 An 8086 programming model.

segment is where the stack must be located, the data segment is where most data are located, and the extra segment is normally used only with the string instructions.

3. Index and Pointer Registers. The index and pointer registers are used to address data within a 64K byte segment of the memory and hold the offset address of the data. The offset address is added to the first location of the segment address to locate the data within a segment. The stack pointer (SP) addresses data within the stack segment for PUSH, POP, CALL, and RET instructions. The base pointer (BP) addresses general purpose data in the stack segment. Both the source index (SI) and destination index registers (DI) address data within the data segment. If a string instruction is executed, the DI register will address data in the extra segment.

Suppose that the DS register holds a 1000H and that the SI register holds a 2000H. If memory data are addressed through the SI register the actual address is 10000H + 2000H or 12000H. Notice how the offset address held in SI is added to the beginning data segment address to obtain the actual physical memory location of the data.

4. Housekeeping Registers. The housekeeping registers include the IP (instruction pointer) and the flags. The instruction pointer is like the program counter in that it addresses the next instruction to be executed. The only difference is that the next instruction is stored in the code segment at the offset address pointed to by the instruction pointer register. For example, when the 8086 is first rest, the IP register contains a 0000H and the CS register contains an FFFFH. This means that the next instruction executed by the 8086, after a reset, is located at memory address FFFF0H, the sum of 0000 and FFFFH.

The flag register holds bits that indicate statistics about the operation of the 8086. The right-most eight bits contain the flags that indicate the outcome of an arithmetic or logic operation and include S (sign), Z (zero), C (carry), P (Parity), and Ac (auxillary carry). The left-most byte of the flag register holds the O (overflow), D (direction), I (interrupt enable), and T (trace) flags. The direction flag is used with the string instructions to indicate auto-increment or auto-decrement operation for SI and/or DI. The interrupt enable flag is used to enable or disable the INTR pin. The trace flag is used to cause a trace interrupt after the execution of each instruction. A more detailed explanation defeats the purpose of this chapter and must be concluded in a course on the 8086 microprocessor.

The Instruction Set

The instruction set of the 8086 microprocessor is similar to the instruction set of the Z80 microprocessor. Table 16-1 lists the instructions found in the 8086 and compares them to the Z80 instructions. Notice that most of the 8086 instructions are implemented in the Z80 with little or no change in the mnemonic opcode. Some of the instructions that aren't implemented include multiplication, division, the ASCII adjust instructions, and some special instructions that are unique to the 8086. For the most part, Z80 instructions are the same as 8086 instructions.

TABLE 16-1.   8086 AND Z80 INSTRUCTIONS

8086	Z80	Function
AAA	—	ASCII adjust for addition
AAD	—	Adjust for division
AAM	—	Adjust for multiplication
AAS	—	ASCII adjust for subtraction
ADD	ADD	addition
ADC	ADC	addition with carry
AND	AND	logical multiplication (AND)
CALL	CALL	call a subroutine
CBW	—	convert signed byte to word
CLC	—	clear carry
CLD	—	select auto-increment for string instructions
CLI	DI	disable interrupts
CMC	CCF	complement carry
CMP	CP	comparison
CMPS	CPI	string memory-to-memory comparison
CWD	—	convert signed word to double word
DAA	DAA	decimal accumulator adjust
DAS	—	decimal accumulator adjust for subtraction
DEC	DEC	decrement
DIV	—	unsigned division
ESC	—	instructions for coprocessors
HLT	HALT	halt
INC	INC	increment
IDIV	—	signed division
IMUL	—	signed multiplication
IN	In	input data
IRET	RETI	return from interrupt
Jcc	JR cc,	conditional jumps
JCXZ	—	jump if CX equals zero
JMP	JP	unconditional jump
LAHF	—	load AH from flags
LOCK	—	lock out coprocessors
LODS	—	load accumulator from string
LOOP	DJNZ	decrement and jump not zero
LOOPE	—	decrement and jump not zero, while an equal condition exists
LOOPNE	—	decrement and jump not zero, while a not equal condition exists
MOV	LD	load or move data
MOVS	LDI	memory-to-memory data transfer
MUL	—	unsigned multiplication
NEG	NEG	change sign
NOP	NOP	no operation
NOT	CPL	invert
OR	OR	logical addition (OR)
OUT	OUT	output data
POP	POP	pop data from the stack
PUSH	PUSH	push data onto the stack
RCL	RL	rotate left through carry
RLR	RR	rotate right through carry

TABLE 16-1.   (Cont.)

8086	Z80	Function
REP	—	repeat a string operation CX times
REPE	—	repeat a string operation CX times while an equal condition exists
REPNE	—	repeat a string operation CX times while a not equal condition exists
RET	RET	return from subroutine
ROL	RLC	rotate left
ROR	RRC	rotate right
SAHF	—	store AH in flags
SAL	SLA	arithmetic left shift
SAR	SRA	arithmetic right shift
SBB	SBC	subtraction with borrow
SCAS	—	accumulator to memory string comparison
SEG	—	segment override prefix
SHL	SLA	shift left logical
SHR	SRL	shift right logical
STC	SCF	set carry flag
STD	—	select auto-decrement for string instructions
STI	EI	enable interrupts
STOS	—	store accumulator in string
SUB	SUB	subtraction
TEST	BIT	test bit (Z80) or bits (8086)
XCHG	EX	exchange
XOR	XOR	exclusive-OR
WAIT	—	waits for a zero on the $\overline{\text{TEST}}$ pin

Addressing Modes

Addressing modes for the 8086 microprocessor are similar to the Z80 microprocessor's and include register addressing, direct addressing, indexed addressing, immediate addressing, and indirect addressing.

By using the MOV instruction to illustrate the addressing modes, a comparison of Z80 and 8086 addressing modes is possible. An 8086 MOV instruction is like the Z80 LD instruction because the contents of the second operand are copied into the first operand. For example, an LD A,B instruction will load the A register with the contents of the B register in the Z80 microprocessor, while the MOV AH,BL instruction will load the AH register with the contents of the BL register.

1. Register Addressing. Register addressed instructions use either 8- or 16-bit registers, but never allow the size of the registers to be mixed. An example of an 8-bit register-to-register move is the MOV AH,AL instruction. This instruction transfers a copy of AL into AH. An example of a 16-bit register-to-register move is the MOV BX,CX instruction. Here the contents of CX is copied into BX. The 8-bit register

set contains AH, AL, BH, BL, CH, CL, DH, and DL. The 16-bit register set contains AX, BX, CX, DX, SP, BP, DI, and SI. The segment registers are only used if a MOV, PUSH, or POP instruction is executed.

2. Direct Addressing. Direct addressed instructions allow data within the data segment to be transferred between any 8- or 16-bit register and memory. For example, the MOV AX,LIST instruction transfers a copy of the 16-bit number stored in memory location LIST and LIST + 1 into AX. A MOV DATA1,BH instruction transfers the contents of BH into data segment memory location DATA1.

3. Immediate Addressing. Immediate addressed instructions allow an immediate byte or word to be used as the source data in an instruction. For example, MOV AL,63H will load AL with a 63H. A MOV CX,1234H will load CX with a 1234H.

4. Indirect Addressing. Indirect addressed instructions allow memory data to be addressed through BP, SI, DI, or BX. This is similar to using the HL register pair to address memory data in the Z80 microprocessor. A MOV AL,[SI] instruction loads AL from the byte of memory addressed by the SI register within the data segment. The SI, DI, and BX registers address data in the data segment and the BP register addresses data in the stack segment.

5. Indexed Addressing. Indexed addressing occurs in a few forms in the 8086 microprocessor. For example, the MOV [BX + 2],CX instruction loads 16-bits of memory width, addressed by the contents of BX plus 2, with the contents of CX. MOV AL,DATA[SI] loads AL with the contents of memory location data plus the contents of SI. Two registers may be used to address the memory data. For example, a MOV AL [BX + DI] instruction loads AL from the memory location addressed by the sum of BX and DI. Recall that memory data are in the data segment unless they are addressed by the SP or the BP registers. The allowable combinations are [BX + DI], [BX + SI], [BP + DI], and [BP + SI].

Table 16-2 summarizes all of the allowable addressing modes with examples of their usage. Most 8086 instructions have two operands, which is different from the Z80 in many cases. For example, the ADD instruction always has two operands. ADD AL,BL will add the contents of BL to AL, while the ADD BL,AL will add the contents of AL to BL. The only difference between these two instructions is where the answer is placed. ADD AL,BL places the sum of AL and BL in AL, while ADD BL,AL places the sum on BL. Notice how flexible the 8086 instruction set is in comparison to the Z80.

The 8088 Microprocessor

The 8088 microprocessor is basically an 8086 with an 8-bit data bus. It is found in many of the IBM-PC and PC compatible computers. In many applications this 8-bit bus version of the 8086 is ideal because ASCII data is 8-bits in width and is used with many of the programs that are executed on personal computers.

TABLE 16-2.   THE 8086 ADDRESSING MODES

Instruction	Mode	Function
MOV AL, BL	register	AL is loaded from BL
MOV AX,CX	register	AX is loaded from CX
MOV BL,34H	immediate	BL is loaded with a 34H
MOV SP,1000H	immediate	SP is loaded with a 1000H
MOV CH,DATA	direct	Ch is loaded from memory byte DATA which is in the data segment
MOV SI,LIST	direct	SI is loaded from memory bytes LIST and LIST + 1 which are in the data segment
MOV AL,[BP]	indirect	load AL from the stack segment byte addressed by BP
MOV BL,[BX]	indirect	load BL from the data segment byte addressed by BX
MOV CX,[DI]	indirect	load CX from data segment memory bytes addressed by DI
MOV [SI],DI	indirect	load data segment memory bytes addressed by SI with the contents of DI
MOV AL,[BX + 200]	indexed	load AL with the data segment memory byte addressed by BX plus 200
MOV AL,LIST[SI]	indexed	load AL with the data segment memory byte addressed by LIST plus SI
MOV BL,[BX + DI]	indexed	load BL with the data segment memory byte addressed by the sum of BX and DI

16-3 THE 16-BIT 68000 MICROPROCESSOR

The 68000 microprocessor is a general purpose 16-bit microprocessor that addresses 16M bytes of memory. When compared to the Z80 microprocessor, the 68000 is much more powerful because data are directly addressed as either 8- or 16-bit words, there are 16M bytes of memory, the instruction set includes multiplication and division, and the execution speed is much higher. Overall the 68000 is a powerful microprocessor which can execute larger programs and operate at a very high rate of speed in comparison to the Z80 microprocessor.

Pinout

The pinout of the 68000 microprocessor is illustrated in Figure 16-5. Notice that the 68000 is contained in a 64-pin DIP—larger than the 40-pin integrated circuit of the Z80 microprocessor. This larger circuit is required because the Motorola 68000 has a 16 bit data bus (D0—D15) and a 24-bit address bus with 23 address pins (A1—A23). The 68000 addresses bytes (8 bits), words (16 bits), or long words (32-bits) of data. Bytes and words are directly addressed, and long words are addressed by two 16-bit read or writes.

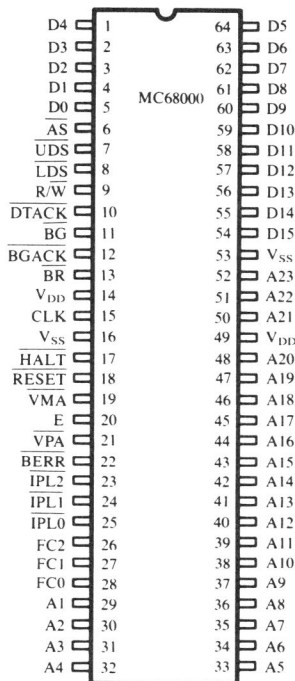

D4	1	64	D5
D3	2	63	D6
D2	3	62	D7
D1	4	61	D8
D0	5	60	D9
AS	6	59	D10
UDS	7	58	D11
LDS	8	57	D12
R/W	9	56	D13
DTACK	10	55	D14
BG	11	54	D15
BGACK	12	53	V$_{SS}$
BR	13	52	A23
V$_{DD}$	14	51	A22
CLK	15	50	A21
V$_{SS}$	16	49	V$_{DD}$
HALT	17	48	A20
RESET	18	47	A19
VMA	19	46	A18
E	20	45	A17
VPA	21	44	A16
BERR	22	43	A15
IPL2	23	42	A14
IPL1	24	41	A13
IPL0	25	40	A12
FC2	26	39	A11
FC1	27	38	A10
FC0	28	37	A9
A1	29	36	A8
A2	30	35	A7
A3	31	34	A6
A4	32	33	A5

MC68000

Figure 16–5   The 68000 pinout. (Courtesy of Motorola, Inc.)

Memory Map

Figure 16-6 illustrates the logical and physical memory maps of the 68000 microprocessor. The logical memory map is a view of the memory as seen by the programmer, and it contains 16M bytes of 8-bit memory. The physical memory map is the memory structure as it exists physically. Here the memory is a set of two 8-bit banks with each bank containing 8M bytes of memory. The memory locations are directly addressed as bytes or as 16-bit words.

Figure 16-7 illustrates the 68000 connected to its memory. Notice that the memory is addressed in banks that are selected by the UDS (upper data strobe) signal and the LDS (lower data strobe) signal. If UDS is a logic 0, the upper memory bank is selected and if LDS is a logic 0, the lower memory bank is selected. The upper memory bank contains all of the odd-numbered memory bytes, and the lower memory bank contains all of the even-numbered memory bytes. This arrangement allows any 8- or 16-bit data to be read or written between the microprocessor and the memory. Again, as far as the programmer is concerned, the memory is 8-bits in width. In this circuit, memory is selected by a separate upper and a lower bank decoder (two 74LS138s). The upper memory bank is selected whenever UDS is a logic 0, and the lower bank is selected whenever LDS is a logic 0. Memory is addressed at locations FF8000H—FFFFFFH by these bank decoders.

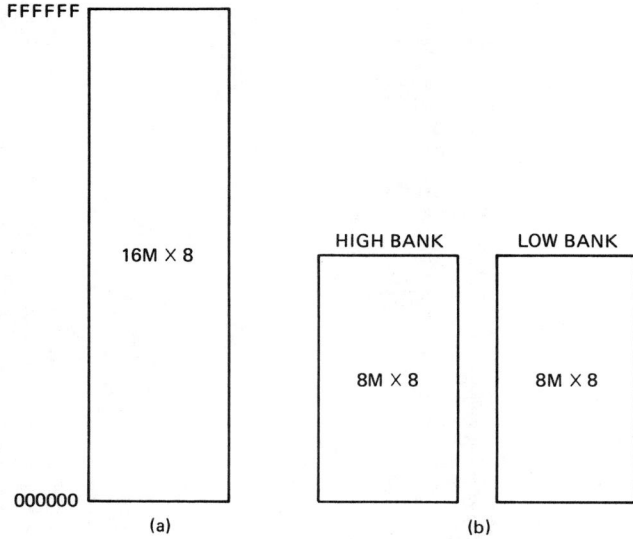

Figure 16–6 The (a) logical and (b) physical memory maps of the 68000 microprocessor.

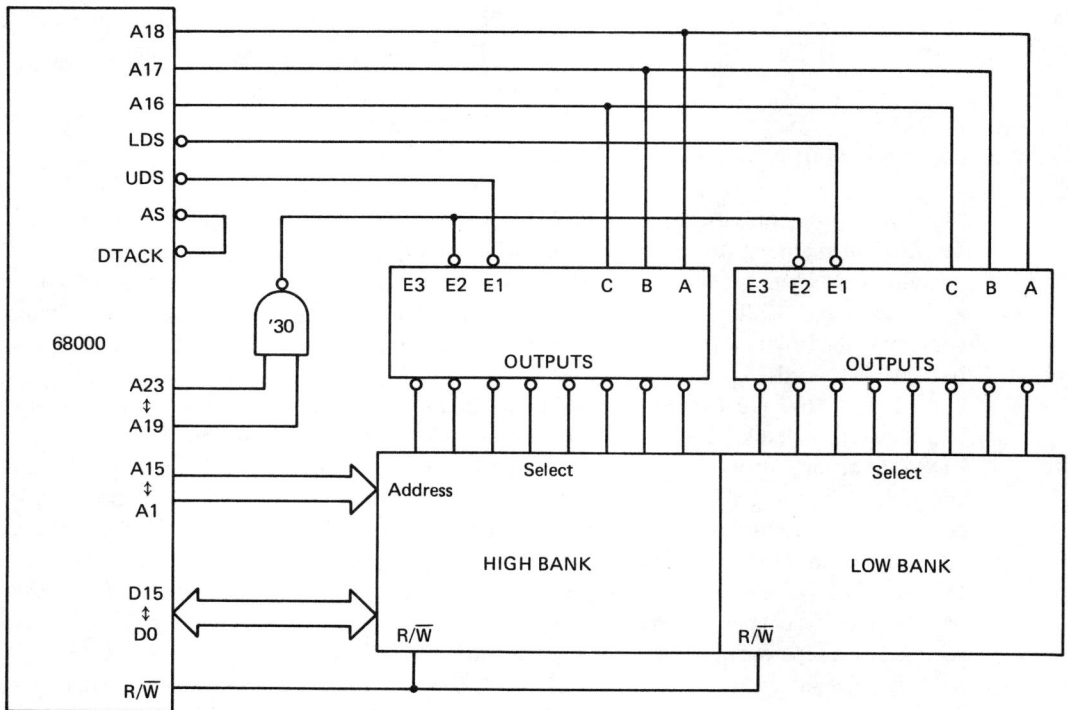

Figure 16–7 Example of a 68000 memory interface.

Programming Model

Figure 16-8 illustrates the programming model of the 68000 microprocessor. The model contains three sections of registers:

1. Data Registers. The 68000 has eight general purpose 32-bit data registers that are labeled D0—D7. These registers are addressed as 32-bit long words, 16-bit words, or as 8-bit bytes. A word is the right-most 16 bits of a data register, and a byte is the right-most 8 bits only.

2. Address Registers. The address registers are used to address memory data and are either 32-bit or 16-bit registers. Seven of them, A0—A6, are general purpose address registers, and the remaining two, A7, and A7′, are used as stack pointers. A7 is the user stack pointer (USP) and A7′ is the supervisor stack pointer (SSP). The 68000 operates in either the supervisor mode or the user mode. The supervisor

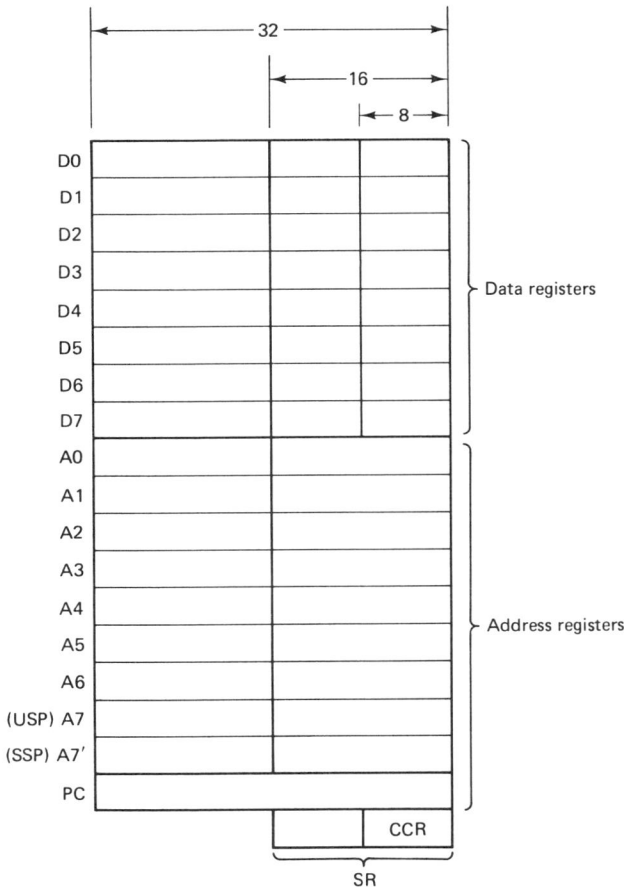

Figure 16–8 The programming model of the 68000 microprocessor.

mode is entered when a hardware reset or an interrupt occurs, giving these system functions their own stack.

3. Housekeeping Registers. The 68000 has two housekeeping registers: the program counter (PC) and the status register (SR). The PC is a 32-bit register that holds the address of the next instruction to be executed by the 68000. Because the address bus is only 24 bits in width, only the right-most 24 bits of the PC are used and the remaining PC bits are ignored. The status register has two parts: the supervisor byte and the CCR (condition code register). The CCR generally indicates the status of the data operated upon by the 68000 and contains the Z (zero), N (negative), V (overflow), C (carry), and X (extend) CCR bits. The supervisor byte, which is accessible only in the supervisor mode, contains the S (supervisor), T (trace), and I2—I0 (interrupt mask) bits.

The Instruction Set

The instruction set of the 68000 microprocessor is similar to the instruction set of the Z80 microprocessor. Table 16-3 lists the instructions found in the 68000 and compares them to the Z80 instructions. Notice that most of the 68000 instructions are implemented in the Z80 with little or no change in the mnemonic opcode. Some of the instructions that aren't implemented include multiplication, division, and some special instructions that are unique to the 68000. For the most part, Z80 instructions are the same as 68000 instructions.

TABLE 16-3. 68000 AND Z80 INSTRUCTIONS

68000	Z80	Function
ABCD	—	BCD addition
ADD	ADD	addition
ADDX	ADC	addition with carry
AND	AND	logical multiplication (AND)
ASL	SLA	arithmetic left shift
ASR	SRA	arithmetic right shift
Bcc	JR cc,	conditional jumps
BCHG	—	invert a bit
BCLR	RES	clear a bit
BRA	JR	relative branch
BSET	SET	set a bit
BSR	—	branch to subroutine
BTST	BIT	test a bit
CLR	—	clear
CMP	CP	comparison
DBcc	—	decrement and branch
DIVS	—	signed division
DIVU	—	unsigned division
EOR	XOR	exclusive-OR
EXG	EX	exchange

TABLE 16-3.   (Cont.)

68000	Z80	Function
EXT.W	—	convert signed byte to word
EXT.L	—	convert signed word to double word
JMP	JP	unconditional jump
JSR	CALL	call a subroutine
LEA	—	load effective address
LSL	SLA	shift left logical
LSR	SRL	shift right logical
MOVE	LD	load or move data
MOVEM	—	multiple register move
MOVEP	—	move peripheral
MOVEQ	—	move quick
MULS	—	signed multiplication
MULU	—	unsigned multiplication
NBCD	—	negate BCD
NEG	NEG	change sign
NEGX	—	change sign plus extend
NOP	NOP	no operation
NOT	CPL	invert
OR	OR	logical addition (OR)
RESET	—	reset peripherals
ROL	RLC	rotate left
ROR	RRC	rotate right
ROXL	RL	rotate left through carry
ROXR	RR	rotate right through carry
RTE	RETI	return from interrupt
RTS	RET	return from subroutine
SBCD	—	subtract BCD
Scc	—	set according to condition
STOP	HALT	halt
SUB	SUB	subtraction
SUBX	SBC	subtraction with borrow
SWAP	—	swap register halves
TAS	—	test and set
TST	—	test operand

Addressing Modes

Addressing modes for the 68000 microprocessor are similar to the Z80 microprocessors and include register addressing, direct addressing, indexed addressing, immediate addressing, program counter addressing, and indirect addressing.

By using the MOVE instruction to illustrate the addressing modes, a comparison of Z80 and 68000 addressing modes is possible. An 68000 MOVE instruction is like the Z80 LD instruction because the contents of the second operand are copied into the first operand. For example, an LD A,B instruction will load the A register with the contents of the B register in the Z80 microprocessor, while the MOVE.B D0,D1 instruction will load the byte of D0 into D1. Notice that the direction of the data flow is the opposite of the Z80 and also note that a .B is a byte operation, .W is a word, and .L is a long word. A MOVE.B will move a byte, a MOVE.W will move a word, and a MOVE.L will move a long word.

1. Register Addressing. Register addressed instructions use either the data or the address registers. Data registers can be 8-, 16-, or 32-bit registers and address registers can be either 16- or 32-bit registers. An example of an 8-bit register-to-register move is the MOVE.B D2,D3 instruction. This instruction transfers a copy of D2 into D3. An example of a 16-bit register-to-register move is the MOVE.W A2,D4 instruction. Here the contents of A2 are copied into D4. The MOVE.L D6,D7 instruction copies D6 into D7.

2. Direct Addressing. Direct addressed instructions allow data to be transferred between any register and memory. For example, the MOVE.L D4,LIST instruction transfers a copy of the 32-bit number stored in D4 into four bytes of memory beginning at memory location LIST. A MOVE.B DATA1,D5 instruction transfers the contents of memory location DATA1 into register D5. Note that only the rightmost eight bits of D5 will change.

3. Immediate Addressing. Immediate addressed instructions allow an immediate byte, word, or long word to be used as the source data in an instruction. For example, MOVE.B #$63,D4 will load the byte in D4 with a 63H. The (#) symbol is used to indicate immediate data, and the ($) symbol is used to indicate hexadecimal data.

4. Indirect Addressing. Indirect addressed instructions allow memory data to be addressed through any address register. This is similar to using the HL register pair to address memory data in the Z80 microprocessor. A MOVE.B D2,(A3) instruction transfers a copy of the byte in D2 to the memory location addressed by the A3 address register. Notice that the address register is surrounded by () to indicate indirect addressing.

5. Post-Increment Indirect Addressing. The post-increment mode is similar to the indirect addressing mode. The only difference is that after the operation is performed, the address register is incremented. For example, a MOVE.B D2,(A1)+ instruction will copy the byte in D2 into the memory location addressed by A1. After the transfer, the contents of address register A1 are incremented. If a byte is transferred 1 is added to the address register, a word adds a 2, and a long word adds a 4.

6. Pre-Decrement Indirect Addressing. The pre-decrement mode of addressing allows the contents of an address register to be decremented before it is used to indirectly address memory data. For example, a MOVE.B −(A2),D1 will decrement A2 by a 1, after which it will copy the byte of data from this new address into the D1 register. As with the post-increment mode, a 1 is subtracted for a byte, a 2 for a word, and a 4 for a long word.

7. Indexed Addressing. Indexed addressing occurs in a few forms in the 68000 micro-

processor. When this mode of addressing is used the contents of an address register are added to the contents of an address or a data register to form the memory address used by the instruction. For example, a MOVE.B D1,(A2 + A3) instruction will copy the byte from D1 into the memory location addressed by the sum of A2 and A3.

8. Program Counter Addressing. The program counter can be used to address memory data. If this mode of addressing is used the data are located in relation to the address of the next instruction because this is where the program counter points. For example, the MOVE.B (PC),D1 instruction will move the next byte of memory into register D1. The next byte of memory is the one following the MOVE.B (PC),D1 instruction. If a byte of data that is 10 bytes past the current instruction is used, then the instruction is written as MOVE.B (PC + 10,D1. The importance of this type of data addressing is that the instruction and data can be relocated without changing a thing except their position in the memory.

Table 16-4 summarizes all of the allowable addressing modes with examples of their usage. Most 68000 instructions have two operands, which is different because the Z80 only uses two operands for some of its instructions. For example, the ADD instruction always has two operands. ADD.B D1,D2 will add the byte contents of D1 to D2, while the ADD.B D2,D1 will add the byte contents of D2 to D1. The only difference between these two instructions is where the answer is placed. ADD.B D1,D2 places the sum of D1 and D2 in D2, while ADD.B D2,D1 places the sum in D1. Notice how flexible the 68000 instruction set is in comparison to the Z80. Instead of leaving the result in the accumulator, the programmer has a choice in the 68000.

TABLE 16-4.   THE 68000 ADDRESSING MODES

Instruction	Mode	Function
MOVE.B D1,D2	register	the byte in D1 is loaded into D2
MOVE.W D1,D2	register	the word in D1 is loaded into D2
MOVE.L D1,D2	register	the long word in D1 is loaded into D2
MOVE.B #$34,D6	immediate	a 34 hexadecimal is loaded into the byte of D6
MOVE.W #1000,D7	immediate	a 1000 decimal is loaded into the word of D7
MOVE.W D3,DATA	direct	the word in D3 is stored in memory locations DATA and DATA + 1
MOVE.W D2,(A5)	indirect	the word in register D2 is stored in the memory at the location addressed by A5
MOVE.L (A4),A6	indirect	load A6 with a long word from the memory location addressed by A4
MOVE.B D1,(A5) +	post-increment	the byte in D1 is stored at the memory location addressed by A5; then the contents of A5 are incremented by 1

TABLE 16-4. (Cont.)

Instruction	Mode	Function
MOVE.L D1,(A2)+	post-increment	the long word in D1 is stored at the memory location addressed by A2; then the contents of A2 are incremented by 4
MOVE.B -(A1),D3	pre-decrement	the contents of A1 are decremented by a 1; then the byte contents of this new memory location are copied into D3
MOVE.W D6,(A2+D4)	indexed	the word contents of D6 are copied into the memory location addressed by the sum of A2 and D4
MOVE.B (PC),D2	program counter	the byte in the memory location addressed by the program counter is copied into D2
MOVE.W A6,(PC+100)	program counter	the word contained in A6 is copied into the memory location addressed by the program counter plus 100 bytes

The 68008 Microprocessor

The 68008 microprocessor is basically a 68000 with an 8-bit data bus. Another difference is that the 68008 addresses only 1M bytes of memory rather than 16M bytes. The 68008 is found in some of the newer 68000-based home or personal computers. In many applications, this 8-bit bus version of the 68000 is ideal because ASCII data are 8-bits in width and are used with many of the programs that are executed on personal computers.

16-4 THE 32-BIT MICROPROCESSORS

The latest entries into the field of microprocessors are the 32-bit machines—the 80368 from Intel and the 68020 from Motorola. The 32-bit microprocessors contain a 32-bit data bus and usually a 32-bit address bus which allows them to address a tremendous number of memory locations. A 32-bit address bus allows the microprocessor to address 4G (4,294,967,296) bytes of memory. 4G bytes of memory are able to hold about 1,000,000 average typewritten pages of information. This is a lot of memory.

Memory Organization

The memory of both the 80386 and 68020 is organized as banks of bytes that can be written or read as bytes, words, or long words. This organization is also common in mainframe computer systems which also address 4G bytes of main memory.

Figure 16-9 illustrates the memory organization found in the 32-bit microprocessors. Notice that this organization is similar to the two memory banks found in the 8086 and

BANK 3   BANK 2   BANK 1   BANK 0

16 X 8   16 X 8   16 X 8   16 X 8

32-bit data bus

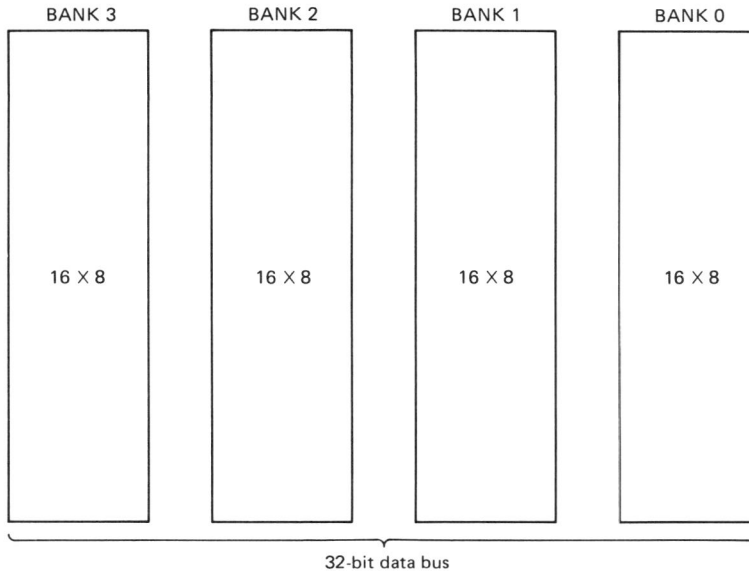

Figure 16–9 Memory organization of the 32-bit microprocessors.

the 68000 except there are four banks of memory. Each of these four memory banks contains 1G bytes of memory. This organization allows the 32-bit data bus to access any byte, any word, or any 32-bit long word of memory. Notice that there are four bank selection lines used to accomplish the memory bank selection.

Programmable Models

The 32-bit versions of the 68000 and the 8086 (68020 and 80386) have essentially the same internal register structure as the 16-bit versions. The 8086 registers have been stretched to 32-bit registers in the 80386, while the 68000 register essentially are and remain 32-bit registers in the 68020.

Figure 16-10 illustrates the modification to the 8086 registers in the 80386. The register set of the 68020 has not been illustrated because it is the same as the 68000 presented in Section 16-3.

Instruction Sets

The instruction sets of the 32-bit microprocessors are very similar to the 16-bit machines. In fact, the only difference is that a few new commands have been added. The main advantage of the 32-bit over the 16-bit microprocessor is that it operates at a much higher rate of speed and that it addresses much more memory. Speeds now approach 16 MHz for most of the 32-bit microprocessors with even higher speeds on the horizon.

	32	16	8
EAX		AH	AL
EBX		BH	BL
ECX		CH	CL
EDX		DH	DL
ESI		SI	
EDI		DI	
EBP		BP	
ESP		SP	

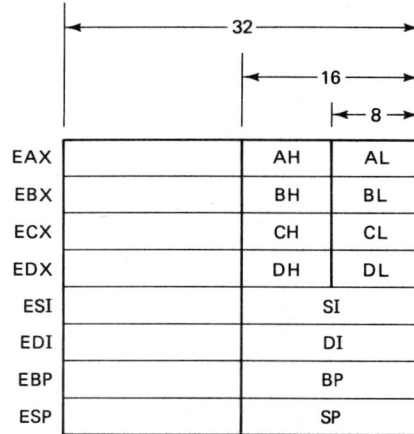

Figure 16–10 Modification to the 8086 registers in the 80386.

16-5 SUMMARY

1. The 8086 microprocessor is a 16-bit microprocessor capable of addressing 1M bytes of memory with its 16-bit data bus and 20-bit address bus.

2. The 8086 uses a multiplexed address/data bus so that it fits onto a 40-pin integrated circuit. The ALE signal is provided to demultiplex the address/data bus.

3. The programming model of the 8086 contains four 16-bit general purpose registers that can be divided into 8-bit registers, four pointer and index registers, four segment registers, and two housekeeping registers.

4. Memory, in the 8086, is addressed by adding an offset address to the contents of a segment register. For example, if the DS register contains a 1000H and an offset address of 0100H exists, then the memory location addressed is 10100H. This is the contents of the segment register with a zero added to the right plus the offset address.

5. The instruction set of the 8086 microprocessor is similar to the Z80 with a few additions. Some of the additional 8086 instructions are multiplication, division, ASCII adjustment commands, and various other instructions. One notable difference in the instructions sets is that the 8086 allows results from arithmetic and logic operations to be placed in registers other than the accumulator.

6. The addressing modes of the 8086 are comparable to the Z80 except there is an additional mode that allows a pointer and an index register to be added together to address memory data.

7. The 8088 microprocessor is an 8-bit data bus version of the 8086 microprocessor.

8. The Motorola 68000 is a 16-bit microprocessor that addresses 16M bytes of memory with its 16-bit data bus and its 24 bit address.

9. The 68000 is packaged in a 64 pin integrated circuit because of the size of its address and data buses.

10. The programming model of the 68000 contains eight 32-bit data registers, eight 32-bit address registers, and two housekeeping registers. The data registers are general purpose registers that hold 8-, 16-, or 32-bit data; the address registers are used to address memory and hold either 16- or 32-bit addresses; and the housekeeping registers are used to hold flags and the program address.

11. The instruction set of the 68000 is enhanced when compared to the Z80 microprocessor. In addition to all the functions of the Z80 the 68000 also includes multiplication and division. Another interesting feature is that the result of an 8-, 16-, or 32-bit operation may be gated into any register.

12. The memory addressing modes of the 68000 are similar to the Z80 except that program counter, pre-increment, and post-increment modes have been added.

13. The 68008 is the 8-bit bus version of the 68000.

14. Both the 68020 and the 80386 are full 32-bit versions of the 68000 and the 8086. Both microprocessors are capable of addressing 4G bytes of memory. The memory is organized as 4 banks of 1G bytes each.

16-6 GLOSSARY

Address register   A register designed to hold a memory address in the 68000 that is often used to indirectly address memory data.

CCR   The condition code register is a register that holds the flag bit for the 68000 microprocessor.

Code segment   A 64K byte section of the 8086 memory used to hold the program.

Coprocessor   A special purpose microprocessor that is designed to function in parallel with a general purpose microprocessor such as the 8086 or the 68000.

Data register   Used to hold general purpose data in the 68000 microprocessor.

Data segment   A 64K byte section of the 8086 memory that is used to hold general purpose data.

Extra segment   A 64K byte section of the 8086 memory that is used during string instructions to hold data addressed by the destination index register.

Instruction pointer register   A register that, when combined with the contents of the code segment register, is used to address the next instruction to be executed by the 8086 microprocessor. This register along with the code segment register functions as the program counter.

Memory bank   An 8-bit wide section of memory.

Offset address   An address that is added to the segment number to obtain the physical memory location in the 8086 microprocessor.

Program counter addressing   A 68000 memory addressing mode that uses the program counter and an offset address to locate memory data.

Segment register   A register whose contents address a 64K byte segment of the memory. The four segment registers are: (1) data, (2) code, (3) stack, and (4) extra.

Stack segment A 64K byte section of the 8086 memory that is used to hold the stack and also data addressed by the base pointer register.

QUESTIONS AND PROBLEMS

16-1. The 8086 microprocessor addresses _____ bytes of memory.

16-2. How can the 8086 fit in a 40-pin integrated circuit?

16-3. Describe how the 8086 memory is organized.

16-4. What is the purpose of the 8086 ALE pin connection?

16-5. What is the purpose of the 8086 $\overline{BHE}$ pin connection?

16-6. How many 16-bit registers are contained in the 8086 programming model?

16-7. List the 8-bit 8086 registers.

16-8. Name the four 8086 segment registers.

16-9. Explain how memory is addressed in the 8086 microprocessor.

16-10. Given the following values for CS and IP, determine the address of the next instruction for each case.
(a) CS = 1000H and IP = 2000H
(b) CS = 2000H and IP = 1230H
(c) CS = 3000H and IP = 2000H
(d) CS = 0020H and IP = FFFFH
(e) CS = A001H and IP = 0020H

16-11. The BP (base pointer) addresses data in which 8086 segment?

16-12. Indicate each of the flag bits in the 8086 flag register and list their purpose.

16-13. Does the 8086 have a multiplication instruction?

16-14. Is there a difference between the 8086 decrement instruction and the Z80 decrement instruction?

16-15. What 8086 opcode is used for a Z80-like LD?

16-16. Which 8086 registers are used to indirectly address memory data?

16-17. What is the main difference between the 8086 microprocessor and the 8088 microprocessor?

16-18. How much memory is addressed by the 68000 microprocessor?

16-19. The 68000 is housed in a _____-pin integrated circuit.

16-20. What are the purposes of the 68000 $\overline{UDS}$ and $\overline{LDS}$ pins?

16-21. How many 32-bit data registers are found in the 68000 microprocessor?

16-22. Can the 68000 address registers be used as 8-bit registers?

16-23. How many stack pointer registers are found in the 68000 microprocessor?

16-24. What two modes of operation are found in the 68000 microprocessor?

16-25. List the CCR bits and define the purpose of each bit.

16-26. The 68000 ADDX instruction is similar to which Z80 instruction?

16-27. How are byte, word, and long word instructions indicated in the 68000 assembly language mnemonics?

16-28. Which 68000 registers are used to indirectly address memory data?

16-29. Describe the 68000 post-increment addressing mode.

16-30. What is 68000 program counter addressing?

16-31. Describe the difference between the 68000 and the 68008.

16-32. The 32-bit microprocessors such as the 68020 and the 80386 address _____ bytes of memory.

16-33. Briefly describe the memory organization of the 32-bit microprocessors.

The Z80 Instruction Set

Instruction	Opcode	Clocks	Comment	Flags					
				S	Z	H	P/V	N	C
ADC A,(HL)	8E	7	A = A + (HL) + Cy	†	†	†	V	O	†
ADC A,(IX + dd)	DD8Edd	19	A = A + (IX + dd) + Cy	†	†	†	V	O	†
ADC A,(IY + dd)	FD8Edd	19	A = A + (IY + dd) + Cy	†	†	†	V	O	†
ADC A,B	88	4	A = A + B + Cy	†	†	†	V	O	†
ADC A,C	89	4	A = A + B + Cy	†	†	†	V	O	†
ADC A,D	8A	4	A = A + D + Cy	†	ï	†	V	O	†
ADC A,E	8B	4	A = A + E = Cy	†	†	†	V	O	†
ADC A,H	8C	4	A = A + H + Cy	†	†	†	V	O	†
ADC A,L	8D	4	A = A + L + Cy	†	†	†	V	O	†
ADC A,A	8F	4	A = A + A + Cy	†	†	†	V	O	†
ADC A,d8	CEd8	7	A = A + d8 + Cy	†	†	†	V	O	†
ADC HL,BC	ED4A	15	HL = HL + BC + Cy	†	†	?	V	O	†
ADC HL,DE	ED5A	15	HL = HL + DE + Cy	†	†	?	V	O	†
ADC HL,HL	ED6A	15	HL = HL + HL + Cy	†	†	?	V	O	†
ADC HL,SP	ED7A	15	HL = HL + SP = Cy	†	†	?	V	O	†
ADD A,(HL)	86	7	A = A + (HL)	†	†	†	V	O	†
ADD A,(IX + dd)	DD86dd	19	A = A + (IX + dd)	†	†	†	V	O	†
ADD A,(IY + dd)	FD86dd	19	A = A + (IY + dd)	†	†	†	V	O	†
ADD A,B	80	4	A = A + B	†	†	†	V	O	†
ADD A,C	81	4	A = A + C	†	†	†	V	O	†
ADD A,D	82	4	A = A + D	†	†	†	V	O	†
ADD A,E	83	4	A = A + E	†	†	†	V	O	†
ADD A,H	84	4	A = A + H	†	†	†	V	O	†

Instruction	Opcode	Clocks	Comment	S	Z	H	P/V	N	C
ADD A,L	85	4	A = A + L	†	†	†	V	O	†
ADD A,A	87	4	A = A + A	†	†	†	V	O	†
ADD A,d8	C6d8	7	A = A + d8	†	†	†	V	O	†
ADD HL,BC	09	11	HL = HL + BC			?		O	†
ADD HL,DE	19	11	HL = HL + DE			?		O	†
ADD HL,HL	29	11	HL = HL + HL			?		O	†
ADD HL,SP	39	11	HL = HL + SP			?		O	†
ADD IX,BC	DD09	15	IX = IX + BC			?		O	†
ADD IX,DE	DD19	15	IX = IX + DE			?		O	†
ADD IX,IX	DD29	15	IX = IX + IX			?		O	†
ADD IX,SP	DD39	15	IX = IX + SP			?		O	†
ADD IY,BC	FD09	15	IY = IY + BC			?		O	†
ADD IY,DE	FD19	15	IY = IY + DE			?		O	†
ADD IY,IY	FD29	15	IY = IY + IY			?		O	†
ADD IY,SP	FD39	15	IY = IY + SP			?		O	†
AND (HL)	A6	7	A = A $\wedge$ (HL)	†	†	1	P	O	O
AND (IX+dd)	DDA6dd	19	A = A $\wedge$ (IX+dd)	†	†	1	P	O	O
AND (IY+dd)	FDA6dd	19	A = A $\wedge$ (IY+dd)	†	†	1	P	O	O
AND B	A0	4	A = A $\wedge$ B	†	†	1	P	O	O
AND C	A1	4	A = A $\wedge$ C	†	†	1	P	O	O
AND D	A2	4	A = A $\wedge$ D	†	†	1	P	O	O
AND E	A3	4	A = A $\wedge$ E	†	†	1	P	O	O
AND H	A4	4	A = A $\wedge$ H	†	†	1	P	O	O
AND L	A5	4	A = A $\wedge$ L	†	†	1	P	O	O
AND A	A7	4	A = A $\wedge$ A	†	†	1	P	O	O
AND D8	E6d8	7	A = A $\wedge$ d8	†	†	1	P	O	O
BIT 0,(HL)	CB46	12	test bit 0 of (HL)	?	†	1	?	0	
Bit 0,(IX+dd)	DDCBdd46	20	test bit 0 of (IX+dd)	?	†	1	?	0	
BIT 0,(IY+dd)	FDCBdd46	20	test bit 0 of (IY+dd)	?	†	1	?	0	
BIT 0,B	CB40	8	test bit 0 of B	?	†	1	?	0	
BIT 0,C	CB41	8	test bit 0 of C	?	†	1	?	0	
BIT 0,D	CB42	8	test bit 0 of D	?	†	1	?	0	
BIT 0,E	CB43	8	test bit 0 of E	?	†	1	?	0	
BIT 0,H	CB44	8	test bit 0 of H	?	†	1	?	0	
BIT 0,L	CB45	8	test bit 0 of L	?	†	1	?	0	
BIT 0,A	CB47	8	test bit 0 of A	?	†	1	?	0	
BIT 1,(HL)	CB4E	12	test bit 1 of (HL)	?	†	1	?	0	
BIT 1,(IX+dd)	DDCBdd4E	20	test bit 1 of (IX+dd)	?	†	1	?	0	
BIT 1,(IY+dd)	FDCBdd4E	20	test bit 1 of (IY+dd)	?	†	1	?	0	
BIT 1,B	CB48	8	test bit 1 of B	?	†	1	?	0	
BIT 1,C	CB49	8	test bit 1 of C	?	†	1	?	0	
BIT 1,D	CB4A	8	test bit 1 of D	?	†	1	?	0	
BIT 1,E	CB4B	8	test bit 1 of E	?	†	1	?	0	
BIT 1,H	CB4C	8	test bit 1 of H	?	†	1	?	0	
BIT 1,L	CB4D	8	test bit 1 of L	?	†	1	?	0	

Instruction	Opcode	Clocks	Comment	Flags					
				S	Z	H	P/V	N	C
BIT 1,A	CB4F	8	test bit 1 of A	?	†	1	?	0	
BIT 2,(HL)	CB56	12	test bit 2 of (HL)	?	†	1	?	0	
BIT 2,(IX + dd)	DDCBdd56	20	test bit 2 of (IX + dd)	?	†	1	?	0	
BIT 2,(IY + dd)	FDCBdd56	20	test bit 2 of (IY + dd)	?	†	1	?	0	
BIT 2,B	CB50	8	test bit 2 of B	?	†	1	?	0	
BIT 2,C	CB51	8	test bit 2 of C	?	†	1	?	0	
BIT 2,D	CB52	8	test bit 2 of D	?	†	1	?	0	
BIT 2,E	CB53	8	test bit 2 of E	?	†	1	?	0	
BIT 2,H	CB54	8	test bit 2 of H	?	†	1	?	0	
BIT 2,L	CB55	8	test bit 2 of L	?	†	1	?	0	
BIT 2,A	CB57	8	test bit 2 of A	?	†	1	?	0	
BIT 3,(HL)	CB5E	12	test bit 3 of (HL)	?	†	1	?	0	
BIT 3,(IX + dd)	DDCBdd5E	20	test bit 3 of (IX + dd)	?	†	1	?	0	
BIT 3,(IY + dd)	FDCBdd5E	20	test bit 3 of (IY + dd)	?	†	1	?	0	
BIT 3,B	CB58	8	test bit 3 of B	?	†	1	?	0	
BIT 3,C	CB59	8	test bit 3 of C	?	†	1	?	0	
BIT 3,D	CB5A	8	test bit 3 of D	?	†	1	?	0	
BIT 3,E	CB5B	8	test bit 3 of E	?	†	1	?	0	
BIT 3,H	CB5C	8	test bit 3 of H	?	†	1	?	0	
BIT 3,L	CB5D	8	test bit 3 of L	?	†	1	?	0	
BIT 3,A	CB5F	8	test bit 3 of A	?	†	1	?	0	
BIT 4,(HL)	CB66	12	test bit 4 of (HL)	?	†	1	?	0	
BIT 4,(IX + dd)	DDCBdd66	20	test bit 4 of (IX + dd)	?	†	1	?	0	
BIT 4,(IY + dd)	FDCBdd66	20	test bit 4 of (IY + dd)	?	†	1	?	0	
BIT 4,B	CB60	8	test bit 4 of B	?	†	1	?	0	
BIT 4,C	CB61	8	test bit 4 of C	?	†	1	?	0	
BIT 4,D	CB62	8	test bit 4 of D	?	†	1	?	0	
BIT 4,E	CB63	8	test bit 4 of E	?	†	1	?	0	
BIT 4,H	CB64	8	test bit 4 of H	?	†	1	?	0	
BIT 4,L	CB65	8	test bit 4 of L	?	†	1	?	0	
BIT 4,A	CB67	8	test bit 4 of A	?	†	1	?	0	
BIT 5,(HL)	CB6E	12	test bit 5 of (HL)	?	†	1	?	0	
BIT 5,(IX + dd)	DDCBdd6E	20	test bit 5 of (IX + dd)	?	†	1	?	0	
BIT 5,(IY + dd)	FDCBdd6E	20	test bit 5 of (IY + dd)	?	†	1	?	0	
BIT 5,B	CB60	8	test bit 5 of B	?	†	1	?	0	
BIT 5,C	CB61	8	test bit 5 of C	?	†	1	?	0	
BIT 5,D	CB62	8	test bit 5 of D	?	†	1	?	0	
BIT 5,E	CB63	8	test bit 5 of E	?	†	1	?	0	
BIT 5,H	CB64	8	test bit 5 of H	?	†	1	?	0	
BIT 5,L	CB65	8	test bit 5 of L	?	†	1	?	0	
BIT 5,A	CB67	8	test bit 5 of A	?	†	1	?	0	
BIT 6,(HL)	CB76	12	test bit 6 of (HL)	?	†	1	?	0	
BIT 6,(IX + dd)	DDCBdd76	20	test bit 6 of (IX + dd)	?	†	1	?	0	
BIT 6,(IY + dd)	FDCBdd76	20	test bit 6 of (IY + dd)	?	†	1	?	0	
BIT 6,B	CB70	8	test bit 6 of B	?	†	1	?	0	

Instruction	Opcode	Clocks	Comment	Flags					
				S	Z	H	P/V	N	C
BIT 6,C	CB71	8	test bit 6 of C	?	†	1	?	0	
BIT 6,D	CB72	8	test bit 6 of D	?	†	1	?	0	
BIT 6,E	CB73	8	test bit 6 of E	?	†	1	?	0	
BIT 6,H	CB74	8	test bit 6 of H	?	†	1	?	0	
BIT 6,L	CB75	8	test bit 6 of L	?	†	1	?	0	
BIT 6,A	CB77	8	test bit 6 of A	?	†	1	?	0	
BIT 7,(HL)	CB7E	12	test bit 7 of (HL)	?	†	1	?	0	
BIT 7,(IX+dd)	DDCBdd7E	20	test bit 7 of (IX+dd)	?	†	1	?	0	
BIT 7,(IX+dd)	FDCBdd7E	20	test bit 7 of (IY+dd)	?	†	1	?	0	
BIT 7,B	CB78	8	test bit 7 of B	?	†	1	?	0	
BIT 7,C	CB79	8	test bit 7 of C	?	†	1	?	0	
BIT 7,D	CB7A	8	test bit 7 of D	?	†	1	?	0	
BIT 7,E	CB7B	8	test bit 7 of E	?	†	1	?	0	
BIT 7,H	CB7C	8	test bit 7 of H	?	†	1	?	0	
BIT 7,L	CB7D	8	test bit 7 of L	?	†	1	?	0	
BIT 7,A	CB7F	8	test bit 7 of A	?	†	1	?	0	
CALL C,adr	DCllhh	10/17	CALL if carry						
CALL M,adr	FCllhh	10/17	CALL if minus						
CALL NC,adr	D4llhh	10/17	CALL if no carry						
CALL adr	CDllhh	17	CALL subroutine						
CALL NZ,adr	C4llhh	10/17	CALL if not zero						
CALL P,adr	F4llhh	10/17	CALL if positive						
CALL PE,adr	ECllhh	10/17	CALL if parity even						
CALL PO,adr	E4llhh	10/17	CALL if parity odd						
CALL Z,adr	CCllhh	10/17	CALL if zero						
CCF	3F	4	complement carry		?			0	†
CP (HL)	BE	7	compare A with (HL)	†	†	†	V	1	†
CP (IX+dd)	DDBEdd	19	compare A with (IX+dd)	†	†	†	V	1	†
CP (IY+dd)	FDBEdd	19	compare A with (IY+dd)	†	†	†	V	1	†
CP B	B8	4	compare A with B	†	†	†	V	1	†
CP C	B9	4	compare A with C	†	†	†	V	1	†
CP D	BA	4	compare A with D	†	†	†	V	1	†
CP E	BB	4	compare A with E	†	†	†	V	1	†
CP H	BC	4	compare A with H	†	†	†	V	1	†
CP L	BD	4	compare A with L	†	†	†	V	1	†
CP A	BF	4	compare A with A	0	1	†	V	1	0
CP d8	FEd8	7	compare A with d8	†	†	†	V	1	†
CPD	EDA9	16	compare A with (HL) then decrement HL and BC	-	†	†	†	1	
CPDR	EDB9	21/16	compare A with (HL) then decrement HL and BC. Repeat until BC = 0 or A = (HL).	-	†	†	†	1	
CPI	EDA1	16	compare A with (HL) then increment HL and decrement BC	†	†	†	†	1	

Instruction	Opcode	Clocks	Comment	S	Z	H	P/V	N	C
							Flags		
CPIR	EDB1	21/16	compare A with (HL) then decrement BC and increment HL. Repeat until BC = 0 or A = (HL).	†	†	†	†	1	
CPL	2F	4	complement A			1		1	
DAA	27	4	decimal adjust A	†	†	†	P		†
DEC (HL)	35	11	(HL) = (HL) − 1	†	†	†	V	1	
DEC (IX + dd)	DD35dd	23	(IX + dd) = (IX + dd) − 1	†	†	†	V	1	
DEC (IY + dd)	FD35dd	23	(IY + dd) = (IY + dd) − 1	†	†	†	V	1	
DEC B	05	4	B = B − 1	†	†	†	V	1	
DEC C	0D	4	C = C − 1	†	†	†	V	1	
DEC D	15	4	D = D − 1	†	†	†	V	1	
DEC E	1D	4	E = E − 1	†	†	†	V	1	
DEC H	25	4	H = H − 1	†	†	†	V	1	
DEC L	2D	4	L = L − 1	†	†	†	V	1	
DEC A	3D	4	A = A − 1	†	†	†	V	1	
DEC BC	0B	6	BC = BC − 1						
DEC DE	1B	6	DE = DE − 1						
DEC HL	2B	6	HL = HL − 1						
DEC SP	3B	6	SP = SP − 1						
DEC IX	DD2B	10	IX + IX − 1						
DEC IY	FD2B	10	IY = IY − 1						
DI	F3	4	disable interrupts						
DJNZ	10dd	8/13	decrement B and jump if B is not zero						
EI	FB	4	enable interrupts						
EX (SP),HL	E3	19	exchange HL with (SP)						
EX (SP),IX	DDE3	23	exchange IX with (SP)						
EX (SP),IY	FDE3	23	exchange IY with (SP)						
EX AF,AF'	08	4	exchange AF with AF'						
EX DE,HL	EB	4	exchange DE with HL						
EXX	D9	4	exchange BC, DE, and HL with BC', DE', and HL'.						
HALT	76	4	halt for interrupt of reset						
IM 0	ED46	8	select interrupt mode 0						
IM 1	ED56	8	select interrupt mode 1						
IM 2	ED5E	8	select interrupt mode 2						
IN A,(C)	ED78	12	input data to A from I/O port (C)	†	†	†	P	0	
IN A,(p8)	DBp8	11	input data to A from I/O port (p8)	†	†	†	P	0	
IN B,(C)	ED40	12	input data to B from I/O port (C)	†	†	†	P	0	
IN C,(C)	ED48	12	input data to C from I/O port (C)	†	†	†	P	0	

Instruction	Opcode	Clocks	Comment	Flags S Z H P/V N C
IN D,(C)	ED50	12	input data to E from I/O port (C)	† † † P 0
IN E,(C)	ED58	12	input data to E from I/O port (C)	† † † P 0
IN H,(C)	ED60	12	input data to H from I/O port (C)	† † † P 0
IN L,(C)	ED68	12	input data to L from I/O port (C)	† † † P 0
INC (HL)	34	11	(HL) = (HL) + 1	† † † V 0
INC (IX+dd)	DD34dd	23	(IX+dd) = (IX+dd) + 1	† † † V 0
INC (IY+dd)	FD34dd	23	(IY+dd) = (IY+dd) + 1	† † † V 0
INC B	04	4	B = B + 1	† † † V 0
INC C	0C	4	C = C + 1	† † † V 0
INC D	14	4	D = D + 1	† † † V 0
INC E	1C	4	E = E + 1	† † † V 0
INC H	24	4	H = H + 1	† † † V 0
INC L	2C	4	L = L + 1	† † † V 0
INC A	3C	4	A = A + 1	† † † V 0
INC BC	03	6	BC = BC + 1	
INC DE	13	6	DE = DE + 1	
INC HL	23	6	HL = HL + 1	
INC SP	33	6	SP = SP + 1	
INC IX	DD23	10	IX = IX + 1	
INC IY	FD23	10	IY = IY + 1	
IND	EDAA	16	input data to (HL) from I/O port (C). Decrement B and HL.	? 1 ? ? 1 ?
INDR	EDBA	21/16	input data to (HL) from I/O port (C). Decrement B and HL. Repeat until B = 0.	? 1 ? ? 1 ?
INI	EDA2	16	input data to (HL) from I/O port (C). Decrement B and increment HL.	? 1 ? ? 1 ?
INIR	EDB2	21/16	input data to (HL) from I/O port (C). Decrement B and increment HL. Repeat until B = 0.	? 1 ? ? 1 ?
JP (HL)	E9	4	jump to address (HL)	
JP (IX)	DDE9	8	jump to address (IX)	
JP (IY)	FDE9	8	jump to address (IY)	
JP C,adr	DAllhh	10	jump if carry	
JP M,adr	FAllhh	10	jump if minus	
JP NC,adr	D2llhh	10	jump if no carry	
JP adr	C3llhh	10	jump	
JP NZ,adr	C2llhh	10	jump if not zero	
JP P,adr	F2llhh	10	jump if positive	

Instruction	Opcode	Clocks	Comment	Flags					
				S	Z	H	P/V	N	C
JP PE,adr	EAllhh	10	jump if parity even						
JP PO,adr	E2llhh	10	jump if parity odd						
JP Z,adr	CAllhh	10	jump if zero						
JR C,dd	38dd	7/12	jump relative if carry						
JR dd	18dd	12	jump relative						
JR NC,dd	30dd	7/12	jump relative if no carry						
JR NZ,dd	20dd	7/12	jump relative if not zero						
JR Z,dd	28dd	7/12	jump relative if zero						
LD (BC),A	02	7	load (BC) from A						
LD (DE),A	12	7	load (DE) from A						
LD (HL),B	70	7	load (HL) from B						
LD (HL),C	71	7	load (HL) from C						
LD (HL),D	72	7	load (HL) from D						
LD (HL),E	73	7	load (HL) from E						
LD (HL),H	74	7	load (HL) from H						
LD (HL),L	75	7	load (HL) from L						
LD (HL),A	77	7	load (HL) from A						
LD (HL),d8	36d8	7	load (HL) with d8						
LD (IX + dd),B	DD70dd	19	load (IX + dd) from B						
LD (IX + dd),C	DD71dd	19	load (IX + dd) from C						
LD (IX + dd),D	DD72dd	19	load (IX + dd) from D						
LD (IX + dd),E	DD73dd	19	load (IX + dd) from E						
LD (IX + dd),H	DD74dd	19	load (IX + dd) from H						
LD (IX + dd),L	DD75dd	19	load (IX + dd) from L						
LD (IX + dd),A	DD77dd	19	load (IX + dd) from A						
LD (IX + dd),d8	DD36ddd8	19	load (IX + dd) with d8						
LD (IY + dd),B	FD70dd	19	load (IY + dd) from B						
LD (IY + dd),C	FD71dd	19	load (IY + dd) from C						
LD (IY + dd),D	FD72dd	19	load (IY + dd) from D						
LD (IY + dd),E	FD73dd	19	load (IY + dd) from E						
LD (IY + dd),H	FD74dd	19	load (IY + dd) from H						
LD (IY + dd),A	FD77dd	19	load (IY + dd) from A						
LD (IY + dd),d8	FD36ddd8	19	load (IY + dd) with d8						
LD (adr),A	32llhh	13	load (adr) from A						
LD (adr),BC	ED43llhh	20	load (adr) from Bc						
LD (adr),DE	ED53llhh	20	load (adr) from DE						
LD (adr),HL	22llhh	16	load (adr) from HL						
LD (adr),IX	DD22llhh	20	load (adr) from IX						
LD (adr),IY	FD22llhh	20	load (adr) from IY						
LD (adr),SP	ED73llhh	20	load (adr) from SP						
LD A,(BC)	0A	7	load A from (BC)						
LD A,(DE)	1A	7	load A from (DE)						
LD A,(HL)	7E	7	load A from (HL)						
LD A,(IX + dd)	DD7Edd	19	load A from (IX + dd)						
LD A,(IY + dd)	FD7Edd	19	load A from (IY + dd)						

Instruction	Opcode	Clocks	Comment	Flags					
				S	Z	H	P/V	N	C
LD A,(adr)	3Allhh	13	load A from (adr)						
LD A,A	7F	4	load A from A						
LD A,B	78	4	load A from B						
LD A,C	79	4	load A from C						
LD A,D	7A	4	load A from D						
LD A,E	7B	4	load A from E						
LD A,H	7C	4	load A from H						
LD A,L	7D	4	load A from L						
LD A,d8	3Ed8	7	load A with d8						
LD A,I	ED57	9	load A from I	†	†	0	†	0	
LD A,R	ED5F	9	load A from R	†	†	0	†		
LD B,(HL)	46	7	load B from (HL)						
LD B,(IX + dd)	DD46nn	19	load B from (IX + dd)						
LD B,(IY + dd)	FD46dd)	19	load B from (IY + dd)						
LD B,A	47	4	load B from A						
LD B,C	48	4	load B from C						
LD B,D	49	4	load B from D						
LD B,E	4A	4	load B from E						
LD B,H	4B	4	load B from H						
LD B,L	4C	4	load B from L						
LD, B,d8	06d8	7	load B with d8						
LD BC,(adr)	ED4Bllhh	20	load BC from (adr)						
LD BC,d16	01llhh	10	load BC with d16						
LD C,(HL)	4E	7	load C from (HL)						
LD C,(IX + dd)	DD4Edd	19	load C from (IX + dd)						
LD C,(IY + dd)	FD4Edd	19	load C from (IY + dd)						
LD C,A	4F	4	load C from A						
LD C,B	48	4	load C from B						
LD C,C	49	4	load C from C						
LD C,D	4A	4	load C from D						
LD C,E	4B	4	load C from E						
LD C,H	4C	4	load C from H						
LD C,L	4D	4	load C from L						
LD C,d8	0Ed8	7	load C with d8						
LD D,(HL)	56	7	load D from (HL)						
LD D,(IX + dd)	DD56dd	19	load D from (IX + dd)						
LD D,(IY + dd)	FD56dd	19	load D from (IY + dd)						
LD D,A	57	7	load D from A						
LD D,B	50	4	load D from B						
LD D,C	51	4	load D from C						
LD D,D	52	4	load D from D						
LD D,E	53	4	load D from E						
LD D,H	54	4	load D from H						
LD D,L	55	4	load D from L						
LD D,d8	16d8	7	load D with d8						

Instruction	Opcode	Clocks	Comment	Flags					
				S	Z	H	P/V	N	C
LD DE(adr)	ED5Bllhh	20	load DE from (adr)						
LD DE,d16	11llhh	10	load DE with d16						
LD E,(HL)	5E	7	load E from (HL)						
LD E,(IX + dd)	DD5Edd	19	load E from (IX + dd)						
LD E,(IY + dd)	FD5Edd	19	load E from (IY + dd)						
LD E,A	5F	4	load E from A						
LD E,B	58	4	load E from B						
LD E,C	59	4	load E from C						
LD E,D	5A	4	load E from D						
LD E,E	5B	4	load E from E						
LD E,H	5C	4	load E from H						
LD E,L	5D	4	load E from L						
LD E,d8	1Ed8	7	load E with d8						
LD H,(HL)	66	7	load H from (HL)						
LD H,(IX + dd)	DD66dd	19	load H from (IX + dd)						
LD H,(IY + dd)	FD66dd	19	load H from (IY + dd)						
LD H,A	67	4	load H from A						
LD H,B	60	4	load H from B						
LD H,C	61	4	load H from C						
LD H,D	62	4	load H from D						
LD H,E	63	4	load H from E						
LD H,H	64	4	load H from H						
LD H,L	65	4	load H from L						
LD H,d8	26d8	4	load H with d8						
LD HL,(adr)	2Allhh	16	load HL from (HL)						
LD HL,d16	21llhh	10	load HL with d16						
LD I,A	ED47	9	load I from A						
LD IX,(adr)	DD2Allhh	20	load IX from (adr)						
LD IX,d16	DD21llhh	14	load IX with d16						
LD IY,(adr)	FD2Allhh	20	load IY from (adr)						
LD IY,d16	FD21llhh	14	load IY with d16						
LD L,(HL)	6E	7	load L from (HL)						
LD L,(IX + dd)	DD6Edd	19	load L from (IX + dd)						
LD L,(IY + dd)	FD6Edd	19	load L from (IY + dd)						
LD L,A	6F	4	load L from A						
LD L,B	68	4	load L from B						
LD L,C	69	4	load L from C						
LD L,D	6A	4	load L from D						
LD L,E	6B	4	load L from E						
LD L,H	6C	4	load L from H						
LD L,L	6D	4	load L from L						
LD L,d8	2Ed8	4	load L with d8						
LD R,A	ED4F	4	load R from A						
LD SP,(adr)	ED7Bllhh	20	load SP from (adr)						
LD SP,HL	F9	6	load SP from HL						

Instruction	Opcode	Clocks	Comment	S	Z	H	P/V	N	C
							Flags		
LD SP,IX	DDF9	10	load SP from IX						
LD SP,IY	FDF9	10	load SP from IY						
LD SP,d16	31llhh	10	load SP with d16						
LDD	EDA8	16	load (HL) from (DE) then decrement BC, DE, and HL.			0	†	0	
LDDR	EDB8	21/16	load (HL) from (DE) then decrement BC, DE, and HL. Repeat until BC = 0.			0	0	0	
LDI	EDA0	16	load (HL) from (DE) then decrement BC and increment DE and HL.			0	†	0	
LDIR	EDB0	21/16	load (HL) from (DE) then decrement BC and increment DE and HL. Repeat until BC = 0.			0	†	0	
NEG	ED44	8	2's complement A	†	†	†	V	1	†
OR (HL)	B6	7	A = A V (HL)	†	†	0	P	0	0
OR (IX + dd)	DDB6dd	19	A = A V (IX + dd)	†	†	0	P	0	0
OR (IY + dd)	FDB6dd	19	A = A V (IY + dd)	†	†	0	P	0	0
OR A	B7	4	A = A V A	†	†	0	P	0	0
OR B	B0	4	A = A V B	†	†	0	P	0	0
OR C	B1	4	A = A V C	†	†	0	P	0	0
OR D	B2	4	A = A V D	†	†	0	P	0	0
OR E	B3	4	A = A V E	†	†	0	P	0	0
OR H	B4	4	A = A V H	†	†	0	P	0	0
OR L	B5	4	A = A V L	†	†	0	P	0	0
OR d8	F6d8	7	A = A V d8	†	†	0	P	0	0
OTDR	EDBB	21/16	output (HL) to I/O port (C). Decrement B and HL. Repeat until B = 0.						
OTIR	EDB3	21/16	output (HL) to I/O port (C). Decrement B and increment HL. Repeat until B = 0.						
OUT (C),A	ED79	12	output A to I/O port (C).						
OUT (C),B	ED41	12	output B to I/O port (C).						
OUT (C),C	ED49	12	output C to I/O port (C).						
OUT (C),D	ED51	12	output D to I/O port (C).						
OUT (C),E	ED59	12	output E to I/O port (C).						
OUT (C),H	ED61	12	output H to I/O port (C).						
OUT (C),L	ED69	12	output L to I/O port (C).						
OUT (p8)	D3p8	11	output A to I/O port (p8)						
OUTD	EDAB	16	output (HL) to I/O port (C) then decrement B and HL.	?	†	?	?	1	?
OUTI	EDA3	16	output (HL) to I/O	?	†	?	?	1	?
POP AF	F1	10	load AF from stack	†	†	†	†	†	†
POP BC	C1	10	load BC from stack						

Instruction	Opcode	Clocks	Comment	Flags					
				S	Z	H	P/V	N	C
POP DE	D1	10	load DE from stack						
POP HL	E1	10	load HL from stack						
POP IX	DDE1	14	load IX from stack						
POP IY	FDE1	14	load IY from stack						
PUSH AF	F5	11	load stack from AF						
PUSH BC	C5	11	load stack from BC						
PUSH DE	D5	11	load stack from DE						
PUSH HL	E5	11	load stack from HL						
PUSH IX	DDE5	15	load stack from IX						
PUSH IY	FDE5	15	load stack from IY						
RES 0,(HL)	CB86	15	bit 0 of (HL) = 0						
RES 0,(IX + dd)	DDCBdd86	23	bit 0 of (IX + dd) = 0						
RES 0,(IY + dd)	FDCBdd86	23	bit 0 of (IY + dd) = 0						
RES 0,A	CB87	8	bit 0 of A = 0						
RES 0,B	CB80	8	bit 0 of B = 0						
RES 0,C	CB81	8	bit 0 of C = 0						
RES 0,D	CB82	8	bit 0 of D = 0						
RES 0,E	CB83	8	bit 0 of E = 0						
RES 0,H	CB84	8	bit 0 of H = 0						
RES 0,L	CB85	8	bit 0 of L = 0						
RES 1,(HL)	CB8E	15	bit 1 of (HL) = 0						
RES 1,(IX + dd)	DDCBdd8E	23	bit 1 of (IX + dd) = 0						
RES 1,(IY + dd)	FDCBdd8E	23	bit 1 of (IY + dd) = 0						
RES 1,A	CB8F	8	bit 1 of A = 0						
RES 1,B	CB88	8	bit 1 of B = 0						
RES 1,C	CB89	8	bit 1 of C = 0						
RES 1,D	CB8A	8	bit 1 of D = 0						
RES 1,E	CB8B	8	bit 1 of E = 0						
RES 1,H	CB8C	8	bit 1 of H = 0						
RES 1,L	CB8D	8	bit 1 of L = 0						
RES 2,(HL)	CB96	15	bit 2 of (HL) = 0						
RES 2,(IX + dd)	DDCBdd96	23	bit 2 of (IX + dd) = 0						
RES 2,(IY + dd)	FDCBdd96	23	bit 2 of (IY + dd) = 0						
RES 2,A	CB97	8	bit 2 of A = 0						
RES 2,B	CB90	8	bit 2 of B = 0						
RES 2,C	CB91	8	bit 2 of C = 0						
RES 2,D	CB92	8	bit 2 of D = 0						
RES 2,E	CB93	8	bit 2 of E = 0						
RES 2,H	CB94	8	bit 2 of H = 0						
RES 2,L	CB95	8	bit 2 of L = 0						
RES 3,(HL)	CB9E	15	bit 3 of (HL) = 0						
RES 3, (IX + dd)	DDCBdd9E	23	bit 3 of (IX + dd) = 0						
RES 3, (IY + dd)	FDCBdd9E	23	bit 3 of (IY + dd) = 0						
RES 3,A	CB9F	8	bit 3 of A = 0						
RES 3,B	CB98	8	bit 3 of B = 0						

Instruction	Opcode	Clocks	Comment	Flags S Z H P/V N C
RES 3,C	CB99	8	bit 3 of C = 0	
RES 3,D	CB9A	8	bit 3 of D = 0	
RES 3,E	CB9B	8	bit 3 of E = 0	
RES 3,H	CB9C	8	bit 3 of H = 0	
RES 3,L	CB9D	8	bit 3 of L = 0	
RES 4,(HL)	CBA6	15	bit 4 of (HL) = 0	
RES 4,(IX + dd)	DDCBddA6	23	bit 4 of (IX + dd) = 0	
RES 4,(IY + dd)	FDCBddA6	23	bit 4 of (IY + dd) = 0	
RES 4,A	CBA7	8	bit 4 of A = 0	
RES 4,B	CBA0	8	bit 4 of B = 0	
RES 4,C	CBA1	8	bit 4 of C = 0	
RES 4,D	CBA2	8	bit 4 of D = 0	
RES 4,E	CBA3	8	bit 4 of E = 0	
RES 4,H	CBA4	8	bit 4 of H = 0	
RES 4,L	CBA5	8	bit 4 of L = 0	
RES 5,(HL)	CBA5	15	bit 5 of (HL) = 0	
RES 5,(IX + dd)	DDCBddAE	23	bit 5 of (IX + dd) = 0	
RES 5,(IY + dd)	FDCBddAE	23	bit 5 of (IY + dd) = 0	
RES 5,A	CBAF	8	bit 5 of A = 0	
RES 5,B	CBA8	8	bit 5 of B = 0	
RES 5,C	CBA9	8	bit 5 of C = 0	
RES 5,D	CBAA	8	bit 5 of D = 0	
RES 5,E	CBAB	8	bit 5 of E = 0	
RES 5,H	CBAC	8	bit 5 of H = 0	
RES 5,L	CBAD	8	bit 5 of L = 0	
RES 6,(HL)	CBB6	15	bit 6 of (HL) = 0	
RES, (IX + dd)	DDCBddB6	23	bit 6 of (IX + dd) = 0	
RES 6,(IY + dd)	FDCBddB6	23	bit 6 of (IY + dd) = 0	
RES 6,A	CBB7	8	bit 6 of A = 0	
RES 6,B	CBB0	8	bit 6 of B = 0	
RES 6,C	CBB1	8	bit 6 of C = 0	
RES 6,D	CBB2	8	bit 6 of D = 0	
RES 6,E	CBB3	8	bit 6 of E = 0	
RES 6,H	CBB4	8	bit 6 of H = 0	
RES 6,L	CBB5	8	bit 6 of L = 0	
RES 7,(HL)	CBBE	15	bit 7 of (HL) = 0	
RES 7,(IX + dd)	DDCBddBE	23	bit 7 of (IX + dd) = 0	
RES 7,(IY + dd)	FDCBddBE	23	bit 7 of (IY + dd) = 0	
RES 7,A	CBBF	8	bit 7 of A = 0	
RES 7,B	CBB8	8	bit 7 of B = 0	
RES 7,C	CBB9	8	bit 7 of C = 0	
RES 7,D	CBBA	8	bit 7 of D = 0	
RES 7,E	CBBB	8	bit 7 of E = 0	
RES 7,H	CBBC	8	bit 7 of H = 0	
RES 7,L	CBBD	8	bit 7 of L = 0	

Instruction	Opcode	Clocks	Comment	S	Z	H	P/V	N	C
RET	C9	10	return						
RET C	D8	5/11	return if carry						
RET M	F8	5/11	return if minus						
RET NC	D0	5/11	return if no carry						
RET NZ	C0	5/11	return if not zero						
RET P	F0	5/11	return if positive						
RET PE	E8	5/11	return if parity even						
RET PO	E0	5/11	return if parity odd						
RET Z	C8	5/11	return if zero						
RETI	ED4D	14	return from interrupt						
RETN	ED45	14	return from nonmaskable interrupt						
RL (HL)	CB16	15	rotate (HL) left through carry	†	†	O	P	O	†
RL (IX + dd)	DDCBdd16	23	rotate (IX + dd) left through carry	†	†	O	P	O	†
RL (IY + dd)	FDCBdd16	23	rotate (IY + dd) left through carry	†	†	O	P	O	†
RL A	CB17	8	rotate A left through carry	†	†	O	P	O	†
RL B	CB10	8	rotate B left through carry	†	†	O	P	O	†
RL C	CB11	8	rotate C left through carry	†	†	O	P	O	†
RL D	CB12	8	rotate D left through carry	†	†	O	P	O	†
RL E	CB13	8	rotate E left through carry	†	†	O	P	O	†
RL H	CB14	8	rotate H left through carry	†	†	O	P	O	†
RL L	CB15	8	rotate L left through carry	†	†	O	P	O	†
RLA	17	4	rotate A left through carry			O		O	†
RLC (HL)	CB06	15	rotate (HL) left	†	†	O	P	O	†
RLC (IX + dd)	DDCBdd06	23	rotate (IX + dd) left	†	†	O	P	O	†
RLC (IY + dd)	FDCBdd06	23	rotate (IY + dd)	†	†	O	P	O	†
RLC A	CB07	8	rotate A left	†	†	O	P	O	†
RLC B	CB00	8	rotate B left	†	†	O	P	O	†
RLC C	CB01	8	rotate C left	†	†	O	P	O	†
RLC D	CB02	8	rotate D left	†	†	O	P	O	†
RLC E	CB03	8	rotate E left	†	†	O	P	O	†
RLC H	CB04	8	rotate H left	†	†	O	P	O	†
RLC L	CB05	8	rotate L left	†	†	O	P	O	†
RLCA	07	4	rotate A left			O		O	†
RLD	ED6F	8	rotate left digit	†	†	O	P	O	
RR (HL)	CB1E	15	rotate (HL) right through carry	†	†	O	P	O	†
RR (IX + dd)	DDCBdd1E	23	rotate (IX + dd) right through carry	†	†	O	P	O	†
RR (IY + dd)	FDCBdd1E	23	rotate (IY + dd) right through carry	†	†	O	P	O	†
RR A	CB1F	8	rotate A right through carry	†	†	O	P	O	†
RR B	CB18	8	rotate B right through carry	†	†	O	P	O	†
RR C	CB19	8	rotate C right through carry	†	†	O	P	O	†

Instruction	Opcode	Clocks	Comment	S	Z	H	P/V	N	C
RR D	CB1A	8	rotate D right through carry	†	†	O	P	O	†
RR E	CB1B	8	rotate E right through carry	†	†	O	P	O	†
RR H	CB1C	8	rotate H right through carry	†	†	O	P	O	†
RR L	CB1D	8	rotate L right through carry	†	†	O	P	O	†
RRA	1F	4	rotate A right through carry			O		O	†
RRC (HL)	CB0E	15	rotate (HL) right	†	†	O	P	O	†
RRC (IX + dd)	DDCBdd0E	23	rotate (IX + dd) right	†	†	O	P	O	†
RRC (IY + dd)	FDCBdd0E	23	rotate (IY + dd) right	†	†	O	P	O	†
RRC A	CB0F	8	rotate A right	†	†	O	P	O	†
RRC B	CB08	8	rotate B right	†	†	O	P	O	†
RRC C	CB09	8	rotate C right	†	†	O	P	O	†
RRC D	CB0A	8	rotate D right	†	†	O	P	O	†
RRC E	CB0B	8	rotate E right	†	†	O	P	O	†
RRC H	CB0C	8	rotate H right	†	†	O	P	O	†
RRC L	CB0D	8	rotate L right	†	†	O	P	O	†
RRCA	0F	4	rotate A right			O		O	†
RRD	ED67	18	rotate digit right	†	†	O	P	O	
RST 00H	C7	11	CALL 0000H						
RST 08H	CF	11	CALL 0008H						
RST 10H	D7	11	CALL 0010H						
RST 18H	DF	11	CALL 0018H						
RST 20H	E7	11	CALL 0020H						
RST 28H	EF	11	CALL 0028H						
RST 30H	F7	11	CALL 0030H						
RST 38H	FF	11	CALL 0038H						
SBC, A(HL)	9E	7	A = A − (HL) − Cy	†	†	†	V	1	†
SBC A,(IX + dd)	DD9Edd	19	A = A − (IX + dd) − Cy	†	†	†	V	1	†
SBC, A,(IY + dd)	FD9Edd	19	A = A − (IY + dd) − Cy	†	†	†	V	1	†
SBC A,A	9F	4	A = A − A − Cy	†	†	†	V	1	†
SBC A,B	98	4	A = A − B − Cy	†	†	†	V	1	†
SBA A,C	99	4	A = A − C − Cy	†	†	†	V	1	†
SBC A,D	9A	4	A = A − D − Cy	†	†	†	V	1	†
SBC A,E	9B	4	A = A − E − Cy	†	†	†	V	1	†
SBC A,H	9C	4	A = A − H − Cy	†	†	†	V	1	†
SBC A,L	9D	4	A = A − L − Cy	†	†	†	V	1	†
SBC A,d8	DEd8	7	A = A − d8 − Cy	†	†	†	V	1	†
SBC HL,BC	ED42	15	HL = HL − BC − Cy	†	†	?	V	1	†
SBC, HL,DE	ED52	15	HL = HL − DE − Cy	†	†	?	V	1	†
SCB HL,HL	ED62	15	HL = HL − HL − Cy	†	†	?	V	1	†
SBC HL,SP	ED72	15	HL = HL − SP − Cy	†	†	?	V	1	†
SCF	37	4	set carry			O		O	1
SET 0,(HL)	CBC6	15	bit 0 or (HL) = 1						
SET 0,(IX + dd)	DDCBddC6	23	bit 0 of (IX + dd) = 1						
SET 0,(IY + dd)	FDCBddC6	23	bit 0 of (IY + dd) = 1						
SET 0,A	CBC7	8	bit 0 of A = 1						

Instruction	Opcode	Clocks	Comment	S	Z	H	P/V	N	C
						Flags			
SET 0,B	CBC0	8	bit 0 of B = 1						
SET 0,C	CBC1	8	bit 0 of C = 1						
SET 0,D	CBC2	8	bit 0 of D = 1						
SET 0,E	CBC3	8	bit 0 of E = 1						
SET 0,H	CBC4	8	bit 0 of H = 1						
SET 0,L	CBC5	8	bit 0 of L = 1						
SET 1,(HL)	CBCE	15	bit 1 of (HL) = 1						
SET 1,(IX + dd)	DDCBddCE	23	bit 1 of (IX + dd) = 1						
SET 1,(IY + dd)	FDCBddCE	23	bit 1 of (IY + dd) = 1						
SET 1,A	CBCF	8	bit 1 of A = 1						
SET 1,B	CBC8	8	bit 1 of B = 1						
SET 1,C	CBC9	8	bit 1 of C = 1						
SET 1,D	CBCA	8	bit 1 of D = 1						
SET 1,E	CBCB	8	bit 1 of E = 1						
SET 1,H	CBCC	8	bit 1 of H = 1						
SET 1,L	CBCD	8	bit 1 of L = 1						
SET 2,(HL)	CBD6	15	bit 2 of (HL) = 1						
SET 2,(IX + dd)	DDCBddD6	23	bit 2 of (IX + dd) = 1						
SET 2,(IY + dd)	FDCBddD6	23	bit 2 of (IY + dd) = 1						
SET 2,A	CBD7	8	bit 2 of A = 1						
SET 2,B	CBD0	8	bit 2 of B = 1						
SET 2,C	CBD1	8	bit 2 of C = 1						
SET 2,D	CBD2	8	bit 2 of D = 1						
SET 2,E	CBD3	8	bit 2 of E = 1						
SET 2,H	CBD4	8	bit 2 of H = 1						
SET 2,L	CBD5	8	bit 2 of L = 1						
SET 3,(HL)	CBDE	15	bit 3 of (HL) = 1						
SET 3,(IX + dd)	DDCBddDE	23	bit 3 of (IX + dd) = 1						
SET 3,(IY + dd)	FDCBddDE	23	bit 3 of (IY + dd) = 1						
SET 3,A	CBDF	8	bit 3 of A = 1						
SET 3,B	CBD8	8	bit 3 of B = 1						
SET 3,C	CBD9	8	bit 3 of C = 1						
SET 3,D	CBDA	8	bit 3 of D = 1						
SET 3,E	CBDB	8	bit 3 of E = 1						
SET 3,H	CBDC	8	bit 3 of H = 1						
SET 3,L	CBDD	8	bit 3 of L = 1						
SET 4,(HL)	CBE6	15	bit 4 of (HL) = 1						
SET 4,(IX − dd)	DDCBddE6	23	bit 4 of (IX + dd) = 1						
SET 4,(IY + dd)	FDCBddE6	23	bit 4 of (IY + dd) = 1						
SET 4,A	CBE7	8	bit 4 of A = 1						
SET 4,B	CBE0	8	bit 4 of B = 1						
SET 4,C	CBE1	8	bit 4 of C = 1						
SET 4,D	CBE2	8	bit 4 of D = 1						
SET 4,E	CBE3	8	bit 4 of E = 1						
SET 4,H	CBE4	8	bit 4 of H = 1						

Instruction	Opcode	Clocks	Comment	Flags					
				S	Z	H	P/V	N	C
SET 4,L	CBE5	8	bit 4 of L = 1						
SET 5,(HL)	CBEE	15	bit 5 of (HL) = 1						
SET 5,(IX + dd)	DDCBddEE	23	bit 5 of (IX + dd) = 1						
SET 5,(IY + dd)	FDCBddEE	23	bit 5 of (IY + dd) = 1						
SET 5,A	CBEF	8	bit 5 of A = 1						
SET 5,B	CBE8	8	bit 5 of B = 1						
SET 5,C	CBE9	8	bit 5 of C = 1						
SET 5,D	CBEA	8	bit 5 of D = 1						
SET 5,E	CBEB	8	bit 5 of E = 1						
SET 5,H	CBEC	8	bit 5 of H = 1						
SET 5,L	CBED	8	bit 5 of L = 1						
SET 6,(HL)	CBF6	15	bit 6 of (HL) = 1						
SET 6,(IX + dd)	DDCBddF6	23	bit 6 of (IX + dd) = 1						
SET 6,(IY + dd)	FDCBddF6	23	bit 6 of (IY + dd) = 1						
SET 6,A	CBF7	8	bit 6 of A = 1						
SET 6,B	CBF0	8	bit 6 of B = 1						
SET 6,C	CBF1	8	bit 6 of C = 1						
SET 6,D	CBF2	8	bit 6 of D = 1						
SET 6,E	CBF3	8	bit 6 of E = 1						
SET 6,H	CBF4	8	bit 6 of H = 1						
SET 6,L	CBF5	8	bit 6 of L = 1						
SET 7,(HL)	CBFE	15	bit 7 of (HL) = 1						
SET 7,(IX + dd)	DDCBddFE	23	bit 7 or (IX + dd) = 1						
SET 7,(IY + dd)	FDCBddFE	23	bit 7 of (IY + dd) = 1						
SET 7,A	CBFF	8	bit 7 of A = 1						
SET 7,B	CBF8	8	bit 7 of B = 1						
SET 7,C	CBF9	8	bit 7 of C = 1						
SET 7,D	CBFA	8	bit 7 of D = 1						
SET 7,E	CBFB	8	bit 7 of E = 1						
SET 7,H	CBFC	8	bit 7 of H = 1						
SET 7,L	CBFD	8	bit 7 or L = 1						
SLA (HL)	CB26	15	shift (HL) left	†	†	O	P	O	†
SLA (IX +dd)	DDCBdd26	23	shift (IX + dd) left	†	†	O	P	O	†
SLA (IY + dd)	FDCBdd26	23	shift (IY + dd) left	†	†	O	P	O	†
SLA A	CB27	8	shift A left	†	†	O	P	O	†
SLA B	CB20	8	shift B left	†	†	O	P	O	†
SLA C	CB21	8	shift C left	†	†	O	P	O	†
SLA D	CB22	8	shift D left	†	†	O	P	O	†
SLA E	CB23	8	shift E left	†	†	O	P	O	†
SLA H	CB24	8	shift H left	†	†	O	P	O	†
SLA L	CB25	8	shift L left	†	†	O	P	O	†
SRA (HL)	CB2E	15	arithmetic shift (HL) right	†	†	O	P	O	†
SRA (IX + dd)	DDCBdd2E	23	arithmetic shift (IX + dd) right	†	†	O	P	O	†
SRA (IY + dd)	FDCBdd2E	23	arithmetic shift (IY + dd) right	†	†	O	P	O	†
SRA A	CB2F	8	arithmetic shift A right	†	†	O	P	O	†

Instruction	Opcode	Clocks	Comment	Flags					
				S	Z	H	P/V	N	C
SRA B	CB28	8	arithmetic shift B right	†	†	O	P	O	†
SRA C	CB29	8	arithmetic shift C right	†	†	O	P	O	†
SRA D	CB2A	8	arithmetic shift D right	†	†	O	P	O	†
SRA E	CB2B	8	arithmetic shift E right	†	†	O	P	O	†
SRA H	CB2C	8	arithmetic shift H right	†	†	O	P	O	†
SRA L	CB2D	8	arithmetic shift	†	†	O	P	O	†
SRL (HL)	CB3E	15	shift (HL) right	†	†	O	P	O	†
SLR (IX + dd)	DDCBdd3E	23	shift (IX + dd) right	†	†	O	P	O	†
SRL (IY + dd)	FDCBdd3E	23	shift (IY + dd) right	†	†	O	P	O	†
SRL A	CB3F	8	shift A right	†	†	O	P	O	†
SRL B	CB38	8	shift B right	†	†	O	P	O	†
SRL C	CB39	8	shift C right	†	†	O	P	O	†
SRL D	CB3A	8	shift D right	†	†	O	P	O	†
SRL E	CB3B	8	shift E right	†	†	O	P	O	†
SRL H	CB3C	8	shift H right	†	†	O	P	O	†
SRL L	CB3D	8	shift L right	†	†	O	P	O	†
SUB (HL)	96	7	A = A − (HL)	†	†	†	V	1	†
SUB (IX + dd)	DD96dd	19	A = A − (IX + dd)	†	†	†	V	1	†
SUB (IY + dd)	FD96dd	19	A = A − (IY + dd)	†	†	†	V	1	†
SUB A	97	4	A = A − A	O	1	O	1	1	O
SUB B	90	4	A = A − B	†	†	†	V	1	†
SUB C	91	4	A = A − C	†	†	†	V	1	†
SUB D	92	4	A = A − D	†	†	†	V	1	†
SUB E	93	4	A = A − E	†	†	†	V	1	†
SUB H	94	4	A = A − H	†	†	†	V	1	†
SUB L	95	4	A = A − L	†	†	†	V	1	†
SUB d8	D6d8	7	A = A − d8	†	†	†	V	1	†
XOR (HL)	AE	7	A = A ∀ (HL)	†	†	O	P	O	O
XOR (IX + dd)	DDAEdd	19	A = A ∀ (IX + dd)	†	†	O	P	O	O
XOR (IY + dd)	FDAEdd	19	A = A ∀ (IY + dd)	†	†	O	P	O	O
XOR A	AF	4	A = A ∀ A	O	1	O	1	O	O
XOR B	A8	4	A = A ∀ B	†	†	O	P	O	O
XOR C	A9	4	A = A ∀ C	†	†	O	P	O	O
XOR D	AA	4	A = A ∀ D	†	†	O	P	O	O
XOR E	AB	4	A = A ∀ E	†	†	O	P	O	O
XOR H	AC	4	A = A ∀ H	†	†	O	P	O	O
XOR L	AD	4	A = A ∀ L	†	†	O	P	O	O
XOR d8	EEd8	7	A = A ∀ d8	†	†	O	P	O	O

Notes: d8 = 8 bits of immediate data; d16 = 16 bits of immediate data; p8 = 8 bits I/O port address; ( ) = indirect addressing; dd = 8 bit displacement; II = low-order address; hh = high-order address; adr = 16 bit memory address; † = any value; ? = undefined; P = parity; V = overflow; and a blank flag means no change.

appendix **B**

The Z80 Data Sheets

T_A = 0°C to 70°C, V_{CC} = +5V ± 5%, Unless Otherwise Noted.

Signal	Symbol	Parameter	Min	Max	Unit	Test Condition
Φ	t_c	Clock Period	.4	[12]	μsec	
	$t_w(ΦH)$	Clock Pulse Width, Clock High	180	∞	nsec	
	$t_w(ΦL)$	Clock Pulse Width, Clock Low	180	2000	nsec	
	$t_{r,f}$	Clock Rise and Fall Time		30	nsec	
A_{0-15}	$t_{D(AD)}$	Address Output Delay		160	nsec	
	$t_{F(AD)}$	Delay to Float		110	nsec	
	t_{acm}	Address Stable Prior to $\overline{MREQ}$ (Memory Cycle)	[1]		nsec	C_L = 100pF
	t_{aci}	Address Stable Prior to $\overline{IORQ}$, $\overline{RD}$ or $\overline{WR}$ (I/O Cycle)	[2]		nsec	
	t_{ca}	Address Stable from $\overline{RD}$ or $\overline{WR}$	[3]		nsec	
	t_{caf}	Address Stable From $\overline{RD}$ or $\overline{WR}$ During Float	[4]		nsec	
D_{0-7}	$t_{D(D)}$	Data Output Delay		260	nsec	
	$t_{F(D)}$	Delay to Float During Write Cycle		90	nsec	
	$t_{SΦ(D)}$	Data Setup Time to Rising Edge of Clock During M1 Cycle	50		nsec	
	$t_{S\overline{Φ}(D)}$	Data Setup Time to Falling Edge of Clock During M2 to M5	60		nsec	C_L = 200pF
	t_{dcm}	Data Stable Prior to $\overline{WR}$ (Memory Cycle)	[5]		nsec	
	t_{dci}	Data Stable Prior to $\overline{WR}$ (I/O Cycle)	[6]		nsec	
	t_{cdf}	Data Stable From $\overline{WR}$	[7]		nsec	
	t_H	Any Hold Time for Setup Time	0		nsec	
$\overline{MREQ}$	$t_{DL\overline{Φ}(MR)}$	$\overline{MREQ}$ Delay From Falling Edge of Clock, $\overline{MREQ}$ Low		100	nsec	
	$t_{DHΦ(MR)}$	$\overline{MREQ}$ Delay From Rising Edge of Clock, $\overline{MREQ}$ High		100	nsec	
	$t_{DH\overline{Φ}(MR)}$	$\overline{MREQ}$ Delay From Falling Edge of Clock, $\overline{MREQ}$ High		100	nsec	C_L = 50pF
	$t_w(\overline{MRL})$	Pulse Width, $\overline{MREQ}$ Low	[8]		nsec	
	$t_w(\overline{MRH})$	Pulse Width, $\overline{MREQ}$ High	[9]		nsec	
$\overline{IORQ}$	$t_{DLΦ(IR)}$	$\overline{IORQ}$ Delay From Rising Edge of Clock, $\overline{IORQ}$ Low		90	nsec	
	$t_{DL\overline{Φ}(IR)}$	$\overline{IORQ}$ Delay From Falling Edge of Clock, $\overline{IORQ}$ Low		110	nsec	
	$t_{DHΦ(IR)}$	$\overline{IORQ}$ Delay From Rising Edge of Clock, $\overline{IORQ}$ High		100	nsec	C_L = 50pF
	$t_{DH\overline{Φ}(IR)}$	$\overline{IORQ}$ Delay From Falling Edge of Clock, $\overline{IORQ}$ High		110	nsec	
$\overline{RD}$	$t_{DLΦ(RD)}$	$\overline{RD}$ Delay From Rising Edge of Clock, $\overline{RD}$ Low		100	nsec	
	$t_{DL\overline{Φ}(RD)}$	$\overline{RD}$ Delay From Falling Edge of Clock, $\overline{RD}$ Low		130	nsec	
	$t_{DHΦ(RD)}$	$\overline{RD}$ Delay From Rising Edge of Clock, $\overline{RD}$ High		100	nsec	C_L = 50pF
	$t_{DH\overline{Φ}(RD)}$	$\overline{RD}$ Delay From Falling Edge of Clock, $\overline{RD}$ High		110	nsec	
$\overline{WR}$	$t_{DLΦ(WR)}$	$\overline{WR}$ Delay From Rising Edge of Clock, $\overline{WR}$ Low		80	nsec	
	$t_{DL\overline{Φ}(WR)}$	$\overline{WR}$ Delay From Falling Edge of Clock, $\overline{WR}$ Low		90	nsec	
	$t_{DHΦ(WR)}$	$\overline{WR}$ Delay From Falling Edge of Clock, $\overline{WR}$ High		100	nsec	C_L = 50pF
	$t_w(\overline{WRL})$	Pulse Width, $\overline{WR}$ Low	[10]		nsec	
$\overline{M1}$	$t_{DL(M1)}$	$\overline{M1}$ Delay From Rising Edge of Clock, $\overline{M1}$ Low		130	nsec	
	$t_{DH(M1)}$	$\overline{M1}$ Delay From Rising Edge of Clock, $\overline{M1}$ High		130	nsec	C_L = 30pF
$\overline{RFSH}$	$t_{DL(RF)}$	$\overline{RFSH}$ Delay From Rising Edge of Clock, $\overline{RFSH}$ Low		180	nsec	
	$t_{DH(RF)}$	$\overline{RFSH}$ Delay From Rising Edge of Clock, $\overline{RFSH}$ High		150	nsec	C_L = 30pF
$\overline{WAIT}$	$t_s(WT)$	$\overline{WAIT}$ Setup Time to Falling Edge of Clock	70		nsec	
$\overline{HALT}$	$t_{D(HT)}$	$\overline{HALT}$ Delay Time From Falling Edge of Clock		300	nsec	C_L = 50pF
$\overline{INT}$	$t_s(IT)$	$\overline{INT}$ Setup Time to Rising Edge of Clock	80		nsec	
$\overline{NMI}$	$t_w(\overline{NML})$	Pulse Width, $\overline{NM1}$ Low	80		nsec	
$\overline{BUSRQ}$	$t_s(BQ)$	$\overline{BUSRQ}$ Setup Time to Rising Edge of Clock	80		nsec	
$\overline{BUSAK}$	$t_{DL(BA)}$	$\overline{BUSAK}$ Delay From Rising Edge of Clock, $\overline{BUSAK}$ Low		120	nsec	
	$t_{DH(BA)}$	$\overline{BUSAK}$ Delay From Falling Edge of Clock, $\overline{BUSAK}$ High		110	nsec	C_L = 50pF
$\overline{RESET}$	$t_s(RS)$	$\overline{RESET}$ Setup Time to Rising Edge of Clock	90		nsec	
	$t_{F(C)}$	Delay to Float ($\overline{MREQ}$, $\overline{IORQ}$, $\overline{RD}$ and $\overline{WR}$)		100	nsec	
	t_{mr}	$\overline{M1}$ Stable Prior to $\overline{IORQ}$ (Interrupt Ack.)	[11]		nsec	

[12] $t_c = t_w(ΦH) + t_w(ΦL) + t_r + t_f$

[1] $t_{acm} = t_w(ΦH) + t_f - 75$

[2] $t_{aci} = t_c - 80$

[3] $t_{ca} = t_w(ΦL) + t_r - 40$

[4] $t_{caf} = t_w(ΦL) + t_r - 60$

[5] $t_{dcm} = t_c - 180$

[6] $t_{dci} = t_w(ΦL) + t_r - 180$

[7] $t_{cdf} = t_w(ΦL) + t_r - 50$

[8] $t_w(\overline{MRL}) = t_c - 40$

[9] $t_w(\overline{MRH}) = t_w(ΦH) + t_f - 30$

[10] $t_w(WR) = t_c - 40$

[11] $t_{mr} = 2t_c + t_w(ΦH) + t_f - 80$

NOTES:

1. Data should be enabled onto the CPU data bus when $\overline{RD}$ is active. During interrupt acknowledge data should be enabled when $\overline{M1}$ and $\overline{IORQ}$ are both active.
2. All control signals are internally synchronized, so they may be totally asynchronous with respect to the clock.
3. The $\overline{RESET}$ signal must be active for a minimum of 3 clock cycles.
4. Output Delay vs. Loaded Capacitance
   T_A = 70°C V_{CC} = +5V ±5%
   (1) ΔC_L = +100pF ($A_0 - A_{15}$ and Control Signals), add 30 ns to timing shown.
   (2) ΔC_L = –50pF ($A_0 - A_{15}$ and Control Signals), subtract 15 ns from timing shown.

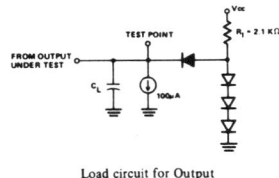

Load circuit for Output

Appendix B   (Courtesy of Zilog Corporation.)

Timing measurements are made at the following
voltages, unless otherwise specified:

	"1"	"0"
CLOCK	4.2 V	.8 V
OUTPUT	2.0 V	.8 V
INPUT	2.0 V	.8 V
FLOAT	Δ V	± 0.5 V

Φ

t_C

t_W (ΦH)

t_W (ΦL)

A_0-A15

t_F (AD)

A_0-15

t_D (AD)

t_SΦ̄ (D)

D_0-7 IN

OUT

t_D (D)

t_SΦ (D) t_H

t_H

t_F (D)

$\overline{M1}$

t_{DL} (M1) t_{DH} (M1)

t_{caf}

t_{ca}

t_{cdf}

$\overline{RFSH}$

t_{DL} (RF) t_{DH} (RF)

t_F (C)

$\overline{MREQ}$

t_{acm} t_{DL}Φ̄ (MR) t_{DH}Φ (MR) t_{DH}Φ̄ (MR) t_{DH}Φ̄ (MR)

t_W (MRL)

$\overline{RD}$

t_{DL}Φ̄ (RD) t_{DH}Φ (RD) t_W (MRH) t_{DH}Φ̄ (RD)

$\overline{WR}$

t_{DL}Φ̄ (WR) t_{DH}Φ̄ (WR)

t_{dcm} t_W ($\overline{WR}$L)

$\overline{IORQ}$

t_{DL}Φ (IR) t_{DH}Φ (IR) t_{DL}Φ (IR) t_{DH}Φ̄ (IR)

t_{mr} t_{aci}

$\overline{RD}$

t_{DL}Φ (RD) t_{DH}Φ̄ (RD)

$\overline{WR}$

t_{DL}Φ (WR) t_{DH}Φ̄ (WR)

t_{dci}

$\overline{WAIT}$

t_S (WT) t_H

$\overline{HALT}$

t_D (HT) t_D (HT)

$\overline{INT}$

t_S (IT) t_H

$\overline{NMI}$

$\overline{BUSRQ}$

t_W ($\overline{NML}$)

t_S (BQ) t_H

$\overline{BUSAK}$

t_{DL} (BA) t_{DH} (BA)

$\overline{RESET}$

t_S (RS) t_H

appendix C

The ASCII Code

Code	No parity	Odd parity	Even parity	Comment
NUL	00	80	00	null
SOH	01	01	81	start of header
STX	02	02	82	start of text
ETX	03	83	03	end of text
EOT	04	04	84	end of transmission
ENQ	05	85	05	enquiry
ACK	06	86	06	acknowledgement
BEL	07	07	87	bell or alarm
BS	08	08	88	backspace
HT	09	89	09	horizontal tab
LF	0A	8A	0A	line feed
VT	0B	0B	8B	vertical tab
FF	0C	8C	0C	form feed
CR	0D	0D	8D	carriage return
SO	0E	0E	8E	shift out
SI	0F	8F	0F	shift in
DLE	10	10	90	data link escape
DC1	11	91	11	direct control 1
DC2	12	92	12	direct control 2
DC3	13	13	93	direct control 3
DC4	14	94	19	direct control 4
NAK	15	15	95	negative acknowledgement

Code	No parity	Odd parity	Even parity	Comment
SYN	16	16	96	synchoronous idle
ETB	17	97	17	end of transmission block
CAN	18	98	18	cancel
EM	19	19	99	end of medium
SUB	1A	1A	9A	substitute
ESC	1B	9B	1B	escape
FS	1C	1C	9C	form separator
GS	1D	9D	1D	group separator
RS	1E	9E	1E	record separator
US	1F	1F	9F	unit separator
SP	20	20	A0	space
!	21	A1	21	
"	22	A2	22	
#	23	23	A3	
$	24	A4	24	
%	25	25	A5	
&	26	26	A6	
'	27	A7	27	apostrophe
(	28	A8	28	
)	29	29	A9	
*	2A	2A	AA	
+	2B	AB	2B	
'	2C	2C	AC	comma
—	2D	AD	2D	minus
/	2F	2F	AF	
0	30	B0	30	
1	31	31	B1	
2	32	32	B2	
3	33	B3	33	
4	34	34	B4	
5	35	B5	35	
6	36	B6	36	
7	37	37	B7	
8	38	38	B8	
9	39	B9	39	
:	3A	BA	3A	colon
;	3B	3B	BB	semicolon
<	3C	BC	3C	
=	3D	3D	BD	
>	3E	3E	BE	
?	3F	BF	3F	
@	40	40	C0	
A	41	C1	41	
B	42	C2	42	
C	43	43	C3	

Code	No parity	Odd parity	Even parity	Comment
D	44	C4	44	
E	45	45	C5	
F	46	46	C6	
G	47	C7	47	
H	48	C8	48	
I	49	49	C9	
J	4A	4A	CA	
K	4B	CB	4B	
L	4C	4C	CC	
M	4D	CD	4D	
N	4E	CE	4E	
O	4F	4F	CF	
P	50	D0	50	
Q	51	51	D1	
R	52	52	D2	
S	53	D3	53	
T	54	54	D4	
U	55	D5	55	
V	56	D6	56	
W	57	57	D7	
X	58	58	D8	
Y	59	D9	59	
Z	5A	DA	5A	
[	5B	5B	DB	
\	5C	DC	5C	
]	5D	5D	DD	
^	5E	5E	DE	
—	5F	DF	5F	
`	60	E0	60	accent grave
a	61	61	E1	
b	62	62	E2	
c	63	E3	63	
d	64	64	E4	
e	65	E5	65	
f	66	E6	66	
g	67	67	E7	
h	68	68	E8	
i	69	E9	69	
j	6A	EA	6A	
k	6B	6B	EB	
l	6C	EC	6C	
m	6D	6D	ED	
n	6E	6E	EE	
o	6F	EF	6F	
p	70	70	F0	

Code	No parity	Odd parity	Even parity	Comment
q	71	F1	71	
r	72	F2	72	
s	73	73	F3	
t	74	F4	74	
u	75	75	F5	
v	76	76	F6	
v	76	76	F6	
w	77	F7	77	
x	78	F8	78	
y	79	79	F9	
z	7A	7A	FA	
{	7B	FB	7B	
|	7C	FC	7C	
}	7D	FD	7D	
~	7E	FE	7E	tilde
DEL	7F	7F	FF	

appendix D

Answers to the Even-Numbered Questions

Chapter 1

1-2. Early applications included: video games, microwave ovens, etc.

1-4. 8.

1-6. NMOS logic.

1-8. 68000, 8086, and the Z8000.

1-10. A microprocessor is a device that transfers data between memory and itself and between I/O and itself. It also performs some basic arithmetic and logic operations and makes some simple decisions based on the outcome of arithmetic and logic operations.

1-12. Data transfer; arithmetic and logic; and decisions.

1-14. Addition, subtraction, AND, and OR.

1-16. Read-only memory (ROM).

1-18. A program is a logical grouping of steps (instructions) that perform a task.

1-20. An I/O device is a device that either accepts an electrical signal from the microprocessor or provides an electrical signal.

1-22. Keyboard, displays, and a breadboarding area.

Chapter 2

2-2. 64K bytes.

2-4. $\overline{\text{RD}}$, $\overline{\text{WR}}$, $\overline{\text{IORQ}}$, and $\overline{\text{MREQ}}$.

2-6. Binary, BCD, and ASCII.

2-8. The accumulator.

2-10. It is called a counter because, as it addresses instructions in a program, it advances its count (contents) by one for each byte.

2-12. IX and IY are additional registers that are used to indirectly address memory data.

2-14. ROM in a Z80 is normally located at the very bottom of the memory beginning at memory location 0000H.

2-16. An I/O port is the number (address) that is used to refer to an I/O device connected to the Z80.

2-18. 0000 0000 1001 1011, 0000 0010 0000 1010, 0000 0011 1110 1000, 0000 0111 1101 1001, and 0010 0111 0001 0000.

2-20. 0000 1100, 1111 0100, 0010 0000, 1100 0001, and 1001 1100.

2-22. By typing the letter H while holding the control key down.

2-24. 0100 0001 0100 0000 0000 0000 0000 0000,
1100 0001 1011 0000 0000 0000 0000 0000,
0100 0001 0010 1000 0000 0000 0000 0000,
0011 1011 0000 0011 0001 0010 0110 1111,
and 1100 0000 1000 1000 0000 0000 0000 0000.

2-26. An opcode is the part of an instruction (the first byte) that tells the microprocessor which operation to perform.

2-28. An operand address is the address of the data.

2-30. 34 12, DC AC, FF 87, 43 34, and 80 90.

2-32. Data transfer instructions.

Chapter 3

3-2. 2 bytes.

3-4. 00 10, 4A 23, CB AB, 00 50, and 6F 45.

3-6. HL is surrounded with parenthesis, (HL).

3-8. 11 00 12, OE 90, 31 34 12, 36 OA, and 36 10.

3-10. See Example D-1.

Example D-1

```
21 00 12      LD HL,1200H
36 16         LD (HL),16H
21 01 12      LD HL,1201H
36 17         LD (HL),17H
```

3-12. 1200H = 44H and 1201H = 22H.

3-14. 1200H = 77H.

3-16. 1212H.

3-18. A 34H is stored into memory location 1233H.

3-20. See Example D-2.

3-22. 16.

3-24. 3000H.

Example D-2

```
DD 21 00 10    LD  IX,1000H
3E 00          LD  A,0
DD 77 00       LD  (IX),A
DD 77 01       LD  (IX+1),A
DD 77 02       LD  (IX+2),A
DD 77 03       LD  (IX+3),A
```

3-26. See Example D-3.

Example D-3

```
21 00 00       LD  HL,0000H
11 00 20       LD  DE,2000H
01 50 00       LD  BC,0050H
ED B0          LDIR
```

3-28. The contents of the accumulator is sent to external I/O device 12H.

3-30. LD SP, (adr); LD SP,HL; LD SP,IX; LD SP,IY; and LD SP,d16.

Chapter 4

4-2.

	S	Z	H	P/V	N	C
12H + 33H	0	0	0	0	0	0
F0H + 33H	0	0	0	0	0	1
0FH + 40H	0	0	0	0	0	0
3FH + ABH	1	0	1	0	0	0

4-4. See Example D-4.

Example D-4

```
7D             LD  A,L
84             ADD A,H
6F             LD  L,A
```

4-6. Whenever numbers that are wider than a byte are added together.

4-8. The contents of the DE register pair is added to the HL register pair.

4-10. It follows the addition or subtraction.

4-12. INC HL. This instruction affects none of the flag bits.

4-14.

	S	Z	H	P/V	N	C
12H + 33H	1	0	1	0	1	1
F0H + 33H	1	0	1	0	1	0
0FH + 40H	1	0	0	0	1	1
3FH + ABH	1	0	0	0	1	1

4-16. SUB (HL).

4-18. See Example D-5.

Example D-5

```
79          LD    A,C
93          SUB   E
4F          LD    C,A
78          LD    A,B
9A          SBC   A,D
47          LD    B,A
```

4-20. False.

4-22. This instruction compares the contents of the accumulator with the contents of the memory location addressed by HL. After the comparison, HL is incremented and BC is decremented. The instruction is repeated until BC = 0 or until A = (HL).

4-24. NEG.

4-26. Clear.

4-28. Invert.

4-30. The contents of the accumulator are tested.

4-32. See Example D-6.

Example D-6

```
CBFF        SET   7,A
CBF7        SET   6,A
CBEF        SET   5,A
CB87        RES   0,A
```

4-34. A logic right shift places a 0 in the left-most bit while the arithmetic shift right copies the sign-bit into the left-most bit.

Chapter 5

5-2. The JR instruction adds the second byte of the instruction to the program counter to determine the jump address.

5-4. It is an infinite loop because it continues to jump to the same instruction at the end.

5-6. Carry and zero flags.

5-8. The carry flag is often used to hold a carry after an addition or a borrow after a subtraction. It also indicates relative magnitude after a comparison.

5-10. Addition or subtraction.

5-12. CALL.

5-14. The return address is stored on the stack, and it is the address of the step after the most recent CALL instruction.

5-16. Program counter.

5-18. See Example D-7.

Example D-7

```
CALL  TRIP
CALL  TRIP
CALL  TRIP
```

5-20. The NOP does absolutely nothing except waste a small amount of time.

5-22. A reset or an interrupt.

5-24. A subroutine that is called in response to an interrupt.

5-26. The RETI instruction is normally used to end an interrupt.

5-28. INT.

Chapter 6

6-2. Source. Object.

6-4. One-pass assemblers allow only reverse references, which makes programming very difficult.

6-6. (a) special characters are not allowed, (c) a label may not start with a number, and (e) a space may not be embedded in a label.

6-8. 12, 120, and 12H.

6-10. 42H, 52H, 45H, and 59H.

6-12. 3.

6-14. DS causes the assembler to set aside bytes of memory.

6-16. EQU is permanent and SET is temporary. Both are used to assign a value to a label.

6-18. GLB allows the programmer to indicate variables that are used by other modules, and EXT allows a module to use a GLB variable.

6-20. (a) V, (b) R, (c) S, and (d) L.

6-22. A macro assembler is one in which the user may define new opcodes.

6-24. MACRO. ENDM.

6-26. Parameters are passed by using the & to identify passed parameters.

Chapter 7

7-2. See Figure D-1.

7-4. A subroutine.

7-6. No, but the questions are usually yes-no or true-false type questions.

7-8. Sequence, if-then, if-then-else, do while, and repeat until.

7-10. See Figure D-2.

7-12. See Figure D-3.

7-14. Yes.

7-16. See Figure D-4.

7-18. See Example D-8.

Example D-8

```
LD    A,0
CP    B
JR    NZ,LOOP
CP    C
JR    NZ,LOOP
```

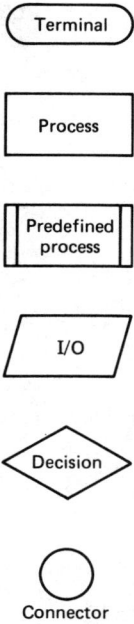

Terminal

Process

Predefined
process

I/O

Decision

Connector

Figure D–1

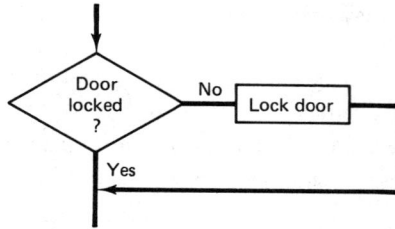

Figure D–2

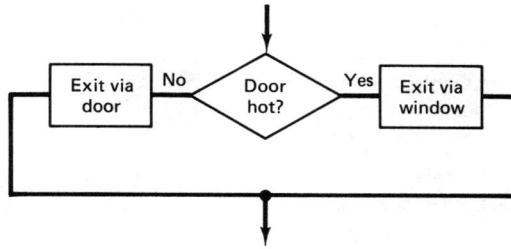

Figure D–3

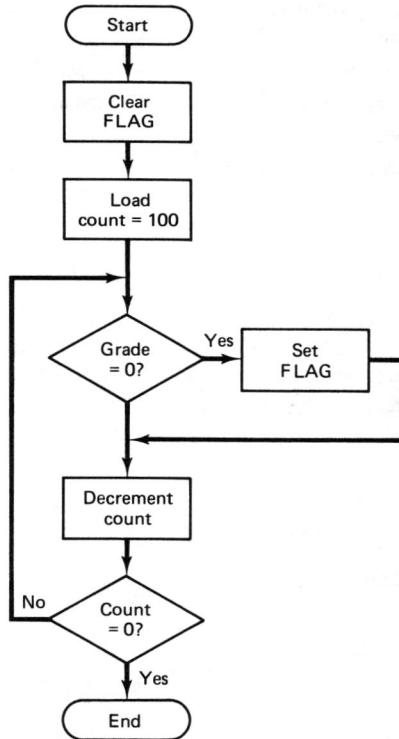

Figure D–4

Chapter 8

8-2. See Example D-9.

Example D-9

```
0100 21 00 28    START:  LD    HL,2800H
0103 11 20 28            LD    DE,2820H
0106 06 05               LD    B,5
0108 7E          LOOP:   LD    A,(HL)
0109 12                  LD    (DE),A
010A 23                  INC   HL
010B 13                  INC   DE
010C 10 FA               DJNZ  LOOP
010E 18 FE       ENDP:   JR    ENDP
```

8-4. The main difference is that words are exchanged in the word exchange program.

8-6. See Example D-10.

Example D-10

```
0100 21 00 00       START:  LD    HL,0000H
0103 11 00 28               LD    DE,2800H
0106 DD 21 00 20            LD    IX,2000H
0109 06 64                  LD    B,100
010B 7E             LOOP:   LD    A,(HL)
010C 12                     LD    (DE),A
010D DD 77 00               LD    (IX),A
0110 23                     INC   HL
0111 13                     INC   DE
0112 DD 23                  INC   IX
0114 10 F5                  DJNZ  LOOP
0116 18 FE          ENDP:   JR    ENDP
```

8-8. No, but in practice the string is limited to 256 characters.

8-10. Repeat-until.

8-12. See Example D-11.

Example D-11

```
0100 EB          START:  EX    DE,HL
0101 09                  ADD   HL,BC
0102 EB                  EX    DE,HL
0103 18 FE       ENDP:   JR    ENDP
```

8-14. See Example D-12.

Example D-12

```
0100 E5        MUL13: PUSH HL
0101 29               ADD  HL,HL
0102 29               ADD  HL,HL
0103 E5               PUSH HL
0104 29               ADD  HL,HL
0105 D1               POP  DE
0106 19               ADD  HL,DE
0107 D1               POP  DE
0108 19               ADD  HL,DE
0109 C9               RET
```

8-16. See Example D-13.

Example D-13

```
0100 06 08     DIVC:  LD   B,8
0102 29        DIVC1: ADD  HL,HL
0103 7C               LD   A,H
0104 91               SUB  C
0105 30 02            JR   NC,DIVC2
0107 67               LD   H,A
0108 23               INC  HL
0109 10 F6     DIVC2: DJNZ DIVC1
010B C9               RET
```

Chapter 9

9-2. 30H.

9-4. A 30H must be added if the original hexadecimal number is between 0-9 and a 37H must be added if it is between A-F.

9-6. 10.

9-8. See Example D-14.

Example D-14

```
;
;the following entries are appended to Example 9-7
;
               DB   54H        ;n
               DB   3EH        ;U
               DB   76H        ;H
               DB   50H        ;r
```

9-10. It sure can.

9-12. (a) 1.75 μs   (b) 1.0 μs   (c) 3.0 μs   (d) 2.5 μs   (e) 2.5 μs

9-14. 182.5 μs.

9-16. 53.2555 μs.

Chapter 10

10-2. 0.1 μF.

10-4. The amount of capacitance that the output pin is capable of driving.

10-6. $\overline{\text{IOR}}$.

10-8. Refresh.

10-10. 0. 0.

10-12. 0066H.

10-14. $\overline{\text{IORQ}}$, $\overline{\text{M1}}$, and $\overline{\text{RD}}$.

10-16. Direct memory access.

10-18. A DMA request.

10-20. 795 ns.

10-22. The refresh address is output so that dynamic RAM can be refreshed during this period of time.

Chapter 11

11-2. The ROM is programmed at the factory during fabrication.

11-4. The EPROM is erased by exposing it to ultraviolet light.

11-6. 27256.

11-8. True.

11-10. 11.

11-12. False.

11-14. It indicates that the Z80 has outputted the refresh address onto the address bus so that DRAM can be refreshed.

11-16. An address bus (A0-A15), a data bus (D0-D7) and a control bus ($\overline{\text{RD}}$, $\overline{\text{WR}}$, and $\overline{\text{MREQ}}$).

11-18. See Figure D-5.

11-20. See Figure D-6.

11-22. The one-to-zero transition of the clock during T2 or TW.

11-24. The address multiplexer is required because the DRAM contains multiplexed address pins which require half the address at a time.

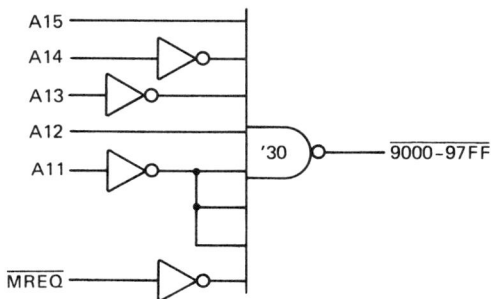

Figure D–5

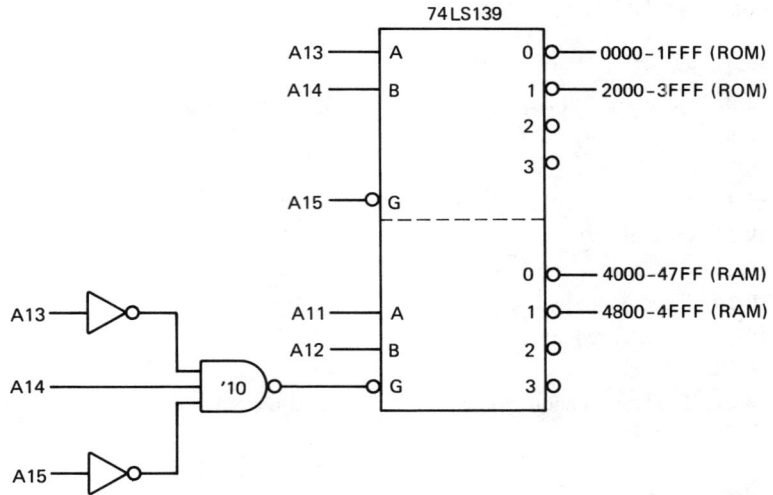

Figure D–6

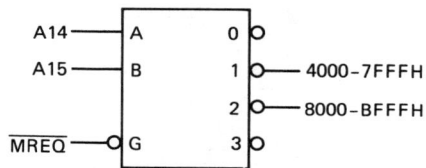

Figure D–7

11-26. $\overline{\text{MREQ}}$.

11-28. See Figure D-7.

Chapter 12

12-2. Address connections A0-A7.

12-4. $\overline{\text{IORQ}}$. $\overline{\text{WR}}$.

12-6. A latch.

12-8. PA0-PA7 and PC4-PC7.

12-10. See Figure D-8.

12-12. See Example D-15.

Example D-15

```
;
;program 8255A so that group A are simple input pins
;and group B are simple output pins
;
PROG:     LD   A,10011000B
          OUT  (43H),A
          RET
```

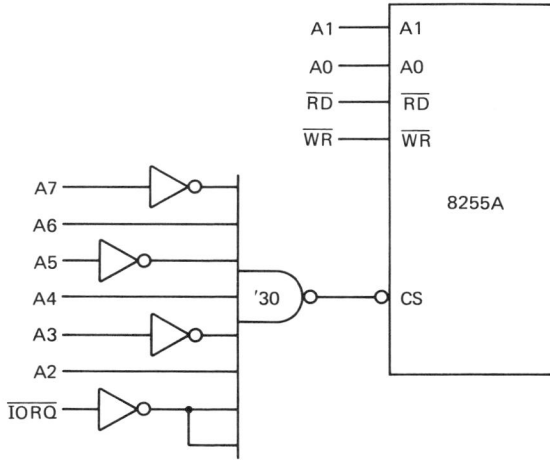

Figure D–8

12-14. See Figure D-9 and Example D-16.

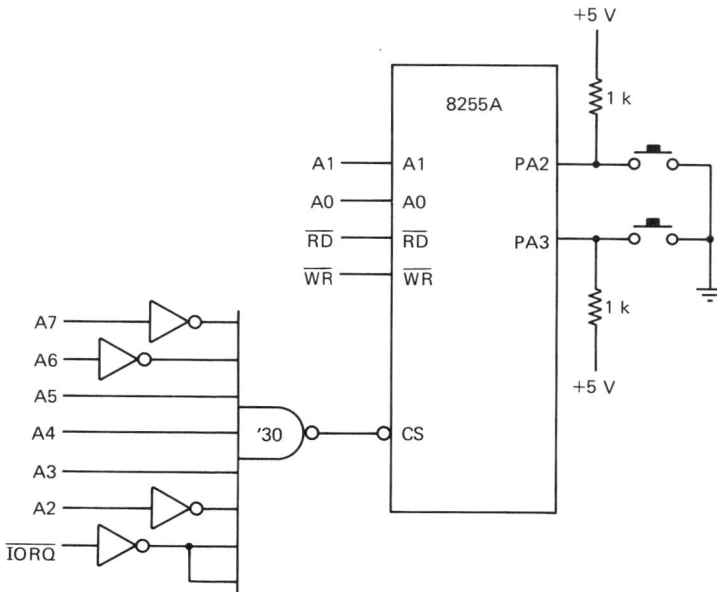

Figure D–9

Example D-16

```
;
;initialize 8255A
;
START:      LD   A,10011000B
            OUT  (3BH),A
;
;wait for release
;
WAIT:       IN   A,(38H)           ;read port A
            CPL
            AND  OCH               ;mask PA3 and PA2
            JR   NZ,WAIT           ;if a switch is closed
            CALL DELAY             ;wait for bouncing to stop
            IN   A,(38H)           ;check again
            CPL
            AND  OCH
                 JR   NZ,WAIT         ;if a switch is closed
;
;wait for a closed switch
;
CLOSED:     IN   A,(38H)           ;read port A
            CPL
            AND  OCH
            JR   Z,CLOSED          ;if no switch is closed
            CALL DELAY             ;wait for bouncing to stop
            IN   A,(38H)           ;check again
            CPL
            AND  OCH
            JR   Z,CLOSED
;
;process closed switch
;
            AND  04H               ;isolate PC2
            JR   Z,PC3             ;if PC3 closed
            LD   A,0FFH
PC3:        LD   (2000H),A         ;save 00 or FF
            JR   WAIT              ;look for next switch
```

12-16. Whenever data are strobed into the port the IBF bit becomes a logic 1 indicating the buffer contains data for the microprocessor. IBF is cleared to 0 whenever the data are removed (IN) from the port.

12-18. Whenever data are output to the port, the $\overline{\text{OBF}}$ signal becomes a logic 0 indicating data are present in the port. The external device responds by sending an $\overline{\text{ACK}}$ to the port to remove the data. The $\overline{\text{ACK}}$ returns the $\overline{\text{OBF}}$ signal to a logic 1.

12-20. Port A.

12-22. The OUT instruction strobes data into port A and then causes the $\overline{\text{OBF}}$ signal to go to a logic 0. $\overline{\text{OBF}}$ indicates data are available to the bidirectional bus from the 8255A.

12-24. 10—15 ms.

12-26. CHECK tests the keyboard to determine if any keys are pressed.

12-28. See Figure D-10.

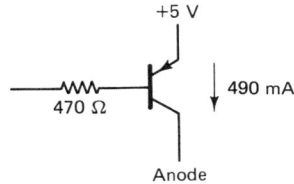

Figure D–10

12-30. Modes 1 and 2.

12-32. Whenever the data are removed from the port with the $\overline{\text{ACK}}$ signal.

Chapter 13

13-2. The receiver searches for the start bit. Once it finds start, it then tests at the center of each subsequent received bit. This process continues until the stop or stops are detected.

13-4. 10.

13-6. 120 per second.

13-8. Zero-to-one.

13-10. 300-3000 Hz.

13-12. Two tones, one for a logic 1 and a second for a logic 0.

13-14. Half duplex operation is communications in one direction at a time, and full duplex is communications in two directions at a time.

13-16. Dibit.

13-18. 0°, 90°, 180°, and 270°.

13-20. A USART is a universal synchronous/asynchronous receiver/transmitter.

13-22. The RxC and TxC inputs.

13-24. After power is applied, three 00H must be sent to the command port followed by an 04H.

13-26. See Example D-17.

Example D-17

```
;
;reset 8251A
;
START:      LD    A,0
            OUT   (13H),A
            OUT   (13H),A
            OUT   (13H),A
            LD    A,4
            OUT   (13H),A
;
;program mode
;
            LD    A,11011011B
            OUT   (13H),A
            RET
```

13-28. See Figure D-11.

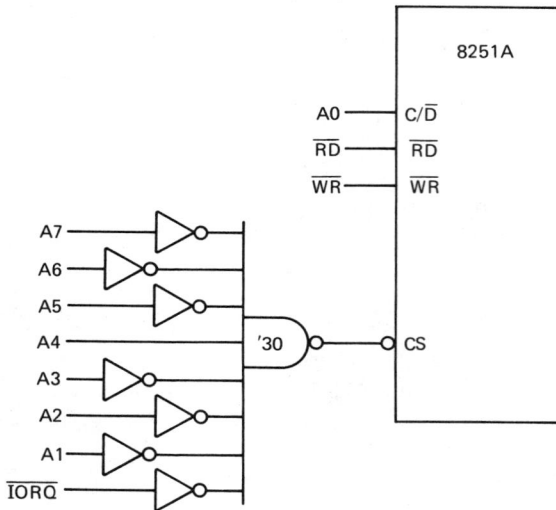

Figure D–11

13-30. An overrun error occurs when the data are not removed from the 8251A before the next character is received.

13-32. RxRDY is active when data are received.

13-34. DCE is the data communications equipment (modem).

13-36. A serial interface standard.

13-38. 50 feet is recommended.

13-40. $\overline{\text{DSR}}$ indicates that the data set is ready.

13-42. $\overline{\text{DCD}}$ indicates that a carrier is detected.

Chapter 14

14-2. 10 MHz.

14-4. 0-65,536 in binary and 0-10,000 in BCD.

14-6. A0 and A1.

14-8. Least significant.

14-10. 6.

14-12. 1.

14-14. 1.

14-16. 5.

14-18. See Example D-18.

Example D-18

```
;
;subroutine that programs timer 2 in mode 5 for
;a count of 100H.
;
FIRE:      LD    A,10111010B    ;program control
           OUT   (FBH),A
           LD    A,0            ;program count LSB
           OUT   (FAH),A
           LD    A,01H          ;program count MSB
           RET
```

14-20. See Example D-19.

Example D-19

```
;
;subroutine to read the count in timer 0 and return
;it in the HL register pair.
;
READ:      LD    A,11010001OB   ;latch timer 0
           OUT   (CONTROL),A
           IN    A,(TIMERO)      ;read LSB count
           LD    L,A
           IN    A,(TIMERO)      ;read MSB count
           LD    H,A
           RET
```

14-22. A count of 0000H is a null count.

14-24. A stepper motor has a permanent magnet armature, and the DC motor has a permanent magnet field.

14-26. A full step moves the armature from one pole (field coil) to the next while the half step moves the armature from a pole to between two poles or from between two poles to a pole.

14-28. Yes, if the current can be reversed in the coils. This would allow the motor to develop much more torque because two coils are energized simultaneously.

14-30. The time of day is calculated by adjusting the current count in the timer by the time that was stored in memory location TIME and TIME + 1. The correct time is obtained by adding the correct time to the count.

Chapter 15

15-2. At the data input connections: DI0-DI7.

15-4. Rfb, IOUT (1), IOUT (2), and Vref.

15-6. $\overline{WR2}$ and $\overline{XFER}$ are both grounded to transfer data into the DAC converter.

15-8. 1.0 μs.

15-10. The data are removed from connections: DB0-DB7.

15-12. The ADC is started by a $\overline{WR}$ with $\overline{CS}$ grounded.

15-14. Data are read from the ADC with $\overline{RD}$ while $\overline{CS}$ is grounded.

15-16. A 100 pF capacitor and 9.1 K resistor.

Chapter 16

16-2. The 8086 fits into a 40-pin integrated circuit because it has a multiplexed address/data bus.

16-4. ALE is used to separate the address from the address/data bus.

16-6. The programming model contains 14, four general purpose, four index and pointers, two housekeeping, and four segment registers.

16-8. Code, data, extra, and stack.

16-10. (a) 12000H, (b) 21230H, (c) 32000H, (d) 001F0H, and (e) A0030H.

16-12. O (overflow): indicates an arithmetic overflow; D (direction): selects either auto-increment or auto-decrement for the string instructions; I (interrupt): enables the INTR pin; T (trace): enables tracing; S (sign): indicates the arithmetic sign; C (carry): holds the carry; AC (auxiliary carry): holds the carry between the right and left nibbles; P (parity): indicates parity; and Z (zero): indicates zero.

16-14. No. Both instructions share the same mnemonic code.

16-16. BX, BP, SI, and DI. Also SP is used with the PUSH, POP, CALL and RET instructions.

16-18. 16 M bytes.

16-20. The $\overline{\text{UDS}}$ and $\overline{\text{LDS}}$ pins are used to select the upper and lower memory banks.

16-22. No.

16-24. User and supervisor.

16-26. ADC.

16-28. The address register (A0—A6) and the stack pointers USP and SSP.

16-30. It addresses the next instruction to be executed by the 68000.

16-32. 4 G bytes.

Index